What's New in This Edition

The second edition of this book covers many new topics including

- ☐ Making your SQL statements more readable
- ☐ Retrieving security information
- ☐ Managing transactions
- ☐ Using Transact-SQL and PL/SQL
- ☐ Troubleshooting SQL errors
- ☐ Retrieving useful information from the data dictionary
- ☐ Using stored procedures, packages, and triggers

The following list summarizes the content of the new days, Days 15 through 21:

- ☐ Day 15, "Streamlining SQL Statements for Improved Performance"—The objective of Day 15 is to recommend methods for improving the performance of an SQL statement.

- ☐ Day 16, "Using Views to Retrieve Useful Information from the Data Dictionary"—To fully understand your relational database management system, you need to understand the information in your data dictionary and how to use it.

- ☐ Day 17, "Using SQL to Generate SQL Statements"—You learn the concept behind generating one or more SQL statements with a single query. Automating the tedious task of code generation enables you to write powerful and flexible code.

- ☐ Day 18, "PL/SQL: An Introduction"—Day 18 shows you how to use PL/SQL to extend the functionality of standard SQL.

- ☐ Day 19, "Transact-SQL: An Introduction"—Learn by example one of the most popular extensions to SQL.

- ☐ Day 20, "SQL*Plus"—Day 20 covers the powerful enhancement that Oracle has added to its implementation, SQL*Plus, which provides database programmers with nearly limitless options for sophisticated output formats.

- ☐ Day 21, "Common SQL Mistakes/Errors and Resolutions"—Day 21 examines several typical errors and their resolutions, common logical shortcomings in SQL programs, and ways to prevent the daily setbacks that errors cause.

Teach Yourself
SQL
in 21 days
Second Edition

Teach Yourself
SQL
in 21 days
Second Edition

Ryan K. Stephens
Ronald R. Plew
Bryan Morgan
Jeff Perkins

SAMS
PUBLISHING

201 West 103rd Street
Indianapolis, Indiana 46290

President, Sams Publishing   Richard K. Swadley
Publishing Manager   Rosemarie Graham
Indexing Manager   Johnna L. VanHoose
Director of Marketing   Kelli S. Spencer
Product Marketing Manager   Wendy Gilbride
Marketing Coordinator   Linda Beckwith

Acquisitions Editor
Elaine Brush

Development Editor
Kristi Asher

Production Editor
June Waldman

Indexer
Tina Trettin

Technical Reviewer
Christopher Stone

Editorial Coordinators
Mandie Rowell
Katie Wise

Technical Edit Coordinator
Lorraine E. Schaffer

Resource Coordinator
Deborah Frisby

Editorial Assistants
Carol Ackerman
Andi Richter
Rhonda Tinch-Mize

Cover Designer
Tim Amrhein

Cover Illustrator
Eric Lindley

Cover Production
Aren Howell

Book Designer
Gary Adair

Copy Writer
David Reichwein

Production Team Supervisors
Brad Chinn
Charlotte Clapp

Production
Georgiana Briggs
Cyndi Davis-Hubler
Elizabeth Deeter
Janet Seib

Overview

Appendixes

Contents

Week 3 In Review   481

Appendixes

Acknowledgments

A special thanks to the following individuals: foremost to my loving wife, Tina, for her tolerance and endless support, to Dan Wilson for his contributions, and to Thomas McCarthy at IUPUI. Also, thank you Jordan for your encouragement over the past few years.

—*Ryan K. Stephens*

Special thanks to my wife for putting up with me through this busiest of times. I apologize to my mom for not seeing her as often as I should (I'll make it up to you). Also, thanks to my loyal dog, Toby. He was with me every night and wouldn't leave my side.

—*Ronald Plew*

Special thanks to the following people: Jeff Perkins, David Blankenbeckler, Shannon Little, Jr., Clint and Linda Morgan, and Shannon and Kaye Little.

This book is dedicated to my beautiful wife, Becky. I am truly appreciative to you for your support, encouragement, and love. Thanks for staying up with me during all those late-night sessions. You are absolutely the best.

—*Bryan Morgan*

Thanks to my family, Leslie, Laura, Kelly, Valerie, Jeff, Mom, and Dad. Their support made working on this book possible.

—*Jeff Perkins*

About the Authors

Ryan K. Stephens

Ryan K. Stephens started using SQL as a programmer/analyst while serving on active duty in the Indiana Army National Guard. Hundreds of programs later, Ryan became a database administrator. He currently works for Unisys Federal Systems, where he is responsible for government-owned databases throughout the United States. In addition to his full-time job, Ryan teaches SQL and various database classes at Indiana University-Purdue University Indianapolis. He also serves part-time as a programmer for the Indiana Army National Guard. Along with Ron Plew and two others, Ryan owns a U.S. patent on a modified chess game. Some of his interests include active sports, chess, nature, and writing. Ryan lives in Indianapolis with his wife, Tina, and their three dogs, Bailey, Onyx, and Sugar.

Ronald R. Plew

Ronald R. Plew is a database administrator for Unisys Federal Systems. He holds a bachelor of science degree in business administration/management from the Indiana Institute of Technology. He is an instructor for Indiana University-Purdue University Indianapolis where he teaches SQL and various database classes. Ron also serves as a programmer for the Indiana Army National Guard. His hobbies include collecting Indy 500 racing memorabilia. He also owns and operates Plew's Indy 500 Museum. He lives in Indianapolis with his wife, Linda. They have four grown children (Leslie, Nancy, Angela, and Wendy) and eight grandchildren (Andy, Ryan, Holly, Morgan, Schyler, Heather, Gavin, and Regan).

Bryan Morgan

Bryan Morgan is a software developer with TASC, Inc., in Fort Walton Beach, Florida. In addition to writing code and chasing the golf balls he hits, Bryan has authored several books for Sams Publishing including *Visual J++ Unleashed*, *Java Developer's Reference*, and *Teach Yourself ODBC Programming in 21 Days*. He lives in Navarre, Florida, with his wife, Becky, and their daughter, Emma.

Jeff Perkins

Jeff Perkins is a senior software engineer with TYBRIN Corporation. He has been a program manager, team leader, project lead, technical lead, and analyst. A graduate of the United States Air Force Academy, he is a veteran with more than 2,500 hours of flying time as a navigator and bombardier in the B-52. He has co-authored three other books, *Teach Yourself NT Workstation in 24 Hours*, *Teach Yourself ODBC Programming in 21 Days*, and *Teach Yourself ActiveX in 21 Days*.

Tell Us What You Think!

As a reader, you are the most important critic and commentator of our books. We value your opinion and want to know what we're doing right, what we could do better, what areas you'd like to see us publish in, and any other words of wisdom you're willing to pass our way. You can help us make strong books that meet your needs and give you the computer guidance you require.

Do you have access to CompuServe or the World Wide Web? Then check out our CompuServe forum by typing **GO SAMS** at any prompt. If you prefer the World Wide Web, check out our site at http://www.mcp.com.

 NOTE

> If you have a technical question about this book, call the technical support line at 317-581-3833 or send e-mail to support@mcp.com.

As the team leader of the group that created this book, I welcome your comments. You can fax, e-mail, or write me directly to let me know what you did or didn't like about this book—as well as what we can do to make our books stronger. Here's the information:

FAX: 317-581-4669

E-mail: enterprise_mgr@sams.mcp.com

Mail: Rosemarie Graham
        Comments Department
        Sams Publishing
        201 W. 103rd Street
        Indianapolis, IN 46290

Introduction

Who Should Read This Book?

Late one Friday afternoon your boss comes into your undersized cubicle and drops a new project on your desk. This project looks just like the others you have been working on except it includes ties to several databases. Recently your company decided to move away from homegrown, flat-file data and is now using a relational database. You have seen terms like SQL, tables, records, queries, and RDBMS, but you don't remember exactly what they all mean. You notice the due date on the program is three, no, make that two, weeks away. (Apparently it had been on your boss's desk for a week!) As you begin looking for definitions and sample code to put those definitions into context, you discover this book.

This book is for people who want to learn the fundamentals of Structured Query Language (SQL)—quickly. Through the use of countless examples, this book depicts all the major components of SQL as well as options that are available with various database implementations. You should be able to apply what you learn here to relational databases in a business setting.

Overview

The first 14 days of this book show you how to use SQL to incorporate the power of modern relational databases into your code. By the end of Week 1, you will be able to use basic SQL commands to retrieve selected data.

> **NOTE**
> If you are familiar with the basics and history of SQL, we suggest you skim the first week's chapters and begin in earnest with Day 8, "Manipulating Data."

At the end of Week 2, you will be able to use the more advanced features of SQL, such as stored procedures and triggers, to make your programs more powerful. Week 3 teaches you how to streamline SQL code; use the data dictionary; use SQL to generate more SQL code; work with PL/SQL, Transact-SQL, and SQL*Plus; and handle common SQL mistakes and errors.

The syntax of SQL is explained and then brought to life in examples using Personal Oracle7, Microsoft Query, and other database tools. You don't need access to any of these products to use this book—it can stand alone as an SQL syntax reference. However, using one of these platforms and walking though the examples will help you understand the nuances.

Conventions Used in This Book

This book uses the following typeface conventions:

- ☐ Menu names are separated from menu options by a vertical bar (|). For example, File | Open means "select the Open option from the File menu."
- ☐ New terms appear in *italic*.

INPUT

- ☐ All code in the listings that you type in (input) appears in **boldface monospace**. Output appears in standard `monospace`.

OUTPUT

- ☐ The input icon and output icon also identify the nature of the code.
- ☐ Many code-related terms within the text also appear in `monospace`.
- ☐ When a line of code is too long to fit on one line of this book, it is broken at a convenient place and continued to the next line. A code continuation character (➥) precedes the continuation of a line of code. (You should type a line of code that has this character as one long line without breaking it.)

ANALYSIS

- ☐ Paragraphs that begin with the analysis icon explain the preceding code sample.
- ☐ The syntax icon identifies syntax statements.

SYNTAX

The following special design features enhance the text:

NOTE

Notes explain interesting or important points that can help you understand SQL concepts and techniques.

TIP

Tips are little pieces of information to begin to help you in real-world situations. Tips often offer shortcuts or information to make a task easier or faster.

WARNING

Warnings provide information about detrimental performance issues or dangerous errors. Pay careful attention to Warnings.

Week
1

1

2

3

4

5

6

7

At A Glance

Let's Get Started

Week 1 introduces SQL from a historical and theoretical perspective. The first statement you learn about is the SELECT statement, which enables you to retrieve data from the database based on various user-specified options. Also during Week 1 you study SQL functions, query joins, and SQL subqueries (a query within a query). Many examples help you understand these important topics. These examples use Oracle7, Sybase SQL Server, Microsoft Access, and Microsoft Query and highlight some of the similarities and differences among the products. The content of the examples should be useful and interesting to a broad group of readers.

Day 1

Introduction to SQL

A Brief History of SQL

The history of SQL begins in an IBM laboratory in San Jose, California, where SQL was developed in the late 1970s. The initials stand for Structured Query Language, and the language itself is often referred to as "sequel." It was originally developed for IBM's DB2 product (a relational database management system, or RDBMS, that can still be bought today for various platforms and environments). In fact, SQL makes an RDBMS possible. SQL is a nonprocedural language, in contrast to the procedural or third-generation languages (3GLs) such as COBOL and C that had been created up to that time.

NOTE

Nonprocedural means *what* rather than *how*. For example, SQL describes what data to retrieve, delete, or insert, rather than how to perform the operation.

The characteristic that differentiates a DBMS from an RDBMS is that the RDBMS provides a set-oriented database language. For most RDBMSs, this set-oriented database language is SQL. *Set oriented* means that SQL processes sets of data in groups.

Two standards organizations, the American National Standards Institute (ANSI) and the International Standards Organization (ISO), currently promote SQL standards to industry. The ANSI-92 standard is the standard for the SQL used throughout this book. Although these standard-making bodies prepare standards for database system designers to follow, all database products differ from the ANSI standard to some degree. In addition, most systems provide some proprietary extensions to SQL that extend the language into a true procedural language. We have used various RDBMSs to prepare the examples in this book to give you an idea of what to expect from the common database systems. (We discuss procedural SQL—known as PL/SQL—on Day 18, "PL/SQL: An Introduction," and Transact-SQL on Day 19, "Transact-SQL: An Introduction.")

A Brief History of Databases

A little background on the evolution of databases and database theory will help you understand the workings of SQL. Database systems store information in every conceivable business environment. From large tracking databases such as airline reservation systems to a child's baseball card collection, database systems store and distribute the data that we depend on. Until the last few years, large database systems could be run only on large mainframe computers. These machines have traditionally been expensive to design, purchase, and maintain. However, today's generation of powerful, inexpensive workstation computers enables programmers to design software that maintains and distributes data quickly and inexpensively.

Dr. Codd's 12 Rules for a Relational Database Model

The most popular data storage model is the relational database, which grew from the seminal paper "A Relational Model of Data for Large Shared Data Banks," written by Dr. E. F. Codd in 1970. SQL evolved to service the concepts of the relational database model. Dr. Codd defined 13 rules, oddly enough referred to as Codd's 12 Rules, for the relational model:

0. A relational DBMS must be able to manage databases entirely through its relational capabilities.

1. Information rule—All information in a relational database (including table and column names) is represented explicitly as values in tables.

2. Guaranteed access—Every value in a relational database is guaranteed to be accessible by using a combination of the table name, primary key value, and column name.

3. Systematic null value support—The DBMS provides systematic support for the treatment of null values (unknown or inapplicable data), distinct from default values, and independent of any domain.

4. Active, online relational catalog—The description of the database and its contents is represented at the logical level as tables and can therefore be queried using the database language.

5. Comprehensive data sublanguage—At least one supported language must have a well-defined syntax and be comprehensive. It must support data definition, manipulation, integrity rules, authorization, and transactions.

6. View updating rule—All views that are theoretically updatable can be updated through the system.

7. Set-level insertion, update, and deletion—The DBMS supports not only set-level retrievals but also set-level inserts, updates, and deletes.

8. Physical data independence—Application programs and ad hoc programs are logically unaffected when physical access methods or storage structures are altered.

9. Logical data independence—Application programs and ad hoc programs are logically unaffected, to the extent possible, when changes are made to the table structures.

10. Integrity independence—The database language must be capable of defining integrity rules. They must be stored in the online catalog, and they cannot be bypassed.

11. Distribution independence—Application programs and ad hoc requests are logically unaffected when data is first distributed or when it is redistributed.

12. Nonsubversion—It must not be possible to bypass the integrity rules defined through the database language by using lower-level languages.

Most databases have had a "parent/child" relationship; that is, a parent node would contain file pointers to its children. (See Figure 1.1.)

Figure 1.1.

Codd's relational database management system.

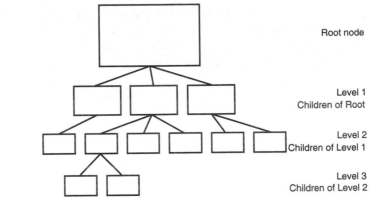

This method has several advantages and many disadvantages. In its favor is the fact that the physical structure of data on a disk becomes unimportant. The programmer simply stores pointers to the next location, so data can be accessed in this manner. Also, data can be added and deleted easily. However, different groups of information could not be easily joined to form new information. The format of the data on the disk could not be arbitrarily changed after the database was created. Doing so would require the creation of a new database structure.

Codd's idea for an RDBMS uses the mathematical concepts of relational algebra to break down data into sets and related common subsets.

Because information can naturally be grouped into distinct sets, Dr. Codd organized his database system around this concept. Under the relational model, data is separated into sets that resemble a table structure. This table structure consists of individual data elements called columns or fields. A single set of a group of fields is known as a record or row. For instance, to create a relational database consisting of employee data, you might start with a table called EMPLOYEE that contains the following pieces of information: Name, Age, and Occupation. These three pieces of data make up the fields in the EMPLOYEE table, shown in Table 1.1.

Table 1.1. The EMPLOYEE table.

Name	Age	Occupation
Will Williams	25	Electrical engineer
Dave Davidson	34	Museum curator
Jan Janis	42	Chef
Bill Jackson	19	Student
Don DeMarco	32	Game programmer
Becky Boudreaux	25	Model

The six rows are the records in the EMPLOYEE table. To retrieve a specific record from this table, for example, Dave Davidson, a user would instruct the database management system to retrieve the records where the NAME field was equal to Dave Davidson. If the DBMS had been instructed to retrieve all the fields in the record, the employee's name, age, and occupation would be returned to the user. SQL is the language that tells the database to retrieve this data. A sample SQL statement that makes this query is

```
SELECT *
FROM EMPLOYEE
```

Remember that the exact syntax is not important at this point. We cover this topic in much greater detail beginning tomorrow.

Because the various data items can be grouped according to obvious relationships (such as the relationship of Employee Name to Employee Age), the relational database model gives the database designer a great deal of flexibility to describe the relationships between the data elements. Through the mathematical concepts of join and union, relational databases can quickly retrieve pieces of data from different sets (tables) and return them to the user or program as one "joined" collection of data. (See Figure 1.2.) The join feature enables the designer to store sets of information in separate tables to reduce repetition.

Figure 1.2.

The join feature.

Set A   Set B

JOIN

Figure 1.3 shows a union. The union would return only data common to both sources.

Figure 1.3.

The union feature.

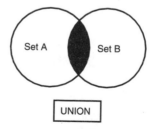

Set A   Set B

UNION

Here's a simple example that shows how data can be logically divided between two tables. Table 1.2 is called RESPONSIBILITIES and contains two fields: NAME and DUTIES.

Table 1.2. The RESPONSIBILITIES table.

Name	Duties
Becky Boudreaux	Smile
Becky Boudreaux	Walk
Bill Jackson	Study
Bill Jackson	Interview for jobs

It would be improper to duplicate the employee's AGE and OCCUPATION fields for each record. Over time, unnecessary duplication of data would waste a great deal of hard disk space and increase access time for the RDBMS. However, if NAME and DUTIES were stored in a separate table named RESPONSIBILITIES, the user could join the RESPONSIBILITIES and EMPLOYEE tables on the NAME field. Instructing the RDBMS to retrieve all fields from the RESPONSIBILITIES and EMPLOYEE tables where the NAME field equals Becky Boudreaux would return Table 1.3.

Table 1.3. Return values from retrieval where NAME equals Becky Boudreaux.

Name	Age	Occupation	Duties
Becky Boudreaux	25	Model	Smile
Becky Boudreaux	25	Model	Walk

More detailed examples of joins begin on Day 6, "Joining Tables."

Designing the Database Structure

The most important decision for a database designer, after the hardware platform and the RDBMS have been chosen, is the structure of the tables. Decisions made at this stage of the design can affect performance and programming later during the development process. The process of separating data into distinct, unique sets is called *normalization*.

Today's Database Landscape

Computing technology has made a permanent change in the ways businesses work around the world. Information that was at one time stored in warehouses full of filing cabinets can now be accessed instantaneously at the click of a mouse button. Orders placed by customers in foreign countries can now be instantly processed on the floor of a manufacturing facility. Although 20 years ago much of this information had been transported onto corporate mainframe databases, offices still operated in a batch-processing environment. If a query needed to be performed, someone notified the management information systems (MIS) department; the requested data was delivered as soon as possible (though often not soon enough).

In addition to the development of the relational database model, two technologies led to the rapid growth of what are now called client/server database systems. The first important technology was the personal computer. Inexpensive, easy-to-use applications such as Lotus 1-2-3 and Word Perfect enabled employees (and home computer users) to create documents and manage data quickly and accurately. Users became accustomed to continually upgrading systems because the rate of change was so rapid, even as the price of the more advanced systems continued to fall.

The second important technology was the local area network (LAN) and its integration into offices across the world. Although users were accustomed to terminal connections to a corporate mainframe, now word processing files could be stored locally within an office and accessed from any computer attached to the network. After the Apple Macintosh introduced a friendly graphical user interface, computers were not only inexpensive and powerful but also easy to use. In addition, they could be accessed from remote sites, and large amounts of data could be off-loaded to departmental data servers.

During this time of rapid change and advancement, a new type of system appeared. Called *client/server development* because processing is split between client computers and a database server, this new breed of application was a radical change from mainframe-based application programming. Among the many advantages of this type of architecture are

- ☐ Reduced maintenance costs
- ☐ Reduced network load (processing occurs on database server or client computer)
- ☐ Multiple operating systems that can interoperate as long as they share a common network protocol
- ☐ Improved data integrity owing to centralized data location

In *Implementing Client/Server Computing,* Bernard H. Boar defines client/server computing as follows:

> *Client/server computing* is a processing model in which a single application is partitioned between multiple processors (front-end and back-end) and the processors cooperate (transparent to the end user) to complete the processing as a single unified task. A client/server bond product ties the processors together to provide a single system image (illusion). Shareable resources are positioned as requestor clients that access authorized services. The architecture is endlessly recursive; in turn, servers can become clients and request services of other servers on the network, and so on and so on.

This type of application development requires an entirely new set of programming skills. User interface programming is now written for graphical user interfaces, whether it be MS Windows, IBM OS/2, Apple Macintosh, or the UNIX X-Window system. Using SQL and a network connection, the application can interface to a database residing on a remote server. The increased power of personal computer hardware enables critical database information to be stored on a relatively inexpensive standalone server. In addition, this server can be replaced later with little or no change to the client applications.

A Cross-Product Language

You can apply the basic concepts introduced in this book in many environments—for example, Microsoft Access running on a single-user Windows application or SQL Server running with 100 user connections. One of SQL's greatest benefits is that it is truly a cross-platform language and a cross-product language. Because it is also what programmers refer to as a high-level or fourth-generation language (4GL), a large amount of work can be done in fewer lines of code.

Early Implementations

Oracle Corporation released the first commercial RDBMS that used SQL. Although the original versions were developed for VAX/VMS systems, Oracle was one of the first vendors to release a DOS version of its RDBMS. (Oracle is now available on more than 70 platforms.) In the mid-1980s Sybase released its RDBMS, SQL Server. With client libraries for database access, support for stored procedures (discussed on Day 14, "Dynamic Uses of SQL"), and interoperability with various networks, SQL Server became a successful product, particularly in client/server environments. One of the strongest points for both of these powerful database systems is their scalability across platforms. C language code (combined with SQL) written for Oracle on a PC is virtually identical to its counterpart written for an Oracle database running on a VAX system.

SQL and Client/Server Application Development

The common thread that runs throughout client/server application development is the use of SQL and relational databases. Also, using this database technology in a single-user business application positions the application for future growth.

An Overview of SQL

SQL is the de facto standard language used to manipulate and retrieve data from these relational databases. SQL enables a programmer or database administrator to do the following:

☐ Modify a database's structure

☐ Change system security settings

- ☐ Add user permissions on databases or tables
- ☐ Query a database for information
- ☐ Update the contents of a database

NOTE

The term SQL can be confusing. The *S*, for Structured, and the *L*, for Language, are straightforward enough, but the *Q* is a little misleading. *Q*, of course, stands for "Query," which—if taken literally—would restrict you to asking the database questions. But SQL does much more than ask questions. With SQL you can also create tables, add data, delete data, splice data together, trigger actions based on changes to the database, and store your queries within your program or database.

Unfortunately, there is no good substitute for *Query*. Obviously, Structured Add Modify Delete Join Store Trigger and Query Language (SAMDJSTQL) is a bit cumbersome. In the interest of harmony, we will stay with SQL. However, you now know that its function is bigger than its name.

The most commonly used statement in SQL is the SELECT statement (see Day 2, "Introduction to the Query: The SELECT Statement"), which retrieves data from the database and returns the data to the user. The EMPLOYEE table example illustrates a typical example of a SELECT statement situation. In addition to the SELECT statement, SQL provides statements for creating new databases, tables, fields, and indexes, as well as statements for inserting and deleting records. ANSI SQL also recommends a core group of data manipulation functions. As you will find out, many database systems also have tools for ensuring data integrity and enforcing security (see Day 11, "Controlling Transactions") that enable programmers to stop the execution of a group of commands if a certain condition occurs.

Popular SQL Implementations

This section introduces some of the more popular implementations of SQL, each of which has its own strengths and weaknesses. Where some implementations of SQL have been developed for PC use and easy user interactivity, others have been developed to accommodate very large databases (VLDB). This sections introduces selected key features of some implementations.

NOTE

In addition to serving as an SQL reference, this book also contains many practical software development examples. SQL is useful only when it solves your real-world problems, which occur inside your code.

Microsoft Access

We use Microsoft Access, a PC-based DBMS, to illustrate some of the examples in this text. Access is very easy to use. You can use GUI tools or manually enter your SQL statements.

Personal Oracle7

We use Personal Oracle7, which represents the larger corporate database world, to demonstrate command-line SQL and database management techniques. (These techniques are important because the days of the standalone machine are drawing to an end, as are the days when knowing one database or one operating system was enough.) In *command-line SQL,* simple standalone SQL statements are entered into Oracle's SQL*Plus tool. This tool then returns data to the screen for the user to see, or it performs the appropriate action on the database.

Most examples are directed toward the beginning programmer or first-time user of SQL. We begin with the simplest of SQL statements and advance to the topics of transaction management and stored procedure programming. The Oracle RDBMS is distributed with a full complement of development tools. It includes a C++ and Visual Basic language library (Oracle Objects for OLE) that can link an application to a Personal Oracle database. It also comes with graphical tools for database, user, and object administration, as well as the SQL*Loader utility, which is used to import and export data to and from Oracle.

NOTE

Personal Oracle7 is a scaled-down version of the full-blown Oracle7 server product. Personal Oracle7 allows only single-user connections (as the name implies). However, the SQL syntax used on this product is identical to that used on the larger, more expensive versions of Oracle. In addition, the tools used in Personal Oracle7 have much in common with the Oracle7 product.

We chose the Personal Oracle7 RDBMS for several reasons:

☐ It includes nearly all the tools needed to demonstrate the topics discussed in this book.

☐ It is available on virtually every platform in use today and is one of the most popular RDBMS products worldwide.

☐ A 90-day trial copy can be downloaded from Oracle Corporation's World Wide Web server (http://www.oracle.com).

Figure 1.4 shows SQL*Plus from this suite of tools.

Figure 1.4.

*Oracle's SQL*Plus.*

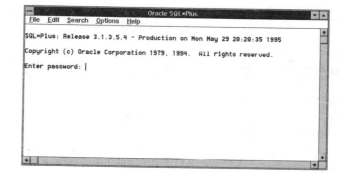

```
                              Oracle SQL*Plus
 File  Edit  Search  Options  Help

SQL*Plus: Release 3.1.3.5.4 - Production on Mon May 29 20:20:35 1995

Copyright (c) Oracle Corporation 1979, 1994.  All rights reserved.

Enter password: |
```

TIP

Keep in mind that nearly all the SQL code given in this book is portable to other database management systems. In cases where syntax differs greatly among different vendors' products, examples are given to illustrate these differences.

Microsoft Query

Microsoft Query (see Figure 1.5) is a useful query tool that comes packaged with Microsoft's Windows development tools, Visual C++, and Visual Basic. It uses the ODBC standard to communicate with underlying databases. Microsoft Query passes SQL statements to a driver, which processes the statements before passing them to a database system.

Figure 1.5.
Microsoft Query.

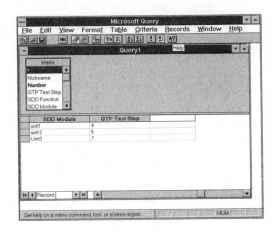

Open Database Connectivity (ODBC)

ODBC is a functional library designed to provide a common Application Programming Interface (API) to underlying database systems. It communicates with the database through a library driver, just as Windows communicates with a printer via a printer driver. Depending on the database being used, a networking driver may be required to connect to a remote database. The architecture of ODBC is illustrated in Figure 1.6.

Figure 1.6.
ODBC structure.

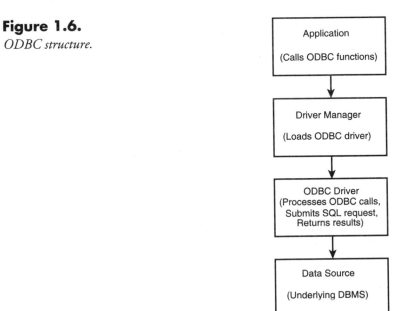

The unique feature of ODBC (as compared to the Oracle or Sybase libraries) is that none of its functions are database-vendor specific. For instance, you can use the same code to perform queries against a Microsoft Access table or an Informix database with little or no modification. Once again, it should be noted that most vendors add some proprietary extensions to the SQL standard, such as Microsoft's and Sybase's Transact-SQL and Oracle's PL/SQL.

You should always consult the documentation before beginning to work with a new data source. ODBC has developed into a standard adopted into many products, including Visual Basic, Visual C++, FoxPro, Borland Delphi, and PowerBuilder. As always, application developers need to weigh the benefit of using the emerging ODBC standard, which enables you to design code without regard for a specific database, versus the speed gained by using a database specific function library. In other words, using ODBC will be more portable but slower than using the Oracle7 or Sybase libraries.

SQL in Application Programming

SQL was originally made an ANSI standard in 1986. The ANSI 1989 standard (often called SQL-89) defines three types of interfacing to SQL within an application program:

- ☐ Module Language—Uses procedures within programs. These procedures can be called by the application program and can return values to the program via parameter passing.
- ☐ Embedded SQL—Uses SQL statements embedded with actual program code. This method often requires the use of a precompiler to process the SQL statements. The standard defines statements for Pascal, FORTRAN, COBOL, and PL/1.
- ☐ Direct Invocation—Left up to the implementor.

Before the concept of dynamic SQL evolved, embedded SQL was the most popular way to use SQL within a program. Embedded SQL, which is still used, uses *static* SQL—meaning that the SQL statement is compiled into the application and cannot be changed at runtime. The principle is much the same as a compiler versus an interpreter. The performance for this type of SQL is good; however, it is not flexible—and cannot always meet the needs of today's changing business environments. Dynamic SQL is discussed shortly.

The ANSI 1992 standard (SQL-92) extended the language and became an international standard. It defines three levels of SQL compliance: entry, intermediate, and full. The new features introduced include the following:

- ☐ Connections to databases
- ☐ Scrollable cursors
- ☐ Dynamic SQL
- ☐ Outer joins

This book covers not only all these extensions but also some proprietary extensions used by RDBMS vendors. Dynamic SQL allows you to prepare the SQL statement at runtime. Although the performance for this type of SQL is not as good as that of embedded SQL, it provides the application developer (and user) with a great degree of flexibility. A call-level interface, such as ODBC or Sybase's DB-Library, is an example of dynamic SQL.

Call-level interfaces should not be a new concept to application programmers. When using ODBC, for instance, you simply fill a variable with your SQL statement and call the function to send the SQL statement to the database. Errors or results can be returned to the program through the use of other function calls designed for those purposes. Results are returned through a process known as the *binding of variables*.

Summary

Day 1 covers some of the history and structure behind SQL. Because SQL and relational databases are so closely linked, Day 1 also covers (albeit briefly) the history and function of relational databases. Tomorrow is devoted to the most important component of SQL: the query.

Q&A

Q Why should I be concerned about SQL?

A Until recently, if you weren't working on a large database system, you probably had only a passing knowledge of SQL. With the advent of client/server development tools (such as Visual Basic, Visual C++, ODBC, Borland's Delphi, and Powersoft's PowerBuilder) and the movement of several large databases (Oracle and Sybase) to the PC platform, most business applications being developed today require a working knowledge of SQL.

Q Why do I need to know anything about relational database theory to use SQL?

A SQL was developed to service relational databases. Without a minimal understanding of relational database theory, you will not be able to use SQL effectively except in the most trivial cases.

Q All the new GUI tools enable me to click a button to write SQL. Why should I spend time learning to write SQL manually?

A GUI tools have their place, and manually writing SQL has its place. Manually written SQL is generally more efficient than GUI-written SQL. Also, a GUI SQL statement is not as easy to read as a manually written SQL statement. Finally, knowing what is going on behind the scenes when you use GUI tools will help you get the most out of them.

Q So, if SQL is standardized, should I be able to program with SQL on any databases?

A No, you will be able to program with SQL only on RDBMS databases that support SQL, such as MS-Access, Oracle, Sybase, and Informix. Although each vendor's implementation will differ slightly from the others, you should be able to use SQL with very few adjustments.

Workshop

The Workshop provides quiz questions to help solidify your understanding of the material covered, as well as exercises to provide you with experience in using what you have learned. Try to answer the quiz and exercise questions before checking the answers in Appendix F, "Answers to Quizzes and Exercises."

Quiz

1. What makes SQL a nonprocedural language?
2. How can you tell whether a database is truly relational?
3. What can you do with SQL?
4. Name the process that separates data into distinct, unique sets.

Exercise

Determine whether the database you use at work or at home is truly relational.

Day 2

Introduction to the Query: The SELECT Statement

Objectives

Welcome to Day 2! By the end of the day you will be able to do the following:

- ☐ Write an SQL query
- ☐ Select and list all rows and columns from a table
- ☐ Select and list selected columns from a table
- ☐ Select and list columns from multiple tables

Background

To fully use the power of a relational database as described briefly on Day 1, "Introduction to SQL," you need to communicate with it. The ultimate communication would be to turn to your computer and say, in a clear, distinct voice, "Show me all the left-handed, brown-eyed bean counters who have worked for this company for at least 10 years." A few of you may already be doing so (talking to your computer, not listing bean counters). Everyone else needs a more conventional way of retrieving information from the database. You can make this vital link through SQL's middle name, "Query."

As mentioned on Day 1, the name *Query* is really a misnomer in this context. An SQL query is not necessarily a question to the database. It can be a command to do one of the following:

- ☐ Build or delete a table
- ☐ Insert, modify, or delete rows or fields
- ☐ Search several tables for specific information and return the results in a specific order
- ☐ Modify security information

A query can also be a simple question to the database. To use this powerful tool, you need to learn how to write an SQL query.

General Rules of Syntax

As you will find, syntax in SQL is quite flexible, although there are rules to follow as in any programming language. A simple query illustrates the basic syntax of an SQL select statement. Pay close attention to the case, spacing, and logical separation of the components of each query by SQL keywords.

```
SELECT NAME, STARTTERM, ENDTERM
FROM PRESIDENTS
WHERE NAME = 'LINCOLN';
```

In this example everything is capitalized, but it doesn't have to be. The preceding query would work just as well if it were written like this:

```
select name, startterm, endterm
from presidents
where name = 'LINCOLN';
```

Notice that LINCOLN appears in capital letters in both examples. Although actual SQL statements are not case sensitive, references to data in a database are. For instance, many companies store their data in uppercase. In the preceding example, assume that the column name stores its contents in uppercase. Therefore, a query searching for 'Lincoln' in the name column would not find any data to return. Check your implementation and/or company policies for any case requirements.

NOTE

Commands in SQL are not case sensitive.

Take another look at the sample query. Is there something magical in the spacing? Again the answer is no. The following code would work as well:

```
select name, startterm, endterm from presidents where name = 'LINCOLN';
```

However, some regard for spacing and capitalization makes your statements much easier to read. It also makes your statements much easier to maintain when they become a part of your project.

Another important feature of the sample query is the semicolon at the end of the expression. This punctuation mark tells the command-line SQL program that your query is complete.

If the magic isn't in the capitalization or the format, then just which elements are important? The answer is *keywords,* or the words in SQL that are reserved as a part of syntax. (Depending on the SQL statement, a keyword can be either a mandatory element of the statement or optional.) The keywords in the current example are

- ☐ SELECT
- ☐ FROM
- ☐ WHERE

Check the table of contents to see some of the SQL keywords you will learn and on what days.

The Building Blocks of Data Retrieval: SELECT and FROM

As your experience with SQL grows, you will notice that you are typing the words SELECT and FROM more than any other words in the SQL vocabulary. They aren't as glamorous as CREATE or as ruthless as DROP, but they are indispensable to any conversation you hope to have with the computer concerning data retrieval. And isn't data retrieval the reason that you entered mountains of information into your very expensive database in the first place?

This discussion starts with SELECT because most of your statements will also start with SELECT:

```
SELECT <COLUMN NAMES>
```

The basic SELECT statement couldn't be simpler. However, SELECT does not work alone. If you typed just SELECT into your system, you might get the following response:

INPUT

```
SQL> SELECT;
```

OUTPUT

```
SELECT
      *
ERROR at line 1:
ORA-00936: missing expression
```

The asterisk under the offending line indicates where Oracle7 thinks the offense occurred. The error message tells you that something is missing. That something is the FROM clause:

```
FROM <TABLE>
```

Together, the statements SELECT and FROM begin to unlock the power behind your database.

NOTE

At this point you may be wondering what the difference is between a keyword, a statement, and a clause. SQL *keywords* refer to individual SQL elements, such as SELECT and FROM. A clause is a part of an SQL statement; for example, SELECT *column1, column2, ...* is a clause. SQL clauses combine to form a complete SQL *statement*. For example, you can combine a SELECT clause and a FROM clause to write an SQL statement.

NOTE

Each implementation of SQL has a unique way of indicating errors. Microsoft Query, for example, says it can't show the query, leaving you to find the problem. Borland's Interbase pops up a dialog box with the error. Personal Oracle7, the engine used in the preceding example, gives you an error number (so you can look up the detailed explanation in your manuals) and a short explanation of the problem.

Examples

Before going any further, look at the sample database that is the basis for the following examples. This database illustrates the basic functions of SELECT and FROM. In the real world you would use the techniques described on Day 8, "Manipulating Data," to build this database, but for the purpose of describing how to use SELECT and FROM, assume it already exists. This example uses the CHECKS table to retrieve information about checks that an individual has written.

The CHECKS table:

```
CHECK# PAYEE                    AMOUNT REMARKS
------ ------------------       ------ --------------------
     1 Ma Bell                     150 Have sons next time
     2 Reading R.R.             245.34 Train to Chicago
     3 Ma Bell                  200.32 Cellular Phone
     4 Local Utilities              98 Gas
```

```
5 Joes Stale $ Dent          150 Groceries
6 Cash                        25 Wild Night Out
7 Joans Gas                 25.1 Gas
```

Your First Query

INPUT

```
SQL> select * from checks;
```

OUTPUT

```
CHECK# PAYEE                 AMOUNT REMARKS
------ --------------------  ------ --------------------
     1 Ma Bell                  150 Have sons next time
     2 Reading R.R.          245.34 Train to Chicago
     3 Ma Bell               200.32 Cellular Phone
     4 Local Utilities           98 Gas
     5 Joes Stale $ Dent        150 Groceries
     6 Cash                      25 Wild Night Out
     7 Joans Gas               25.1 Gas

7 rows selected.
```

ANALYSIS This output looks just like the code in the example. Notice that columns 1 and 3 in the output statement are right-justified and that columns 2 and 4 are left-justified. This format follows the alignment convention in which numeric data types are right-justified and character data types are left-justified. Data types are discussed on Day 9, "Creating and Maintaining Tables."

The asterisk (*) in select * tells the database to return all the columns associated with the given table described in the FROM clause. The database determines the order in which to return the columns.

Terminating an SQL Statement

In some implementations of SQL, the semicolon at the end of the statement tells the interpreter that you are finished writing the query. For example, Oracle's SQL*PLUS won't execute the query until it finds a semicolon (or a slash). On the other hand, some implementations of SQL do not use the semicolon as a terminator. For example, Microsoft Query and Borland's ISQL don't require a terminator, because your query is typed in an edit box and executed when you push a button.

Changing the Order of the Columns

The preceding example of an SQL statement used the * to select all columns from a table, the order of their appearance in the output being determined by the database. To specify the order of the columns, you could type something like:

INPUT

```
SQL> SELECT payee, remarks, amount, check# from checks;
```

Notice that each column name is listed in the SELECT clause. The order in which the columns are listed is the order in which they will appear in the output. Notice both the commas that separate the column names and the space between the final column name and the subsequent clause (in this case FROM). The output would look like this:

OUTPUT

```
PAYEE                   REMARKS                 AMOUNT   CHECK#
--------------------    -------------------     -------- --------
Ma Bell                 Have sons next time        150        1
Reading R.R.            Train to Chicago        245.34        2
Ma Bell                 Cellular Phone          200.32        3
Local Utilities         Gas                         98        4
Joes Stale $ Dent       Groceries                  150        5
Cash                    Wild Night Out              25        6
Joans Gas               Gas                       25.1        7

7 rows selected.
```

Another way to write the same statement follows.

INPUT

```
SELECT payee, remarks, amount, check#
FROM checks;
```

Notice that the FROM clause has been carried over to the second line. This convention is a matter of personal taste when writing SQL code. The output would look like this:

OUTPUT

```
PAYEE                   REMARKS                 AMOUNT  CHECK#
--------------------    -------------------     ------- --------
Ma Bell                 Have sons next time        150       1
Reading R.R.            Train to Chicago        245.34       2
Ma Bell                 Cellular Phone          200.32       3
Local Utilities         Gas                         98       4
Joes Stale $ Dent       Groceries                  150       5
Cash                    Wild Night Out              25       6
Joans Gas               Gas                       25.1       7

7 rows selected.
```

ANALYSIS The output is identical because only the *format* of the statement changed. Now that you have established control over the order of the columns, you will be able to specify which columns you want to see.

Selecting Individual Columns

Suppose you do not want to see every column in the database. You used SELECT * to find out what information was available, and now you want to concentrate on the check number and the amount. You type

INPUT

```
SQL> SELECT CHECK#, amount from checks;
```

which returns

OUTPUT

```
   CHECK#    AMOUNT
---------  ---------
        1        150
        2     245.34
        3     200.32
        4         98
        5        150
        6         25
        7       25.1
```

7 rows selected.

ANALYSIS   Now you have the columns you want to see. Notice the use of upper- and lowercase in the query. It did not affect the result.

What if you need information from a different table?

Selecting Different Tables

Suppose you had a table called DEPOSITS with this structure:

```
DEPOSIT# WHOPAID              AMOUNT REMARKS
-------- --------------------  ------ --------------------
       1 Rich Uncle              200 Take off Xmas list
       2 Employer               1000 15 June Payday
       3 Credit Union            500 Loan
```

You would simply change the FROM clause to the desired table and type the following statement:

SQL> **select * from deposits**

   The result is

```
DEPOSIT# WHOPAID              AMOUNT REMARKS
-------- --------------------  ------ --------------------
       1 Rich Uncle              200 Take off Xmas list
       2 Employer               1000 15 June Payday
       3 Credit Union            500 Loan
```

ANALYSIS   With a single change you have a new data source.

Queries with Distinction

If you look at the original table, CHECKS, you see that some of the data repeats. For example, if you looked at the AMOUNT column using

INPUT   SQL> **select amount from checks;**

you would see

OUTPUT

```
        AMOUNT
        --------
           150
        245.34
        200.32
            98
           150
            25
          25.1
```

Notice that the amount 150 is repeated. What if you wanted to see how may different amounts were in this column? Try this:

INPUT

```
SQL> select DISTINCT amount from checks;
```

The result would be

OUTPUT

```
        AMOUNT
        --------
            25
          25.1
            98
           150
        200.32
        245.34

6 rows selected.
```

ANALYSIS Notice that only six rows are selected. Because you specified DISTINCT, only one instance of the duplicated data is shown, which means that one less row is returned. ALL is a keyword that is implied in the basic SELECT statement. You almost never see ALL because SELECT <Table> and SELECT ALL <Table> have the same result.

Try this example—for the first (and only!) time in your SQL career:

INPUT

```
SQL> SELECT ALL AMOUNT
  2  FROM CHECKS;
```

OUTPUT

```
        AMOUNT
        --------
           150
        245.34
        200.32
            98
           150
            25
          25.1

7 rows selected.
```

 ANALYSIS It is the same as a SELECT <Column>. Who needs the extra keystrokes?

Summary

The keywords SELECT and FROM enable the query to retrieve data. You can make a broad statement and include all tables with a SELECT * statement, or you can rearrange or retrieve specific tables. The keyword DISTINCT limits the output so that you do not see duplicate values in a column. Tomorrow you learn how to make your queries even more selective.

Q&A

Q Where did this data come from and how do I connect to it?

A The data was created using the methods described on Day 8. The database connection depends on how you are using SQL. The method shown is the traditional command-line method used on commercial-quality databases. These databases have traditionally been the domain of the mainframe or the workstation, but recently they have migrated to the PC.

Q OK, but if I don't use one of these databases, how will I use SQL?

A You can also use SQL from within a programming language. *Embedded SQL* is normally a language extension, most commonly seen in COBOL, in which SQL is written inside of and compiled with the program. Microsoft has created an entire Application Programming Interface (API) that enables programmers to use SQL from inside Visual Basic, C, or C++. Libraries available from Sybase and Oracle also enable you to put SQL in your programs. Borland has encapsulated SQL into database objects in Delphi. The concepts in this book apply in all these languages.

Workshop

The Workshop provides quiz questions to help solidify your understanding of the material covered, as well as exercises to provide you with experience in using what you have learned. Try to answer the quiz and exercise questions before checking the answers in Appendix F, "Answers to Quizzes and Exercises," and make sure you understand the answers before starting tomorrow's work.

Quiz

1. Do the following statements return the same or different output:
```
SELECT * FROM CHECKS;
select * from checks;?
```

2. The following queries do not work. Why not?

    a. `Select *`

    b. `Select * from checks`

    c. `Select amount name payee FROM checks;`

3. Which of the following SQL statements will work?

    a. `select *`
       `from checks;`

    b. `select * from checks;`

    c. `select * from checks`
       `/`

Exercises

1. Using the CHECKS table from earlier today, write a query to return just the check numbers and the remarks.

2. Rewrite the query from exercise 1 so that the remarks will appear as the first column in your query results.

3. Using the CHECKS table, write a query to return all the unique remarks.

Day 3

Expressions, Conditions, and Operators

Objectives

On Day 2, "Introduction to the Query: The SELECT Statement," you used SELECT and FROM to manipulate data in interesting (and useful) ways. Today you learn more about SELECT and FROM and expand the basic query with some new terms to go with query, table, and row, as well as a new clause and a group of handy items called operators. When the sun sets on Day 3, you will

- ☐ Know what an expression is and how to use it
- ☐ Know what a condition is and how to use it
- ☐ Be familiar with the basic uses of the WHERE clause
- ☐ Be able to use arithmetic, comparison, character, logical, and set operators
- ☐ Have a working knowledge of some miscellaneous operators

NOTE

We used Oracle's Personal Oracle7 to generate today's examples. Other implementations of SQL may differ slightly in the way in which commands are entered or output is displayed, but the results are basically the same for all implementations that conform to the ANSI standard.

Expressions

The definition of an expression is simple: An *expression* returns a value. Expression types are very broad, covering different data types such as String, Numeric, and Boolean. In fact, pretty much anything following a clause (SELECT or FROM, for example) is an expression. In the following example amount is an expression that returns the value contained in the amount column.

```
SELECT amount FROM checks;
```

In the following statement NAME, ADDRESS, PHONE and ADDRESSBOOK are expressions:

```
SELECT NAME, ADDRESS, PHONE
FROM ADDRESSBOOK;
```

Now, examine the following expression:

```
WHERE NAME = 'BROWN'
```

It contains a condition, NAME = 'BROWN', which is an example of a Boolean expression. NAME = 'BROWN' will be either TRUE or FALSE, depending on the condition =.

Conditions

If you ever want to find a particular item or group of items in your database, you need one or more conditions. Conditions are contained in the WHERE clause. In the preceding example, the condition is

```
NAME = 'BROWN'
```

To find everyone in your organization who worked more than 100 hours last month, your condition would be

```
NUMBEROFHOURS > 100
```

Conditions enable you to make selective queries. In their most common form, conditions comprise a variable, a constant, and a comparison operator. In the first example the variable is NAME, the constant is 'BROWN', and the comparison operator is =. In the second example the variable is NUMBEROFHOURS, the constant is 100, and the comparison operator is >. You need to know about two more elements before you can write conditional queries: the WHERE clause and operators.

The WHERE Clause

The syntax of the WHERE clause is

SYNTAX

```
WHERE <SEARCH CONDITION>
```

SELECT, FROM, and WHERE are the three most frequently used clauses in SQL. WHERE simply causes your queries to be more selective. Without the WHERE clause, the most useful thing you could do with a query is display all records in the selected table(s). For example:

INPUT

```
SQL> SELECT * FROM BIKES;
```

lists all rows of data in the table BIKES.

OUTPUT

```
NAME            FRAMESIZE COMPOSITION    MILESRIDDEN TYPE
-------------   --------- -------------- ----------- --------
TREK 2300            22.5 CARBON FIBER          3500 RACING
BURLEY                 22 STEEL                 2000 TANDEM
GIANT                 19 STEEL                 1500 COMMUTER
FUJI                  20 STEEL                  500 TOURING
SPECIALIZED           16 STEEL                  100 MOUNTAIN
CANNONDALE          22.5 ALUMINUM              3000 RACING
6 rows selected.
```

If you wanted a particular bike, you could type

INPUT/OUTPUT

```
SQL> SELECT *
     FROM BIKES
     WHERE NAME = 'BURLEY';
```

which would yield only one record:

```
NAME            FRAMESIZE COMPOSITION    MILESRIDDEN TYPE
-------------   --------- -------------- ----------- --------
BURLEY                 22 STEEL                 2000 TANDEM
```

ANALYSIS This simple example shows how you can place a condition on the data that you want to retrieve.

Operators

Operators are the elements you use inside an expression to articulate how you want specified conditions to retrieve data. Operators fall into six groups: arithmetic, comparison, character, logical, set, and miscellaneous.

Arithmetic Operators

The arithmetic operators are plus (+), minus (–), divide (/), multiply (*), and modulo (%). The first four are self-explanatory. Modulo returns the integer remainder of a division. Here are two examples:

```
5 % 2 = 1
6 % 2 = 0
```

The modulo operator does not work with data types that have decimals, such as Real or Number.

If you place several of these arithmetic operators in an expression without any parentheses, the operators are resolved in this order: multiplication, division, modulo, addition, and subtraction. For example, the expression

```
2*6+9/3
```

equals

```
12 + 3 = 15
```

However, the expression

```
2 * (6 + 9) / 3
```

equals

```
2 * 15 / 3 = 10
```

Watch where you put those parentheses! Sometimes the expression does exactly what you tell it to do, rather than what you want it to do.

The following sections examine the arithmetic operators in some detail and give you a chance to write some queries.

Plus (+)

You can use the plus sign in several ways. Type the following statement to display the PRICE table:

INPUT

```
SQL> SELECT * FROM PRICE;
```

OUTPUT

```
ITEM            WHOLESALE
--------------  ----------
TOMATOES             .34
POTATOES             .51
BANANAS              .67
TURNIPS              .45
CHEESE               .89
APPLES               .23
6 rows selected.
```

3

Now type:

```
SQL> SELECT ITEM, WHOLESALE, WHOLESALE + 0.15
       FROM PRICE;
```

Here the + adds 15 cents to each price to produce the following:

```
ITEM            WHOLESALE WHOLESALE+0.15
-------------   --------- --------------
TOMATOES             .34            .49
POTATOES             .51            .66
BANANAS              .67            .82
TURNIPS              .45            .60
CHEESE               .89           1.04
APPLES               .23            .38
6 rows selected.
```

ANALYSIS What is this last column with the unattractive column heading WHOLESALE+0.15? It's not in the original table. (Remember, you used * in the SELECT clause, which causes all the columns to be shown.) SQL allows you to create a virtual or derived column by combining or modifying existing columns.

Retype the original entry:

```
SQL> SELECT * FROM PRICE;
```

The following table results:

```
ITEM            WHOLESALE
-------------   ---------
TOMATOES             .34
POTATOES             .51
BANANAS              .67
TURNIPS              .45
CHEESE               .89
APPLES               .23
6 rows selected.
```

ANALYSIS The output confirms that the original data has not been changed and that the column heading WHOLESALE+0.15 is not a permanent part of it. In fact, the column heading is so unattractive that you should do something about it.

Type the following:

```
SQL> SELECT ITEM, WHOLESALE, (WHOLESALE + 0.15) RETAIL
       FROM PRICE;
```

Here's the result:

```
ITEM            WHOLESALE RETAIL
-------------   --------- ------
TOMATOES             .34    .49
POTATOES             .51    .66
BANANAS              .67    .82
TURNIPS              .45    .60
CHEESE               .89   1.04
APPLES               .23    .38
6 rows selected.
```

ANALYSIS This is wonderful! Not only can you create new columns, but you can also rename them on the fly. You can rename any of the columns using the syntax `column_name alias` (note the space between `column_name` and `alias`).

For example, the query

INPUT/ OUTPUT
```
SQL> SELECT ITEM PRODUCE, WHOLESALE, WHOLESALE + 0.25 RETAIL
     FROM PRICE;
```

renames the columns as follows:

```
PRODUCE         WHOLESALE   RETAIL
--------------- --------- ---------
TOMATOES             .34       .59
POTATOES             .51       .76
BANANAS              .67       .92
TURNIPS              .45       .70
CHEESE               .89      1.14
APPLES               .23       .48
```

 NOTE

Some implementations of SQL use the syntax `<column name = alias>`. The preceding example would be written as follows:

```
SQL> SELECT ITEM = PRODUCE,
     WHOLESALE,
     WHOLESALE + 0.25 = RETAIL,
     FROM PRICE;
```

Check your implementation for the exact syntax.

You might be wondering what use aliasing is if you are not using command-line SQL. Fair enough. Have you ever wondered how report builders work? Someday, when you are asked to write a report generator, you'll remember this and not spend weeks reinventing what Dr. Codd and IBM have wrought.

So far, you have seen two uses of the plus sign. The first instance was the use of the plus sign in the SELECT clause to perform a calculation on the data and display the calculation. The second use of the plus sign is in the WHERE clause. Using operators in the WHERE clause gives you more flexibility when you specify conditions for retrieving data.

In some implementations of SQL, the plus sign does double duty as a character operator. You'll see that side of the plus a little later today.

Minus (-)

Minus also has two uses. First, it can change the sign of a number. You can use the table HILOW to demonstrate this function.

INPUT
```
SQL> SELECT * FROM HILOW;
```

OUTPUT

```
STATE       HIGHTEMP    LOWTEMP
----------  --------    --------
CA              -50         120
FL               20         110
LA               15          99
ND              -70         101
NE              -60         100
```

For example, here's a way to manipulate the data:

INPUT/OUTPUT

```
SQL> SELECT STATE, -HIGHTEMP LOWS, -LOWTEMP HIGHS
        FROM HILOW;

STATE        LOWS      HIGHS
----------  --------  --------
CA             50       -120
FL            -20       -110
LA            -15        -99
ND             70       -101
NE             60       -100
```

The second (and obvious) use of the minus sign is to subtract one column from another. For example:

INPUT/OUTPUT

```
SQL> SELECT STATE,
  2    HIGHTEMP LOWS,
  3    LOWTEMP HIGHS,
  4    (LOWTEMP - HIGHTEMP) DIFFERENCE
  5    FROM HILOW;

STATE        LOWS      HIGHS   DIFFERENCE
----------  --------  --------  ----------
CA             -50       120        170
FL              20       110         90
LA              15        99         84
ND             -70       101        171
NE             -60       100        160
```

ANALYSIS Notice the use of aliases to fix the data that was entered incorrectly. This remedy is merely a temporary patch, though, and not a permanent fix. You should see to it that the data is corrected and entered correctly in the future. On Day 21, "Common SQL Mistakes/Errors and Resolutions," you'll learn how to correct bad data.

This query not only fixed (at least visually) the incorrect data but also created a new column containing the difference between the highs and lows of each state.

If you accidentally use the minus sign on a character field, you get something like this:

INPUT/OUTPUT

```
SQL> SELECT -STATE FROM HILOW;

ERROR:
ORA-01722: invalid number
no rows selected
```

The exact error message varies with implementation, but the result is the same.

Divide (/)

The division operator has only the one obvious meaning. Using the table PRICE, type the following:

INPUT

```
SQL> SELECT * FROM PRICE;
```

OUTPUT

```
ITEM            WHOLESALE
--------------  ---------
TOMATOES             .34
POTATOES             .51
BANANAS              .67
TURNIPS              .45
CHEESE               .89
APPLES               .23
6 rows selected.
```

You can show the effects of a two-for-one sale by typing the next statement:

INPUT/ OUTPUT

```
SQL> SELECT ITEM, WHOLESALE, (WHOLESALE/2) SALEPRICE
  2  FROM PRICE;

ITEM            WHOLESALE SALEPRICE
--------------  --------- ---------
TOMATOES             .34       .17
POTATOES             .51      .255
BANANAS              .67      .335
TURNIPS              .45      .225
CHEESE               .89      .445
APPLES               .23      .115
6 rows selected.
```

The use of division in the preceding SELECT statement is straightforward (except that coming up with half pennies can be tough).

Multiply (*)

The multiplication operator is also straightforward. Again, using the PRICE table, type the following:

INPUT

```
SQL> SELECT * FROM PRICE;
```

OUTPUT

```
ITEM            WHOLESALE
--------------  ---------
TOMATOES             .34
POTATOES             .51
BANANAS              .67
TURNIPS              .45
CHEESE               .89
APPLES               .23
6 rows selected.
```

This query changes the table to reflect an across-the-board 10 percent discount:

```
INPUT/    SQL> SELECT ITEM, WHOLESALE, WHOLESALE * 0.9 NEWPRICE
OUTPUT         FROM PRICE;

          ITEM            WHOLESALE  NEWPRICE
          -------------   ---------  --------
          TOMATOES              .34      .306
          POTATOES              .51      .459
          BANANAS               .67      .603
          TURNIPS               .45      .405
          CHEESE                .89      .801
          APPLES                .23      .207
          6 rows selected.
```

These operators enable you to perform powerful calculations in a SELECT statement.

Modulo (%)

The modulo operator returns the integer remainder of the division operation. Using the table REMAINS, type the following:

```
INPUT     SQL> SELECT * FROM REMAINS;

OUTPUT    NUMERATOR  DENOMINATOR
          ---------  -----------
                 10            5
                  8            3
                 23            9
                 40           17
               1024           16
                 85           34
          6 rows selected.
```

You can also create a new column, REMAINDER, to hold the values of NUMERATOR % DENOMINATOR:

```
INPUT/    SQL> SELECT NUMERATOR,
OUTPUT         DENOMINATOR,
               NUMERATOR%DENOMINATOR REMAINDER
               FROM REMAINS;

          NUMERATOR DENOMINATOR REMAINDER
          --------- ----------- ---------
                 10           5         0
                  8           3         2
                 23           9         5
                 40          17         6
               1024          16         0
                 85          34        17
          6 rows selected.
```

Some implementations of SQL implement modulo as a function called MOD (see Day 4, "Functions: Molding the Data You Retrieve"). The following statement produces results that are identical to the results in the preceding statement:

```
SQL> SELECT NUMERATOR,
     DENOMINATOR,
     MOD(NUMERATOR,DENOMINATOR) REMAINDER
     FROM REMAINS;
```

Precedence

This section examines the use of precedence in a SELECT statement. Using the database PRECEDENCE, type the following:

```
SQL> SELECT * FROM PRECEDENCE;
     N1          N2          N3          N4
- - - - - - - -  - - - - - - -  - - - - - - -  - - - - -
      1           2           3           4
     13          24          35          46
      9           3          23           5
     63           2          45           3
      7           2           1           4
```

Use the following code segment to test precedence:

INPUT/OUTPUT

```
SQL> SELECT
  2  N1+N2*N3/N4,
  3  (N1+N2)*N3/N4,
  4  N1+(N2*N3)/N4
  5  FROM PRECEDENCE;

N1+N2*N3/N4  (N1+N2)*N3/N4 N1+(N2*N3)/N4
- - - - - - - - - - -  - - - - - - - - - - - - -  - - - - - - - - - - -
        2.5          2.25          2.5
   31.26087     28.152174     31.26087
       22.8          55.2         22.8
         93           975           93
        7.5          2.25          7.5
```

Notice that the first and last columns are identical. If you added a fourth column N1+N2*(N3/N4), its values would also be identical to those of the current first and last columns.

Comparison Operators

True to their name, comparison operators compare expressions and return one of three values: TRUE, FALSE, or Unknown. Wait a minute! Unknown? TRUE and FALSE are self-explanatory, but what is Unknown?

To understand how you could get an Unknown, you need to know a little about the concept of NULL. In database terms NULL is the absence of data in a field. It does not mean a column has a zero or a blank in it. A zero or a blank is a value. NULL means nothing is in that field. If you make a comparison like Field = 9 and the only value for Field is NULL, the comparison will come back Unknown. Because Unknown is an uncomfortable condition, most flavors of SQL change Unknown to FALSE and provide a special operator, IS NULL, to test for a NULL condition.

Here's an example of NULL: Suppose an entry in the PRICE table does not contain a value for WHOLESALE. The results of a query might look like this:

INPUT

```
SQL> SELECT * FROM PRICE;
```

OUTPUT

```
ITEM            WHOLESALE
-------------   ----------
TOMATOES             .34
POTATOES             .51
BANANAS              .67
TURNIPS              .45
CHEESE               .89
APPLES               .23
ORANGES
```

Notice that nothing is printed out in the WHOLESALE field position for oranges. The value for the field WHOLESALE for oranges is NULL. The NULL is noticeable in this case because it is in a numeric column. However, if the NULL appeared in the ITEM column, it would be impossible to tell the difference between NULL and a blank.

Try to find the NULL:

INPUT/OUTPUT

```
SQL> SELECT *
  2  FROM PRICE
  3  WHERE WHOLESALE IS NULL;

ITEM            WHOLESALE
-------------   ----------
ORANGES
```

ANALYSIS

As you can see by the output, ORANGES is the only item whose value for WHOLESALE is NULL or does not contain a value. What if you use the equal sign (=) instead?

INPUT/OUTPUT

```
SQL> SELECT *
     FROM PRICE
     WHERE WHOLESALE = NULL;

no rows selected
```

ANALYSIS

You didn't find anything because the comparison WHOLESALE = NULL returned a FALSE—the result was unknown. It would be more appropriate to use an IS NULL instead of =, changing the WHERE statement to WHERE WHOLESALE IS NULL. In this case you would get all the rows where a NULL existed.

This example also illustrates both the use of the most common comparison operator, the equal sign (=), and the playground of all comparison operators, the WHERE clause. You already know about the WHERE clause, so here's a brief look at the equal sign.

Equal (=)

Earlier today you saw how some implementations of SQL use the equal sign in the SELECT clause to assign an alias. In the WHERE clause, the equal sign is the most commonly used comparison operator. Used alone, the equal sign is a very convenient way of selecting one value out of many. Try this:

```
SQL> SELECT * FROM FRIENDS;
```

```
LASTNAME         FIRSTNAME        AREACODE PHONE     ST ZIP
--------------   --------------   -------- --------  -- -----
BUNDY            AL                    100 555-1111  IL 22333
MEZA             AL                    200 555-2222  UK
MERRICK          BUD                   300 555-6666  CO 80212
MAST             JD                    381 555-6767  LA 23456
BULHER           FERRIS                345 555-3223  IL 23332
```

Let's find JD's row. (On a short list this task appears trivial, but you may have more friends than we do—or you may have a list with thousands of records.)

```
SQL> SELECT *
     FROM FRIENDS
     WHERE FIRSTNAME = 'JD';

LASTNAME         FIRSTNAME        AREACODE PHONE     ST ZIP
--------------   --------------   -------- --------  -- -----
MAST             JD                    381 555-6767  LA 23456
```

We got the result that we expected. Try this:

```
SQL> SELECT *
     FROM FRIENDS
     WHERE FIRSTNAME = 'AL';

LASTNAME         FIRSTNAME        AREACODE PHONE     ST ZIP
--------------   --------------   -------- --------  -- -----
BUNDY            AL                    100 555-1111  IL 22333
MEZA             AL                    200 555-2222  UK
```

NOTE

Here you see that = can pull in multiple records. Notice that ZIP is blank on the second record. ZIP is a character field (you learn how to create and populate tables on Day 8, "Manipulating Data"), and in this particular record the NULL demonstrates that a NULL in a character field is impossible to differentiate from a blank field.

Here's another very important lesson concerning case sensitivity:

```
SQL> SELECT * FROM FRIENDS
     WHERE FIRSTNAME = 'BUD';

FIRSTNAME
--------------
BUD
1 row selected.
```

Now try this:

INPUT/OUTPUT
```
SQL> select * from friends
        where firstname = 'Bud';

no rows selected.
```

ANALYSIS Even though SQL syntax is not case sensitive, data is. Most companies prefer to store data in uppercase to provide data consistency. You should always store data either in all uppercase or in all lowercase. Mixing case creates difficulties when you try to retrieve accurate data.

Greater Than (>) and Greater Than or Equal To (>=)

The greater than operator (>) works like this:

INPUT
```
SQL> SELECT *
        FROM FRIENDS
        WHERE AREACODE > 300;
```

OUTPUT

LASTNAME	FIRSTNAME	AREACODE	PHONE	ST	ZIP
MAST	JD	381	555-6767	LA	23456
BULHER	FERRIS	345	555-3223	IL	23332

ANALYSIS This example found all the area codes greater than (but not including) 300. To include 300, type this.

INPUT/OUTPUT
```
SQL> SELECT *
   2  FROM FRIENDS
   3  WHERE AREACODE >= 300;
```

LASTNAME	FIRSTNAME	AREACODE	PHONE	ST	ZIP
MERRICK	BUD	300	555-6666	CO	80212
MAST	JD	381	555-6767	LA	23456
BULHER	FERRIS	345	555-3223	IL	23332

ANALYSIS With this change you get area codes starting at 300 and going up. You could achieve the same results with the statement AREACODE > 299.

NOTE Notice that no quotes surround 300 in this SQL statement. Number-defined fields do not require quotes.

Less Than (<) and Less Than or Equal To (<=)

As you might expect, these comparison operators work the same way as > and >= work, only in reverse:

INPUT
```
SQL> SELECT *
   2  FROM FRIENDS
   3  WHERE STATE < 'LA';
```

OUTPUT

```
LASTNAME         FIRSTNAME        AREACODE PHONE     ST ZIP
---------------  ---------------  -------- --------  -- -----
BUNDY            AL                    100 555-1111  IL 22333
MERRICK          BUD                   300 555-6666  CO 80212
BULHER           FERRIS                345 555-3223  IL 23332
```

NOTE

How did STATE get changed to ST? Because the column has only two characters, the column name is shortened to two characters in the returned rows. If the column name had been COWS, it would come out CO. The widths of AREACODE and PHONE are wider than their column names, so they are not truncated.

ANALYSIS

Wait a minute. Did you just use < on a character field? Of course you did. You can use any of these operators on any data type. The result varies by data type. For example, use lowercase in the following state search:

INPUT/ OUTPUT

```
SQL> SELECT *
  2  FROM FRIENDS
  3  WHERE STATE < 'la';

LASTNAME         FIRSTNAME        AREACODE PHONE     ST ZIP
---------------  ---------------  -------- --------  -- -----
BUNDY            AL                    100 555-1111  IL 22333
MEZA             AL                    200 555-2222  UK
MERRICK          BUD                   300 555-6666  CO 80212
MAST             JD                    381 555-6767  LA 23456
BULHER           FERRIS                345 555-3223  IL 23332
```

ANALYSIS

Uppercase is usually sorted before lowercase; therefore, the uppercase codes returned are less than 'la'. Again, to be safe, check your implementation.

TIP

To be sure of how these operators will behave, check your language tables. Most PC implementations use the ASCII tables. Some other platforms use EBCDIC.

To include the state of Louisiana in the original search, type

INPUT/ OUTPUT

```
SQL> SELECT *
  2  FROM FRIENDS
  3  WHERE STATE <= 'LA';

LASTNAME         FIRSTNAME        AREACODE PHONE     ST ZIP
---------------  ---------------  -------- --------  -- -----
BUNDY            AL                    100 555-1111  IL 22333
MERRICK          BUD                   300 555-6666  CO 80212
MAST             JD                    381 555-6767  LA 23456
BULHER           FERRIS                345 555-3223  IL 23332
```

Inequalities (< > or !=)

When you need to find everything except for certain data, use the inequality symbol, which can be either < > or !=, depending on your SQL implementation. For example, to find everyone who is not AL, type this:

INPUT

```
SQL> SELECT *
  2  FROM FRIENDS
  3  WHERE FIRSTNAME <> 'AL';
```

OUTPUT

```
LASTNAME          FIRSTNAME          AREACODE PHONE      ST ZIP
--------------    --------------     -------- --------   -- -----
MERRICK           BUD                     300 555-6666   CO 80212
MAST              JD                      381 555-6767   LA 23456
BULHER            FERRIS                  345 555-3223   IL 23332
```

To find everyone not living in California, type this:

**INPUT/
OUTPUT**

```
SQL> SELECT *
  2  FROM FRIENDS
  3  WHERE STATE != 'CA';
```

```
LASTNAME          FIRSTNAME          AREACODE PHONE      ST ZIP
--------------    --------------     -------- --------   -- -----
BUNDY             AL                      100 555-1111   IL 22333
MEZA              AL                      200 555-2222   UK
MERRICK           BUD                     300 555-6666   CO 80212
MAST              JD                      001 555-0707   LA 23456
BULHER            FERRIS                  345 555-3223   IL 23332
```

NOTE

Notice that both symbols, <> and !=, can express "not equals."

Character Operators

You can use character operators to manipulate the way character strings are represented, both in the output of data and in the process of placing conditions on data to be retrieved. This section describes two character operators: the LIKE operator and the || operator, which conveys the concept of character concatenation.

I Want to Be Like LIKE

What if you wanted to select parts of a database that fit a pattern but weren't quite exact matches? You could use the equal sign and run through all the possible cases, but that process would be boring and time-consuming. Instead, you could use LIKE. Consider the following:

INPUT

```
SQL> SELECT * FROM PARTS;
```

	NAME	LOCATION	PARTNUMBER
OUTPUT			
	APPENDIX	MID-STOMACH	1
	ADAMS APPLE	THROAT	2
	HEART	CHEST	3
	SPINE	BACK	4
	ANVIL	EAR	5
	KIDNEY	MID-BACK	6

How can you find all the parts located in the back? A quick visual inspection of this simple table shows that it has two parts, but unfortunately the locations have slightly different names. Try this:

INPUT/OUTPUT
```
SQL> SELECT *
  2  FROM PARTS
  3  WHERE LOCATION LIKE '%BACK%';
```

NAME	LOCATION	PARTNUMBER
SPINE	BACK	4
KIDNEY	MID-BACK	6

ANALYSIS You can see the use of the percent sign (%) in the statement after LIKE. When used inside a LIKE expression, % is a wildcard. What you asked for was any occurrence of BACK in the column location. If you queried

INPUT
```
SQL> SELECT *
     FROM PARTS
     WHERE LOCATION LIKE 'BACK%';
```

you would get any occurrence that started with BACK:

	NAME	LOCATION	PARTNUMBER
OUTPUT			
	SPINE	BACK	4

If you queried

INPUT
```
SQL> SELECT *
     FROM PARTS
     WHERE NAME LIKE 'A%';
```

you would get any name that starts with A:

	NAME	LOCATION	PARTNUMBER
OUTPUT			
	APPENDIX	MID-STOMACH	1
	ADAMS APPLE	THROAT	2
	ANVIL	EAR	5

Is LIKE case sensitive? Try the next query to find out.

INPUT/OUTPUT
```
SQL> SELECT *
     FROM PARTS
     WHERE NAME LIKE 'a%';
```

```
no rows selected
```

3

ANALYSIS The answer is yes. References to data are always case sensitive.

What if you want to find data that matches all but one character in a certain pattern? In this case you could use a different type of wildcard: the underscore.

Underscore (_)

The underscore is the single-character wildcard. Using a modified version of the table FRIENDS, type this:

INPUT
```
SQL> SELECT * FROM FRIENDS;
```

OUTPUT
```
LASTNAME         FIRSTNAME        AREACODE PHONE     ST ZIP
--------------   --------------   -------- --------  -- -----
BUNDY            AL                    100 555-1111  IL 22333
MEZA             AL                    200 555-2222  UK
MERRICK          UD                    300 555-6666  CO 80212
MAST             JD                    381 555-6767  LA 23456
BULHER           FERRIS                345 555-3223  IL 23332
PERKINS          ALTON                 011 555-3116  CA 95633
BOSS             SIR                   204 555-2345  CT 95633
```

To find all the records where STATE starts with C, type the following:

INPUT/OUTPUT
```
SQL> SELECT *
  2  FROM FRIENDS
  3  WHERE STATE LIKE 'C_';

LASTNAME         FIRSTNAME        AREACODE PHONE     ST ZIP
--------------   --------------   -------- --------  -- -----
MERRICK          DUD                   300 555-6666  CO 80212
PERKINS          ALTON                 911 555-3116  CA 95633
BOSS             SIR                   204 555-2345  CT 95633
```

You can use several underscores in a statement:

INPUT/OUTPUT
```
SQL> SELECT *
  2  FROM FRIENDS
  3  WHERE PHONE LIKE'555-6_6_';

LASTNAME         FIRSTNAME        AREACODE PHONE     ST ZIP
--------------   --------------   -------- --------  -- -----
MERRICK          BUD                   300 555-6666  CO 80212
MAST             JD                    381 555-6767  LA 23456
```

The previous statement could also be written as follows:

INPUT/OUTPUT
```
SQL> SELECT *
  2  FROM FRIENDS
  3  WHERE PHONE LIKE '555-6%';

LASTNAME         FIRSTNAME        AREACODE PHONE     ST ZIP
--------------   --------------   -------- --------  -- -----
MERRICK          BUD                   300 555-6666  CO 80212
MAST             JD                    381 555-6767  LA 23456
```

Notice that the results are identical. These two wildcards can be combined. The next example finds all records with L as the second character:

```
SQL> SELECT *
  2   FROM FRIENDS
  3   WHERE FIRSTNAME LIKE '_L%';

LASTNAME         FIRSTNAME        AREACODE PHONE    ST ZIP
--------------   --------------   -------- -------- -- -----
BUNDY            AL                    100 555-1111 IL 22333
MEZA             AL                    200 555-2222 UK
PERKINS          ALTON                 911 555-3116 CA 95633
```

Concatenation (¦¦)

The ¦¦ (double pipe) symbol concatenates two strings. Try this:

INPUT

```
SQL> SELECT FIRSTNAME ¦¦ LASTNAME ENTIRENAME
  2   FROM FRIENDS;
```

OUTPUT

```
ENTIRENAME
--------------------
AL          BUNDY
AL          MEZA
BUD         MERRICK
JD          MAST
FERRIS      BULHER
ALTON       PERKINS
SIR         BOSS
7 rows selected.
```

ANALYSIS Notice that ¦¦ is used instead of +. If you use + to try to concatenate the strings, the SQL interpreter used for this example (Personal Oracle7) returns the following error:

INPUT/OUTPUT

```
SQL> SELECT FIRSTNAME + LASTNAME ENTIRENAME
     FROM FRIENDS;

ERROR:
ORA-01722: invalid number
```

It is looking for two numbers to add and throws the error invalid number when it doesn't find any.

NOTE Some implementations of SQL use the plus sign to concatenate strings. Check your implementation.

Here's a more practical example using concatenation:

INPUT/OUTPUT

```
SQL> SELECT LASTNAME ¦¦ ',' ¦¦ FIRSTNAME NAME
     FROM FRIENDS;
```

```
NAME
- - - - - - - - - - - - - - - - - - - - - - - - - - - - - - - - - - - - - - - - - - - - - -
BUNDY     , AL
MEZA      , AL
MERRICK   , BUD
MAST      , JD
BULHER    , FERRIS
PERKINS   , ALTON
BOSS      , SIR
7 rows selected.
```

ANALYSIS This statement inserted a comma between the last name and the first name.

NOTE

Notice the extra spaces between the first name and the last name in these examples. These spaces are actually part of the data. With certain data types, spaces are right-padded to values less than the total length allocated for a field. See your implementation. Data types will be discussed on Day 9, "Creating and Maintaining Tables."

So far you have performed the comparisons one at a time. That method is fine for some problems, but what if you need to find all the people at work with last names starting with *P* who have less than three days of vacation time?

Logical Operators

Logical operators separate two or more conditions in the WHERE clause of an SQL statement.

Vacation time is always a hot topic around the workplace. Say you designed a table called VACATION for the accounting department:

INPUT `SQL> SELECT * FROM VACATION;`

OUTPUT

```
LASTNAME      EMPLOYEENUM   YEARS  LEAVETAKEN
- - - - - - - -   - - - - - - - - -   - - -   - - - - - -
ABLE              101         2         4
BAKER             104         5        23
BLEDSOE           107         8        45
BOLIVAR           233         4        80
BOLD              210        15       100
COSTALES          211        10        78
6 rows selected.
```

Suppose your company gives each employee 12 days of leave each year. Using what you have learned and a logical operator, find all the employees whose names start with B and who have more than 50 days of leave coming.

```
SQL> SELECT LASTNAME,
  2  YEARS * 12 - LEAVETAKEN REMAINING
  3  FROM VACATION
  4  WHERE LASTNAME LIKE 'B%'
  5  AND
  6  YEARS * 12 - LEAVETAKEN > 50;

LASTNAME        REMAINING
--------------- ---------
BLEDSOE                51
BOLD                   80
```

ANALYSIS This query is the most complicated you have done so far. The SELECT clause (lines 1 and 2) uses arithmetic operators to determine how many days of leave each employee has remaining. The normal precedence computes YEARS * 12 - LEAVETAKEN. (A clearer approach would be to write (YEARS * 12) - LEAVETAKEN.)

LIKE is used in line 4 with the wildcard % to find all the B names. Line 6 uses the > to find all occurrences greater than 50.

The new element is on line 5. You used the logical operator AND to ensure that you found records that met the criteria in lines 4 *and* 6.

AND

AND means that the expressions on both sides must be true to return TRUE. If either expression is false, AND returns FALSE. For example, to find out which employees have been with the company for 5 years or less and have taken more than 20 days leave, try this:

INPUT
```
SQL> SELECT LASTNAME
  2  FROM VACATION
  3  WHERE YEARS <= 5
  4  AND
  5  LEAVETAKEN > 20 ;
```

OUTPUT
```
LASTNAME
--------
BAKER
BOLIVAR
```

If you want to know which employees have been with the company for 5 years or more and have taken less than 50 percent of their leave, you could write:

INPUT/ OUTPUT
```
SQL> SELECT LASTNAME WORKAHOLICS
  2  FROM VACATION
  3  WHERE YEARS >= 5
  4  AND
  5  ((YEARS *12)-LEAVETAKEN)/(YEARS * 12) < 0.50;

WORKAHOLICS
---------------
BAKER
BLEDSOE
```

3

Check these people for burnout. Also check out how we used the AND to combine these two conditions.

OR

You can also use OR to sum up a series of conditions. If any of the comparisons is true, OR returns TRUE. To illustrate the difference, run the last query with OR instead of with AND:

```
SQL> SELECT LASTNAME WORKAHOLICS
  2  FROM VACATION
  3  WHERE YEARS >= 5
  4  OR
  5  ((YEARS *12)-LEAVETAKEN)/(YEARS * 12) >= 0.50;
```

OUTPUT

```
WORKAHOLICS
---------------
ABLE
BAKER
BLEDSOE
DOLD
COSTALES
```

ANALYSIS The original names are still in the list, but you have three new entries (who would probably resent being called workaholics). These three new names made the list because they satisfied one of the conditions. OR requires that only one of the conditions be true in order for data to be returned.

NOT

NOT means just that. If the condition it applies to evaluates to TRUE, NOT make it FALSE. If the condition after the NOT is FALSE, it becomes TRUE. For example, the following SELECT returns the only two names not beginning with B in the table:

INPUT

```
SQL> SELECT *
  2  FROM VACATION
  3  WHERE LASTNAME NOT LIKE 'B%';
```

OUTPUT

LASTNAME	EMPLOYEENUM	YEARS	LEAVETAKEN
ABLE	101	2	4
COSTALES	211	10	78

NOT can also be used with the operator IS when applied to NULL. Recall the PRICES table where we put a NULL value in the WHOLESALE column opposite the item ORANGES.

INPUT/ OUTPUT

```
SQL> SELECT * FROM PRICE;
```

ITEM	WHOLESALE
TOMATOES	.34
POTATOES	.51
BANANAS	.67
TURNIPS	.45
CHEESE	.89
APPLES	.23
ORANGES	

```
7 rows selected.
```

To find the non-NULL items, type this:

```
SQL> SELECT *
  2  FROM PRICE
  3  WHERE WHOLESALE IS NOT NULL;

ITEM           WHOLESALE
-------------- ---------
TOMATOES            .34
POTATOES            .51
BANANAS             .67
TURNIPS             .45
CHEESE              .89
APPLES              .23
6 rows selected.
```

Set Operators

On Day 1, "Introduction to SQL," you learned that SQL is based on the theory of sets. The following sections examine set operators.

UNION and UNION ALL

UNION returns the results of two queries minus the duplicate rows. The following two tables represent the rosters of teams:

```
SQL> SELECT * FROM FOOTBALL;

NAME
-------------------
ABLE
BRAVO
CHARLIE
DECON
EXITOR
FUBAR
GOOBER
7 rows selected.
```

```
SQL> SELECT * FROM SOFTBALL;

NAME
-------------------
ABLE
BAKER
CHARLIE
DEAN
EXITOR
FALCONER
GOOBER
7 rows selected.
```

How many different people play on one team or another?

```
SQL> SELECT NAME FROM SOFTBALL
  2  UNION
  3  SELECT NAME FROM FOOTBALL;
```

```
NAME
- - - - - - - - - - - - - - - - - - -
ABLE
BAKER
BRAVO
CHARLIE
DEAN
DECON
EXITOR
FALCONER
FUBAR
GOOBER
10 rows selected.
```

UNION returns 10 distinct names from the two lists. How many names are on both lists (including duplicates)?

INPUT/ OUTPUT
```
SQL> SELECT NAME FROM SOFTBALL
  2  UNION ALL
  3  SELECT NAME FROM FOOTBALL;

NAME
- - - - - - - - - - - - - - - - - - -
ABLE
BAKER
CHARLIE
DEAN
EXITOR
FALCONER
GOOBER
ABLE
BRAVO
CHARLIE
DECON
EXITOR
FUBAR
GOOBER
14 rows selected.
```

ANALYSIS
The combined list—courtesy of the UNION ALL statement—has 14 names. UNION ALL works just like UNION except it does not eliminate duplicates. Now show me a list of players who are on both teams. You can't do that with UNION—you need to learn INTERSECT.

INTERSECT

INTERSECT returns only the rows found by both queries. The next SELECT statement shows the list of players who play on both teams:

INPUT
```
SQL> SELECT * FROM FOOTBALL
  2  INTERSECT
  3  SELECT * FROM SOFTBALL;
NAME
```

```
OUTPUT  - - - - - - - - - - - - - - - - - - -
        ABLE
        CHARLIE
        EXITOR
        GOOBER
```

In this example INTERSECT finds the short list of players who are on both teams by combining the results of the two SELECT statements.

MINUS (Difference)

Minus returns the rows from the first query that were not present in the second. For example:

```
INPUT   SQL> SELECT * FROM FOOTBALL
          2  MINUS
          3  SELECT * FROM SOFTBALL;
```

```
OUTPUT  NAME
        - - - - - - - - - - - - - - - - - - -
        BRAVO
        DECON
        FUBAR
```

The preceding query shows the three football players who are not on the softball team. If you reverse the order, you get the three softball players who aren't on the football team:

```
INPUT/   SQL> SELECT * FROM SOFTBALL
OUTPUT     2  MINUS
           3  SELECT * FROM FOOTBALL;

         NAME
         - - - - - - - - - - - - - - - - - - -
         BAKER
         DEAN
         FALCONER
```

Miscellaneous Operators: IN and BETWEEN

The two operators IN and BETWEEN provide a shorthand for functions you already know how to do. If you wanted to find friends in Colorado, California, and Louisiana, you could type the following:

```
INPUT   SQL> SELECT *
          2  FROM FRIENDS
          3  WHERE STATE= 'CA'
          4  OR
          5  STATE ='CO'
          6  OR
          7  STATE = 'LA';
```

```
OUTPUT  LASTNAME        FIRSTNAME       AREACODE PHONE     ST ZIP
        - - - - - - - - - - - -  - - - - - - - - - - - -  - - - - - - - - -  - - - - - - - -  - -  - - - - -
        MERRICK         BUD                  300 555-6666 CO 80212
        MAST            JD                   381 555-6767 LA 23456
        PERKINS         ALTON                911 555-3116 CA 95633
```

Or you could type this:

INPUT/
OUTPUT

```
SQL> SELECT *
  2  FROM FRIENDS
  3  WHERE STATE IN('CA','CO','LA');

LASTNAME        FIRSTNAME        AREACODE PHONE     ST ZIP
--------------- ---------------- -------- -------- -- -----
MERRICK         BUD                   300 555-6666 CO 80212
MAST            JD                    381 555-6767 LA 23456
PERKINS         ALTON                 911 555-3116 CA 95633
```

ANALYSIS The second example is shorter and more readable than the first. You never know when you might have to go back and work on something you wrote months ago. IN also works with numbers. Consider the following, where the column AREACODE is a number:

INPUT/
OUTPUT

```
SQL> SELECT *
  2  FROM FRIENDS
  3  WHERE AREACODE IN(100,381,204);

LASTNAME        FIRSTNAME        AREACODE PHONE     ST ZIP
--------------- ---------------- -------- -------- -- -----
BUNDY           AL                    100 555-1111 IL 22333
MAST            JD                    381 555-6767 LA 23456
BOSS            SIR                   204 555-2345 CT 95633
```

If you needed a range of things from the PRICE table, you could write the following:

INPUT/
OUTPUT

```
SQL> SELECT *
  2  FROM PRICE
  3  WHERE WHOLESALE > 0.25
  4  AND
  5  WHOLESALE < 0.75;

ITEM            WHOLESALE
--------------- ---------
TOMATOES              .34
POTATOES             .51
BANANAS              .67
TURNIPS              .45
```

Or using BETWEEN, you would write this:

INPUT/
OUTPUT

```
SQL> SELECT *
  2  FROM PRICE
  3  WHERE WHOLESALE BETWEEN 0.25 AND 0.75;

ITEM            WHOLESALE
--------------- ---------
TOMATOES              .34
POTATOES             .51
BANANAS              .67
TURNIPS              .45
```

Again, the second example is a cleaner, more readable solution than the first.

NOTE If a WHOLESALE value of 0.25 existed in the PRICE table, that record would have been retrieved also. Parameters used in the BETWEEN operator are inclusive.

Summary

At the beginning of Day 3, you knew how to use the basic SELECT and FROM clauses. Now you know how to use a host of operators that enable you to fine-tune your requests to the database. You learned how to use arithmetic, comparison, character, logical, and set operators. This powerful set of tools provides the cornerstone of your SQL knowledge.

Q&A

Q How does all of this information apply to me if I am not using SQL from the command line as depicted in the examples?

A Whether you use SQL in COBOL as Embedded SQL or in Microsoft's Open Database Connectivity (ODBC), you use the same basic constructions. You will use what you learned today and yesterday repeatedly as you work with SQL.

Q Why are you constantly telling me to check my implementation? I thought there was a standard!

A There is an ANSI standard (the most recent version is 1992); however, most vendors modify it somewhat to suit their databases. The basics are similar if not identical, and each instance has extensions that other vendors copy and improve. We have chosen to use ANSI as a starting point but point out the differences as we go along.

Workshop

The Workshop provides quiz questions to help solidify your understanding of the material covered, as well as exercises to provide you with experience in using what you have learned. Try to answer the quiz and exercise questions before checking the answers in Appendix F, "Answers to Quizzes and Exercises."

Quiz

Use the FRIENDS table to answer the following questions.

LASTNAME	FIRSTNAME	AREACODE	PHONE	ST	ZIP
BUNDY	AL	100	555-1111	IL	22333
MEZA	AL	200	555-2222	UK	
MERRICK	BUD	300	555-6666	CO	80212
MAST	JD	381	555-6767	LA	23456
BULHER	FERRIS	345	555-3223	IL	23332
PERKINS	ALTON	911	555-3116	CA	95633
BOSS	SIR	204	555-2345	CT	95633

1. Write a query that returns everyone in the database whose last name begins with M.

2. Write a query that returns everyone who lives in Illinois with a first name of AL.

3. Given two tables (PART1 and PART2) containing columns named PARTNO, how would you find out which part numbers are in both tables? Write the query.

4. What shorthand could you use instead of WHERE a >= 10 AND a <=30?

5. What will this query return?

```
SELECT FIRSTNAME
FROM FRIENDS
WHERE FIRSTNAME = 'AL'
  AND LASTNAME = 'BULHER';
```

Exercises

1. Using the FRIENDS table, write a query that returns the following:

```
NAME               ST
------------------ --
AL                 FROM IL
```

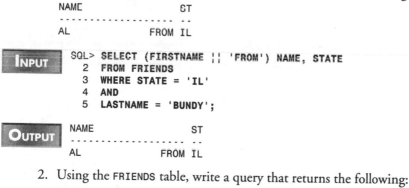

INPUT
```
SQL> SELECT (FIRSTNAME || 'FROM') NAME, STATE
  2  FROM FRIENDS
  3  WHERE STATE = 'IL'
  4  AND
  5  LASTNAME = 'BUNDY';
```

OUTPUT
```
NAME               ST
------------------ --
AL                 FROM IL
```

2. Using the FRIENDS table, write a query that returns the following:

```
NAME                         PHONE
---------------------------- -------------
MERRICK, BUD                 300-555-6666
MAST, JD                     381-555-6767
BULHER, FERRIS               345-555-3223
```

Day 4

Functions: Molding the Data You Retrieve

Objectives

Today we talk about functions. Functions in SQL enable you to perform feats such as determining the sum of a column or converting all the characters of a string to uppercase. By the end of the day, you will understand and be able to use all the following:

- ☐ Aggregate functions
- ☐ Date and time functions
- ☐ Arithmetic functions
- ☐ Character functions
- ☐ Conversion functions
- ☐ Miscellaneous functions

These functions greatly increase your ability to manipulate the information you retrieved using the basic functions of SQL that were described earlier this week.

The first five aggregate functions, COUNT, SUM, AVG, MAX, and MIN, are defined in the ANSI standard. Most implementations of SQL have extensions to these aggregate functions, some of which are covered today. Some implementations may use different names for these functions.

Aggregate Functions

These functions are also referred to as *group functions*. They return a value based on the values in a column. (After all, you wouldn't ask for the average of a single field.) The examples in this section use the table TEAMSTATS:

INPUT

```
SQL> SELECT * FROM TEAMSTATS;
```

OUTPUT

NAME	POS	AB	HITS	WALKS	SINGLES	DOUBLES	TRIPLES	HR	SO
JONES	1B	145	45	34	31	8	1	5	10
DONKNOW	3B	175	65	23	50	10	1	4	15
WORLEY	LF	157	49	15	35	8	3	3	16
DAVID	OF	187	70	24	48	4	0	17	42
HAMHOCKER	3B	50	12	10	10	2	0	0	13
CASEY	DH	1	0	0	0	0	0	0	1

```
6 rows selected.
```

COUNT

The function COUNT returns the number of rows that satisfy the condition in the WHERE clause. Say you wanted to know how many ball players were hitting under 350. You would type

INPUT/OUTPUT

```
SQL> SELECT COUNT(*)
  2    FROM TEAMSTATS
  3    WHERE HITS/AB < .35;

COUNT(*)
--------
       4
```

To make the code more readable, try an alias:

INPUT/OUTPUT

```
SQL> SELECT COUNT(*) NUM_BELOW_350
  2    FROM TEAMSTATS
  3    WHERE HITS/AB < .35;

NUM_BELOW_350
-------------
            4
```

4

Would it make any difference if you tried a column name instead of the asterisk? (Notice the use of parentheses around the column names.) Try this:

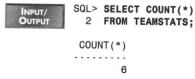

```
SQL> SELECT COUNT(NAME) NUM_BELOW_350
  2    FROM TEAMSTATS
  3    WHERE HITS/AB < .35;

NUM_BELOW_350
-------------
            4
```

The answer is no. The NAME column that you selected was not involved in the WHERE statement. If you use COUNT without a WHERE clause, it returns the number of records in the table.

```
SQL> SELECT COUNT(*)
  2    FROM TEAMSTATS;

  COUNT(*)
----------
         6
```

SUM

SUM does just that. It returns the sum of all values in a column. To find out how many singles have been hit, type

```
SQL> SELECT SUM(SINGLES) TOTAL_SINGLES
  2    FROM TEAMSTATS;
```

```
TOTAL_SINGLES
-------------
          174
```

To get several sums, use

```
SQL> SELECT SUM(SINGLES) TOTAL_SINGLES, SUM(DOUBLES) TOTAL_DOUBLES,
SUM(TRIPLES) TOTAL_TRIPLES, SUM(HR) TOTAL_HR
  2    FROM TEAMSTATS;

TOTAL_SINGLES TOTAL_DOUBLES TOTAL_TRIPLES TOTAL_HR
------------- ------------- ------------- --------
          174            32             5       29
```

To collect similar information on all 300 or better players, type

```
SQL> SELECT SUM(SINGLES) TOTAL_SINGLES, SUM(DOUBLES) TOTAL_DOUBLES,
SUM(TRIPLES) TOTAL_TRIPLES, SUM(HR) TOTAL_HR
  2    FROM TEAMSTATS
  3    WHERE HITS/AB >= .300;

TOTAL_SINGLES TOTAL_DOUBLES TOTAL_TRIPLES TOTAL_HR
------------- ------------- ------------- --------
          164            30             5       29
```

To compute a team batting average, type

```
SQL> SELECT SUM(HITS)/SUM(AB) TEAM_AVERAGE
  2  FROM TEAMSTATS;

TEAM_AVERAGE
------------
    .33706294
```

SUM works only with numbers. If you try it on a nonnumerical field, you get

```
SQL> SELECT SUM(NAME)
  2  FROM TEAMSTATS;

ERROR:
ORA-01722: invalid number
no rows selected
```

This error message is logical because you cannot sum a group of names.

AVG

The AVG function computes the average of a column. To find the average number of strike outs, use this:

```
SQL> SELECT AVG(SO) AVE_STRIKE_OUTS
  2  FROM TEAMSTATS;
```

```
AVE_STRIKE_OUTS
---------------
       16.166667
```

The following example illustrates the difference between SUM and AVG:

```
SQL> SELECT AVG(HITS/AB) TEAM_AVERAGE
  2  FROM TEAMSTATS;

TEAM_AVERAGE
------------
    .26803448
```

The team was batting over 300 in the previous example! What happened? AVG computed the average of the combined column hits divided by at bats, whereas the example with SUM divided the total number of hits by the number of at bats. For example, player A gets 50 hits in 100 at bats for a .500 average. Player B gets 0 hits in 1 at bat for a 0.0 average. The average of 0.0 and 0.5 is .250. If you compute the combined average of 50 hits in 101 at bats, the answer is a respectable .495. The following statement returns the correct batting average:

```
SQL> SELECT AVG(HITS)/AVG(AB) TEAM_AVERAGE
  2  FROM TEAMSTATS;
TEAM_AVERAGE
------------
    .33706294
```

Like the SUM function, AVG works only with numbers.

MAX

If you want to find the largest value in a column, use MAX. For example, what is the highest number of hits?

INPUT
```
SQL> SELECT MAX(HITS)
  2  FROM TEAMSTATS;
```

OUTPUT
```
MAX(HITS)
---------
       70
```

Can you find out who has the most hits?

INPUT/OUTPUT
```
SQL> SELECT NAME
  2  FROM TEAMSTATS
  3  WHERE HITS = MAX(HITS);

ERROR at line 3:
ORA-00934: group function is not allowed here
```

Unfortunately, you can't. The error message is a reminder that this group function (remember that *aggregate functions* are also called *group functions*) does not work in the WHERE clause. Don't despair, Day 7, "Subqueries: The Embedded SELECT Statement," covers the concept of subqueries and explains a way to find who has the MAX hits.

What happens if you try a nonnumerical column?

INPUT/OUTPUT
```
SQL> SELECT MAX(NAME)
  2  FROM TEAMSTATS;


MAX(NAME)
---------------
WORLEY
```

Here's something new. MAX returns the highest (closest to Z) string. Finally, a function that works with both characters and numbers.

MIN

MIN does the expected thing and works like MAX except it returns the lowest member of a column. To find out the fewest at bats, type

INPUT
```
SQL> SELECT MIN(AB)
  2  FROM TEAMSTATS;
```

OUTPUT
```
MIN(AB)
---------
      1
```

The following statement returns the name closest to the beginning of the alphabet:

```
SQL> SELECT MIN(NAME)
  2  FROM TEAMSTATS;

MIN(NAME)
- - - - - - - - - - - - - -
CASEY
```

You can combine MIN with MAX to give a range of values. For example:

```
SQL> SELECT MIN(AB), MAX(AB)
  2  FROM TEAMSTATS;

  MIN(AB)  MAX(AB)
- - - - - - - -  - - - - - - - -
        1      187
```

This sort of information can be useful when using statistical functions.

NOTE

> As we mentioned in the introduction, the first five aggregate functions are described in the ANSI standard. The remaining aggregate functions have become de facto standards, present in all important implementations of SQL. We use the Oracle7 names for these functions. Other implementations may use different names.

VARIANCE

VARIANCE produces the square of the standard deviation, a number vital to many statistical calculations. It works like this:

```
SQL> SELECT VARIANCE(HITS)
  2  FROM TEAMSTATS;
```

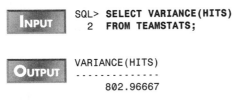

```
VARIANCE(HITS)
- - - - - - - - - - - - -
    802.96667
```

If you try a string

```
SQL> SELECT VARIANCE(NAME)
  2  FROM TEAMSTATS;

ERROR:
ORA-01722: invalid number
no rows selected
```

you find that VARIANCE is another function that works exclusively with numbers.

STDDEV

The final group function, STDDEV, finds the standard deviation of a column of numbers, as demonstrated by this example:

INPUT

```
SQL> SELECT STDDEV(HITS)
  2  FROM TEAMSTATS;
```

OUTPUT

```
STDDEV(HITS)
------------
   28.336666
```

It also returns an error when confronted by a string:

INPUT/OUTPUT

```
SQL> SELECT STDDEV(NAME)
  2  FROM TEAMSTATS;

ERROR:
ORA-01722: invalid number
no rows selected
```

These aggregate functions can also be used in various combinations:

INPUT/OUTPUT

```
SQL> SELECT COUNT(AB),
  2  AVG(AB),
  3  MIN(AB),
  4  MAX(AB),
  5  STDDEV(AB),
  6  VARIANCE(AB),
  7  SUM(AB)
  8  FROM TEAMSTATS;
```

COUNT(AB)	AVG(AB)	MIN(AB)	MAX(AB)	STDDEV(AB)	VARIANCE(AB)	SUM(AB)
6	119.167	1	187	75.589	5712.97	715

The next time you hear a sportscaster use statistics to fill the time between plays, you will know that SQL is at work somewhere behind the scenes.

Date and Time Functions

We live in a civilization governed by times and dates, and most major implementations of SQL have functions to cope with these concepts. This section uses the table PROJECT to demonstrate the time and date functions.

INPUT

```
SQL> SELECT * FROM PROJECT;
```

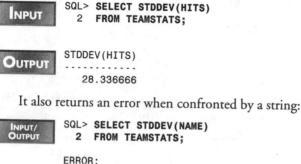

```
TASK              STARTDATE ENDDATE
--------------    --------- ---------
KICKOFF MTG       01-APR-95 01-APR-95
TECH SURVEY       02-APR-95 01-MAY-95
USER MTGS         15-MAY-95 30-MAY-95
DESIGN WIDGET     01-JUN-95 30-JUN-95
CODE WIDGET       01-JUL-95 02-SEP-95
TESTING           03-SEP-95 17-JAN-96

6 rows selected.
```

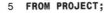

NOTE

> This table used the Date data type. Most implementations of SQL have a Date data type, but the exact syntax may vary.

ADD_MONTHS

This function adds a number of months to a specified date. For example, say something extraordinary happened, and the preceding project slipped to the right by two months. You could make a new schedule by typing

INPUT

```
SQL> SELECT TASK,
  2  STARTDATE,
  3  ENDDATE ORIGINAL_END,
  4  ADD_MONTHS(ENDDATE,2)
  5  FROM PROJECT;
```

```
TASK              STARTDATE ORIGINAL_ ADD_MONTH
--------------    --------- --------- ---------
KICKOFF MTG       01-APR-95 01-APR-95 01-JUN-95
TECH SURVEY       02-APR-95 01-MAY-95 01-JUL-95
USER MTGS         15-MAY-95 30-MAY-95 30-JUL-95
DESIGN WIDGET     01-JUN-95 30-JUN-95 31-AUG-95
CODE WIDGET       01-JUL-95 02-SEP-95 02-NOV-95
TESTING           03-SEP-95 17-JAN-96 17-MAR-96

6 rows selected.
```

Not that a slip like this is possible, but it's nice to have a function that makes it so easy. ADD_MONTHS also works outside the SELECT clause. Typing

INPUT

```
SQL> SELECT TASK TASKS_SHORTER_THAN_ONE_MONTH
  2  FROM PROJECT
  3  WHERE ADD_MONTHS(STARTDATE,1) > ENDDATE;
```

produces the following result:

Output

```
TASKS_SHORTER_THAN_ONE_MONTH
---------------------------
KICKOFF MTG
TECH SURVEY
USER MTGS
DESIGN WIDGET
```

Analysis You will find that all the functions in this section work in more than one place. However, ADD MONTHS does not work with other data types like character or number without the help of functions TO_CHAR and TO_DATE, which are discussed later today.

LAST_DAY

LAST_DAY returns the last day of a specified month. It is for those of us who haven't mastered the "Thirty days has September..." rhyme—or at least those of us who have not yet taught it to our computers. If, for example, you need to know what the last day of the month is in the column ENDDATE, you would type

Input

```
SQL> SELECT ENDDATE, LAST_DAY(ENDDATE)
  2  FROM PROJECT;
```

Here's the result:

Output

```
ENDDATE    LAST_DAY(ENDDATE)
---------  -----------------
01-APR-95  30-APR-95
01-MAY-95  31-MAY-95
30-MAY-95  31-MAY-95
30-JUN-95  30-JUN-95
02-SEP-95  30-SEP-95
17-JAN-96  31-JAN-96

6 rows selected.
```

How does LAST DAY handle leap years?

Input/ Output

```
SQL> SELECT LAST_DAY('1-FEB-95') NON_LEAP,
  2  LAST_DAY('1-FEB-96') LEAP
  3  FROM PROJECT;

NON_LEAP   LEAP
---------  ---------
28-FEB-95  29-FEB-96
28-FEB-95  29-FEB-96
28-FEB-95  29-FEB-96
28-FEB-95  29-FEB-96
28-FEB-95  29-FEB-96
28-FEB-95  29-FEB-96

6 rows selected.
```

4

You got the right result, but why were so many rows returned? Because you didn't specify an existing column or any conditions, the SQL engine applied the date functions in the statement to each existing row. Let's get something less redundant by using the following:

```
SQL> SELECT DISTINCT LAST_DAY('1-FEB-95') NON_LEAP,
  2    LAST_DAY('1-FEB-96') LEAP
  3    FROM PROJECT;
```

This statement uses the word DISTINCT (see Day 2, "Introduction to the Query: The SELECT Statement") to produce the singular result

OUTPUT

```
NON_LEAP   LEAP
--------- ---------
28-FEB-95 29-FEB-96
```

Unlike me, this function knows which years are leap years. But before you trust your own or your company's financial future to this or any other function, check your implementation!

MONTHS_BETWEEN

If you need to know how many months fall between month x and month y, use MONTHS_BETWEEN like this:

INPUT

```
SQL> SELECT TASK, STARTDATE, ENDDATE,MONTHS_BETWEEN(STARTDATE,ENDDATE)
         DURATION
  2    FROM PROJECT;
```

OUTPUT

```
TASK           STARTDATE ENDDATE   DURATION
-------------- --------- --------- ---------
KICKOFF MTG    01-APR-95 01-APR-95         0
TECH SURVEY    02-APR-95 01-MAY-95 -.9677419
USER MTGS      15-MAY-95 30-MAY-95  -.483871
DESIGN WIDGET  01-JUN-95 30-JUN-95 -.9354839
CODE WIDGET    01-JUL-95 02-SEP-95 -2.032258
TESTING        03-SEP-95 17-JAN-96 -4.451613

6 rows selected.
```

Wait a minute—that doesn't look right. Try this:

INPUT/OUTPUT

```
SQL> SELECT TASK, STARTDATE, ENDDATE,
  2    MONTHS_BETWEEN(ENDDATE,STARTDATE) DURATION
  3    FROM PROJECT;

TASK           STARTDATE ENDDATE   DURATION
-------------- --------- --------- ---------
KICKOFF MTG    01-APR-95 01-APR-95         0
TECH SURVEY    02-APR-95 01-MAY-95 .96774194
USER MTGS      15-MAY-95 30-MAY-95 .48387097
DESIGN WIDGET  01-JUN-95 30-JUN-95 .93548387
CODE WIDGET    01-JUL-95 02-SEP-95 2.0322581
TESTING        03-SEP-95 17-JAN-96 4.4516129

6 rows selected.
```

ANALYSIS That's better. You see that MONTHS_BETWEEN is sensitive to the way you order the months. Negative months might not be bad. For example, you could use a negative result to determine whether one date happened before another. For example, the following statement shows all the tasks that started before May 19, 1995:

INPUT
```
SQL> SELECT *
  2  FROM PROJECT
  3  WHERE MONTHS_BETWEEN('19 MAY 95', STARTDATE) > 0;
```

OUTPUT
```
TASK            STARTDATE ENDDATE
--------------- --------- ---------
KICKOFF MTG     01-APR-95 01-APR-95
TECH SURVEY     02-APR-95 01-MAY-95
USER MTGS       15-MAY-95 30-MAY-95
```

NEW_TIME

If you need to adjust the time according to the time zone you are in, the NEW_TIME function is for you. Here are the time zones you can use with this function:

Abbreviation	Time Zone
AST or ADT	Atlantic standard or daylight time
BST or BDT	Bering standard or daylight time
CST or CDT	Central standard or daylight time
EST or EDT	Eastern standard or daylight time
GMT	Greenwich mean time
HST or HDT	Alaska-Hawaii standard or daylight time
MST or MDT	Mountain standard or daylight time
NST	Newfoundland standard time
PST or PDT	Pacific standard or daylight time
YST or YDT	Yukon standard or daylight time

You can adjust your time like this:

INPUT
```
SQL> SELECT ENDDATE EDT,
  2  NEW_TIME(ENDDATE, 'EDT','PDT')
  3  FROM PROJECT;
```

OUTPUT
```
EDT               NEW_TIME(ENDDATE
----------------- ----------------
01-APR-95 1200AM 31-MAR-95 0900PM
01-MAY-95 1200AM 30-APR-95 0900PM
30-MAY-95 1200AM 29-MAY-95 0900PM
30-JUN-95 1200AM 29-JUN-95 0900PM
02-SEP-95 1200AM 01-SEP-95 0900PM
17-JAN-96 1200AM 16-JAN-96 0900PM

6 rows selected.
```

Like magic, all the times are in the new time zone and the dates are adjusted.

NEXT_DAY

NEXT_DAY finds the name of the first day of the week that is equal to or later than another specified date. For example, to send a report on the Friday following the first day of each event, you would type

```
SQL> SELECT STARTDATE,
  2    NEXT_DAY(STARTDATE, 'FRIDAY')
  3  FROM PROJECT;
```

which would return

OUTPUT

```
STARTDATE NEXT_DAY(
--------- ---------
01-APR-95 07-APR-95
02-APR-95 07-APR-95
15-MAY-95 19-MAY-95
01-JUN-95 02-JUN-95
01-JUL-95 07-JUL-95
03-SEP-95 08-SEP-95

6 rows selected.
```

ANALYSIS The output tells you the date of the first Friday that occurs after your STARTDATE.

SYSDATE

SYSDATE returns the system time and date:

INPUT

```
SQL> SELECT DISTINCT SYSDATE
  2  FROM PROJECT;
```

OUTPUT

```
SYSDATE
---------------
18-JUN-95 1020PM
```

If you wanted to see where you stood today in a certain project, you could type

INPUT/ OUTPUT

```
SQL> SELECT *
  2  FROM PROJECT
  3  WHERE STARTDATE > SYSDATE;

TASK            STARTDATE ENDDATE
--------------  --------- ---------
CODE WIDGET     01-JUL-95 02-SEP-95
TESTING         03-SEP-95 17-JAN-96
```

Now you can see what parts of the project start after today.

Arithmetic Functions

Many of the uses you have for the data you retrieve involve mathematics. Most implementations of SQL provide arithmetic functions similar to the functions covered here. The examples in this section use the NUMBERS table:

INPUT
```
SQL> SELECT *
  2  FROM NUMBERS;
```

OUTPUT
```
         A         B
.......... ..........
    3.1415         4
       -45      .707
         5         9
   -57.667        42
        15        55
      -7.2       5.3

6 rows selected.
```

ABS

The ABS function returns the absolute value of the number you point to. For example:

INPUT
```
SQL> SELECT ABS(A) ABSOLUTE_VALUE
  2  FROM NUMBERS;
```

OUTPUT
```
ABSOLUTE_VALUE
.............
       3.1415
           45
            5
       57.667
           15
          7.2

6 rows selected.
```

ANALYSIS ABS changes all the negative numbers to positive and leaves positive numbers alone.

CEIL and FLOOR

CEIL returns the smallest integer greater than or equal to its argument. FLOOR does just the reverse, returning the largest integer equal to or less than its argument. For example:

INPUT
```
SQL> SELECT B, CEIL(B) CEILING
  2  FROM NUMBERS;
```

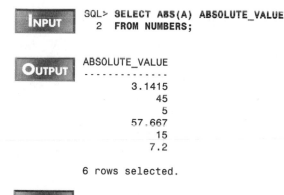

OUTPUT

```
          B    CEILING
      --------  --------
          4          4
       .707          1
          9          9
         42         42
         55         55
        5.3          6
```

6 rows selected.

And

INPUT/OUTPUT

```
SQL> SELECT A, FLOOR(A) FLOOR
  2  FROM NUMBERS;

          A      FLOOR
      --------  --------
     3.1415          3
        -45        -45
          5          5
    -57.667        -58
         15         15
       -7.2         -8
```

6 rows selected.

COS, COSH, SIN, SINH, TAN, and TANH

The COS, SIN, and TAN functions provide support for various trigonometric concepts. They all work on the assumption that *n* is in radians. The following statement returns some unexpected values if you don't realize COS expects A to be in radians.

INPUT

```
SQL> SELECT A, COS(A)
  2  FROM NUMBERS;
```

OUTPUT

```
          A     COS(A)
      --------  --------
     3.1415         -1
        -45  .52532199
          5  .28366219
    -57.667    .437183
         15  -.7596879
       -7.2  .60835131
```

ANALYSIS You would expect the COS of 45 degrees to be in the neighborhood of .707, not .525. To make this function work the way you would expect it to in a degree-oriented world, you need to convert degrees to radians. (When was the last time you heard a news broadcast report that a politician had done a π-radian turn? You hear about a 180-degree turn.) Because 360 degrees = 2π radians, you can write

```
SQL> SELECT A, COS(A* 0.01745329251994)
  2  FROM NUMBERS;
         A COS(A*0.01745329251994)
--------- ------------------------
    3.1415                .99849724
       -45                .70710678
         5                 .9961947
   -57.667                .5348391
        15                .96592583
      -7.2                .9921147
```

ANALYSIS Note that the number `0.01745329251994` is radians divided by degrees. The trigonometric functions work as follows:

```
SQL> SELECT A, COS(A*0.017453), COSH(A*0.017453)
  2  FROM NUMBERS;
         A COS(A*0.017453) COSH(A*0.017453)
--------- --------------- ----------------
    3.1415       .99849729        1.0015035
       -45       .70711609        1.3245977
         5       .99619483          1.00381
   -57.667       .53485335        1.5507072
        15       .96592696        1.0344645
      -7.2       .99211497        1.0079058

6 rows selected.
```

And

```
SQL> SELECT A, SIN(A*0.017453), SINH(A*0.017453)
  2  FROM NUMBERS;
         A SIN(A*0.017453) SINH(A*0.017453)
--------- --------------- ----------------
    3.1415       .05480113        .05485607
       -45       -.7070975        -.8686535
         5       .08715429        .0873758
   -57.667       -.8449449        -1.186197
        15       .25881481        .26479569
      -7.2       -.1253311        -.1259926

6 rows selected.
```

And

```
SQL> SELECT A, TAN(A*0.017453), TANH(A*0.017453)
  2  FROM NUMBERS;

         A TAN(A*0.017453) TANH(A*0.017453)
--------- --------------- ----------------
    3.1415       .05488361        .05477372
       -45       -.9999737        -.6557867
         5       .08748719        .08704416
   -57.667       -1.579769        -.7642948
        15       .26794449        .25597369
      -7.2       -.1263272        -.1250043

6 rows selected.
```

EXP

EXP enables you to raise *e* (*e* is a mathematical constant used in various formulas) to a power. Here's how EXP raises *e* by the values in column A:

INPUT
```
SQL> SELECT A, EXP(A)
  2  FROM NUMBERS;
```

OUTPUT
```
         A     EXP(A)
--------- ----------
    3.1415  23.138549
      -45   2.863E-20
        5   148.41316
  -57.667   9.027E-26
       15   3269017.4
     -7.2   .00074659
```

```
6 rows selected.
```

LN and LOG

These two functions center on logarithms. LN returns the natural logarithm of its argument. For example:

INPUT
```
SQL> SELECT A, LN(A)
  2  FROM NUMBERS;
```

OUTPUT
```
ERROR:
ORA-01428: argument '-45' is out of range
```

Did we neglect to mention that the argument had to be positive? Write

INPUT/ OUTPUT
```
SQL> SELECT A, LN(ABS(A))
  2  FROM NUMBERS;

         A LN(ABS(A))
--------- ----------
    3.1415  1.1447004
      -45   3.8066625
        5   1.6094379
  -57.667   4.0546851
       15   2.7080502
     -7.2   1.974081
```

```
6 rows selected.
```

ANALYSIS Notice how you can embed the function ABS inside the LN call. The other logarithmic function, LOG, takes two arguments, returning the logarithm of the first argument in the base of the second. The following query returns the logarithms of column B in base 10.

```
SQL> SELECT B, LOG(B, 10)
  2   FROM NUMBERS;

         B LOG(B,10)
---------- ----------
         4  1.660964
      .707 -6.640962
         9 1.0479516
        42 .61604832
        55 .57459287
       5.3 1.3806894

6 rows selected.
```

MOD

You have encountered MOD before. On Day 3, "Expressions, Conditions, and Operators," you saw that the ANSI standard for the modulo operator % is sometimes implemented as the function MOD. Here's a query that returns a table showing the remainder of A divided by B:

```
SQL> SELECT A, B, MOD(A,B)
  2   FROM NUMBERS;
```

```
         A         B  MOD(A,B)
---------- --------- ---------
    3.1415         4    3.1415
       -45      .707     -.459
         5         9         5
   -57.667        42   -15.667
        15        55        15
      -7.2       5.3      -1.9

6 rows selected.
```

POWER

To raise one number to the power of another, use POWER. In this function the first argument is raised to the power of the second:

```
SQL> SELECT A, B, POWER(A,B)
  2   FROM NUMBERS;
```

```
ERROR:
ORA-01428: argument '-45' is out of range
```

At first glance you are likely to think that the first argument can't be negative. But that impression can't be true, because a number like –4 can be raised to a power. Therefore, if the first number in the POWER function is negative, the second must be an integer. You can work around this problem by using CEIL (or FLOOR):

INPUT
```
SQL> SELECT A, CEIL(B), POWER(A,CEIL(B))
  2  FROM NUMBERS;
```

OUTPUT
```
         A  CEIL(B) POWER(A,CEIL(B))
--------- -------- ----------------
    3.1415        4          97.3976
      -45         1              -45
        5         9          1953125
  -57.667        42        9.098E+73
       15        55        4.842E+64
     -7.2         6        139314.07

6 rows selected.
```

That's better!

SIGN

SIGN returns -1 if its argument is less than 0, 0 if its argument is equal to 0, and 1 if its argument is greater than 0, as shown in the following example:

INPUT
```
SQL> SELECT A, SIGN(A)
  2  FROM NUMBERS;
```

OUTPUT
```
         A  SIGN(A)
--------- --------
    3.1415        1
      -45        -1
        5         1
  -57.667        -1
       15         1
     -7.2        -1
        0         0

7 rows selected.
```

You could also use SIGN in a SELECT WHERE clause like this:

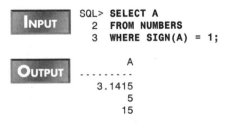

INPUT
```
SQL> SELECT A
  2  FROM NUMBERS
  3  WHERE SIGN(A) = 1;
```

OUTPUT
```
         A
---------
    3.1415
        5
       15
```

SQRT

The function SQRT returns the square root of an argument. Because the square root of a negative number is undefined, you cannot use SQRT on negative numbers.

INPUT

```
SQL> SELECT A, SQRT(A)
  2  FROM NUMBERS;
```

OUTPUT

```
ERROR:
ORA-01428: argument '-45' is out of range
```

However, you can fix this limitation with ABS:

INPUT/
OUTPUT

```
SQL> SELECT ABS(A), SQRT(ABS(A))
  2  FROM NUMBERS;

   ABS(A) SQRT(ABS(A))
--------- ------------
   3.1415    1.7724277
       45    6.7082039
        5     2.236068
   57.667    7.5938791
       15    3.8729833
      7.2    2.6832816
        0            0

7 rows selected.
```

Character Functions

Many implementations of SQL provide functions to manipulate characters and strings of characters. This section covers the most common character functions. The examples in this section use the table CHARACTERS.

INPUT

```
SQL> SELECT * FROM CHARACTERS;
```

OUTPUT

```
LASTNAME          FIRSTNAME         M     CODE
---------------   ---------------   -    -------
PURVIS            KELLY             A       32
TAYLOR            CHUCK             J       67
CHRISTINE         LAURA             C       65
ADAMS             FESTER            M       87
COSTALES          ARMANDO           A       77
KONG              MAJOR             G       52

6 rows selected.
```

CHR

CHR returns the character equivalent of the number it uses as an argument. The character it returns depends on the character set of the database. For this example the database is set to ASCII. The column CODE includes numbers.

INPUT

```
SQL> SELECT CODE, CHR(CODE)
  2  FROM CHARACTERS;
```

OUTPUT

```
     CODE CH
--------- --
       32
       67 C
       65 A
       87 W
       77 M
       52 4
```

```
6 rows selected.
```

The space opposite the 32 shows that 32 is a *space* in the ASCII character set.

CONCAT

You used the equivalent of this function on Day 3, when you learned about operators. The ¦¦ symbol splices two strings together, as does CONCAT. It works like this:

INPUT

```
SQL> SELECT CONCAT(FIRSTNAME, LASTNAME) "FIRST AND LAST NAMES"
  2  FROM CHARACTERS;
```

OUTPUT

```
FIRST AND LAST NAMES
--------------------
KELLY          PURVIS
CHUCK          TAYLOR
LAURA          CHRISTINE
FESTER         ADAMS
ARMANDO        COSTALES
MAJOR          KONG
```

```
6 rows selected.
```

ANALYSIS Quotation marks surround the multiple-word alias FIRST AND LAST NAMES. Again, it is safest to check your implementation to see if it allows multiple-word aliases.

Also notice that even though the table looks like two separate columns, what you are seeing is one column. The first value you concatenated, FIRSTNAME, is 15 characters wide. This operation retained all the characters in the field.

INITCAP

INITCAP capitalizes the first letter of a word and makes all other characters lowercase.

INPUT

```
SQL> SELECT FIRSTNAME BEFORE, INITCAP(FIRSTNAME) AFTER
  2  FROM CHARACTERS;
```

```
Output   BEFORE        AFTER
         --------------  ----------
         KELLY         Kelly
         CHUCK         Chuck
         LAURA         Laura
         FESTER        Fester
         ARMANDO       Armando
         MAJOR         Major

         6 rows selected.
```

LOWER and UPPER

As you might expect, LOWER changes all the characters to lowercase; UPPER does just the reverse.

The following example starts by doing a little magic with the UPDATE function (you learn more about this next week) to change one of the values to lowercase:

```
Input    SQL> UPDATE CHARACTERS
           2   SET FIRSTNAME = 'kelly'
           3   WHERE FIRSTNAME = 'KELLY';
```

```
Output   1 row updated.
```

```
Input/    SQL> SELECT FIRSTNAME
Output      2   FROM CHARACTERS;

         FIRSTNAME
         --------------
         kelly
         CHUCK
         LAURA
         FESTER
         ARMANDO
         MAJOR

         6 rows selected.
```

Then you write

```
Input/    SQL> SELECT FIRSTNAME, UPPER(FIRSTNAME), LOWER(FIRSTNAME)
Output      2   FROM CHARACTERS;

         FIRSTNAME       UPPER(FIRSTNAME LOWER(FIRSTNAME
         --------------  --------------- ---------------
         kelly           KELLY           kelly
         CHUCK           CHUCK           chuck
         LAURA           LAURA           laura
         FESTER          FESTER          fester
         ARMANDO         ARMANDO         armando
         MAJOR           MAJOR           major

         6 rows selected.
```

Now you see the desired behavior.

LPAD **and** RPAD

LPAD and RPAD take a minimum of two and a maximum of three arguments. The first argument is the character string to be operated on. The second is the number of characters to pad it with, and the optional third argument is the character to pad it with. The third argument defaults to a blank, or it can be a single character or a character string. The following statement adds five pad characters, assuming that the field LASTNAME is defined as a 15-character field:

```
SQL> SELECT LASTNAME, LPAD(LASTNAME,20,'*')
  2  FROM CHARACTERS;
```

OUTPUT

```
LASTNAME           LPAD(LASTNAME,20,'*'
--------------     --------------------
PURVIS             *****PURVIS
TAYLOR             *****TAYLOR
CHRISTINE          *****CHRISTINE
ADAMS              *****ADAMS
COSTALES           *****COSTALES
KONG               *****KONG

6 rows selected.
```

ANALYSIS Why were only five pad characters added? Remember that the LASTNAME column is 15 characters wide and that LASTNAME includes the blanks to the right of the characters that make up the name. Some column data types eliminate padding characters if the width of the column value is less than the total width allocated for the column. Check your implementation. Now try the right side:

INPUT/ OUTPUT

```
SQL> SELECT LASTNAME, RPAD(LASTNAME,20,'*')
  2  FROM CHARACTERS;

LASTNAME           RPAD(LASTNAME,20,'*'
--------------     --------------------
PURVIS             PURVIS          *****
TAYLOR             TAYLOR          *****
CHRISTINE          CHRISTINE       *****
ADAMS              ADAMS           *****
COSTALES           COSTALES        *****
KONG               KONG            *****

6 rows selected.
```

ANALYSIS Here you see that the blanks are considered part of the field name for these operations. The next two functions come in handy in this type of situation.

LTRIM **and** RTRIM

LTRIM and RTRIM take at least one and at most two arguments. The first argument, like LPAD and RPAD, is a character string. The optional second element is either a character or character string or defaults to a blank. If you use a second argument that is not a blank, these trim functions will trim that character the same way they trim the blanks in the following examples.

INPUT

```
SQL> SELECT LASTNAME, RTRIM(LASTNAME)
  2  FROM CHARACTERS;
```

OUTPUT

```
LASTNAME          RTRIM(LASTNAME)
---------------   ---------------
PURVIS            PURVIS
TAYLOR            TAYLOR
CHRISTINE         CHRISTINE
ADAMS             ADAMS
COSTALES          COSTALES
KONG              KONG

6 rows selected.
```

You can make sure that the characters have been trimmed with the following statement:

INPUT/ OUTPUT

```
SQL> SELECT LASTNAME, RPAD(RTRIM(LASTNAME),20,'*')
  2  FROM CHARACTERS;

LASTNAME          RPAD(RTRIM(LASTNAME)
---------------   --------------------
PURVIS            PURVIS**************
TAYLOR            TAYLOR**************
CHRISTINE         CHRISTINE**********
ADAMS             ADAMS**************
COSTALES          COSTALES***********
KONG              KONG***************

6 rows selected.
```

The output proves that trim is working. Now try LTRIM:

INPUT/ OUTPUT

```
SQL> SELECT LASTNAME, LTRIM(LASTNAME, 'C')
  2  FROM CHARACTERS;

LASTNAME          LTRIM(LASTNAME,
---------------   ---------------
PURVIS            PURVIS
TAYLOR            TAYLOR
CHRISTINE         HRISTINE
ADAMS             ADAMS
COSTALES          OSTALES
KONG              KONG

6 rows selected.
```

Note the missing *C*s in the third and fifth rows.

REPLACE

REPLACE does just that. Of its three arguments, the first is the string to be searched. The second is the search key. The last is the optional replacement string. If the third argument is left out or NULL, each occurrence of the search key on the string to be searched is removed and is not replaced with anything.

```
SQL> SELECT LASTNAME, REPLACE(LASTNAME, 'ST') REPLACEMENT
  2  FROM CHARACTERS;
```

OUTPUT

```
LASTNAME          REPLACEMENT
---------------   ---------------
PURVIS            PURVIS
TAYLOR            TAYLOR
CHRISTINE         CHRIINE
ADAMS             ADAMS
COSTALES          COALES
KONG              KONG

6 rows selected.
```

If you have a third argument, it is substituted for each occurrence of the search key in the target string. For example:

INPUT/OUTPUT

```
SQL> SELECT LASTNAME, REPLACE(LASTNAME, 'ST','**') REPLACEMENT
  2  FROM CHARACTERS;

LASTNAME          REPLACEMENT
---------------   ------------
PURVIS            PURVIS
TAYLOR            TAYLOR
CHRISTINE         CHRI**INE
ADAMS             ADAMS
COSTALES          CO**ALES
KONG              KONG

6 rows selected.
```

If the second argument is NULL, the target string is returned with no changes.

INPUT/OUTPUT

```
SQL> SELECT LASTNAME, REPLACE(LASTNAME, NULL) REPLACEMENT
  2  FROM CHARACTERS;

LASTNAME          REPLACEMENT
---------------   ---------------
PURVIS            PURVIS
TAYLOR            TAYLOR
CHRISTINE         CHRISTINE
ADAMS             ADAMS
COSTALES          COSTALES
KONG              KONG

6 rows selected.
```

SUBSTR

This three-argument function enables you to take a piece out of a target string. The first argument is the target string. The second argument is the position of the first character to be output. The third argument is the number of characters to show.

INPUT

```
SQL> SELECT FIRSTNAME, SUBSTR(FIRSTNAME,2,3)
  2  FROM CHARACTERS;
```

OUTPUT

```
FIRSTNAME        SUB
---------------  ---
kelly            ell
CHUCK            HUC
LAURA            AUR
FESTER           EST
ARMANDO          RMA
MAJOR            AJO

6 rows selected.
```

If you use a negative number as the second argument, the starting point is determined by counting backwards from the end, like this:

INPUT/OUTPUT

```
SQL> SELECT FIRSTNAME, SUBSTR(FIRSTNAME,-13,2)
  2  FROM CHARACTERS;

FIRSTNAME        SU
---------------  --
kelly            ll
CHUCK            UC
LAURA            UR
FESTER           ST
ARMANDO          MA
MAJOR            JO

6 rows selected.
```

ANALYSIS Remember the character field FIRSTNAME in this example is 15 characters long. That is why you used a -13 to start at the third character. Counting back from 15 puts you at the start of the third character, not at the start of the second. If you don't have a third argument, use the following statement instead:

INPUT/OUTPUT

```
SQL> SELECT FIRSTNAME, SUBSTR(FIRSTNAME,3)
  2  FROM CHARACTERS;

FIRSTNAME        SUBSTR(FIRSTN
---------------  -------------
kelly            lly
CHUCK            UCK
LAURA            URA
FESTER           STER
ARMANDO          MANDO
MAJOR            JOR

6 rows selected.
```

The rest of the target string is returned.

4

```
SQL> SELECT * FROM SSN_TABLE;

SSN_____
300541117
301457111
459789998
3 rows selected.
```

 Reading the results of the preceding output is difficult—Social Security numbers usually have dashes. Now try something fancy and see whether you like the results:

```
SQL> SELECT SUBSTR(SSN,1,3)||'-'||SUBSTR(SSN,4,2)||'-'||SUBSTR(SSN,6,4)
SSN
  2  FROM SSN_TABLE;

SSN_____
300-54-1117
301-45-7111
459-78-9998
3 rows selected.
```

> This particular use of the substr function could come in very handy with large numbers using commas such as 1,343,178,128 and in area codes and phone numbers such as 317-787-2915 using dashes.

Here is another good use of the SUBSTR function. Suppose you are writing a report and a few columns are more than 50 characters wide. You can use the SUBSTR function to reduce the width of the columns to a more manageable size if you know the nature of the actual data. Consider the following two examples:

```
SQL> SELECT NAME, JOB, DEPARTMENT FROM JOB_TBL;

NAME_____
JOB_____DEPARTMENT_____
ALVIN SMITH
VICEPRESIDENT                        MARKETING
1 ROW SELECTED.
```

 Notice how the columns wrapped around, which makes reading the results a little too difficult. Now try this select:

```
SQL> SELECT SUBSTR(NAME, 1,15) NAME, SUBSTR(JOB,1,15) JOB,
                DEPARTMENT
  2  FROM JOB_TBL;

NAME_____JOB_____DEPARTMENT_____
ALVIN SMITH        VICEPRESIDENT      MARKETING
```

Much better!

TRANSLATE

The function TRANSLATE takes three arguments: the target string, the FROM string, and the TO string. Elements of the target string that occur in the FROM string are translated to the corresponding element in the TO string.

INPUT

```
SQL> SELECT FIRSTNAME, TRANSLATE(FIRSTNAME
  2  '0123456789ABCDEFGHIJKLMNOPQRSTUVWXYZ
  3  'NNNNNNNNNNAAAAAAAAAAAAAAAAAAAAAAAAAAAA)
  4  FROM CHARACTERS;
```

OUTPUT

```
FIRSTNAME        TRANSLATE(FIRST
---------------  ---------------
kelly            kelly
CHUCK            AAAAA
LAURA            AAAAA
FESTER           AAAAAA
ARMANDO          AAAAAAA
MAJOR            AAAAA

0 rows selected.
```

Notice that the function is case sensitive.

INSTR

To find out where in a string a particular pattern occurs, use INSTR. Its first argument is the target string. The second argument is the pattern to match. The third and forth are numbers representing where to start looking and which match to report. This example returns a number representing the first occurrence of 0 starting with the second character:

INPUT

```
SQL> SELECT LASTNAME, INSTR(LASTNAME, 'O', 2, 1)
  2  FROM CHARACTERS;
```

OUTPUT

```
LASTNAME         INSTR(LASTNAME,'O',2,1)
---------------  -----------------------
PURVIS                                 0
TAYLOR                                 5
CHRISTINE                              0
ADAMS                                  0
COSTALES                               2
KONG                                   2

6 rows selected.
```

ANALYSIS

The default for the third and fourth arguments is 1. If the third argument is negative, the search starts at a position determined from the end of the string, instead of from the beginning.

4

LENGTH

LENGTH returns the length of its lone character argument. For example:

INPUT
```
SQL> SELECT FIRSTNAME, LENGTH(RTRIM(FIRSTNAME))
  2  FROM CHARACTERS;
```

OUTPUT
```
FIRSTNAME        LENGTH(RTRIM(FIRSTNAME))
---------------  ------------------------
kelly                                   5
CHUCK                                   5
LAURA                                   5
FESTER                                  6
ARMANDO                                 7
MAJOR                                   5

6 rows selected.
```

ANALYSIS Note the use of the RTRIM function. Otherwise, LENGTH would return 15 for every value.

Conversion Functions

These three conversion functions provide a handy way of converting one type of data to another. These examples use the table CONVERSIONS.

INPUT
```
SQL> SELECT * FROM CONVERSIONS;
```

OUTPUT
```
NAME              TESTNUM
---------------   ---------
40                     95
13                     23
74                     68
```

The NAME column is a character string 15 characters wide, and TESTNUM is a number.

TO_CHAR

The primary use of TO_CHAR is to convert a number into a character. Different implementations may also use it to convert other data types, like Date, into a character, or to include different formatting arguments. The next example illustrates the primary use of TO_CHAR:

INPUT
```
SQL> SELECT TESTNUM, TO_CHAR(TESTNUM)
  2  FROM CONVERT;
```

OUTPUT
```
TESTNUM TO_CHAR(TESTNUM)
--------- ----------------
     95               95
     23               23
     68               68
```

4

Not very exciting, or convincing. Here's how to verify that the function returned a character string:

```
SQL> SELECT TESTNUM, LENGTH(TO_CHAR(TESTNUM))
  2  FROM CONVERT;

   TESTNUM LENGTH(TO_CHAR(TESTNUM))
---------- ------------------------
        95                        2
        23                        2
        68                        2
```

ANALYSIS LENGTH of a number would have returned an error. Notice the difference between TO CHAR and the CHR function discussed earlier. CHR would have turned this number into a character or a symbol, depending on the character set.

TO_NUMBER

TO_NUMBER is the companion function to TO_CHAR, and of course, it converts a string into a number. For example:

INPUT
```
SQL> SELECT NAME, TESTNUM, TESTNUM*TO_NUMBER(NAME)
  2  FROM CONVERT;
```

OUTPUT
```
NAME                TESTNUM TESTNUM*TO_NUMBER(NAME)
---------------- ---------- -----------------------
40                       95                    3800
13                       23                     299
74                       68                    5032
```

ANALYSIS This test would have returned an error if TO_NUMBER had returned a character.

Miscellaneous Functions

Here are three miscellaneous functions you may find useful.

GREATEST and LEAST

These functions find the GREATEST or the LEAST member from a series of expressions. For example:

INPUT
```
SQL> SELECT GREATEST('ALPHA', 'BRAVO','FOXTROT', 'DELTA')
  2  FROM CONVERT;
```

OUTPUT
```
GREATEST
-------
FOXTROT
FOXTROT
FOXTROT
```

ANALYSIS Notice GREATEST found the word closest to the end of the alphabet. Notice also a seemingly unnecessary FROM and three occurrences of FOXTROT. If FROM is missing, you will get an error. Every SELECT needs a FROM. The particular table used in the FROM has three rows, so the function in the SELECT clause is performed for each of them.

INPUT/ OUTPUT
```
SQL> SELECT LEAST(34, 567, 3, 45, 1090)
  2  FROM CONVERT;

LEAST(34,567,3,45,1090)
-----------------------
                      3
                      3
                      3
```

As you can see, GREATEST and LEAST also work with numbers.

USER

USER returns the character name of the current user of the database.

INPUT
```
SQL> SELECT USER FROM CONVERT;
```

OUTPUT
```
USER
-------------------------------
PERKINS
PERKINS
PERKINS
```

ANALYSIS There really is only one of me. Again, the echo occurs because of the number of rows in the table. USER is similar to the date functions explained earlier today. Even though USER is not an actual column in the table, it is selected for each row that is contained in the table.

Summary

It has been a long day. We covered 47 functions—from aggregates to conversions. You don't have to remember every function—just knowing the general types (aggregate functions, date and time functions, arithmetic functions, character functions, conversion functions, and miscellaneous functions) is enough to point you in the right direction when you build a query that requires a function.

Q&A

Q Why are so few functions defined in the ANSI standard and so many defined by the individual implementations?

A ANSI standards are broad strokes and are not meant to drive companies into bankruptcy by forcing all implementations to have dozens of functions. On the other hand, when company X adds a statistical package to its SQL and it sells well, you can bet company Y and Z will follow suit.

Q I thought you said SQL was simple. Will I really use all of these functions?

A The answer to this question is similar to the way a trigonometry teacher might respond to the question, Will I ever need to know how to figure the area of an isosceles triangle in real life? The answer, of course, depends on your profession. The same concept applies with the functions and all the other options available with SQL. How you use functions in SQL depends mostly on you company's needs. As long as you understand how functions work as a whole, you can apply the same concepts to your own queries.

Workshop

The Workshop provides quiz questions to help solidify your understanding of the material covered, as well as exercises to provide you with experience in using what you have learned. Try to answer the quiz and exercise questions before checking the answers in Appendix F, "Answers to Quizzes and Exercises."

Quiz

1. Which function capitalizes the first letter of a character string and makes the rest lowercase?

2. Which functions are also known by the name *group functions*?

3. Will this query work?

```
SQL> SELECT COUNT(LASTNAME) FROM CHARACTERS;
```

4. How about this one?

```
SQL> SELECT SUM(LASTNAME) FROM CHARACTERS;
```

5. Assuming that they are separate columns, which function(s) would splice together FIRSTNAME and LASTNAME?

6. What does the answer 6 mean from the following SELECT?

 SQL> SELECT COUNT(*) FROM TEAMSTATS;

OUTPUT COUNT(*)

7. Will the following statement work?

```
SQL> SELECT SUBSTR LASTNAME,1,5 FROM NAME_TBL;
```

Exercises

1. Using today's TEAMSTATS table, write a query to determine who is batting under .25. (For the baseball-challenged reader, batting average is hits/ab.)

2. Using today's CHARACTERS table, write a query that will return the following:

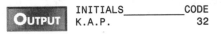

```
INITIALS_____CODE
K.A.P.                 32

1 row selected.
```

Day **5**

Clauses in SQL

Objectives

Today's topic is clauses—not the kind that distribute presents during the holidays, but the ones you use with a SELECT statement. By the end of the day you will understand and be able to use the following clauses:

- [ ] WHERE
- [ ] STARTING WITH
- [ ] ORDER BY
- [ ] GROUP BY
- [ ] HAVING

To get a feel for where these functions fit in, examine the general syntax for a SELECT statement:

```
SELECT [DISTINCT ¦ ALL] { *                           .
                        ¦ { [schema.]{table ¦ view ¦ snapshot}.*
                        ¦ expr } [ [AS] c_alias ]
                       [, { [schema.]{table ¦ view ¦ snapshot}.*
                        ¦ expr } [ [AS] c_alias ] ] ... }
FROM [schema.]{table ¦ view ¦ snapshot}[@dblink] [t_alias]
[, [schema.]{table ¦ view ¦ snapshot}[@dblink] [t_alias] ] ...
    [WHERE condition ]
    [GROUP BY expr [, expr] ... [HAVING condition] ]
    [{UNION ¦ UNION ALL ¦ INTERSECT ¦ MINUS} SELECT command ]
    [ORDER BY {expr¦position} [ASC ¦ DESC]
            [, {expr¦position} [ASC ¦ DESC]] ...]
```

NOTE

In my experience with SQL, the ANSI standard is really more of an ANSI "suggestion." The preceding syntax will generally work with any SQL engine, but you may find some slight variations.

NOTE

You haven't yet had to deal with a complicated syntax diagram. Because many people find syntax diagrams more puzzling than illuminating when learning something new, this book has used simple examples to illustrate particular points. However, we are now at the point where a syntax diagram can help tie the familiar concepts to today's new material.

Don't worry about the exact syntax—it varies slightly from implementation to implementation anyway. Instead, focus on the relationships. At the top of this statement is SELECT, which you have used many times in the last few days. SELECT is followed by FROM, which should appear with every SELECT statement you typed. (You learn a new use for FROM tomorrow.) WHERE, GROUP BY, HAVING, and ORDER BY all follow. (The other clauses in the diagram—UNION, UNION ALL, INTERSECT, and MINUS—were covered in Day 3, "Expressions, Conditions, and Operators.") Each clause plays an important part in selecting and manipulating data.

NOTE

We have used two implementations of SQL to prepare today's examples. One implementation has an SQL> prompt and line numbers (Personal Oracle7), and the other (Borland's ISQL) does not. You will also notice that the output displays vary slightly, depending on the implementation.

5

The WHERE Clause

Using just SELECT and FROM, you are limited to returning every row in a table. For example, using these two key words on the CHECKS table, you get all seven rows:

INPUT
```
SQL> SELECT *
  2  FROM CHECKS;
```

OUTPUT
```
CHECK# PAYEE                    AMOUNT REMARKS
------ -----------------------  ------ ------------------
     1 Ma Bell                     150 Have sons next time
     2 Reading R.R.             245.34 Train to Chicago
     3 Ma Bell                  200.32 Cellular Phone
     4 Local Utilities              98 Gas
     5 Joes Stale $ Dent           150 Groceries
    16 Cash                         25 Wild Night Out
    17 Joans Gas                  25.1 Gas

7 rows selected.
```

With WHERE in your vocabulary, you can be more selective. To find all the checks you wrote with a value of more than 100 dollars, write this:

INPUT
```
SQL> SELECT *
  2  FROM CHECKS
  3  WHERE AMOUNT > 100;
```

The WHERE clause returns the four instances in the table that meet the required condition:

OUTPUT
```
CHECK# PAYEE                    AMOUNT REMARKS
------ -----------------------  ------ ------------------
     1 Ma Bell                     150 Have sons next time
     2 Reading R.R.             245.34 Train to Chicago
     3 Ma Bell                  200.32 Cellular Phone
     5 Joes Stale $ Dent           150 Groceries
```

WHERE can also solve other popular puzzles. Given the following table of names and locations, you can ask that popular question, Where's Waldo?

INPUT/OUTPUT
```
SQL> SELECT *
  2  FROM PUZZLE;

NAME           LOCATION
-------------- --------------
TYLER          BACKYARD
MAJOR          KITCHEN
SPEEDY         LIVING ROOM
WALDO          GARAGE
LADDIE         UTILITY CLOSET
ARNOLD         TV ROOM

6 rows selected.
```

5

```
SQL> SELECT LOCATION AS "WHERE'S WALDO?"
  2   FROM PUZZLE
  3   WHERE NAME = 'WALDO';

WHERE'S WALDO?
--------------
GARAGE
```

Sorry, we couldn't resist. We promise no more corny queries. (We're saving those for that SQL bathroom humor book everyone's been wanting.) Nevertheless, this query shows that the column used in the condition of the WHERE statement does not have to be mentioned in the SELECT clause. In this example you selected the location column but used WHERE on the name, which is perfectly legal. Also notice the AS on the SELECT line. AS is an optional assignment operator, assigning the alias WHERE'S WALDO? to LOCATION. You might never see the AS again, because it involves extra typing. In most implementations of SQL you can type

```
SQL> SELECT LOCATION "WHERE'S WALDO?"
  2   FROM PUZZLE
  3   WHERE NAME ='WALDO';
```

and get the same result as the previous query without using AS:

```
WHERE'S WALDO?
--------------
GARAGE
```

After SELECT and FROM, WHERE is the third most frequently used SQL term.

The STARTING WITH Clause

STARTING WITH is an addition to the WHERE clause that works exactly like LIKE(<exp>%). Compare the results of the following query:

```
SELECT PAYEE, AMOUNT, REMARKS
FROM CHECKS
WHERE PAYEE LIKE('Ca%');
```

```
PAYEE                        AMOUNT REMARKS
===================== =============== ==============

Cash                             25 Wild Night Out
Cash                             60 Trip to Boston
Cash                             34 Trip to Dayton
```

with the results from this query:

```
SELECT PAYEE, AMOUNT, REMARKS
FROM CHECKS
WHERE PAYEE STARTING WITH('Ca');

PAYEE                        AMOUNT REMARKS
===================== =============== ==============

Cash                             25 Wild Night Out
Cash                             60 Trip to Boston
Cash                             34 Trip to Dayton
```

The results are identical. You can even use them together, as shown here:

```
SELECT PAYEE, AMOUNT, REMARKS
FROM CHECKS
WHERE PAYEE STARTING WITH('Ca')
OR
REMARKS LIKE 'G%';
```

```
PAYEE                       AMOUNT REMARKS
===================== ================ ================

Local Utilities                 98 Gas
Joes Stale $ Dent              150 Groceries
Cash                            25 Wild Night Out
Joans Gas                     25.1 Gas
Cash                            60 Trip to Boston
Cash                            34 Trip to Dayton
Joans Gas                    15.75 Gas
```

WARNING

STARTING WITH is a common feature of many implementations of SQL.
Check your implementation before you grow fond of it.

Order from Chaos: The ORDER BY Clause

From time to time you will want to present the results of your query in some kind of order.
As you know, however, SELECT FROM gives you a listing, and unless you have defined a primary
key (see Day 10, "Creating Views and Indexes"), your query comes out in the order the rows
were entered. Consider a beefed-up CHECKS table:

INPUT

```
SQL> SELECT * FROM CHECKS;
```

OUTPUT

```
CHECK# PAYEE                   AMOUNT REMARKS
------- -------------------    -------- --------------------
     1 Ma Bell                    150 Have sons next time
     2 Reading R.R.            245.34 Train to Chicago
     3 Ma Bell                 200.32 Cellular Phone
     4 Local Utilities             98 Gas
     5 Joes Stale $ Dent          150 Groceries
    16 Cash                        25 Wild Night Out
    17 Joans Gas                 25.1 Gas
     9 Abes Cleaners            24.35 X-Tra Starch
    20 Abes Cleaners             10.5 All Dry Clean
     8 Cash                        60 Trip to Boston
    21 Cash                        34 Trip to Dayton

11 rows selected.
```

ANALYSIS   You're going to have to trust me on this one, but the order of the output is exactly the same order as the order in which the data was entered. After you read Day 8, "Manipulating Data," and know how to use INSERT to create tables, you can test how data is ordered by default on your own.

The ORDER BY clause gives you a way of ordering your results. For example, to order the preceding listing by check number, you would use the following ORDER BY clause:

INPUT/ OUTPUT

```
SQL> SELECT *
  2    FROM CHECKS
  3    ORDER BY CHECK#;

    CHECK# PAYEE                      AMOUNT REMARKS
   ------- -------------------- --------- ------------------
         1 Ma Bell                        150 Have sons next time
         2 Reading R.R.                245.34 Train to Chicago
         3 Ma Bell                     200.32 Cellular Phone
         4 Local Utilities                 98 Gas
         5 Joes Stale $ Dent              150 Groceries
         8 Cash                            60 Trip to Boston
         9 Abes Cleaners                24.35 X-Tra Starch
        16 Cash                            25 Wild Night Out
        17 Joans Gas                     25.1 Gas
        20 Abes Cleaners                 10.5 All Dry Clean
        21 Cash                            34 Trip to Dayton

11 rows selected.
```

Now the data is ordered the way you want it, not the way in which it was entered. As the following example shows, ORDER requires BY; BY is not optional.

INPUT/ OUTPUT

```
SQL> SELECT * FROM CHECKS ORDER CHECK#;

SELECT * FROM CHECKS ORDER CHECK#
                             *
ERROR at line 1:
ORA-00924: missing BY keyword
```

What if you want to list the data in reverse order, with the highest number or letter first? You're in luck! The following query generates a list of PAYEEs that stars at the end of the alphabet:

INPUT/ OUTPUT

```
SQL> SELECT *
  2    FROM CHECKS
  3    ORDER BY PAYEE DESC;

    CHECK# PAYEE                      AMOUNT REMARKS
   ------- -------------------- --------- ------------------
         2 Reading R.R.                245.34 Train to Chicago
         1 Ma Bell                        150 Have sons next time
         3 Ma Bell                     200.32 Cellular Phone
         4 Local Utilities                 98 Gas
         5 Joes Stale $ Dent              150 Groceries
        17 Joans Gas                     25.1 Gas
        16 Cash                            25 Wild Night Out
```

```
        8 Cash                    60 Trip to Boston
       21 Cash                    34 Trip to Dayton
        9 Abes Cleaners        24.35 X-Tra Starch
       20 Abes Cleaners         10.5 All Dry Clean
```

11 rows selected.

ANALYSIS The DESC at the end of the ORDER BY clause orders the list in descending order instead of the default (ascending) order. The rarely used, optional keyword ASC appears in the following statement:

INPUT/OUTPUT
```
SQL> SELECT PAYEE, AMOUNT
  2  FROM CHECKS
  3  ORDER BY CHECK# ASC;
```

```
PAYEE                    AMOUNT
-------------------- ----------
Ma Bell                     150
Reading R.R.             245.34
Ma Bell                  200.32
Local Utilities              98
Joes Stale $ Dent           150
Cash                         60
Abes Cleaners             24.35
Cash                         25
Joans Gas                  25.1
Abes Cleaners              10.5
Cash                         34
```

11 rows selected.

ANALYSIS The ordering in this list is identical to the ordering of the list at the beginning of the section (without ASC) because ASC is the default. This query also shows that the expression used after the ORDER BY clause does not have to be in the SELECT statement. Although you selected only PAYEE and AMOUNT, you were still able to order the list by CHECK#.

You can also use ORDER BY on more than one field. To order CHECKS by PAYEE and REMARKS, you would query as follows:

INPUT/OUTPUT
```
SQL> SELECT *
  2  FROM CHECKS
  3  ORDER BY PAYEE, REMARKS;
```

```
CHECK# PAYEE                 AMOUNT REMARKS
------- -------------------- ------- -------------------
    20 Abes Cleaners           10.5 All Dry Clean
     9 Abes Cleaners          24.35 X-Tra Starch
     8 Cash                      60 Trip to Boston
    21 Cash                      34 Trip to Dayton
    16 Cash                      25 Wild Night Out
    17 Joans Gas               25.1 Gas
     5 Joes Stale $ Dent        150 Groceries
     4 Local Utilities           98 Gas
     3 Ma Bell                200.32 Cellular Phone
     1 Ma Bell                  150 Have sons next time
     2 Reading R.R.           245.34 Train to Chicago
```

5

Notice the entries for Cash in the PAYEE column. In the previous ORDER BY, the CHECK#s were in the order 16, 21, 8. Adding the field REMARKS to the ORDER BY clause puts the entries in alphabetical order according to REMARKS. Does the order of multiple columns in the ORDER BY clause make a difference? Try the same query again but reverse PAYEE and REMARKS:

```
SQL> SELECT *
  2  FROM CHECKS
  3  ORDER BY REMARKS, PAYEE;

CHECK# PAYEE                    AMOUNT REMARKS
------ --------------------    ------- --------------------
    20 Abes Cleaners             10.5 All Dry Clean
     3 Ma Bell                 200.32 Cellular Phone
    17 Joans Gas                 25.1 Gas
     4 Local Utilities             98 Gas
     5 Joes Stale $ Dent          150 Groceries
     1 Ma Bell                    150 Have sons next time
     2 Reading R.R.            245.34 Train to Chicago
     8 Cash                        60 Trip to Boston
    21 Cash                        34 Trip to Dayton
    16 Cash                        25 Wild Night Out
     9 Abes Cleaners            24.35 X-Tra Starch

11 rows selected.
```

As you probably guessed, the results are completely different. Here's how to list one column in alphabetical order and list the second column in reverse alphabetical order:

```
SQL> SELECT *
  2  FROM CHECKS
  3  ORDER BY PAYEE ASC, REMARKS DESC;

CHECK# PAYEE                    AMOUNT REMARKS
------ --------------------    ------- --------------------
     9 Abes Cleaners            24.35 X-Tra Starch
    20 Abes Cleaners             10.5 All Dry Clean
    16 Cash                        25 Wild Night Out
    21 Cash                        34 Trip to Dayton
     8 Cash                        60 Trip to Boston
    17 Joans Gas                 25.1 Gas
     5 Joes Stale $ Dent          150 Groceries
     4 Local Utilities             98 Gas
     1 Ma Bell                    150 Have sons next time
     3 Ma Bell                 200.32 Cellular Phone
     2 Reading R.R.            245.34 Train to Chicago

11 rows selected.
```

In this example PAYEE is sorted alphabetically, and REMARKS appears in descending order. Note how the remarks in the three checks with a PAYEE of Cash are sorted.

5

TIP

If you know that a column you want to order your results by is the first column in a table, then you can type ORDER BY 1 in place of spelling out the column name. See the following example.

**INPUT/
OUTPUT**

```
SQL> SELECT *
  2  FROM CHECKS
  3  ORDER BY 1;

    CHECK# PAYEE                  AMOUNT REMARKS
-------- -------------------- -------- ------------------
       1 Ma Bell                   150 Have sons next time
       2 Reading R.R.           245.34 Train to Chicago
       3 Ma Bell                200.32 Cellular Phone
       4 Local Utilities            98 Gas
       5 Joes Stale $ Dent         150 Groceries
       8 Cash                       60 Trip to Boston
       9 Abes Cleaners           24.35 X-Tra Starch
      16 Cash                       25 Wild Night Out
      17 Joans Gas                25.1 Gas
      20 Abes Cleaners            10.5 All Dry Clean
      21 Cash                       34 Trip to Dayton

11 rows selected.
```

ANALYSIS This result is identical to the result produced by the SELECT statement that you used earlier today:

```
SELECT * FROM CHECKS ORDER BY CHECK#;
```

The GROUP BY Clause

On Day 3 you learned how to use aggregate functions (COUNT, SUM, AVG, MIN, and MAX). If you wanted to find the total amount of money spent from the slightly changed CHECKS table, you would type:

INPUT

```
SELECT *
FROM CHECKS;
```

Here's the modified table:

OUTPUT

```
CHECKNUM PAYEE              AMOUNT   REMARKS
======== =========== =============== =======================
       1 Ma Bell                150  Have sons next time
       2 Reading R.R.        245.34  Train to Chicago
       3 Ma Bell             200.33  Cellular Phone
       4 Local Utilities         98  Gas
       5 Joes Stale $ Dent      150  Groceries
      16 Cash                    25  Wild Night Out
```

5

```
17 Joans Gas            25.1  Gas
 9 Abes Cleaners       24.35  X-Tra Starch
20 Abes Cleaners        10.5  All Dry Clean
 8 Cash                   60  Trip to Boston
21 Cash                   34  Trip to Dayton
30 Local Utilities      87.5  Water
31 Local Utilities        34  Sewer
25 Joans Gas           15.75  Gas
```

Then you would type:

```
SELECT SUM(AMOUNT)
FROM CHECKS;

            SUM
===============

       1159.87
```

 This statement returns the sum of the column AMOUNT. What if you wanted to find out how much you have spent on each PAYEE? SQL helps you with the GROUP BY clause. To find out whom you have paid and how much, you would query like this:

```
SELECT PAYEE, SUM(AMOUNT)
FROM CHECKS
GROUP BY PAYEE;

PAYEE                           SUM
==================== ===============

Abes Cleaners              34.849998
Cash                             119
Joans Gas                  40.849998
Joes Stale $ Dent                150
Local Utilities                219.5
Ma Bell                    350.33002
Reading R.R.                  245.34
```

 The SELECT clause has a normal column selection, PAYEE, followed by the aggregate function SUM(AMOUNT). If you had tried this query with only the FROM CHECKS that follows, here's what you would see:

```
SELECT PAYEE, SUM(AMOUNT)
FROM CHECKS;

Dynamic SQL Error
-SQL error code = -104
-invalid column reference
```

 SQL is complaining about the combination of the normal column and the aggregate function. This condition requires the GROUP BY clause. GROUP BY runs the aggregate function described in the SELECT statement for each grouping of the column that follows the GROUP BY clause. The table CHECKS returned 14 rows when queried with SELECT * FROM CHECKS. The query on the same table, SELECT PAYEE, SUM(AMOUNT) FROM CHECKS GROUP BY PAYEE, took the 14 rows in the table and made seven groupings, returning the SUM of each grouping.

Suppose you wanted to know how much you gave to whom with how many checks. Can you use more than one aggregate function?

INPUT/ OUTPUT

```
SELECT PAYEE, SUM(AMOUNT), COUNT(PAYEE)
FROM CHECKS
GROUP BY PAYEE;
```

PAYEE	SUM	COUNT
Abes Cleaners	34.849998	2
Cash	119	3
Joans Gas	40.849998	2
Joes Stale $ Dent	150	1
Local Utilities	219.5	3
Ma Bell	350.33002	2
Reading R.R.	245.34	1

ANALYSIS This SQL is becoming increasingly useful! In the preceding example, you were able to perform group functions on unique groups using the GROUP BY clause. Also notice that the results were ordered by payee. GROUP BY also acts like the ORDER BY clause. What would happen if you tried to group by more than one column? Try this:

INPUT/ OUTPUT

```
SELECT PAYEE, SUM(AMOUNT), COUNT(PAYEE)
FROM CHECKS
GROUP BY PAYEE, REMARKS;
```

PAYEE	SUM	COUNT
Abes Cleaners	10.5	1
Abes Cleaners	24.35	1
Cash	60	1
Cash	34	1
Cash	25	1
Joans Gas	40.849998	2
Joes Stale $ Dent	150	1
Local Utilities	98	1
Local Utilities	34	1
Local Utilities	87.5	1
Ma Bell	200.33	1
Ma Bell	150	1
Reading R.R.	245.34	1

ANALYSIS The output has gone from 7 groupings of 14 rows to 13 groupings. What is different about the one grouping with more than one check associated with it? Look at the entries for Joans Gas:

INPUT/ OUTPUT

```
SELECT PAYEE, REMARKS
FROM CHECKS
WHERE PAYEE = 'Joans Gas';
```

```
PAYEE                    REMARKS
====================     ====================

Joans Gas                Gas
Joans Gas                Gas
```

ANALYSIS You see that the combination of PAYEE and REMARKS creates identical entities, which SQL groups together into one line with the GROUP BY clause. The other rows produce unique combinations of PAYEE and REMARKS and are assigned their own unique groupings.

The next example finds the largest and smallest amounts, grouped by REMARKS:

INPUT/ OUTPUT
```
SELECT MIN(AMOUNT), MAX(AMOUNT)
FROM CHECKS
GROUP BY REMARKS;
```

```
           MIN                MAX
================    ================

        245.34             245.34
         10.5               10.5
        200.33             200.33
         15.75               98
        150                150
        150                150
         34                 34
         60                 60
         34                 34
         87.5               87.5
         25                 25
         24.35              24.35
```

Here's what will happen if you try to include in the select statement a column that has several different values within the group formed by GROUP BY:

INPUT/ OUTPUT
```
SELECT PAYEE, MAX(AMOUNT), MIN(AMOUNT)
FROM CHECKS
GROUP BY REMARKS;
```

```
Dynamic SQL Error
-SQL error code = -104
-invalid column reference
```

ANALYSIS This query tries to group CHECKS by REMARK. When the query finds two records with the same REMARK but different PAYEEs, such as the rows that have GAS as a REMARK but have PAYEEs of LOCAL UTILITIES and JOANS GAS, it throws an error.

The rule is, Don't use the SELECT statement on columns that have multiple values for the GROUP BY clause column. The reverse is not true. You can use GROUP BY on columns not mentioned in the SELECT statement. For example:

INPUT/ OUTPUT
```
SELECT PAYEE, COUNT(AMOUNT)
FROM CHECKS
GROUP BY PAYEE, AMOUNT;
```

```
PAYEE                     COUNT
===================== ===========

Abes Cleaners                 1
Abes Cleaners                 1
Cash                          1
Cash                          1
Cash                          1
Joans Gas                     1
Joans Gas                     1
Joes Stale $ Dent             1
Local Utilities               1
Local Utilities               1
Local Utilities               1
Ma Bell                       1
Ma Bell                       1
Reading R.R.                  1
```

ANALYSIS   This silly query shows how many checks you had written for identical amounts to the same PAYEE. Its real purpose is to show that you can use AMOUNT in the GROUP BY clause, even though it is not mentioned in the SELECT clause. Try moving AMOUNT out of the GROUP BY clause and into the SELECT clause, like this:

INPUT/ OUTPUT
```
SELECT PAYEE, AMOUNT, COUNT(AMOUNT)
FROM CHECKS
GROUP BY PAYEE;
```

```
Dynamic SQL Error
 SQL error code = -104
-invalid column reference
```

ANALYSIS   SQL cannot run the query, which makes sense if you play the part of SQL for a moment. Say you had to group the following lines:

INPUT/ OUTPUT
```
SELECT PAYEE, AMOUNT, REMARKS
FROM CHECKS
WHERE PAYEE ='Cash';
```

```
PAYEE                         AMOUNT REMARKS
===================== ================ ================

Cash                              25 Wild Night Out
Cash                              60 Trip to Boston
Cash                              34 Trip to Dayton
```

If the user asked you to output all three columns and group by PAYEE only, where would you put the unique remarks? Remember you have only one row per group when you use GROUP BY. SQL can't do two things at once, so it complains: Error #31: Can't do two things at once.

The HAVING Clause

How can you qualify the data used in your GROUP BY clause? Use the table ORGCHART and try this:

INPUT

```
SELECT * FROM ORGCHART;
```

OUTPUT

NAME	TEAM	SALARY	SICKLEAVE	ANNUALLEAVE
======	======	========	===========	=============
ADAMS	RESEARCH	34000.00	34	12
WILKES	MARKETING	31000.00	40	9
STOKES	MARKETING	36000.00	20	19
MEZA	COLLECTIONS	40000.00	30	27
MERRICK	RESEARCH	45000.00	20	17
RICHARDSON	MARKETING	42000.00	25	18
FURY	COLLECTIONS	35000.00	22	14
PRECOURT	PR	37500.00	24	24

If you wanted to group the output into divisions and show the average salary in each division, you would type:

INPUT/ OUTPUT

```
SELECT TEAM, AVG(SALARY)
FROM ORGCHART
GROUP BY TEAM;
```

TEAM	AVG
======	=====
COLLECTIONS	37500.00
MARKETING	36333.33
PR	37500.00
RESEARCH	39500.00

The following statement qualifies this query to return only those departments with average salaries under 38000:

INPUT/ OUTPUT

```
SELECT TEAM, AVG(SALARY)
FROM ORGCHART
WHERE AVG(SALARY) < 38000
GROUP BY TEAM;

Dynamic SQL Error
-SQL error code = -104
-Invalid aggregate reference
```

ANALYSIS This error occurred because WHERE does not work with aggregate functions. To make this query work, you need something new: the HAVING clause. If you type the following query, you get what you ask for:

```
SELECT TEAM, AVG(SALARY)
FROM ORGCHART
GROUP BY TEAM
HAVING AVG(SALARY) < 38000;

TEAM                 AVG
=============== ===========

COLLECTIONS          37500.00
MARKETING            36333.33
PR                   37500.00
```

ANALYSIS HAVING enables you to use aggregate functions in a comparison statement, providing for aggregate functions what WHERE provides for individual rows. Does HAVING work with nonaggregate expressions? Try this:

```
SELECT TEAM, AVG(SALARY)
FROM ORGCHART
GROUP BY TEAM
HAVING SALARY < 38000;

TEAM                 AVG
=============== ===========

PR                   37500.00
```

ANALYSIS Why is this result different from the last query? The HAVING AVG(SALARY) < 38000 clause evaluated each grouping and returned only those with an average salary of under 38000, just what you expected. HAVING SALARY < 38000, on the other hand, had a different outcome. Take on the role of the SQL engine again. If the user asks you to evaluate and return groups of divisions where SALARY < 38000, you would examine each group and reject those where an individual SALARY is greater than 38000. In each division except PR, you would find at least one salary greater than 38000:

```
SELECT NAME, TEAM, SALARY
FROM ORGCHART
ORDER BY TEAM;

NAME             TEAM             SALARY
=============== ================ ===========

FURY             COLLECTIONS      35000.00
MEZA             COLLECTIONS      40000.00
WILKES           MARKETING        31000.00
STOKES           MARKETING        36000.00
RICHARDSON       MARKETING        42000.00
PRECOURT         PR               37500.00
ADAMS            RESEARCH         34000.00
MERRICK          RESEARCH         45000.00
```

ANALYSIS Therefore, you would reject all other groups except PR. What you really asked was Select all groups where no individual makes more than 38000. Don't you just hate it when the computer does exactly what you tell it to?

WARNING

> Some implementations of SQL return an error if you use anything other than an aggregate function in a HAVING clause. Don't bet the farm on using the previous example until you check the implementation of the particular SQL you use.

Can you use more than one condition in your HAVING clause? Try this:

INPUT

```
SELECT TEAM, AVG(SICKLEAVE),AVG(ANNUALLEAVE)
FROM ORGCHART
GROUP BY TEAM
HAVING AVG(SICKLEAVE)>25 AND
AVG(ANNUALLEAVE)<20;
```

 ANALYSIS The following table is grouped by TEAM. It shows all the teams with SICKLEAVE averages above 25 days and ANNUALLEAVE averages below 20 days.

OUTPUT

TEAM	AVG	AVG
===============	===========	===========
MARKETING	28	15
RESEARCH	27	15

You can also use an aggregate function in the HAVING clause that was not in the SELECT statement. For example:

INPUT/ OUTPUT

```
SELECT TEAM, AVG(SICKLEAVE),AVG(ANNUALLEAVE)
FROM ORGCHART
GROUP BY TEAM
HAVING COUNT(TEAM) > 1;
```

TEAM	AVG	AVG
===============	===========	===========
COLLECTIONS	26	21
MARKETING	28	15
RESEARCH	27	15

ANALYSIS This query returns the number of TEAMs with more than one member. COUNT(TEAM) is not used in the SELECT statement but still functions as expected in the HAVING clause.

The other logical operators all work well within the HAVING clause. Consider this:

INPUT/ OUTPUT

```
SELECT TEAM,MIN(SALARY),MAX(SALARY)
FROM ORGCHART
GROUP BY TEAM
HAVING AVG(SALARY) > 37000
OR
MIN(SALARY) > 32000;
```

5

```
TEAM                    MIN          MAX
=============== =========== ===========

COLLECTIONS        35000.00    40000.00
PR                 37500.00    37500.00
RESEARCH           34000.00    45000.00
```

The operator IN also works in a HAVING clause, as demonstrated here:

INPUT/ OUTPUT
```
SELECT TEAM,AVG(SALARY)
FROM ORGCHART
GROUP BY TEAM
HAVING TEAM IN ('PR','RESEARCH');

TEAM                    AVG
=============== ===========

PR                 37500.00
RESEARCH           39500.00
```

Combining Clauses

Nothing exists in a vacuum, so this section takes you through some composite examples that demonstrate how combinations of clauses perform together.

Example 5.1

Find all the checks written for Cash and Gas in the CHECKS table and order them by REMARKS.

INPUT
```
SELECT PAYEE, REMARKS
FROM CHECKS
WHERE PAYEE = 'Cash'
OR REMARKS LIKE'Ga%'
ORDER BY REMARKS;
```

OUTPUT
```
PAYEE                   REMARKS
==================== ====================

Joans Gas            Gas
Joans Gas            Gas
Local Utilities      Gas
Cash                 Trip to Boston
Cash                 Trip to Dayton
Cash                 Wild Night Out
```

ANALYSIS Note the use of LIKE to find the REMARKS that started with Ga. With the use of OR, data was returned if the WHERE clause met either one of the two conditions.

What if you asked for the same information and group it by PAYEE? The query would look something like this:

INPUT
```
SELECT PAYEE, REMARKS
FROM CHECKS
```

```
WHERE PAYEE = 'Cash'
OR REMARKS LIKE'Ga%'

GROUP BY PAYEE
ORDER BY REMARKS;
```

 ANALYSIS This query would not work because the SQL engine would not know what to do with the remarks. Remember that whatever columns you put in the SELECT clause must also be in the GROUP BY clause—unless you don't specify any columns in the SELECT clause.

Example 5.2

Using the table ORGCHART, find the salary of everyone with less than 25 days of sick leave. Order the results by NAME.

 INPUT
```
SELECT NAME, SALARY
FROM ORGCHART
WHERE SICKLEAVE < 25
ORDER BY NAME;
```

 OUTPUT
```
NAME                  SALARY
================ ===========

FURY                35000.00
MERRICK             45000.00
PRECOURT            37500.00
STOKES              36000.00
```

 ANALYSIS This query is straightforward and enables you to use your new-found skills with WHERE and ORDER BY.

Example 5.3

Again, using ORGCHART, display TEAM, AVG(SALARY), AVG(SICKLEAVE), and AVG(ANNUALLEAVE) on each team:

 INPUT
```
SELECT TEAM,
AVG(SALARY),
AVG(SICKLEAVE),
AVG(ANNUALLEAVE)
FROM ORGCHART
GROUP BY TEAM;
```

 OUTPUT

TEAM	AVG	AVG	AVG
COLLECTIONS	37500.00	26	21
MARKETING	36333.33	28	15
PR	37500.00	24	24
RESEARCH	39500.00	26	15

An interesting variation on this query follows. See if you can figure out what happened:

**INPUT/
OUTPUT**

```
SELECT TEAM,
AVG(SALARY),
AVG(SICKLEAVE),
AVG(ANNUALLEAVE)
FROM ORGCHART
GROUP BY TEAM
ORDER BY NAME;
```

TEAM	AVG	AVG	AVG
RESEARCH	39500.00	27	15
COLLECTIONS	37500.00	26	21
PR	37500.00	24	24
MARKETING	36333.33	28	15

A simpler query using ORDER BY might offer a clue:

**INPUT/
OUTPUT**

```
SELECT NAME, TEAM
FROM ORGCHART
ORDER BY NAME, TEAM;
```

NAME	TEAM
ADAMS	RESEARCH
FURY	COLLECTIONS
MERRICK	RESEARCH
MEZA	COLLECTIONS
PRECOURT	PR
RICHARDSON	MARKETING
STOKES	MARKETING
WILKES	MARKETING

ANALYSIS When the SQL engine got around to ordering the results of the query, it used the NAME column (remember, it is perfectly legal to use a column not specified in the SELECT statement), ignored duplicate TEAM entries, and came up with the order RESEARCH, COLLECTIONS, PR, and MARKETING. Including TEAM in the ORDER BY clause is unnecessary, because you have unique values in the NAME column. You can get the same result by typing this statement:

**INPUT/
OUTPUT**

```
SELECT NAME, TEAM
FROM ORGCHART
ORDER BY NAME;
```

NAME	TEAM
ADAMS	RESEARCH
FURY	COLLECTIONS
MERRICK	RESEARCH
MEZA	COLLECTIONS
PRECOURT	PR
RICHARDSON	MARKETING
STOKES	MARKETING
WILKES	MARKETING

5

While you are looking at variations, don't forget you can also reverse the order:

```
SELECT NAME, TEAM
FROM ORGCHART
ORDER BY NAME DESC;
```

```
NAME            TEAM
=============== ============

WILKES          MARKETING
STOKES          MARKETING
RICHARDSON      MARKETING
PRECOURT        PR
MEZA            COLLECTIONS
MERRICK         RESEARCH
FURY            COLLECTIONS
ADAMS           RESEARCH
```

Example 5.4: The Big Finale

Is it possible to use everything you have learned in one query? It is, but the results will be convoluted because in many ways you are working with apples and oranges—or aggregates and nonaggregates. For example, WHERE and ORDER BY are usually found in queries that act on single rows, such as this:

INPUT

```
SELECT *
FROM ORGCHART
ORDER BY NAME DESC;
```

OUTPUT

```
NAME            TEAM        SALARY   SICKLEAVE ANNUALLEAVE
=============== ======== =========== =========== ===========

WILKES          MARKETING   31000.00         40           9
STOKES          MARKETING   36000.00         20          19
RICHARDSON      MARKETING   42000.00         25          18
PRECOURT        PR          37500.00         24          24
MEZA            COLLECTIONS 40000.00         30          27
MERRICK         RESEARCH    45000.00         20          17
FURY            COLLECTIONS 35000.00         22          14
ADAMS           RESEARCH    34000.00         34          12
```

GROUP BY and HAVING are normally seen in the company of aggregates:

```
SELECT PAYEE,
SUM(AMOUNT) TOTAL,
COUNT(PAYEE) NUMBER_WRITTEN
FROM CHECKS
GROUP BY PAYEE
HAVING SUM(AMOUNT) > 50;
```

```
PAYEE                          TOTAL NUMBER_WRITTEN
==================== =============== ==============

Cash                             119              3
Joes Stale $ Dent                150              1
Local Utilities                219.5              3
Ma Bell                    350.33002              2
Reading R.R.                  245.34              1
```

You have seen that combining these two groups of clauses can have unexpected results, including the following:

INPUT

```
SELECT PAYEE,
SUM(AMOUNT) TOTAL,
COUNT(PAYEE) NUMBER_WRITTEN
FROM CHECKS
WHERE AMOUNT >= 100
GROUP BY PAYEE
HAVING SUM(AMOUNT) > 50;
```

OUTPUT

```
PAYEE                           TOTAL NUMBER_WRITTEN
==================== ================ ==============

Joes Stale $ Dent                 150              1
Ma Bell                     350.33002              2
Reading R.R.                   245.34              1
```

Compare these two result sets and examine the raw data.

INPUT/OUTPUT

```
SELECT PAYEE, AMOUNT
FROM CHECKS
ORDER BY PAYEE;

PAYEE                          AMOUNT
==================== ================

Abes Cleaners                    10.5
Abes Cleaners                   24.35
Cash                               25
Cash                               34
Cash                               60
Joans Gas                       15.75
Joans Gas                        25.1
Joes Stale $ Dent                 150
Local Utilities                    34
Local Utilities                  87.5
Local Utilities                    98
Ma Bell                           150
Ma Bell                        200.33
Reading R.R.                   245.34
```

ANALYSIS

You see how the WHERE clause filtered out all the checks less than 100 dollars before the GROUP BY was performed on the query. We are not trying to tell you not to mix these groups—you may have a requirement that this sort of construction will meet. However, you should not casually mix aggregate and nonaggregate functions. The previous examples have been tables with only a handful of rows. (Otherwise, you would need a cart to carry this book.) In the real world you will be working with thousands and thousands (or billions and billions) of rows, and the subtle changes caused by mixing these clauses might not be so apparent.

Summary

Today you learned all the clauses you need to exploit the power of a SELECT statement. Remember to be careful what you ask for because you just might get it. Your basic SQL education is complete. You already know enough to work effectively with single tables. Tomorrow (Day 6, "Joining Tables") you will have the opportunity to work with multiple tables.

Q&A

Q I thought we covered some of these functions earlier this week? If so, why are we covering them again?

A We did indeed cover WHERE on Day 3. You needed a knowledge of WHERE to understand how certain operators worked. WHERE appears again today because it is a clause, and today's topic is clauses.

Workshop

The Workshop provides quiz questions to help solidify your understanding of the material covered, as well as exercises to provide you with experience in using what you have learned. Try to answer the quiz and exercise questions before checking the answers in Appendix F, "Answers to Quizzes and Exercises."

Quiz

1. Which clause works just like LIKE(<exp>%)?

2. What is the function of the GROUP BY clause, and what other clause does it act like?

3. Will this SELECT work?

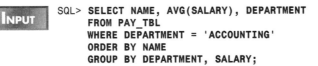

```
SQL> SELECT NAME, AVG(SALARY), DEPARTMENT
     FROM PAY_TBL
     WHERE DEPARTMENT = 'ACCOUNTING'
     ORDER BY NAME
     GROUP BY DEPARTMENT, SALARY;
```

4. When using the HAVING clause, do you always have to use a GROUP BY also?

5. Can you use ORDER BY on a column that is not one of the columns in the SELECT statement?

Exercises

1. Using the ORGCHART table from the preceding examples, find out how many people on each team have 30 or more days of sick leave.

2. Using the CHECKS table, write a SELECT that will return the following:

OUTPUT	CHECK#	PAYEE	AMOUNT
	1	MA BELL	150

5

Week 1

Day 6

Joining Tables

Objectives

Today you will learn about joins. This information will enable you to gather and manipulate data across several tables. By the end of the day, you will understand and be able to do the following:

- [ ] Perform an outer join
- [ ] Perform a left join
- [ ] Perform a right join
- [ ] Perform an equi-join
- [ ] Perform a non-equi-join
- [ ] Join a table to itself

Introduction

One of the most powerful features of SQL is its capability to gather and manipulate data from across several tables. Without this feature you would have to store all the data elements necessary for each application in one table. Without common tables you would need to store the same data in several tables. Imagine having to redesign, rebuild, and repopulate your tables and databases every time your user needed a query with a new piece of information. The JOIN statement of SQL enables you to design smaller, more specific tables that are easier to maintain than larger tables.

Multiple Tables in a Single SELECT Statement

Like Dorothy in *The Wizard of Oz*, you have had the power to join tables since Day 2, "Introduction to the Query: The SELECT Statement," when you learned about SELECT and FROM. Unlike Dorothy, you don't have to click you heels together three times to perform a join. Use the following two tables, named, cleverly enough, TABLE1 and TABLE2.

NOTE

The queries in today's examples were produced using Borland's ISQL tool. You will notice some differences between these queries and the ones that we used earlier in the book. For example, these queries do not begin with an SQL prompt. Another difference is that ISQL does not require a semicolon at the end of the statement. (The semicolon is optional in ISQL.) But the SQL basics are still the same.

INPUT

```
SELECT *
FROM TABLE1
```

OUTPUT

```
ROW          REMARKS
==========  =======

row 1        Table 1
row 2        Table 1
row 3        Table 1
row 4        Table 1
row 5        Table 1
row 6        Table 1
```

INPUT/OUTPUT

```
SELECT *
FROM TABLE2

ROW          REMARKS
==========  ========

row 1        table 2
row 2        table 2
```

```
row 3      table 2
row 4      table 2
row 5      table 2
row 6      table 2
```

To join these two tables, type this:

INPUT

```
SELECT *
FROM TABLE1,TABLE2
```

```
ROW          REMARKS      ROW          REMARKS
==========   ==========   ==========   ========

row 1        Table 1      row 1        table 2
row 1        Table 1      row 2        table 2
row 1        Table 1      row 3        table 2
row 1        Table 1      row 4        table 2
row 1        Table 1      row 5        table 2
row 1        Table 1      row 6        table 2
row 2        Table 1      row 1        table 2
row 2        Table 1      row 2        table 2
row 2        Table 1      row 3        table 2
row 2        Table 1      row 4        table 2
row 2        Table 1      row 5        table 2
row 2        Table 1      row 6        table 2
row 3        Table 1      row 1        table 2
row 3        Table 1      row 2        table 2
row 3        Table 1      row 3        table 2
row 3        Table 1      row 4        table 2
row 3        Table 1      row 5        table 2
row 3        Table 1      row 6        table 2
row 4        Table 1      row 1        table 2
row 4        Table 1      row 2        table 2
row 4        Table 1      row 3        table 2
row 4        Table 1      row 4        table 2
row 4        Table 1      row 5        table 2
row 4        Table 1      row 6        table 2
row 5        Table 1      row 1        table 2
row 5        Table 1      row 2        table 2
row 5        Table 1      row 3        table 2
row 5        Table 1      row 4        table 2
row 5        Table 1      row 5        table 2
row 5        Table 1      row 6        table 2
row 6        Table 1      row 1        table 2
row 6        Table 1      row 2        table 2
row 6        Table 1      row 3        table 2
row 6        Table 1      row 4        table 2
row 6        Table 1      row 5        table 2
row 6        Table 1      row 6        table 2
```

Thirty-six rows! Where did they come from? And what kind of join is this?

ANALYSIS   A close examination of the result of your first join shows that each row from TABLE1 was added to each row from TABLE2. An extract from this join shows what happened:

```
ROW           REMARKS     ROW         REMARKS
=====         ==========  =========   ========

row 1         Table 1     row 1       table 2
row 1         Table 1     row 2       table 2
row 1         Table 1     row 3       table 2
row 1         Table 1     row 4       table 2
row 1         Table 1     row 5       table 2
row 1         Table 1     row 6       table 2
```

Notice how each row in TABLE2 was combined with row 1 in TABLE1. Congratulations! You have performed your first join. But what kind of join? An inner join? an outer join? or what? Well, actually this type of join is called a *cross-join*. A cross-join is not normally as useful as the other joins covered today, but this join does illustrate the basic combining property of all joins: Joins bring tables together.

Suppose you sold parts to bike shops for a living. When you designed your database, you built one big table with all the pertinent columns. Every time you had a new requirement, you added a new column or started a new table with all the old data plus the new data required to create a specific query. Eventually, your database would collapse from its own weight—not a pretty sight. An alternative design, based on a relational model, would have you put all related data into one table. Here's how your customer table would look:

```
SELECT *
FROM CUSTOMER
```

```
NAME        ADDRESS     STATE  ZIP         PHONE       REMARKS
==========  ==========  ======  ==========  =========  ==========

TRUE WHEEL  550 HUSKER  NE      58702       555-4545   NONE
BIKE SPEC   CPT SHRIVE  LA      45678       555-1234   NONE
LE SHOPPE   HOMETOWN    KS      54678       555-1278   NONE
AAA BIKE    10 OLDTOWN  NE      56784       555-3421   JOHN-MGR
JACKS BIKE  24 EGLIN    FL      34567       555-2314   NONE
```

This table contains all the information you need to describe your customers. The items you sold would go into another table:

```
SELECT *
FROM PART

    PARTNUM DESCRIPTION              PRICE
=========== ====================  ===========

         54 PEDALS                     54.25
         42 SEATS                      24.50
         46 TIRES                      15.25
         23 MOUNTAIN BIKE             350.45
         76 ROAD BIKE                 530.00
         10 TANDEM                   1200.00
```

And the orders you take would have their own table:

INPUT/ OUTPUT

```
SELECT *
FROM ORDERS
```

ORDEREDON	NAME	PARTNUM	QUANTITY	REMARKS
15-MAY-1996	TRUE WHEEL	23	6	PAID
19-MAY-1996	TRUE WHEEL	76	3	PAID
2-SEP-1996	TRUE WHEEL	10	1	PAID
30-JUN-1996	TRUE WHEEL	42	8	PAID
30-JUN-1996	BIKE SPEC	54	10	PAID
30-MAY-1996	BIKE SPEC	10	2	PAID
30-MAY-1996	BIKE SPEC	23	8	PAID
17-JAN-1996	BIKE SPEC	76	11	PAID
17-JAN-1996	LE SHOPPE	76	5	PAID
1-JUN-1996	LE SHOPPE	10	3	PAID
1-JUN-1996	AAA BIKE	10	1	PAID
1-JUL-1996	AAA BIKE	76	4	PAID
1-JUL-1996	AAA BIKE	46	14	PAID
11-JUL-1996	JACKS BIKE	76	14	PAID

One advantage of this approach is that you can have three specialized people or departments responsible for maintaining their own data. You don't need a database administrator who is conversant with all aspects of your project to shepherd one gigantic, multidepartmental database. Another advantage is that in the age of networks, each table could reside on a different machine. People who understand the data could maintain it, and it could reside on an appropriate machine (rather than that nasty corporate mainframe protected by legions of system administrators).

Now join PARTS and ORDERS:

INPUT/ OUTPUT

```
SELECT  O.ORDEREDON, O.NAME, O.PARTNUM,
P.PARTNUM, P.DESCRIPTION
FROM ORDERS O, PART P
```

ORDEREDON	NAME	PARTNUM	PARTNUM	DESCRIPTION
15-MAY-1996	TRUE WHEEL	23	54	PEDALS
19-MAY-1996	TRUE WHEEL	76	54	PEDALS
2-SEP-1996	TRUE WHEEL	10	54	PEDALS
30-JUN-1996	TRUE WHEEL	42	54	PEDALS
30-JUN-1996	BIKE SPEC	54	54	PEDALS
30-MAY-1996	BIKE SPEC	10	54	PEDALS
30-MAY-1996	BIKE SPEC	23	54	PEDALS
17-JAN-1996	BIKE SPEC	76	54	PEDALS
17-JAN-1996	LE SHOPPE	76	54	PEDALS
1-JUN-1996	LE SHOPPE	10	54	PEDALS
1-JUN-1996	AAA BIKE	10	54	PEDALS
1-JUL-1996	AAA BIKE	76	54	PEDALS
1-JUL-1996	AAA BIKE	46	54	PEDALS
11-JUL-1996	JACKS BIKE	76	54	PEDALS

...

6

ANALYSIS The preceding code is just a portion of the result set. The actual set is 14 (number of rows in ORDERS) × 6 (number of rows in PART), or 84 rows. It is similar to the result from joining TABLE1 and TABLE2 earlier today, and it is still one statement shy of being useful. Before we reveal that statement, we need to regress a little and talk about another use for the alias.

Finding the Correct Column

When you joined TABLE1 and TABLE2, you used SELECT *, which returned all the columns in both tables. In joining ORDERS to PART, the SELECT statement is a bit more complicated:

```
SELECT  O.ORDEREDON, O.NAME, O.PARTNUM,
P.PARTNUM, P.DESCRIPTION
```

SQL is smart enough to know that ORDEREDON and NAME exist only in ORDERS and that DESCRIPTION exists only in PART, but what about PARTNUM, which exists in both? If you have a column that has the same name in two tables, you must use an alias in your SELECT clause to specify which column you want to display. A common technique is to assign a single character to each table, as you did in the FROM clause:

```
FROM ORDERS O, PART P
```

You use that character with each column name, as you did in the preceding SELECT clause. The SELECT clause could also be written like this:

```
SELECT  ORDEREDON, NAME, O.PARTNUM, P.PARTNUM, DESCRIPTION
```

But remember, someday you might have to come back and maintain this query. It doesn't hurt to make it more readable. Now back to the missing statement.

Equi-Joins

An extract from the PART/ORDERS join provides a clue as to what is missing:

```
30-JUN-1996 TRUE WHEEL          42          54 PEDALS
30-JUN-1996 BIKE SPEC           54          54 PEDALS
30-MAY-1996 BIKE SPEC           10          54 PEDALS
```

Notice the PARTNUM fields that are common to both tables. What if you wrote the following?

INPUT
```
SELECT  O.ORDEREDON, O.NAME, O.PARTNUM,
P.PARTNUM, P.DESCRIPTION
FROM ORDERS O, PART P
WHERE O.PARTNUM = P.PARTNUM
```

OUTPUT

ORDEREDON	NAME	PARTNUM	PARTNUM	DESCRIPTION
===========	==========	===========	=========	===============
1-JUN-1996	AAA BIKE	10	10	TANDEM
30-MAY-1996	BIKE SPEC	10	10	TANDEM
2-SEP-1996	TRUE WHEEL	10	10	TANDEM

6

```
 1-JUN-1996 LE SHOPPE        10        10 TANDEM
30-MAY-1996 BIKE SPEC        23        23 MOUNTAIN BIKE
15-MAY-1996 TRUE WHEEL       23        23 MOUNTAIN BIKE
30-JUN-1996 TRUE WHEEL       42        42 SEATS
 1-JUL-1996 AAA BIKE         46        46 TIRES
30-JUN-1996 BIKE SPEC        54        54 PEDALS
 1-JUL-1996 AAA BIKE         76        76 ROAD BIKE
17-JAN-1996 BIKE SPEC        76        76 ROAD BIKE
19-MAY-1996 TRUE WHEEL       76        76 ROAD BIKE
11-JUL-1996 JACKS BIKE       76        76 ROAD BIKE
17-JAN-1996 LE SHOPPE        76        76 ROAD BIKE
```

ANALYSIS Using the column PARTNUM that exists in both of the preceding tables, you have just combined the information you had stored in the ORDERS table with information from the PART table to show a description of the parts the bike shops have ordered from you. The join that was used is called an equi-join because the goal is to match the values of a column in one table to the corresponding values in the second table.

You can further qualify this query by adding more conditions in the WHERE clause. For example:

INPUT/OUTPUT
```
SELECT  O.ORDEREDON, O.NAME, O.PARTNUM,
P.PARTNUM, P.DESCRIPTION
FROM ORDERS O, PART P
WHERE O.PARTNUM = P.PARTNUM
AND O.PARTNUM = 76

ORDEREDON NAME        PARTNUM    PARTNUM DESCRIPTION
=========== =========== =========== =========== =============

 1-JUL-1996 AAA BIKE         76        76 ROAD BIKE
17-JAN-1996 BIKE SPEC        76        76 ROAD BIKE
19-MAY-1996 TRUE WHEEL       76        76 ROAD BIKE
11-JUL-1996 JACKS BIKE       76        76 ROAD BIKE
17-JAN-1996 LE SHOPPE        76        76 ROAD BIKE
```

The number 76 is not very descriptive, and you wouldn't want your sales people to have to memorize a part number. (We have had the misfortune to see many data information systems in the field that require the end user to know some obscure code for something that had a perfectly good name. Please don't write one of those!) Here's another way to write the query:

INPUT/OUTPUT
```
SELECT  O.ORDEREDON, O.NAME, O.PARTNUM,
P.PARTNUM, P.DESCRIPTION
FROM ORDERS O, PART P
WHERE O.PARTNUM = P.PARTNUM
AND P.DESCRIPTION = 'ROAD BIKE'

ORDEREDON NAME        PARTNUM    PARTNUM DESCRIPTION
=========== =========== =========== =========== =============

 1-JUL-1996 AAA BIKE         76        76 ROAD BIKE
17-JAN-1996 BIKE SPEC        76        76 ROAD BIKE
19-MAY-1996 TRUE WHEEL       76        76 ROAD BIKE
11-JUL-1996 JACKS BIKE       76        76 ROAD BIKE
17-JAN-1996 LE SHOPPE        76        76 ROAD BIKE
```

6

Along the same line, take a look at two more tables to see how they can be joined. In this example the `employee_id` column should obviously be unique. You could have employees with the same name, they could work in the same department, and earn the same salary. However, each employee would have his or her own `employee_id`. To join these two tables, you would use the `employee_id` column.

EMPLOYEE_TABLE	EMPLOYEE_PAY_TABLE
employee_id	employee_id
last_name	salary
first_name	department
middle_name	supervisor
	marital_status

INPUT
```
SELECT E.EMPLOYEE_ID, E.LAST_NAME, EP.SALARY
FROM EMPLOYEE_TBL E,
        EMPLOYEE_PAY_TBL EP
WHERE E.EMPLOYEE_ID = EP.EMPLOYEE_ID
  AND E.LAST_NAME = 'SMITH';
```

OUTPUT
```
E.EMPLOYEE_ID  E.LAST_NAME  EP.SALARY

=============  ===========  =========
       13245   SMITH         35000.00
```

 TIP
When you join two tables without the use of a WHERE clause, you are performing a Cartesian join. This join combines all rows from all the tables in the FROM clause. If each table has 200 rows, then you will end up with 40,000 rows in your results (200 × 200). Always join your tables in the WHERE clause unless you have a real need to join all the rows of all the selected tables.

Back to the original tables. Now you are ready to use all this information about joins to do something really useful: finding out how much money you have made from selling road bikes:

INPUT/OUTPUT
```
SELECT SUM(O.QUANTITY * P.PRICE) TOTAL
FROM ORDERS O, PART P
WHERE O.PARTNUM = P.PARTNUM
AND P.DESCRIPTION = 'ROAD BIKE'

        TOTAL
===========

   19610.00
```

ANALYSIS With this setup, the sales people can keep the ORDERS table updated, the production department can keep the PART table current, and you can find your bottom line without redesigning your database.

NOTE Notice the consistent use of table and column aliases in the SQL statement examples. You will save many, many keystrokes by using aliases. They also help to make your statement more readable.

Can you join more than one table? For example, to generate information to send out an invoice, you could type this statement:

```
INPUT/
OUTPUT   SELECT C.NAME, C.ADDRESS, (O.QUANTITY * P.PRICE) TOTAL
         FROM ORDER O, PART P, CUSTOMER C
         WHERE O.PARTNUM = P.PARTNUM
         AND O.NAME = C.NAME

         NAME         ADDRESS         TOTAL
         ==========   ==========   ============

         TRUE WHEEL   550 HUSKER      1200.00
         BIKE SPEC    CPT SHRIVE      2400.00
         LE SHOPPE    HOMETOWN        3600.00
         AAA BIKE     10 OLDTOWN      1200.00
         TRUE WHEEL   550 HUSKER      2102.70
         BIKE SPEC    CPT SHRIVE      2803.60
         TRUE WHEEL   550 HUSKER       196.00
         AAA BIKE     10 OLDTOWN       213.50
         BIKE SPEC    CPT SHRIVE       542.50
         TRUE WHEEL   550 HUSKER      1590.00
         BIKE SPEC    CPT SHRIVE      5830.00
         JACKS BIKE   24 EGLIN        7420.00
         LE SHOPPE    HOMETOWN        2650.00
         AAA BIKE     10 OLDTOWN      2120.00
```

You could make the output more readable by writing the statement like this:

```
INPUT/
OUTPUT   SELECT C.NAME, C.ADDRESS,
         O.QUANTITY * P.PRICE TOTAL
         FROM ORDERS O, PART P, CUSTOMER C
         WHERE O.PARTNUM = P.PARTNUM
         AND O.NAME = C.NAME
         ORDER BY C.NAME

         NAME         ADDRESS         TOTAL
         ==========   ==========   ============

         AAA BIKE     10 OLDTOWN       213.50
         AAA BIKE     10 OLDTOWN      2120.00
         AAA BIKE     10 OLDTOWN      1200.00
```

6

```
BIKE SPEC  CPT SHRIVE     542.50
BIKE SPEC  CPT SHRIVE    2803.60
BIKE SPEC  CPT SHRIVE    5830.00
BIKE SPEC  CPT SHRIVE    2400.00
JACKS BIKE 24 EGLIN      7420.00
LE SHOPPE  HOMETOWN      2650.00
LE SHOPPE  HOMETOWN      3600.00
TRUE WHEEL 550 HUSKER     196.00
TRUE WHEEL 550 HUSKER    2102.70
TRUE WHEEL 550 HUSKER    1590.00
TRUE WHEEL 550 HUSKER    1200.00
```

NOTE

Notice that when joining the three tables (ORDERS, PART, and CUSTOMER) that the ORDERS table was used in two joins and the other tables were used only once. Tables that will return the fewest rows with the given conditions are commonly referred to as *driving tables,* or *base tables.* Tables other than the base table in a query are usually joined to the base table for more efficient data retrieval. Consequently, the ORDERS table is the base table in this example. In most databases a few base tables join (either directly or indirectly) all the other tables. (See Day 15, "Streamlining SQL Statements for Improved Performance," for more on base tables.)

You can make the previous query more specific, thus more useful, by adding the DESCRIPTION column as in the following example:

INPUT/OUTPUT

```
SELECT C.NAME, C.ADDRESS,
O.QUANTITY * P.PRICE TOTAL,
P.DESCRIPTION
FROM ORDERS O, PART P, CUSTOMER C
WHERE O.PARTNUM = P.PARTNUM
AND O.NAME = C.NAME
ORDER BY C.NAME

NAME        ADDRESS         TOTAL DESCRIPTION
==========  ==========  ========== ===============

AAA BIKE    10 OLDTOWN    213.50 TIRES
AAA BIKE    10 OLDTOWN   2120.00 ROAD BIKE
AAA BIKE    10 OLDTOWN   1200.00 TANDEM
BIKE SPEC   CPT SHRIVE    542.50 PEDALS
BIKE SPEC   CPT SHRIVE   2803.60 MOUNTAIN BIKE
BIKE SPEC   CPT SHRIVE   5830.00 ROAD BIKE
BIKE SPEC   CPT SHRIVE   2400.00 TANDEM
JACKS BIKE  24 EGLIN     7420.00 ROAD BIKE
LE SHOPPE   HOMETOWN     2650.00 ROAD BIKE
LE SHOPPE   HOMETOWN     3600.00 TANDEM
TRUE WHEEL  550 HUSKER    196.00 SEATS
TRUE WHEEL  550 HUSKER   2102.70 MOUNTAIN BIKE
TRUE WHEEL  550 HUSKER   1590.00 ROAD BIKE
TRUE WHEEL  550 HUSKER   1200.00 TANDEM
```

ANALYSIS This information is a result of joining three tables. You can now use this information to create an invoice.

 NOTE In the example at the beginning of the day, SQL grouped TABLE1 and TABLE2 to create a new table with X (rows in TABLE1) × Y (rows in TABLE2) number of rows. A physical table is not created by the join, but rather in a virtual sense. The join between the two tables produces a new set that meets all conditions in the WHERE clause, including the join itself. The SELECT statement has reduced the number of rows displayed, but to evaluate the WHERE clause SQL still creates all the possible rows. The sample tables in today's examples have only a handful of rows. Your actual data may have thousands of rows. If you are working on a platform with lots of horsepower, using a multiple-table join might not visibly affect performance. However, if you are working in a slower environment, joins could cause a significant slowdown.

We aren't telling you not to use joins, because you have seen the advantages to be gained from a relational design. Just be aware of the platform you are using and your customer's requirements for speed versus reliability.

Non-Equi-Joins

Because SQL supports an equi-join, you might assume that SQL also has a non-equi-join. You would be right! Whereas the equi-join uses an = sign in the WHERE statement, the non-equi-join uses everything but an = sign. For example:

INPUT
```
SELECT O.NAME, O.PARTNUM, P.PARTNUM,
O.QUANTITY * P.PRICE TOTAL
FROM ORDERS O, PART P
WHERE O.PARTNUM > P.PARTNUM
```

OUTPUT
```
NAME          PARTNUM       PARTNUM         TOTAL
==========    ===========   ===========   ===========

TRUE WHEEL         76            54         162.75
BIKE SPEC          76            54         596.75
LE SHOPPE          76            54         271.25
AAA BIKE           76            54         217.00
JACKS BIKE         76            54         759.50
TRUE WHEEL         76            42          73.50
BIKE SPEC          54            42         245.00
BIKE SPEC          76            42         269.50
LE SHOPPE          76            42         122.50
AAA BIKE           76            42          98.00
```

6

```
AAA BIKE               46        42        343.00
JACKS BIKE             76        42        343.00
TRUE WHEEL             76        46         45.75
BIKE SPEC              54        46        152.50
BIKE SPEC              76        46        167.75
LE SHOPPE              76        46         76.25
AAA BIKE               76        46         61.00
JACKS BIKE             76        46        213.50
TRUE WHEEL             76        23       1051.35
TRUE WHEEL             42        23       2803.60
...
```

This listing goes on to describe all the rows in the join WHERE O.PARTNUM > P.PARTNUM. In the context of your bicycle shop, this information doesn't have much meaning, and in the real world the equi-join is far more common than the non-equi-join. However, you may encounter an application in which a non-equi-join produces the perfect result.

Outer Joins versus Inner Joins

Just as the non-equi-join balances the equi-join, an outer join complements the inner join. An inner join is where the rows of the tables are combined with each other, producing a number of new rows equal to the product of the number of rows in each table. Also, the inner join uses these rows to determine the result of the WHERE clause. An outer join groups the two tables in a slightly different way. Using the PART and ORDERS tables from the previous examples, perform the following inner join:

```
SELECT P.PARTNUM, P.DESCRIPTION,P.PRICE,
O.NAME, O.PARTNUM
FROM PART P
JOIN ORDERS O ON ORDERS.PARTNUM = 54
```

OUTPUT

```
PARTNUM DESCRIPTION                  PRICE NAME         PARTNUM
======= ====================  =========== ==========  ===========

     54 PEDALS                     54.25 BIKE SPEC          54
     42 SEATS                      24.50 BIKE SPEC          54
     46 TIRES                      15.25 BIKE SPEC          54
     23 MOUNTAIN BIKE             350.45 BIKE SPEC          54
     76 ROAD BIKE                 530.00 BIKE SPEC          54
     10 TANDEM                   1200.00 BIKE SPEC          54
```

NOTE

The syntax you used to get this join—JOIN ON—is not ANSI standard. The implementation you used for this example has additional syntax. You are using it here to specify an inner and an outer join. Most implementations of SQL have similar extensions. Notice the absence of the WHERE clause in this type of join.

ANALYSIS The result is that all the rows in PART are spliced on to specific rows in ORDERS where the column PARTNUM is 54. Here's a RIGHT OUTER JOIN statement:

INPUT/OUTPUT
```
SELECT P.PARTNUM, P.DESCRIPTION,P.PRICE,
O.NAME, O.PARTNUM
FROM PART P
RIGHT OUTER JOIN ORDERS O ON ORDERS.PARTNUM = 54
```

PARTNUM	DESCRIPTION	PRICE	NAME	PARTNUM
<null>	<null>	<null>	TRUE WHEEL	23
<null>	<null>	<null>	TRUE WHEEL	76
<null>	<null>	<null>	TRUE WHEEL	10
<null>	<null>	<null>	TRUE WHEEL	42
54	PEDALS	54.25	BIKE SPEC	54
42	SEATS	24.50	BIKE SPEC	54
46	TIRES	15.25	BIKE SPEC	54
23	MOUNTAIN BIKE	350.45	BIKE SPEC	54
76	ROAD BIKE	530.00	BIKE SPEC	54
10	TANDEM	1200.00	BIKE SPEC	54
<null>	<null>	<null>	BIKE SPEC	10
<null>	<null>	<null>	BIKE SPEC	23
<null>	<null>	<null>	BIKE SPEC	76
<null>	<null>	<null>	LE SHOPPE	76
<null>	<null>	<null>	LE SHOPPE	10
<null>	<null>	<null>	AAA BIKE	10
<null>	<null>	<null>	AAA BIKE	76
<null>	<null>	<null>	AAA BIKE	46
<null>	<null>	<null>	JACKS BIKE	76

ANALYSIS This type of query is new. First you specified a RIGHT OUTER JOIN, which caused SQL to return a full set of the right table, ORDERS, and to place nulls in the fields where ORDERS.PARTNUM <> 54. Following is a LEFT OUTER JOIN statement:

INPUT/OUTPUT
```
SELECT P.PARTNUM, P.DESCRIPTION,P.PRICE,
O.NAME, O.PARTNUM
FROM PART P
LEFT OUTER JOIN ORDERS O ON ORDERS.PARTNUM = 54
```

PARTNUM	DESCRIPTION	PRICE	NAME	PARTNUM
54	PEDALS	54.25	BIKE SPEC	54
42	SEATS	24.50	BIKE SPEC	54
46	TIRES	15.25	BIKE SPEC	54
23	MOUNTAIN BIKE	350.45	BIKE SPEC	54
76	ROAD BIKE	530.00	BIKE SPEC	54
10	TANDEM	1200.00	BIKE SPEC	54

ANALYSIS You get the same six rows as the INNER JOIN. Because you specified LEFT (the LEFT table), PART determined the number of rows you would return. Because PART is smaller than ORDERS, SQL saw no need to pad those other fields with blanks.

6

Don't worry too much about inner and outer joins. Most SQL products determine the optimum JOIN for your query. In fact, if you are placing your query into a stored procedure (or using it inside a program (both stored procedures and Embedded SQL covered on Day 13, "Advanced SQL Topics"), you should not specify a join type even if your SQL implementation provides the proper syntax. If you do specify a join type, the optimizer chooses your way instead of the optimum way.

Some implementations of SQL use the + sign instead of an OUTER JOIN statement. The + simply means "Show me everything even if something is missing." Here's the syntax:

SYNTAX

```
SQL> select e.name, e.employee_id, ep.salary,
            ep.marital_status
     from e,ployee_tbl e,
          employee_pay_tbl ep
     where e.employee_id = ep.employee_id(+)
      and e.name like '%MITH';
```

ANALYSIS This statement is joining the two tables. The + sign on the ep.employee_id column will return all rows even if they are empty.

Joining a Table to Itself

Today's final topic is the often-used technique of joining a table to itself. The syntax of this operation is similar to joining two tables. For example, to join table TABLE1 to itself, type this:

INPUT

```
SELECT *
FROM TABLE1, TABLE1
```

OUTPUT

ROW	REMARKS	ROW	REMARKS
=====	=========	=====	========
row 1	Table 1	row 1	Table 1
row 1	Table 1	row 2	Table 1
row 1	Table 1	row 3	Table 1
row 1	Table 1	row 4	Table 1
row 1	Table 1	row 5	Table 1
row 1	Table 1	row 6	Table 1
row 2	Table 1	row 1	Table 1
row 2	Table 1	row 2	Table 1
row 2	Table 1	row 3	Table 1
row 2	Table 1	row 4	Table 1
row 2	Table 1	row 5	Table 1
row 2	Table 1	row 6	Table 1
row 3	Table 1	row 1	Table 1
row 3	Table 1	row 2	Table 1
row 3	Table 1	row 3	Table 1
row 3	Table 1	row 4	Table 1
row 3	Table 1	row 5	Table 1
row 3	Table 1	row 6	Table 1
row 4	Table 1	row 1	Table 1
row 4	Table 1	row 2	Table 1
...			

ANALYSIS In its complete form, this join produces the same number of combinations as joining two 6-row tables. This type of join could be useful to check the internal consistency of data. What would happen if someone fell asleep in the production department and entered a new part with a PARTNUM that already existed? That would be bad news for everybody: Invoices would be wrong; your application would probably blow up; and in general you would be in for a very bad time. And the cause of all your problems would be the duplicate PARTNUM in the following table:

INPUT/ OUTPUT
```
SELECT * FROM PART

    PARTNUM DESCRIPTION              PRICE
    =========== ==================== ===========

         54 PEDALS                   54.25
         42 SEATS                    24.50
         46 TIRES                    15.25
         23 MOUNTAIN BIKE           350.45
         76 ROAD BIKE               530.00
         10 TANDEM                  1200.00
         76 CLIPPLESS SHOE            65.00 <-NOTE SAME #
```

You saved your company from this bad situation by checking PART before anyone used it:

INPUT/ OUTPUT
```
SELECT F.PARTNUM, F.DESCRIPTION,
S.PARTNUM,S.DESCRIPTION
FROM PART F, PART S
WHERE F.PARTNUM = S.PARTNUM
AND F.DESCRIPTION <> S.DESCRIPTION

    PARTNUM DESCRIPTION                  PARTNUM DESCRIPTION
    ========== ========================= ======= ============

         76 ROAD BIKE                        76 CLIPPLESS SHOE
         76 CLIPPLESS SHOE                   76 ROAD BIKE
```

ANALYSIS Now you are a hero until someone asks why the table has only two entries. You, remembering what you have learned about JOINs, retain your hero status by explaining how the join produced two rows that satisfied the condition WHERE F.PARTNUM = S.PARTNUM AND F.DESCRIPTION <> S.DESCRIPTION. Of course, at some point, the row of data containing the duplicate PARTNUM would have to be corrected.

Summary

Today you learned that a join combines all possible combinations of rows present in the selected tables. These new rows are then available for selection based on the information that you want.

Congratulations—you have learned almost everything there is to know about the SELECT clause. The one remaining item, subqueries, is covered tomorrow (Day 7, "Subqueries: The Embedded SELECT Statement").

6

Q&A

Q Why cover outer, inner, left, and right joins when I probably won't ever use them?

A A little knowledge is a dangerous thing, and no knowledge can be expensive. You now know enough to understand the basics of what your SQL engine might try while optimizing you queries.

Q How many tables can you join on?

A That depends on the implementation. Some implementations have a 25-table limit, whereas others have no limit. Just remember, the more tables you join on, the slower the response time will be. To be safe, check your implementation to find out the maximum number of tables allowed in a query.

Q Would it be fair to say that when tables are joined, they actually become one table?

A Very simply put, that is just about what happens. When you join the tables, you can select from any of the columns in either table.

Workshop

The Workshop provides quiz questions to help solidify your understanding of the material covered, as well as exercises to provide you with experience in using what you have learned. Try to answer the quiz and exercise questions before checking the answers in Appendix F, "Answers to Quizzes and Exercises."

Quiz

1. How many rows would a two-table join produce if one table had 50,000 rows and the other had 100,000?

2. What type of join appears in the following SELECT statement?

```
select e.name, e.employee_id, ep.salary
from employee_tbl e,
     employee_pay_tbl ep
where e.employee_id = ep.employee_id;
```

3. Will the following SELECT statements work?

```
a. select name, employee_id, salary
   from employee_tbl e,
        employee_pay_tbl ep
   where employee_id = employee_id
     and name like '%MITH';
```

6

b.
```
select e.name, e.employee_id, ep.salary
from employee_tbl e,
     employee_pay_tbl ep
where name like '%MITH';
```

c.
```
select e.name, e.employee_id, ep.salary
from employee_tbl e,
     employee_pay_tbl ep
where e.employee_id = ep.employee_id
  and e.name like '%MITH';
```

4. In the WHERE clause, when joining the tables, should you do the join first or the conditions?

5. In joining tables are you limited to one-column joins, or can you join on more than one column?

Exercises

1. In the section on joining tables to themselves, the last example returned two combinations. Rewrite the query so only one entry comes up for each redundant part number.

2. Rewrite the following query to make it more readable and shorter.

INPUT
```
select orders.orderedon, orders.name, part.partnum,
       part.price, part.description from orders, part
where orders.partnum = part.partnum and
orders.orderedon
between '1-SEP 06' and '30-3EP-90'
order by part.partnum;
```

3. From the PART table and the ORDERS table, make up a query that will return the following:

OUTPUT

ORDEREDON	NAME	PARTNUM	QUANTITY
===================	===================	========	========
2-SEP-96	TRUE WHEEL	10	1

6

Week 1

Day 7

Subqueries: The Embedded SELECT Statement

Objectives

A *subquery* is a query whose results are passed as the argument for another query. Subqueries enable you to bind several queries together. By the end of the day, you will understand and be able to do the following:

- ☐ Build a subquery
- ☐ Use the keywords EXISTS, ANY, and ALL with your subqueries
- ☐ Build and use correlated subqueries

NOTE

The examples for today's lesson were created using Borland's ISQL, the same implementation used on Day 6, "Joining Tables." Remember, this implementation does not use the SQL> prompt or line numbers.

Building a Subquery

Simply put, a subquery lets you tie the result set of one query to another. The general syntax is as follows:

 SYNTAX

```
SELECT *
FROM TABLE1
WHERE TABLE1.SOMECOLUMN =
(SELECT SOMEOTHERCOLUMN
FROM TABLE2
WHERE SOMEOTHERCOLUMN = SOMEVALUE)
```

Notice how the second query is nested inside the first. Here's a real-world example that uses the PART and ORDERS tables:

INPUT
```
SELECT *
FROM PART
```

OUTPUT

PARTNUM	DESCRIPTION	PRICE
54	PEDALS	54.25
42	SEATS	24.50
46	TIRES	15.25
23	MOUNTAIN BIKE	350.45
76	ROAD BIKE	530.00
10	TANDEM	1200.00

INPUT/OUTPUT
```
SELECT *
FROM ORDERS
```

ORDEREDON	NAME	PARTNUM	QUANTITY	REMARKS
15-MAY-1996	TRUE WHEEL	23	6	PAID
19-MAY-1996	TRUE WHEEL	76	3	PAID
2-SEP-1996	TRUE WHEEL	10	1	PAID
30-JUN-1996	TRUE WHEEL	42	8	PAID
30-JUN-1996	BIKE SPEC	54	10	PAID
30-MAY-1996	BIKE SPEC	10	2	PAID
30-MAY-1996	BIKE SPEC	23	8	PAID
17-JAN-1996	BIKE SPEC	76	11	PAID
17-JAN-1996	LE SHOPPE	76	5	PAID
1-JUN-1996	LE SHOPPE	10	3	PAID
1-JUN-1996	AAA BIKE	10	1	PAID

```
            1-JUL-1996 AAA BIKE          76           4 PAID
            1-JUL-1996 AAA BIKE          46          14 PAID
           11-JUL-1996 JACKS BIKE        76          14 PAID
```

ANALYSIS   The tables share a common field called PARTNUM. Suppose that you didn't know (or
didn't want to know) the PARTNUM, but instead wanted to work with the description
of the part. Using a subquery, you could type this:

INPUT/
OUTPUT

```
SELECT *
FROM ORDERS
WHERE PARTNUM =
(SELECT PARTNUM
FROM PART
WHERE DESCRIPTION LIKE "ROAD%")

    ORDEREDON NAME            PARTNUM     QUANTITY REMARKS
    =========== ========== =========== =========== ========

    19-MAY-1996 TRUE WHEEL        76           3 PAID
    17-JAN-1996 BIKE SPEC         76          11 PAID
    17-JAN-1996 LE SHOPPE         76           5 PAID
     1-JUL-1996 AAA BIKE          76           4 PAID
    11-JUL-1996 JACKS BIKE        76          14 PAID
```

ANALYSIS   Even better, if you use the concepts you learned on Day 6, you could enhance the
PARTNUM column in the result by including the DESCRIPTION, making PARTNUM clearer
for anyone who hasn't memorized it. Try this:

INPUT/
OUTPUT

```
SELECT O.ORDEREDON, O.PARTNUM,
P.DESCRIPTION, O.QUANTITY, O.REMARKS
FROM ORDERS O, PART P
WHERE O.PARTNUM = P.PARTNUM
AND
O.PARTNUM =
(SELECT PARTNUM
FROM PART
WHERE DESCRIPTION LIKE "ROAD%")

    ORDEREDON     PARTNUM DESCRIPTION     QUANTITY REMARKS
    =========== =========== ============= =========== =========

    19-MAY-1996        76 ROAD BIKE            3 PAID
     1-JUL-1996        76 ROAD BIKE            4 PAID
    17-JAN-1996        76 ROAD BIKE            5 PAID
    17-JAN-1996        76 ROAD BIKE           11 PAID
    11-JUL-1996        76 ROAD BIKE           14 PAID
```

ANALYSIS   The first part of the query is very familiar:

```
SELECT O.ORDEREDON, O.PARTNUM,
P.DESCRIPTION, O.QUANTITY, O.REMARKS
FROM ORDERS O, PART P
```

7

Here you are using the aliases O and P for tables ORDERS and PART to select the five columns you are interested in. In this case the aliases were not necessary because each of the columns you asked to return is unique. However, it is easier to make a readable query now than to have to figure it out later. The first WHERE clause you encounter

```
WHERE O.PARTNUM = P.PARTNUM
```

is standard language for the join of tables PART and ORDERS specified in the FROM clause. If you didn't use this WHERE clause, you would have all the possible row combinations of the two tables. The next section includes the subquery. The statement

```
AND
O.PARTNUM =
(SELECT PARTNUM
FROM PART
WHERE DESCRIPTION LIKE "ROAD%")
```

adds the qualification that O.PARTNUM must be equal to the result of your simple subquery. The subquery is straightforward, finding all the part numbers that are LIKE "ROAD%". The use of LIKE was somewhat lazy, saving you the keystrokes required to type ROAD BIKE. However, it turns out you were lucky this time. What if someone in the Parts department had added a new part called ROADKILL? The revised PART table would look like this:

INPUT/OUTPUT
```
SELECT *
FROM PART
```

```
     PARTNUM DESCRIPTION              PRICE
     =========== ==================== ===========

          54 PEDALS                   54.25
          42 SEATS                    24.50
          46 TIRES                    15.25
          23 MOUNTAIN BIKE           350.45
          76 ROAD BIKE               530.00
          10 TANDEM                 1200.00
          77 ROADKILL                  7.99
```

Suppose you are blissfully unaware of this change and try your query after this new product was added. If you enter this:

```
SELECT O.ORDEREDON, O.PARTNUM,
P.DESCRIPTION, O.QUANTITY, O.REMARKS
FROM ORDERS O, PART P
WHERE O.PARTNUM = P.PARTNUM
AND
O.PARTNUM =
(SELECT PARTNUM
FROM PART
WHERE DESCRIPTION LIKE "ROAD%")
```

the SQL engine complains

```
multiple rows in singleton select
```

and you don't get any results. The response from your SQL engine may vary, but it still complains and returns nothing.

To find out why you get this undesirable result, assume the role of the SQL engine. You will probably evaluate the subquery first. You would return this:

```
SELECT PARTNUM
FROM PART
WHERE DESCRIPTION LIKE "ROAD%"

        PARTNUM
    ===========

        76
        77
```

You would take this result and apply it to O.PARTNUM =, which is the step that causes the problem.

ANALYSIS How can PARTNUM be equal to both 76 and 77? This must be what the engine meant when it accused you of being a simpleton. When you used the LIKE clause, you opened yourself up for this error. When you combine the results of a relational operator with another relational operator, such as =, <, or >, you need to make sure the result is singular. In the case of the example we have been using, the solution would be to rewrite the query using an = instead of the LIKE, like this:

```
SELECT O.ORDEREDON, O.PARTNUM,
P.DESCRIPTION, O.QUANTITY, O.REMARKS
FROM ORDERS O, PART P
WHERE O.PARTNUM = P.PARTNUM
AND
O.PARTNUM =
(SELECT PARTNUM
FROM PART
WHERE DESCRIPTION = "ROAD BIKE")
```

ORDEREDON	PARTNUM	DESCRIPTION	QUANTITY	REMARKS
19-MAY-1996	76	ROAD BIKE	3	PAID
1-JUL-1996	76	ROAD BIKE	4	PAID
17-JAN-1996	76	ROAD BIKE	5	PAID
17-JAN-1996	76	ROAD BIKE	11	PAID
11-JUL-1996	76	ROAD BIKE	14	PAID

ANALYSIS This subquery returns only one unique result; therefore narrowing your = condition to a single value. How can you be sure the subquery won't return multiple values if you are looking for only one value?

Avoiding the use of LIKE is a start. Another approach is to ensure the uniqueness of the search field during table design. If you are the untrusting type, you could use the method (described yesterday) for joining a table to itself to check a given field for uniqueness. If you design the

7

table yourself (see Day 9, "Creating and Maintaining Tables") or trust the person who designed the table, you could require the column you are searching to have a unique value. You could also use a part of SQL that returns only one answer: the aggregate function.

Using Aggregate Functions with Subqueries

The aggregate functions SUM, COUNT, MIN, MAX, and AVG all return a single value. To find the average amount of an order, type this:

INPUT
```
SELECT AVG(O.QUANTITY * P.PRICE)
FROM ORDERS O, PART P
WHERE O.PARTNUM = P.PARTNUM
```

OUTPUT
```
        AVG
===========

     2419.16
```

ANALYSIS This statement returns only one value. To find out which orders were above average, use the preceding SELECT statement for your subquery. The complete query and result are as follows:

INPUT/ OUTPUT
```
SELECT O.NAME, O.ORDEREDON,
O.QUANTITY * P.PRICE TOTAL
FROM ORDERS O, PART P
WHERE O.PARTNUM = P.PARTNUM
AND
O.QUANTITY * P.PRICE >
(SELECT AVG(O.QUANTITY * P.PRICE)
FROM ORDERS O, PART P
WHERE O.PARTNUM = P.PARTNUM)

NAME        ORDEREDON       TOTAL
==========  ===========  ===========

LE SHOPPE    1-JUN-1996     3600.00
BIKE SPEC   30-MAY-1996     2803.60
LE SHOPPE   17-JAN-1996     2650.00
BIKE SPEC   17-JAN-1996     5830.00
JACKS BIKE  11-JUL-1996     7420.00
```

ANALYSIS This example contains a rather unremarkable SELECT/FROM/WHERE clause:

```
SELECT O.NAME, O.ORDEREDON,
O.QUANTITY * P.PRICE TOTAL
FROM ORDERS O, PART P
WHERE O.PARTNUM = P.PARTNUM
```

These lines represent the common way of joining these two tables. This join is necessary because the price is in PART and the quantity is in ORDERS. The WHERE ensures that you examine only the join-formed rows that are related. You then add the subquery:

```
AND
O.QUANTITY * P.PRICE  >
(SELECT AVG(O.QUANTITY * P.PRICE)
FROM ORDERS O, PART P
WHERE O.PARTNUM = P.PARTNUM)
```

The preceding condition compares the total of each order with the average you computed in the subquery. Note that the join in the subquery is required for the same reasons as in the main SELECT statement. This join is also constructed exactly the same way. There are no secret handshakes in subqueries; they have exactly the same syntax as a standalone query. In fact, most subqueries start out as standalone queries and are incorporated as subqueries after their results are tested.

Nested Subqueries

Nesting is the act of embedding a subquery within another subquery. For example:

```
Select * FROM SOMETHING WHERE ( SUBQUERY(SUBQUERY(SUBQUERY)));
```

Subqueries can be nested as deeply as your implementation of SQL allows. For example, to send out special notices to customers who spend more than the average amount of money, you would combine the information in the table CUSTOMER

INPUT
```
SELECT *
FROM CUSTOMER
```

OUTPUT

NAME	ADDRESS	STATE	ZIP	PHONE	REMARKS
TRUE WHEEL	550 HUSKER	NE	58702	555-4545	NONE
BIKE SPEC	CPT SHRIVE	LA	45678	555-1234	NONE
LE SHOPPE	HOMETOWN	KS	54678	555-1278	NONE
AAA BIKE	10 OLDTOWN	NE	56784	555-3421	JOHN-MGR
JACKS BIKE	24 EGLIN	FL	34567	555-2314	NONE

with a slightly modified version of the query you used to find the above-average orders:

INPUT/
OUTPUT
```
SELECT ALL C.NAME, C.ADDRESS, C.STATE,C.ZIP
FROM CUSTOMER C
WHERE C.NAME IN
(SELECT O.NAME
FROM ORDERS O, PART P
WHERE O.PARTNUM = P.PARTNUM
AND
O.QUANTITY * P.PRICE  >
(SELECT AVG(O.QUANTITY * P.PRICE)
FROM ORDERS O, PART P
WHERE O.PARTNUM = P.PARTNUM))
```

7

```
NAME        ADDRESS     STATE  ZIP
==========  ==========  ====== ==========

BIKE SPEC   CPT SHRIVE  LA     45678
LE SHOPPE   HOMETOWN    KS     54678
JACKS BIKE  24 EGLIN    FL     34567
```

ANALYSIS Here's a look at what you asked for. In the innermost set of parentheses, you find a familiar statement:

```
SELECT AVG(O.QUANTITY * P.PRICE)
FROM ORDERS O, PART P
WHERE O.PARTNUM = P.PARTNUM
```

This result feeds into a slightly modified version of the SELECT clause you used before:

```
SELECT O.NAME
FROM ORDERS O, PART P
WHERE O.PARTNUM = P.PARTNUM
AND
O.QUANTITY * P.PRICE  >
(...)
```

Note the SELECT clause has been modified to return a single column, NAME, which, not so coincidentally, is common with the table CUSTOMER. Running this statement by itself you get:

INPUT/ OUTPUT

```
SELECT O.NAME
FROM ORDERS O, PART P
WHERE O.PARTNUM = P.PARTNUM
AND
O.QUANTITY * P.PRICE  >
(SELECT AVG(O.QUANTITY * P.PRICE)
FROM ORDERS O, PART P
WHERE O.PARTNUM = P.PARTNUM)

NAME
==========

LE SHOPPE
BIKE SPEC
LE SHOPPE
BIKE SPEC
JACKS BIKE
```

ANALYSIS We just spent some time discussing why your subqueries should return just one value. The reason this query was able to return more than one value becomes apparent in a moment.

You bring these results to the statement:

```
SELECT C.NAME, C.ADDRESS, C.STATE,C.ZIP
FROM CUSTOMER C
WHERE C.NAME IN
(...)
```

ANALYSIS The first two lines are unremarkable. The third reintroduces the keyword IN, last seen on Day 2, "Introduction to the Query: The SELECT Statement." IN is the tool that enables you to use the multiple-row output of your subquery. IN, as you remember, looks for matches in the following set of values enclosed by parentheses, which in the this case produces the following values:

```
LE SHOPPE
BIKE SPEC
LE SHOPPE
BIKE SPEC
JACKS BIKE
```

This subquery provides the conditions that give you the mailing list:

```
NAME        ADDRESS      STATE  ZIP
==========  ==========   ====== ======

BIKE SPEC   CPT SHRIVE   LA     45678
LE SHOPPE   HOMETOWN     KS     54678
JACKS BIKE  24 EGLIN     FL     34567
```

This use of IN is very common in subqueries. Because IN uses a set of values for its comparison, it does not cause the SQL engine to feel conflicted and inadequate.

Subqueries can also be used with GROUP BY and HAVING clauses. Examine the following query:

INPUT/ OUTPUT
```
SELECT NAME, AVG(QUANTITY)
FROM ORDERS
GROUP BY NAME
HAVING AVG(QUANTITY) >
(SELECT AVG(QUANTITY)
FROM ORDERS)

NAME               AVG
==========  ===========

BIKE SPEC          8
JACKS BIKE         14
```

 ANALYSIS Let's examine this query in the order the SQL engine would. First, look at the subquery:

INPUT/ OUTPUT
```
SELECT AVG(QUANTITY)
FROM ORDERS

            AVG
===========
```

6

7

By itself, the query is as follows:

INPUT/
OUTPUT

```
SELECT NAME, AVG(QUANTITY)
FROM ORDERS
GROUP BY NAME
```

```
NAME               AVG
==========   ===========

AAA BIKE             6
BIKE SPEC            8
JACKS BIKE          14
LE SHOPPE            4
TRUE WHEEL           5
```

When combined through the HAVING clause, the subquery produces two rows that have above-average QUANTITY.

INPUT/
OUTPUT

```
HAVING AVG(QUANTITY) >
(SELECT AVG(QUANTITY)
FROM ORDERS)
```

```
NAME               AVG
==========   ===========

BIKE SPEC           8
JACKS BIKE         14
```

Correlated Subqueries

The subqueries you have written so far are *self-contained*. None of them have used a reference from outside the subquery. *Correlated subqueries* enable you to use an outside reference with some strange and wonderful results. Look at the following query:

INPUT

```
SELECT *
FROM ORDERS O
WHERE 'ROAD BIKE' =
(SELECT DESCRIPTION
FROM PART P
WHERE P.PARTNUM = O.PARTNUM)
```

OUTPUT

ORDEREDON	NAME	PARTNUM	QUANTITY	REMARKS
19-MAY-1996	TRUE WHEEL	76	3	PAID
17-JAN-1996	BIKE SPEC	76	11	PAID
17-JAN-1996	LE SHOPPE	76	5	PAID
1-JUL-1996	AAA BIKE	76	4	PAID
11-JUL-1996	JACKS BIKE	76	14	PAID

This query actually resembles the following JOIN:

INPUT/
OUTPUT

```
SELECT O.ORDEREDON, O.NAME,
O.PARTNUM, O.QUANTITY, O.REMARKS
FROM ORDERS O, PART P
WHERE P.PARTNUM = O.PARTNUM
AND P.DESCRIPTION = 'ROAD BIKE'
```

ORDEREDON	NAME	PARTNUM	QUANTITY	REMARKS
19-MAY-1996	TRUE WHEEL	76	3	PAID
1-JUL-1996	AAA BIKE	76	4	PAID
17-JAN-1996	LE SHOPPE	76	5	PAID
17-JAN-1996	BIKE SPEC	76	11	PAID
11-JUL-1996	JACKS BIKE	76	14	PAID

ANALYSIS   In fact, except for the order, the results are identical. The correlated subquery acts very much like a join. The correlation is established by using an element from the query in the subquery. In this example the correlation was established by the statement

```
WHERE P.PARTNUM = O.PARTNUM
```

in which you compare P.PARTNUM, from the table inside your subquery, to O.PARTNUM, from the table outside your query. Because O.PARTNUM can have a different value for every row, the correlated subquery is executed for each row in the query. In the next example each row in the table ORDERS

INPUT/
OUTPUT

```
SELECT *
FROM ORDERS
```

ORDEREDON	NAME	PARTNUM	QUANTITY	REMARKS
15-MAY-1996	TRUE WHEEL	23	6	PAID
19-MAY-1996	TRUE WHEEL	76	3	PAID
2-SEP-1996	TRUE WHEEL	10	1	PAID
30-JUN-1996	TRUE WHEEL	42	8	PAID
30-JUN-1996	BIKE SPEC	54	10	PAID
30-MAY-1996	BIKE SPEC	10	2	PAID
30-MAY-1996	BIKE SPEC	23	8	PAID
17-JAN-1996	BIKE SPEC	76	11	PAID
17-JAN-1996	LE SHOPPE	76	5	PAID
1-JUN-1996	LE SHOPPE	10	3	PAID
1-JUN-1996	AAA BIKE	10	1	PAID
1-JUL-1996	AAA BIKE	76	4	PAID
1-JUL-1996	AAA BIKE	46	14	PAID
11-JUL-1996	JACKS BIKE	76	14	PAID

is processed against the subquery criteria:

```
SELECT DESCRIPTION
FROM PART P
WHERE P.PARTNUM = O.PARTNUM
```

7

ANALYSIS This operation returns the DESCRIPTION of every row in PART where P.PARTNUM = O.PARTNUM. These descriptions are then compared in the WHERE clause:

```
WHERE 'ROAD BIKE' =
```

Because each row is examined, the subquery in a correlated subquery can have more than one value. However, don't try to return multiple columns or columns that don't make sense in the context of the WHERE clause. The values returned still must match up against the operation specified in the WHERE clause. For example, in the query you just did, returning the PRICE to compare with ROAD BIKE would have the following result:

INPUT/OUTPUT
```
SELECT *
FROM ORDERS O
WHERE 'ROAD BIKE' =
(SELECT PRICE
FROM PART P
WHERE P.PARTNUM = O.PARTNUM)

conversion error from string "ROAD BIKE"
```

Here's another example of something not to do:

```
SELECT *
FROM ORDERS O
WHERE 'ROAD BIKE' =
(SELECT *
FROM PART P
WHERE P.PARTNUM = O.PARTNUM)
```

ANALYSIS This SELECT caused a General Protection Fault on my Windows operating system. The SQL engine simply can't correlate all the columns in PART with the operator =.

Correlated subqueries can also be used with the GROUP BY and HAVING clauses. The following query uses a correlated subquery to find the average total order for a particular part and then applies that average value to filter the total order grouped by PARTNUM:

INPUT/OUTPUT
```
SELECT O.PARTNUM, SUM(O.QUANTITY*P.PRICE), COUNT(PARTNUM)
FROM ORDERS O, PART P
WHERE P.PARTNUM = O.PARTNUM
GROUP BY O.PARTNUM
HAVING SUM(O.QUANTITY*P.PRICE) >
(SELECT AVG(O1.QUANTITY*P1.PRICE)
FROM PART P1, ORDERS O1
WHERE P1.PARTNUM = O1.PARTNUM
AND P1.PARTNUM = O.PARTNUM)
```

```
    PARTNUM          SUM         COUNT
    ===========  ===========  ===========

         10       8400.00            4
         23       4906.30            2
         76      19610.00            5
```

ANALYSIS The subquery does not just compute one

```
AVG(O1.QUANTITY*P1.PRICE)
```

Because of the correlation between the query and the subquery,

```
AND P1.PARTNUM = O.PARTNUM
```

this average is computed for every group of parts and then compared:

```
HAVING SUM(O.QUANTITY*P.PRICE) >
```

> **TIP**
>
> When using correlated subqueries with GROUP BY and HAVING, the columns in the HAVING clause must exist in either the SELECT clause or the GROUP BY clause. Otherwise, you get an error message along the lines of invalid column reference because the subquery is evoked for each group, not each row. You cannot make a valid comparison to something that is not used in forming the group.

Using EXISTS, ANY, and ALL

The usage of the keywords EXISTS, ANY, and ALL is not intuitively obvious to the casual observer. EXISTS takes a subquery as an argument and returns TRUE if the subquery returns anything and FALSE if the result set is empty. For example:

 INPUT/ OUTPUT
```
SELECT NAME, ORDEREDON
FROM ORDERS
WHERE EXISTS
(SELECT *
FROM ORDERS
WHERE NAME ='TRUE WHEEL')

NAME        ORDEREDON
==========  ===========

TRUE WHEEL  15-MAY-1996
TRUE WHEEL  19-MAY-1996
TRUE WHEEL   2-SEP-1996
TRUE WHEEL  30-JUN-1996
BIKE SPEC   30-JUN-1996
BIKE SPEC   30-MAY-1996
BIKE SPEC   30-MAY-1996
BIKE SPEC   17-JAN-1996
LE SHOPPE   17-JAN-1996
LE SHOPPE    1-JUN-1996
```

7

```
AAA BIKE     1-JUN-1996
AAA BIKE     1-JUL-1996
AAA BIKE     1-JUL-1996
JACKS BIKE 11-JUL-1996
```

 Not what you might expect. The subquery inside EXISTS is evaluated only once in this uncorrelated example. Because the return from the subquery has at least one row, EXISTS evaluates to TRUE and all the rows in the query are printed. If you change the subquery as shown next, you don't get back any results.

```
SELECT NAME, ORDEREDON
FROM ORDERS
WHERE EXISTS
(SELECT *
FROM ORDERS
WHERE NAME ='MOSTLY HARMLESS')
```

 EXISTS evaluates to FALSE. The subquery does not generate a result set because MOSTLY HARMLESS is not one of your names.

NOTE

Notice the use of SELECT * in the subquery inside the EXISTS. EXISTS does not care how many columns are returned.

You could use EXISTS in this way to check on the existence of certain rows and control the output of your query based on whether they exist.

If you use EXISTS in a correlated subquery, it is evaluated for every case implied by the correlation you set up. For example:

INPUT/ OUTPUT

```
SELECT NAME, ORDEREDON
FROM ORDERS O
WHERE EXISTS
(SELECT *
FROM CUSTOMER C
WHERE STATE ='NE'
AND C.NAME = O.NAME)

NAME         ORDEREDON
==========  ===========

TRUE WHEEL  15-MAY-1996
TRUE WHEEL  19-MAY-1996
TRUE WHEEL   2-SEP-1996
TRUE WHEEL  30-JUN-1996
AAA BIKE     1-JUN-1996
AAA BIKE     1-JUL-1996
AAA BIKE     1-JUL-1996
```

This slight modification of your first, uncorrelated query returns all the bike shops from Nebraska that made orders. The following subquery is run for every row in the query correlated on the CUSTOMER name and ORDERS name:

```
(SELECT *
FROM CUSTOMER C
WHERE STATE ='NE'
AND C.NAME = O.NAME)
```

ANALYSIS EXISTS is TRUE for those rows that have corresponding names in CUSTOMER located in NE. Otherwise, it returns FALSE.

Closely related to EXISTS are the keywords ANY, ALL, and SOME. ANY and SOME are identical in function. An optimist would say this feature provides the user with a choice. A pessimist would see this condition as one more complication. Look at this query:

INPUT
```
SELECT NAME, ORDEREDON
FROM ORDERS
WHERE NAME = ANY
(SELECT NAME
FROM ORDERS
WHERE NAME ='TRUE WHEEL')
```

OUTPUT
```
NAME          ORDEREDON
==========    ===========

TRUE WHEEL  15-MAY-1996
TRUE WHEEL  19-MAY-1996
TRUE WHEEL   2-SEP-1996
TRUE WHEEL  30-JUN-1996
```

ANALYSIS ANY compared the output of the following subquery to each row in the query, returning TRUE for each row of the query that has a result from the subquery.

```
(SELECT NAME
FROM ORDERS
WHERE NAME ='TRUE WHEEL')
```

Replacing ANY with SOME produces an identical result:

INPUT/OUTPUT
```
SELECT NAME, ORDEREDON
FROM ORDERS
WHERE NAME = SOME
(SELECT NAME
FROM ORDERS
WHERE NAME ='TRUE WHEEL')

NAME          ORDEREDON
==========    ===========

TRUE WHEEL  15-MAY-1996
TRUE WHEEL  19-MAY-1996
TRUE WHEEL   2-SEP-1996
TRUE WHEEL  30-JUN-1996
```

7

ANALYSIS You may have already noticed the similarity to IN. The same query using IN is as follows:

 INPUT/OUTPUT
```
SELECT NAME, ORDEREDON
FROM ORDERS
WHERE NAME IN
(SELECT NAME
FROM ORDERS
WHERE NAME ='TRUE WHEEL')

NAME         ORDEREDON
=========== ===========

TRUE WHEEL  15-MAY-1996
TRUE WHEEL  19-MAY-1996
TRUE WHEEL   2-SEP-1996
TRUE WHEEL  30-JUN-1996
```

 ANALYSIS As you can see, IN returns the same result as ANY and SOME. Has the world gone mad? Not yet. Can IN do this?

INPUT/OUTPUT
```
SELECT NAME, ORDEREDON
FROM ORDERS
WHERE NAME > ANY
(SELECT NAME
FROM ORDERS
WHERE NAME ='JACKS BIKE')

NAME         ORDEREDON
=========== ===========

TRUE WHEEL  15-MAY-1996
TRUE WHEEL  19-MAY-1996
TRUE WHEEL   2-SEP-1996
TRUE WHEEL  30-JUN-1996
LE SHOPPE   17-JAN-1996
LE SHOPPE    1-JUN-1996
```

The answer is no. IN works like multiple equals. ANY and SOME can be used with other relational operators such as greater than or less than. Add this tool to your kit.

ALL returns TRUE only if all the results of a subquery meet the condition. Oddly enough, ALL is used most commonly as a double negative, as in this query:

INPUT/OUTPUT
```
SELECT NAME, ORDEREDON
FROM ORDERS
WHERE NAME <> ALL
(SELECT NAME
FROM ORDERS
WHERE NAME ='JACKS BIKE')

NAME         ORDEREDON
=========== ===========

TRUE WHEEL  15-MAY-1996
TRUE WHEEL  19-MAY-1996
TRUE WHEEL   2-SEP-1996
```

```
TRUE WHEEL 30-JUN-1996
BIKE SPEC  30-JUN-1996
BIKE SPEC  30-MAY-1996
BIKE SPEC  30-MAY-1996
BIKE SPEC  17-JAN-1996
LE SHOPPE  17-JAN-1996
LE SHOPPE   1-JUN-1996
AAA BIKE    1-JUN-1996
AAA BIKE    1-JUL-1996
AAA BIKE    1-JUL-1996
```

ANALYSIS This statement returns everybody except JACKS BIKE. <>ALL evaluates to TRUE only if the result set does not contain what is on the left of the <>.

Summary

Today you performed dozens of exercises involving subqueries. You learned how to use one of the most important parts of SQL. You also tackled one of the most difficult parts of SQL: a correlated subquery. The correlated subquery creates a relationship between the query and the subquery that is evaluated for every instance of that relationship. Don't be intimidated by the length of the queries. You can easily examine them one subquery at a time.

Q&A

Q In some cases SQL offers several ways to get the same result. Isn't this flexibility confusing?

A No, not really. Having so many ways to achieve the same result enables you to create some really neat statements. Flexibility is the virtue of SQL.

Workshop

The Workshop provides quiz questions to help solidify your understanding of the material covered, as well as exercises to provide you with experience in using what you have learned. Try to answer the quiz and exercise questions before checking the answers in Appendix F, "Answers to Quizzes and Exercises."

Quiz

1. In the section on nested subqueries, the sample subquery returned several values:

```
LE SHOPPE
BIKE SPEC
LE SHOPPE
BIKE SPEC
JACKS BIKE
```

Some of these are duplicates. Why aren't these duplicates in the final result set?

7

2. Are the following statements true or false?

The aggregate functions SUM, COUNT, MIN, MAX, and AVG all return multiple values.

The maximum number of subqueries that can be nested is two.

Correlated subqueries are completely self-contained.

3. Will the following subqueries work using the ORDERS table and the PART table?

```
SQL> SELECT *
     FROM PART;

PARTNUM   DESCRIPTION     PRICE
     54   PEDALS          54.25
     42   SEATS           24.50
     46   TIRES           15.25
     23   MOUNTAIN BIKE   350.45
     76   ROAD BIKE       530.00
     10   TANDEM          1200.00
6 rows selected.
```

```
SQL> SELECT *
     FROM ORDERS;

ORDEREDON    NAME         PARTNUM   QUANITY   REMARKS
15-MAY-96    TRUE WHEEL     23         6      PAID
19-MAY-96    TRUE WHEEL     76         3      PAID
2-SEP-96     TRUE WHEEL     10         1      PAID
30-JUN-96    BIKE SPEC      54        10      PAID
30-MAY-96    BIKE SPEC      10         2      PAID
30-MAY-96    BIKE SPEC      23         8      PAID
17-JAN-96    BIKE SPEC      76        11      PAID
17-JAN-96    LE SHOPPE      76         5      PAID
1-JUN-96     LE SHOPPE      10         3      PAID
1-JUN-96     AAA BIKE       10         1      PAID
1-JUN-96     AAA BIKE       76         4      PAID
1-JUN-96     AAA BIKE       46        14      PAID
11-JUL-96    JACKS BIKE     76        14      PAID
13 rows selected.
```

a.
```
SQL> SELECT * FROM ORDERS
     WHERE PARTNUM =
     SELECT PARTNUM FROM PART
     WHERE DESCRIPTION = 'TRUE WHEEL';
```

b.
```
SQL> SELECT PARTNUM
     FROM ORDERS
     WHERE PARTNUM =
     (SELECT * FROM PART
     WHERE DESCRIPTION = 'LE SHOPPE');
```

```
c. SQL> SELECT NAME, PARTNUM
        FROM ORDERS
        WHERE EXISTS
        (SELECT * FROM ORDERS
        WHERE NAME = 'TRUE WHEEL');
```

Exercise

Write a query using the table ORDERS to return all the NAMEs and ORDEREDON dates for every store that comes after JACKS BIKE in the alphabet.

WEEK 1

In Review

After setting the stage with a quick survey of database history and theory, Week 1 moved right into the heart of SQL with the SELECT statement. The following summary of the SELECT statement syntax includes cross-references to the days on which the particular aspect was covered:

- ☐ SELECT [DISTINCT | ALL] (Day 2)—Columns (Day 1), Functions (Day 4)
- ☐ FROM (Day 2)—Tables or Views (Day 1), Aggregate Functions (Day 4)
- ☐ WHERE (Day 5)—Condition (Day 3), Join (Day 6), Subquery (Day 7)
- ☐ GROUP BY (Day 5)—Columns (Day 3)
- ☐ HAVING (Day 5)—Aggregate Function (Day 4)

1

2

3

4

5

6

7

☐ UNION ¦ INTERSECT (Day 3)—(Placed between two SELECT statements)

☐ ORDER BY (Day 5)—Columns (Day 1)

If you build a million queries in your programming career, more than 80 percent of them will begin with SELECT. The other 20 percent will fall into the categories covered in Week 2.

Preview

The new skills you learn in Week 2 cover database administration. During Week 2 you will learn how to

☐ Create and destroy tables

☐ Assign permissions to your friends and prevent your enemies from even looking at your data

☐ Update and delete data in tables

WEEK

2

8

9

10

11

12

13

14

At A Glance

What's Covered This Week

Week 1 covered the basic SQL query using the SELECT statement. Beginning with the simplest SELECT statement, you learned how to retrieve data from the database. Then you moved on to the SQL functions, which are useful in converting to money or date formats, for example. You quickly learned that you can retrieve data from a database in many ways. Clauses such as WHERE, ORDER BY, and GROUP BY enable you to tailor a query to return a specific set of records. You can use a join to return a set of data from a group of tables. Subqueries are especially useful when you need to execute several queries, each of which depends on data returned from an earlier query.

Week 2 moves on to the more advanced uses of SQL:

☐ Day 8 shows you how to modify data within a database. You may have been dreading the idea of typing in all your data, but manually entering data is not always necessary. Modern database systems often supply useful tools for importing and exporting data from various database formats. In addition, SQL provides several useful statements for manipulating data within a database.

☐ Day 9 teaches you how to create and maintain tables within a database. You also learn how to create a database and manage that database's disk space.

☐ Day 10 explains how to create, maintain, and use views and indexes within a database.

☐ Day 11 covers transaction control. Transactions commit and roll back changes to a database, and the use of transactions is essential in online transaction processing (OLTP) applications.

☐ Day 12 focuses on database security. A knowledge of your database's security capabilities is essential to manage a database effectively.

☐ Day 13 describes how to use SQL within larger application programs. Embedded SQL is often used to execute SQL within a host language such as C or COBOL. In addition, the open database connectivity (ODBC) standard enables application programmers to write code that can use database drivers to connect with many database management systems. Day 13 also covers various advanced SQL topics.

☐ Day 14 discusses dynamic uses of SQL and provides numerous examples that illustrate how SQL is used in applications.

Week 2

Day 8

Manipulating Data

Objectives

Today we discuss data manipulation. By the end of the day, you should understand:

- [ ] How to manipulate data using the INSERT, UPDATE, and DELETE commands
- [ ] The importance of using the WHERE clause when you are manipulating data
- [ ] The basics of importing and exporting data from foreign data sources

Introduction to Data Manipulation Statements

Up to this point you have learned how to retrieve data from a database using every selection criterion imaginable. After this data is retrieved, you can use it in an application program or edit it. Week 1 focused on retrieving data. However, you may have wondered how to enter data into the database in the first place. You may also be wondering what to do with data that has been edited. Today we discuss three SQL statements that enable you to manipulate the data within a database's table. The three statements are as follows:

- [ ] The INSERT statement
- [ ] The UPDATE statement
- [ ] The DELETE statement

You may have used a PC-based product such as Access, dBASE IV, or FoxPro to enter your data in the past. These products come packaged with excellent tools to enter, edit, and delete records from databases. One reason that SQL provides data manipulation statements is that it is primarily used within application programs that enable the user to edit the data using the application's own tools. The SQL programmer needs to be able to return the data to the database using SQL. In addition, most large-scale database systems are not designed with the database designer or programmer in mind. Because these systems are designed to be used in high-volume, multiuser environments, the primary design emphasis is placed on the query optimizer and data retrieval engines.

Most commercial relational database systems also provide tools for importing and exporting data. This data is traditionally stored in a delimited text file format. Often a format file is stored that contains information about the table being imported. Tools such as Oracle's SQL*Loader, SQL Server's bcp (bulk copy), and Microsoft Access Import/Export are covered at the end of the day.

NOTE Today's examples were generated with Personal Oracle7. Please note the minor differences in the appearance of commands and the way data is displayed in the various implementations.

The INSERT Statement

The INSERT statement enables you to enter data into the database. It can be broken down into two statements:

INSERT...VALUES

and

INSERT...SELECT

The INSERT...VALUES Statement

The INSERT...VALUES statement enters data into a table one record at a time. It is useful for small operations that deal with just a few records. The syntax of this statement is as follows:

```
INSERT INTO table_name
(col1, col2...)
VALUES(value1, value2...)
```

The basic format of the INSERT...VALUES statement adds a record to a table using the columns you give it and the corresponding values you instruct it to add. You must follow three rules when inserting data into a table with the INSERT...VALUES statement:

☐ The values used must be the same data type as the fields they are being added to.

☐ The data's size must be within the column's size. For instance, you cannot add an 80-character string to a 40-character column.

☐ The data's location in the VALUES list must correspond to the location in the column list of the column it is being added to. (That is, the first value must be entered into the first column, the second value into the second column, and so on.)

Example 8.1

Assume you have a COLLECTION table that lists all the important stuff you have collected. You can display the table's contents by writing

INPUT

```
SQL> SELECT * FROM COLLECTION;
```

which would yield this:

OUTPUT

```
ITEM                      WORTH REMARKS
-------------------- ---------- ------------------------------
NBA ALL STAR CARDS          300 SOME STILL IN BIKE SPOKES
MALIBU BARBIE               150 TAN NEEDS WORK
STAR WARS GLASS             5.5 HANDLE CHIPPED
LOCK OF SPOUSES HAIR          1 HASN'T NOTICED BALD SPOT YET
```

If you wanted to add a new record to this table, you would write

INPUT/ OUTPUT

```
SQL> INSERT INTO COLLECTION
  2  (ITEM, WORTH, REMARKS)
  3  VALUES('SUPERMANS CAPE', 250.00, 'TUGGED ON IT');

1 row created.
```

You can execute a simple SELECT statement to verify the insertion:

```
SQL> SELECT * FROM COLLECTION;

ITEM                    WORTH REMARKS
--------------------    ----- -----------------------------
NBA ALL STAR CARDS        300 SOME STILL IN BIKE SPOKES
MALIBU BARBIE             150 TAN NEEDS WORK
STAR WARS GLASS           5.5 HANDLE CHIPPED
LOCK OF SPOUSES HAIR        1 HASN'T NOTICED BALD SPOT YET
SUPERMANS CAPE            250 TUGGED ON IT
```

The INSERT statement does not require column names. If the column names are not entered, SQL lines up the values with their corresponding column numbers. In other words, SQL inserts the first value into the first column, the second value into the second column, and so on.

Example 8.2

The following statement inserts the values from Example 8.1 into the table:

```
SQL> INSERT INTO COLLECTION VALUES
  2  ('STRING',1000.00,'SOME DAY IT WILL BE VALUABLE');

1 row created.
```

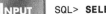

By issuing the same SELECT statement as you did in Example 8.1, you can verify that the insertion worked as expected:

```
SQL> SELECT * FROM COLLECTION;
```

OUTPUT

```
ITEM                    WORTH REMARKS
--------------------    ----- -----------------------------
NBA ALL STAR CARDS        300 SOME STILL IN BIKE SPOKES
MALIBU BARBIE             150 TAN NEEDS WORK
STAR WARS GLASS           5.5 HANDLE CHIPPED
LOCK OF SPOUSES HAIR        1 HASN'T NOTICED BALD SPOT YET
SUPERMANS CAPE            250 TUGGED ON IT
STRING                   1000 SOME DAY IT WILL BE VALUABLE

6 rows selected.
```

Inserting NULL Values

On Day 9, "Creating and Maintaining Tables," you learn how to create tables using the SQL CREATE TABLE statement. For now, all you need to know is that when a column is created, it can have several different limitations placed upon it. One of these limitations is that the column should (or should not) be allowed to contain NULL values. A NULL value means that the value is empty. It is neither a zero, in the case of an integer, nor a space, in the case of a string. Instead, no data at all exists for that record's column. If a column is defined as NOT NULL (that column is not allowed to contain a NULL value), you *must* insert a value for that column when using the INSERT statement. The INSERT is canceled if this rule is broken, and you should receive a descriptive error message concerning your error.

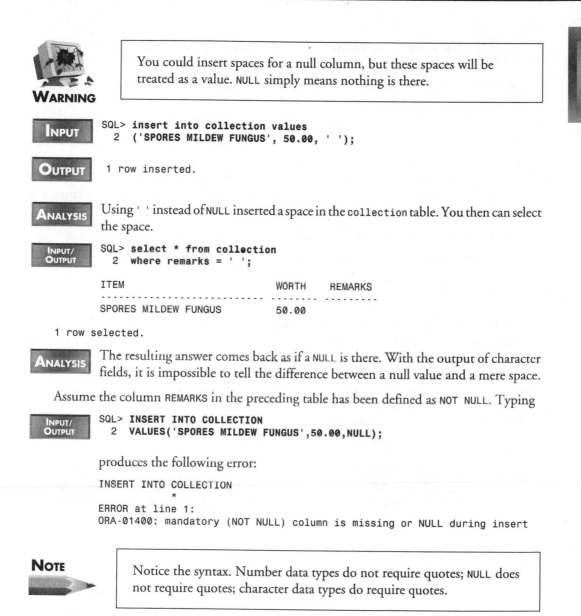

WARNING

You could insert spaces for a null column, but these spaces will be treated as a value. NULL simply means nothing is there.

INPUT
```
SQL> insert into collection values
  2  ('SPORES MILDEW FUNGUS', 50.00, ' ');
```

OUTPUT
```
1 row inserted.
```

ANALYSIS   Using ' ' instead of NULL inserted a space in the collection table. You then can select the space.

INPUT/ OUTPUT
```
SQL> select * from collection
  2  where remarks = ' ';

ITEM                              WORTH    REMARKS
-----------------------------     -------- ---------
SPORES MILDEW FUNGUS              50.00
```

```
1 row selected.
```

ANALYSIS   The resulting answer comes back as if a NULL is there. With the output of character fields, it is impossible to tell the difference between a null value and a mere space.

Assume the column REMARKS in the preceding table has been defined as NOT NULL. Typing

INPUT/ OUTPUT
```
SQL> INSERT INTO COLLECTION
  2  VALUES('SPORES MILDEW FUNGUS',50.00,NULL);
```

produces the following error:
```
INSERT INTO COLLECTION
             *
ERROR at line 1:
ORA-01400: mandatory (NOT NULL) column is missing or NULL during insert
```

NOTE

Notice the syntax. Number data types do not require quotes; NULL does not require quotes; character data types do require quotes.

Inserting Unique Values

Many database management systems also allow you to create a UNIQUE column attribute. This attribute means that within the current table, the values within this column must be completely unique and cannot appear more than once. This limitation can cause problems when inserting or updating values into an existing table, as the following exchange demonstrates:

INPUT   SQL> **INSERT INTO COLLECTION VALUES('STRING', 50, 'MORE STRING');**

OUTPUT INSERT INTO COLLECTION VALUES('STRING', 50, 'MORE STRING')
                       *
            ERROR at line 1:
            ORA-00001: unique constraint (PERKINS.UNQ_COLLECTION_ITEM) violated

ANALYSIS   In this example you tried to insert another ITEM called STRING into the COLLECTION
table. Because this table was created with ITEM as a unique value, it returned the
appropriate error. ANSI SQL does not offer a solution to this problem, but several
commercial implementations include extensions that would allow you to use something like
the following:

```
IF NOT EXISTS (SELECT * FROM COLLECTION WHERE NAME = 'STRING'
```

```
INSERT INTO COLLECTION VALUES('STRING', 50, 'MORE STRING')
```

This particular example is supported in the Sybase system.

A properly normalized table should have a unique, or key, field. This field is useful for joining
data between tables, and it often improves the speed of your queries when using indexes. (See
Day 10, "Creating Views and Indexes.")

NOTE   Here's an INSERT statement that inserts a new employee into a table:

```
SQL> insert into employee_tbl values
     ('300500177', 'SMITHH', 'JOHN');
```

```
1 row inserted.
```

After hitting Enter, you noticed that you misspelled SMITH. Not to fret!
All you have to do is issue the ROLLBACK command, and the row will not
be inserted. See Day 11, "Controlling Transactions," for more on the
ROLLBACK command.

The INSERT...SELECT Statement

The INSERT...VALUES statement is useful when adding single records to a database table, but
it obviously has limitations. Would you like to use it to add 25,000 records to a table? In
situations like this, the INSERT...SELECT statement is much more beneficial. It enables the
programmer to copy information from a table or group of tables into another table. You will
want to use this statement in several situations. Lookup tables are often created for
performance gains. Lookup tables can contain data that is spread out across multiple tables
in multiple databases. Because multiple-table joins are slower to process than simple queries,
it is much quicker to execute a SELECT query against a lookup table than to execute a long,

8

complicated joined query. Lookup tables are often stored on the client machines in client/server environments to reduce network traffic.

Many database systems also support temporary tables. (See Day 14, "Dynamic Uses of SQL.") Temporary tables exist for the life of your database connection and are deleted when your connection is terminated. The INSERT...SELECT statement can take the output of a SELECT statement and insert these values into a temporary table.

Here is an example:

INPUT
```
SQL> insert into tmp_tbl
   2  select * from table;
```

OUTPUT
```
19,999 rows inserted.
```

ANALYSIS You are selecting all the rows that are in table and inserting them into tmp_tbl.

NOTE
Not all database management systems support temporary tables. Check the documentation for the specific system you are using to determine if this feature is supported. Also, see Day 14 for a more detailed treatment of this topic.

The syntax of the INSERT...SELECT statement is as follows:

SYNTAX
```
INSERT INTO table_name
(col1, col2...)
SELECT col1, col2...
FROM tablename
WHERE search_condition
```

Essentially, the output of a standard SELECT query is then input into a database table. The same rules that applied to the INSERT...VALUES statement apply to the INSERT...SELECT statement. To copy the contents of the COLLECTION table into a new table called INVENTORY, execute the set of statements in Example 8.3.

Example 8.3

This example creates the new table INVENTORY.

INPUT
```
SQL> CREATE TABLE INVENTORY
   2  (ITEM CHAR(20),
   3   COST NUMBER,
   4   ROOM CHAR(20),
   5   REMARKS CHAR(40));
```

OUTPUT
```
Table created.
```

The following INSERT fills the new INVENTORY table with data from COLLECTION.

```
SQL> INSERT INTO INVENTORY (ITEM, COST, REMARKS)
  2  SELECT ITEM, WORTH, REMARKS
  3  FROM COLLECTION;
```

6 rows created.

You can verify that the INSERT works with this SELECT statement:

```
SQL> SELECT * FROM INVENTORY;
```

ITEM	COST	ROOM	REMARKS
NBA ALL STAR CARDS	300		SOME STILL IN BIKE SPOKES
MALIBU BARBIE	150		TAN NEEDS WORK
STAR WARS GLASS	5.5		HANDLE CHIPPED
LOCK OF SPOUSES HAIR	1		HASN'T NOTICED BALD SPOT YET
SUPERMANS CAPE	250		TUGGED ON IT
STRING	1000		SOME DAY IT WILL BE VALUABLE

6 rows selected.

> **NOTE**
>
> The data appears to be in the table; however, the transaction is not finalized until a COMMIT is issued. The transaction can be committed either by issuing the COMMIT command or by simply exiting. See Day 11 for more on the COMMIT command.

ANALYSIS You have successfully, and somewhat painlessly, moved the data from the COLLECTION table to the new INVENTORY table!

The INSERT...SELECT statement requires you to follow several new rules:

☐ The SELECT statement cannot select rows from the table that is being inserted into.

☐ The number of columns in the INSERT INTO statement must equal the number of columns returned from the SELECT statement.

☐ The data types of the columns in the INSERT INTO statement must be the same as the data types of the columns returned from the SELECT statement.

Another use of the INSERT...SELECT statement is to back up a table that you are going to drop, truncate for repopulation, or rebuild. The process requires you to create a temporary table and insert data that is contained in your original table into the temporary table by selecting everything from the original table. For example:

```
SQL> insert into copy_table
  2  select * from original_table;
```

Now you can make changes to the original table with a clear conscience.

NOTE Later today you learn how to input data into a table using data from another database format. Nearly all businesses use a variety of database formats to store data for their organizations. The applications programmer is often expected to convert these formats, and you will learn some common methods for doing just that.

The UPDATE Statement

The purpose of the UPDATE statement is to change the values of existing records. The syntax is

```
UPDATE table_name
SET columnname1 = value1
[, columnname2 = value2]...
WHERE search_condition
```

This statement checks the WHERE clause first. For all records in the given table in which the WHERE clause evaluates to TRUE, the corresponding value is updated.

Example 8.4

This example illustrates the use of the UPDATE statement:

INPUT
```
SQL> UPDATE COLLECTION
  2   SET WORTH = 900
  3   WHERE ITEM = 'STRING';
```

OUTPUT   1 row updated.

To confirm the change, the query

INPUT/ OUTPUT
```
SQL> SELECT * FROM COLLECTION
  2   WHERE ITEM = 'STRING';
```

yields

```
ITEM                      WORTH REMARKS
-------------------- ---------- ------------------------------
STRING                      900 SOME DAY IT WILL BE VALUABLE
```

Here is a multiple-column update:

INPUT/ OUTPUT
```
SQL> update collection
  2   set worth = 900, item = ball
  3   where item = 'STRING';

1 row updated.
```

NOTE

Your implementation might use a different syntax for multiple-row updates.

 NOTE

Notice in the set that 900 does not have quotes, because it is a numeric data type. On the other hand, String is a character data type, which requires the quotes.

Example 8.5

If the WHERE clause is omitted, every record in the COLLECTION table is updated with the value given.

INPUT
```
SQL> UPDATE COLLECTION
  2  SET WORTH = 555;
```

OUTPUT
6 rows updated.

Performing a SELECT query shows that every record in the database was updated with that value:

INPUT/OUTPUT
```
SQL> SELECT * FROM COLLECTION;

ITEM                     WORTH REMARKS
-------------------- --------- ------------------------------
NBA ALL STAR CARDS         555 SOME STILL IN BIKE SPOKES
MALIBU BARBIE              555 TAN NEEDS WORK
STAR WARS GLASS            555 HANDLE CHIPPED
LOCK OF SPOUSES HAIR       555 HASN'T NOTICED BALD SPOT YET
SUPERMANS CAPE            555 TUGGED ON IT
STRING                    555 SOME DAY IT WILL BE VALUABLE

6 rows selected.
```

You, of course, should check whether the column you are updating allows unique values only.

 WARNING

If you omit the WHERE clause from the UPDATE statement, all records in the given table are updated.

Some database systems provide an extension to the standard UPDATE syntax. SQL Server's Transact-SQL language, for instance, enables programmers to update the contents of a table based on the contents of several other tables by using a FROM clause. The extended syntax looks like this:

```
UPDATE table_name
SET columnname1 = value1
[, columnname2 = value2]...
FROM table_list
WHERE search_condition
```

Example 8.6

Here's an example of the extension:

INPUT
```
SQL> UPDATE COLLECTION
  2   SET WORTH = WORTH * 0.005;
```

that changes the table to this:

**INPUT/
OUTPUT**
```
SQL> SELECT * FROM COLLECTION;

ITEM                      WORTH REMARKS
-------------------- --------- -----------------------------
NBA ALL STAR CARDS        2.775 SOME STILL IN BIKE SPOKES
MALIBU BARBIE             2.775 TAN NEEDS WORK
STAR WARS GLASS           2.775 HANDLE CHIPPED
LOCK OF SPOUSES HAIR      2.775 HASN'T NOTICED BALD SPOT YET
SUPERMANS CAPE            2.775 TUGGED ON IT
STRING                    2.775 SOME DAY IT WILL BE VALUABLE

6 rows selected.
```

ANALYSIS This syntax is useful when the contents of one table need to be updated following the manipulation of the contents of several other tables. Keep in mind that this syntax is nonstandard and that you need to consult the documentation for your particular database management system before you use it.

The UPDATE statement can also update columns based on the result of an arithmetic expression. When using this technique, remember the requirement that the data type of the result of the expression must be the same as the data type of the field that is being modified. Also, the size of the value must fit within the size of the field that is being modified.

Two problems can result from the use of calculated values: truncation and overflow. *Truncation* results when the database system converts a fractional number to an integer, for instance. *Overflow* results when the resulting value is larger than the capacity of the modified column, which will cause an error to be returned by your database system.

NOTE   Some database systems handle the overflow problem for you. Oracle7 converts the number to exponential notation and presents the number that way. You should keep this potential error in mind when using number data types.

TIP   If you update a column(s) and notice an error after you run the update, issue the ROLLBACK command (as you would for an incorrect insert) to void the update. See Day 11 for more on the ROLLBACK command.

The DELETE Statement

In addition to adding data to a database, you will also need to delete data from a database. The syntax for the DELETE statement is

```
DELETE FROM tablename
WHERE condition
```

The first thing you will probably notice about the DELETE command is that it doesn't have a prompt. Users are accustomed to being prompted for assurance when, for instance, a directory or file is deleted at the operating system level. Are you sure? (Y/N) is a common question asked before the operation is performed. Using SQL, when you instruct the DBMS to delete a group of records from a table, it obeys your command without asking. That is, when you tell SQL to delete a group of records, it will really do it!

On Day 11 you will learn about transaction control. Transactions are database operations that enable programmers to either COMMIT or ROLLBACK changes to the database. These operations are very useful in online transaction-processing applications in which you want to execute a batch of modifications to the database in one logical execution. Data integrity problems will occur if operations are performed while other users are modifying the data at the same time. For now, assume that no transactions are being undertaken.

NOTE   Some implementations, for example, Oracle, automatically issue a COMMIT command when you exit SQL.

Depending on the use of the DELETE statement's WHERE clause, SQL can do the following:

- ☐ Delete single rows
- ☐ Delete multiple rows
- ☐ Delete all rows
- ☐ Delete no rows

Here are several points to remember when using the DELETE statement:

- ☐ The DELETE statement cannot delete an individual field's values (use UPDATE instead). The DELETE statement deletes entire records from a single table.

- ☐ Like INSERT and UPDATE, deleting records from one table can cause referential integrity problems within other tables. Keep this potential problem area in mind when modifying data within a database.

- ☐ Using the DELETE statement deletes only records, not the table itself. Use the DROP TABLE statement (see Day 9) to remove an entire table.

Example 8.7

This example shows you how to delete all the records from COLLECTION where WORTH is less than 275.

INPUT

```
SQL> DELETE FROM COLLECTION
  2   WHERE WORTH < 275;

4 rows deleted.
```

The result is a table that looks like this:

**INPUT/
OUTPUT**

```
SQL> SELECT * FROM COLLECTION;

ITEM                      WORTH REMARKS
------------------------- ----- ----------------------------------
NBA ALL STAR CARDS          300 SOME STILL IN BIKE SPOKES
STRING                     1000 SOME DAY IT WILL BE VALUABLE
```

WARNING

Like the UPDATE statement, if you omit a WHERE clause from the DELETE statement, all rows in that particular table will be deleted.

Example 8.8 uses all three data manipulation statements to perform a set of database operations.

Example 8.8

This example inserts some new rows into the COLLECTION table you used earlier today.

INPUT

```
SQL> INSERT INTO COLLECTION
  2  VALUES('CHIA PET', 5,'WEDDING GIFT');
```

OUTPUT

```
1 row created.
```

INPUT/ OUTPUT

```
SQL> INSERT INTO COLLECTION
  2  VALUES('TRS MODEL III', 50, 'FIRST COMPUTER');
```

```
1 row created.
```

Now create a new table and copy this data to it:

INPUT/ OUTPUT

```
SQL> CREATE TABLE TEMP
  2  (NAME CHAR(20),
  3  VALUE NUMBER,
  4  REMARKS CHAR(40));
```

```
Table created.
```

INPUT/ OUTPUT

```
SQL> INSERT INTO TEMP(NAME, VALUE, REMARKS)
  2  SELECT ITEM, WORTH, REMARKS
  3  FROM COLLECTION;
```

```
4 rows created.
```

INPUT/ OUTPUT

```
SQL> SELECT * FROM TEMP;

NAME                      VALUE REMARKS
-------------------- ---------- --------------------------------
NBA ALL STAR CARDS          300 SOME STILL IN BIKE SPOKES
STRING                     1000 SOME DAY IT WILL BE VALUABLE
CHIA PET                      5 WEDDING GIFT
TRS MODEL III                50 FIRST COMPUTER
```

Now change some values:

INPUT/ OUTPUT

```
SQL> UPDATE TEMP
  2  SET VALUE = 100
  3  WHERE NAME = 'TRS MODEL III';
```

```
1 row updated.
```

INPUT/ OUTPUT

```
SQL> UPDATE TEMP
  2  SET VALUE = 8
  3  WHERE NAME = 'CHIA PET';
```

```
1 row updated.
```

```
SQL> SELECT * FROM TEMP;

NAME                          VALUE REMARKS
--------------------          ----- ------------------------------
NBA ALL STAR CARDS              300 SOME STILL IN BIKE SPOKES
STRING                         1000 SOME DAY IT WILL BE VALUABLE
CHIA PET                          8 WEDDING GIFT
TRS MODEL III                   100 FIRST COMPUTER
```

And update these values back to the original table:

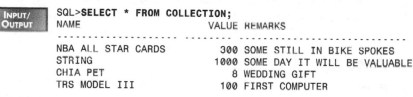

```
INSERT COLLECTION
SELECT * FROM TEMP;
DROP TABLE TEMP;
```

ANALYSIS The DROP TABLE and CREATE TABLE statements are discussed in greater detail on Day 9. For now, these statements basically do what their names suggest. CREATE TABLE builds a new table with the format you give it, and DROP TABLE deletes the table. Keep in mind that DROP TABLE permanently removes a table, whereas DELETE FROM <TableName> removes only the records from a table.

To check what you have done, select out the records from the COLLECTION table. You will see that the changes you made now exist in the COLLECTION table.

```
SQL>SELECT * FROM COLLECTION;
NAME                          VALUE REMARKS
--------------------          ----- ------------------------------
NBA ALL STAR CARDS              300 SOME STILL IN BIKE SPOKES
STRING                         1000 SOME DAY IT WILL BE VALUABLE
CHIA PET                          8 WEDDING GIFT
TRS MODEL III                   100 FIRST COMPUTER
```

ANALYSIS The previous example used all three data manipulation commands—INSERT, UPDATE, and DELETE—to perform a set of operations on a table. The DELETE statement is the easiest of the three to use.

WARNING

> Always keep in mind that any modifications can affect the referential integrity of your database. Think through all your database editing steps to make sure that you have updated all tables correctly.

Importing and Exporting Data from Foreign Sources

The INSERT, UPDATE, and DELETE statements are extremely useful from within a database program. They are used with the SELECT statement to provide the foundation for all other database operations you will perform. However, SQL as a language does not have a way to import or export of data from foreign data sources. For instance, your office may have been using a dBASE application for several years now that has outgrown itself. Now your manager wants to convert this application to a client/server application using the Oracle RDBMS. Unfortunately for you, these dBASE files contain thousands of records that must be converted to an Oracle database. Obviously, the INSERT, UPDATE, and DELETE commands will help you after your Oracle database has been populated, but you would rather quit than retype 300,000 records. Fortunately, Oracle and other manufacturers provide tools that will assist you in this task.

Nearly all database systems allow you to import and export data using ASCII text file formats. Although the SQL language does not include this feature, SQL will not do you (or your boss) much good when you have an empty database. We will examine the import/export tools available in the following products: Microsoft Access, Microsoft and Sybase SQL Server, and Personal Oracle7.

Microsoft Access

Microsoft Access is a PC-only database product that contains many of the features of a relational database management system. Access also includes powerful reporting tools, a macro language similar to Visual Basic, and the capability to import and export data from various database and text file formats. This section examines this last feature, particularly the capability to export to delimited text files. *Delimited* means that each field is separated, or delimited, by some special character. This character is often a comma, a quotation mark, or a space.

Access allows you to import and export various database formats, including dBASE, FoxPro, and SQL Database. The SQL Database option is actually an ODBC data source connection. (Microsoft ODBC is covered on Day 13, "Advanced SQL Topics.") For this discussion, you want to select the Export option and then choose the Text (Fixed Width) option.

After opening an Access database (with the File I Open), select Export. A Destination dialog box (for Exporting) is displayed. Select the Text (Fixed Width) option. This option allows you to output your Access tables to text files in which each data type is a fixed width. For example, a character data field of length 30 will be output to the file as a field 30 characters long. If the field's data takes up less space than 30 characters, it will be padded with spaces.

Eventually, you will be asked to set up the export file format. Figure 8.1 shows the Import/ Export Setup dialog box.

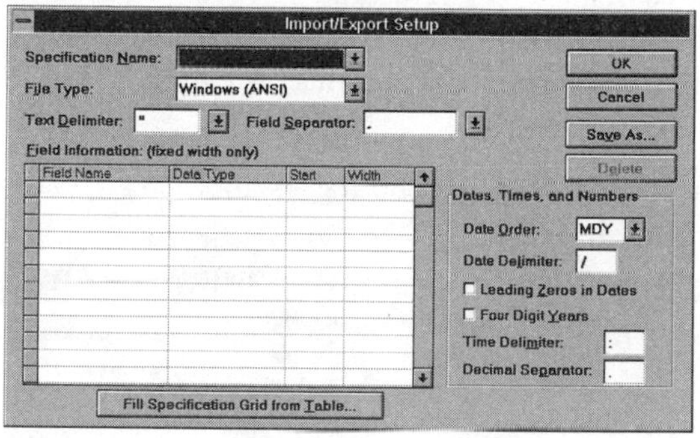

Figure 8.1.

The Import/Export Setup dialog box.

Notice that in this dialog box you can select the Text Delimiter and the Field Separator for your export file. As a final step, save the specification for use later. This specification is stored internally within the database.

Microsoft and Sybase SQL Server

Microsoft and Sybase have jointly developed a powerful database system that is very popular in client/server application development. The name of this system is SQL Server. Microsoft has agreed to develop versions of the RDBMS for some platforms, and Sybase has developed its version for all the other platforms (usually the larger ones). Although the arrangement has changed somewhat in recent years, we mention this agreement here to help you avoid confusion when you begin examining the various database systems available on the market today.

SQL Server provides file import/export capabilities with the bcp tool. *bcp* is short for "bulk copy." The basic concept behind bcp is the same as that behind Microsoft Access. Unfortunately, the bcp tool requires you to issue commands from the operating system command prompt, instead of through dialog boxes or windows.

Bcp imports and exports fixed-width text files. It is possible to export a file using the Microsoft Access method described earlier and then import that same file directly into an SQL Server table using bcp. bcp uses format files (usually with an .FMT extension) to store the import specification. This specification tells bcp the column names, field widths, and field delimiters. You can run bcp from within an SQL database build script to completely import data after the database has been built.

Personal Oracle7

Personal Oracle7 allows you to import and export data from ASCII text files containing delimited or fixed-length records. The tool you use is SQL*Loader. This graphical tool uses a control file (with the .CTL extension). This file is similar to SQL Server's format (FMT) file. The information contained in this file tells SQL*Loader what it needs to know to load the data from the file.

The SQL*Loader dialog box appears in Figure 8.2.

Figure 8.2.

*The SQL*Loader dialog box.*

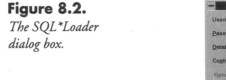

Summary

SQL provides three statements that you can use to manipulate data within a database.

The INSERT statement has two variations. The INSERT...VALUES statement inserts a set of values into one record. The INSERT...SELECT statement is used in combination with a SELECT statement to insert multiple records into a table based on the contents of one or more tables. The SELECT statement can join multiple tables, and the results of this join can be added to another table.

The UPDATE statement changes the values of one or more columns based on some condition. This updated value can also be the result of an expression or calculation.

The DELETE statement is the simplest of the three statements. It deletes all rows from a table based on the result of an optional WHERE clause. If the WHERE clause is omitted, all records from the table are deleted.

Modern database systems supply various tools for data manipulation. Some of these tools enable developers to import or export data from foreign sources. This feature is particularly useful when a database is upsized or downsized to a different system. Microsoft Access, Microsoft and Sybase SQL Server, and Personal Oracle7 include many options that support the migration of data between systems.

Q&A

Q **Does SQL have a statement for file import/export operations?**

A No. Import and export are implementation-specific operations. In other words, the ANSI committee allows individual manufacturers to create whatever features or enhancements they feel are necessary.

Q **Can I copy data from a table into itself using the INSERT command? I would like to make duplicate copies of all the existing records and change the value of one field.**

A No, you cannot insert data into the same table that you selected from. However, you can select the original data into a temporary table. (True temporary tables are discussed on Day 14.) Then modify the data in this temporary table and select back into the original table. Make sure that you watch out for unique fields you may have already created. A unique field means that the particular field must contain a unique value for each row of data that exists in its table.

Q **You have stressed using caution when issuing INSERT, UPDATE, and DELETE commands, but simple fixes seem to be available to correct whatever I did wrong. Is that a fair statement?**

A Yes. For example, a simple way to fix a misspelled name is to issue a ROLLBACK command and redo the insert. Another fix would be to do an update to fix the name. Or you could delete the row and redo the insert with the corrected spelling of the name.

But suppose you inserted a million rows into a table and didn't notice that you had misspelled a name when you issued the COMMIT command. A few weeks later, someone notices some bad data. You have had two weeks' worth of database activity. You would more than likely have to issue individual updates to make individual corrections, instead of making any type of global change. In most cases you probably will not know what to change. You may have to restore the database.

Workshop

The Workshop provides quiz questions to help solidify your understanding of the material covered, as well as exercises to provide you with experience in using what you have learned. Try to answer the quiz and exercise questions before checking the answers in Appendix F, "Answers to Quizzes and Exercises."

Quiz

1. What is wrong with the following statement?

   ```
   DELETE COLLECTION;
   ```

2. What is wrong with the following statement?

   ```
   INSERT INTO COLLECTION
   SELECT * FROM TABLE_2
   ```

3. What is wrong with the following statement?

   ```
   UPDATE COLLECTION ("HONUS WAGNER CARD",
   25000, "FOUND IT");
   ```

4. What would happen if you issued the following statement?

   ```
   SQL> DELETE * FROM COLLECTION;
   ```

5. What would happen if you issued the following statement?

   ```
   SQL> DELETE FROM COLLECTION;
   ```

6. What would happen if you issued the following statement?

   ```
   SQL> UPDATE COLLECTION
       SET WORTH = 555
       SET REMARKS = 'UP FROM 525';
   ```

7. Will the following SQL statement work?

   ```
   SQL> INSERT INTO COLLECTION
       SET VALUES = 900
       WHERE ITEM = 'STRING';
   ```

8. Will the following SQL statement work?

   ```
   SQL> UPDATE COLLECTION
       SET VALUES = 900
       WHERE ITEM = 'STRING';
   ```

Exercises

1. Try inserting values with incorrect data types into a table. Note the errors and then insert values with correct data types into the same table.

2. Using your database system, try exporting a table (or an entire database) to some other format. Then import the data back into your database. Familiarize yourself with this capability. Also, export the tables to another database format if your DBMS supports this feature. Then use the other system to open these files and examine them.

Week 2

Day 9

Creating and Maintaining Tables

Objectives

Today you learn about creating databases. Day 9 covers the CREATE DATABASE, CREATE TABLE, ALTER TABLE, DROP TABLE, and DROP DATABASE statements, which are collectively known as *data definition statements*. (In contrast, the SELECT, UPDATE, INSERT, and DELETE statements are often described as *data manipulation statements*.) By the end of the day, you will understand and be able to do the following:

- ☐ Create key fields
- ☐ Create a database with its associated tables
- ☐ Create, alter, and drop a table
- ☐ Add data to the database
- ☐ Modify the data in a database
- ☐ Drop databases

You now know much of the SQL vocabulary and have examined the SQL query in some detail, beginning with its basic syntax. On Day 2, "Introduction to the Query: The SELECT Statement," you learned how to select data from the database. On Day 8, "Manipulating Data," you learned how to insert, update, and delete data from the database. Now, nine days into the learning process, you probably have been wondering just where these databases come from. For simplicity's sake, we have been ignoring the process of creating databases and tables. We have assumed that these data objects existed currently on your system. Today you finally create these objects.

The syntax of the CREATE statements can range from the extremely simple to the complex, depending on the options your database management system (DBMS) supports and how detailed you want to be when building a database.

NOTE   The examples used today were generated using Personal Oracle7. Please see the documentation for your specific SQL implementation for any minor differences in syntax.

The CREATE DATABASE **Statement**

The first data management step in any database project is to create the database. This task can range from the elementary to the complicated, depending on your needs and the database management system you have chosen. Many modern systems (including Personal Oracle7) include graphical tools that enable you to completely build the database with the click of a mouse button. This time-saving feature is certainly helpful, but you should understand the SQL statements that execute in response to the mouse clicks.

Through personal experience, we have learned the importance of creating a good SQL install script. This script file contains the necessary SQL code to completely rebuild a database or databases; the script often includes database objects such as indexes, stored procedures, and triggers. You will see the value of this script during development as you continually make changes to the underlying database and on occasion want to completely rebuild the database with all the latest changes. Using the graphical tools each time you need to perform a rebuild can become extremely time-consuming. In addition, knowing the SQL syntax for this procedure enables you to apply your knowledge to other database systems.

The syntax for the typical CREATE DATABASE statement looks like this:

```
CREATE DATABASE database_name
```

Because the syntax varies so widely from system to system, we will not expand on the CREATE DATABASE statement's syntax. Many systems do not even support an SQL CREATE DATABASE command. However, all the popular, more powerful, relational database management systems (RDBMSs) do provide it. Instead of focusing on its syntax, we will spend some time discussing the options to consider when creating a database.

CREATE DATABASE Options

The syntax for the CREATE DATABASE statement can vary widely. Many SQL texts skip over the CREATE DATABASE statement and move directly on to the CREATE TABLE statement. Because you must create a database before you can build a table, this section focuses on some of the concepts a developer must consider when building a database. The first consideration is your level of permission. If you are using a relational database management system (RDBMS) that supports user permissions, you must make sure that either you have system administrator-level permission settings or the system administrator has granted you CREATE DATABASE permission. Refer to your RDBMS documentation for more information.

Most RDBMSs also allow you to specify a default database size, usually in terms of hard disk space (such as megabytes). You will need to understand how your database system stores and locates data on the disk to accurately estimate the size you need. The responsibility for managing this space falls primarily to system administrators, and possibly at your location a database administrator will build you a test database.

Don't let the CREATE DATABASE statement intimidate you. At its simplest, you can create a database named PAYMENTS with the following statement:

```
SQL> CREATE DATABASE PAYMENTS;
```

NOTE

> Again, be sure to consult your database management system's documentation to learn the specifics of building a database, as the CREATE DATABASE statement can and does vary for the different implementations. Each implementation also has some unique options.

Database Design

Designing a database properly is extremely important to the success of your application. The introductory material on Day 1, "Introduction to SQL," touched on the topics of relational database theory and database normalization.

Normalization is the process of breaking your data into separate components to reduce the repetition of data. Each level of normalization reduces the repetition of data. Normalizing your data can be an extremely complex process, and numerous database design tools enable you to plan this process in a logical fashion.

Many factors can influence the design of your database, including the following:

☐ Security

☐ Disk space available

☐ Speed of database searches and retrievals

☐ Speed of database updates

☐ Speed of multiple-table joins to retrieve data

☐ RDBMS support for temporary tables

Disk space is always an important factor. Although you may not think that disk space is a major concern in an age of multigigabyte storage, remember that the bigger your database is, the longer it takes to retrieve records. If you have done a poor job of designing your table structure, chances are that you have needlessly repeated much of your data.

Often the opposite problem can occur. You may have sought to completely normalize your tables' design with the database and in doing so created many tables. Although you may have approached database-design nirvana, any query operations done against this database may take a very long time to execute. Databases designed in this manner are sometimes difficult to maintain because the table structure might obscure the designer's intent. This problem underlines the importance of always documenting your code or design so that others can come in after you (or work with you) and have some idea of what you were thinking at the time you created your database structure. In database designer's terms, this documentation is known as a *data dictionary*.

Creating a Data Dictionary

A data dictionary is the database designer's most important form of documentation. It performs the following functions:

☐ Describes the purpose of the database and who will be using it.

☐ Documents the specifics behind the database itself: what device it was created on, the database's default size, or the size of the log file (used to store database operations information in some RDBMSs).

☐ Contains SQL source code for any database install or uninstall scripts, including documentation on the use of import/export tools, such as those introduced yesterday (Day 8).

☐ Provides a detailed description of each table within the database and explains its purpose in business process terminology.

☐ Documents the internal structure of each table, including all fields and their data types with comments, all indexes, and all views. (See Day 10, "Creating Views and Indexes.")

☐ Contains SQL source code for all stored procedures and triggers.

☐ Describes database constraints such as the use of unique values or NOT NULL values. The documentation should also mention whether these constraints are enforced at the RDBMS level or whether the database programmer is expected to check for these constraints within the source code.

Many computer-aided software engineering (CASE) tools aid the database designer in the creation of this data dictionary. For instance, Microsoft Access comes prepackaged with a database documenting tool that prints out a detailed description of every object in the database. See Day 17, "Using SQL to Generate SQL Statements," for more details on the data dictionary.

NOTE   Most of the major RDBMS packages come with either the data dictionary installed or scripts to install it.

Creating Key Fields

Along with documenting your database design, the most important design goal you should have is to create your table structure so that each table has a primary key and a foreign key. The primary key should meet the following goals:

☐ Each record is unique within a table (no other record within the table has all of its columns equal to any other).

☐ For a record to be unique, all the columns are necessary; that is, data in one column should not be repeated anywhere else in the table.

Regarding the second goal, the column that has completely unique data throughout the table is known as the *primary key field.* A *foreign key field* is a field that links one table to another table's primary or foreign key. The following example should clarify this situation.

Assume you have three tables: BILLS, BANK_ACCOUNTS, and COMPANY. Table 9.1 shows the format of these three tables.

Table 9.1. Table structure for the PAYMENTS database.

Bills	Bank_Accounts	Company
NAME, CHAR(30)	ACCOUNT_ID, NUMBER	NAME, CHAR(30)
AMOUNT, NUMBER	TYPE, CHAR(30)	ADDRESS, CHAR(50)
ACCOUNT_ID, NUMBER	BALANCE, NUMBER	CITY, CHAR(20)
	BANK, CHAR(30)	STATE, CHAR(2)

Take a moment to examine these tables. Which fields do you think are the primary keys? Which are the foreign keys?

The primary key in the BILLS table is the NAME field. This field should not be duplicated because you have only one bill with this amount. (In reality, you would probably have a check number or a date to make this record truly unique, but assume for now that the NAME field works.) The ACCOUNT_ID field in the BANK_ACCOUNTS table is the primary key for that table. The NAME field is the primary key for the COMPANY table.

The foreign keys in this example are probably easy to spot. The ACCOUNT_ID field in the BILLS table joins the BILLS table with the BANK_ACCOUNTS table. The NAME field in the BILLS table joins the BILLS table with the COMPANY table. If this were a full-fledged database design, you would have many more tables and data breakdowns. For instance, the BANK field in the BANK_ACCOUNTS table could point to a BANK table containing bank information such as addresses and phone numbers. The COMPANY table could be linked with another table (or database for that matter) containing information about the company and its products.

Exercise 9.1

Let's take a moment to examine an incorrect database design using the same information contained in the BILLS, BANK_ACCOUNTS, and COMPANY tables. A mistake many beginning users make is not breaking down their data into as many logical groups as possible. For instance, one poorly designed BILLS table might look like this:

Column Names	Comments
NAME, CHAR(30)	Name of company that bill is owed to
AMOUNT, NUMBER	Amount of bill in dollars
ACCOUNT_ID, NUMBER	Bank account number of bill (linked to BANK_ACCOUNTS table)
ADDRESS, CHAR(30)	Address of company that bill is owed to
CITY, CHAR(15)	City of company that bill is owed to
STATE, CHAR(2)	State of company that bill is owed to

The results may look correct, but take a moment to really look at the data here. If over several months you wrote several bills to the company in the NAME field, each time a new record was added for a bill, the company's ADDRESS, CITY, and STATE information would be duplicated. Now multiply that duplication over several hundred or thousand records and then multiply that figure by 10, 20, or 30 tables. You can begin to see the importance of a properly normalized database.

Before you actually fill these tables with data, you will need to know how to create a table.

The CREATE TABLE Statement

The process of creating a table is far more standardized than the CREATE DATABASE statement. Here's the basic syntax for the CREATE TABLE statement:

SYNTAX

```
CREATE TABLE table_name
(      field1 datatype [ NOT NULL ],
       field2 datatype [ NOT NULL ],
       field3 datatype [ NOT NULL ]...)
```

A simple example of a CREATE TABLE statement follows.

INPUT/ OUTPUT

```
SQL>    CREATE TABLE BILLS (
  2     NAME CHAR(30),
  3     AMOUNT NUMBER,
  4     ACCOUNT_ID NUMBER);

Table created.
```

ANALYSIS This statement creates a table named BILLS. Within the BILLS table are three fields: NAME, AMOUNT, and ACCOUNT_ID. The NAME field has a data type of character and can store strings up to 30 characters long. The AMOUNT and ACCOUNT_ID fields can contain number values only.

The following section examines components of the CREATE TABLE command.

The Table Name

When creating a table using Personal Oracle7, several constraints apply when naming the table. First, the table name can be no more than 30 characters long. Because Oracle is case insensitive, you can use either uppercase or lowercase for the individual characters. However, the first character of the name must be a letter between A and Z. The remaining characters can be letters or the symbols _, #, $, and @. Of course, the table name must be unique within its schema. The name also cannot be one of the Oracle or SQL reserved words (such as SELECT).

NOTE

You can have duplicate table names as long as the owner or schema is different. Table names in the same schema must be unique.

The Field Name

The same constraints that apply to the table name also apply to the field name. However, a field name can be duplicated within the database. The restriction is that the field name must be unique within its table. For instance, assume that you have two tables in your database: TABLE1 and TABLE2. Both of these tables could have fields called ID. You cannot, however, have two fields within TABLE1 called ID, even if they are of different data types.

The Field's Data Type

If you have ever programmed in any language, you are familiar with the concept of data types, or the type of data that is to be stored in a specific field. For instance, a character data type constitutes a field that stores only character string data. Table 9.2 shows the data types supported by Personal Oracle7.

Table 9.2. Data types supported by Personal Oracle7.

Data Type	Comments
CHAR	Alphanumeric data with a length between 1 and 255 characters. Spaces are padded to the right of the value to supplement the total allocated length of the column.
DATE	Included as part of the date are century, year, month, day, hour, minute, and second.
LONG	Variable-length alphanumeric strings up to 2 gigabytes. (See the following note.)
LONG RAW	Binary data up to 2 gigabytes. (See the following note.)
NUMBER	Numeric 0, positive or negative fixed or floating-point data.
RAW	Binary data up to 255 bytes.
ROWID	Hexadecimal string representing the unique address of a row in a table. (See the following note.)
VARCHAR2	Alphanumeric data that is variable length; this field must be between 1 and 2,000 characters long.

NOTE

> The LONG data type is often called a MEMO data type in other database management systems. It is primarily used to store large amounts of text for retrieval at some later time.
>
> The LONG RAW data type is often called a binary large object (BLOB) in other database management systems. It is typically used to store graphics, sound, or video data. Although relational database management systems were not originally designed to serve this type of data, many multimedia systems today store their data in LONG RAW, or BLOB, fields.
>
> The ROWID field type is used to give each record within your table a unique, nonduplicating value. Many other database systems support this concept with a COUNTER field (Microsoft Access) or an IDENTITY field (SQL Server).

NOTE

Check your implementation for supported data types as they may vary.

The NULL Value

SQL also enables you to identify what can be stored within a column. A NULL value is almost an oxymoron, because having a field with a value of NULL means that the field actually has no value stored in it.

When building a table, most database systems enable you to denote a column with the NOT NULL keywords. NOT NULL means the column cannot contain any NULL values for any records in the table. Conversely, NOT NULL means that every record must have an actual value in this column. The following example illustrates the use of the NOT NULL keywords.

INPUT

```
SQL>   CREATE TABLE BILLS (
2        NAME CHAR(30) NOT NULL,
3        AMOUNT NUMBER,
4        ACCOUNT_ID NOT NULL);
```

ANALYSIS

In this table you want to save the name of the company you owe the money to, along with the bill's amount. If the NAME field and/or the ACCOUNT_ID were not stored, the record would be meaningless. You would end up with a record with a bill, but you would have no idea whom you should pay.

The first statement in the next example inserts a valid record containing data for a bill to be sent to Joe's Computer Service for $25.

INPUT/ OUTPUT

```
SQL> INSERT INTO BILLS VALUES("Joe's Computer Service", 25, 1);

1 row inserted.

SQL> INSERT INTO BILLS VALUES("", 25000, 1);

1 row inserted.
```

ANALYSIS

Notice that the second record in the preceding example does not contain a NAME value. (You might think that a missing payee is to your advantage because the bill amount is $25,000, but we won't consider that.) If the table had been created with a NOT NULL value for the NAME field, the second insert would have raised an error.

A good rule of thumb is that the primary key field and all foreign key fields should never contain NULL values.

Unique Fields

One of your design goals should be to have one unique column within each table. This column or field is a primary key field. Some database management systems allow you to set a field as unique. Other database management systems, such as Oracle and SQL Server, allow you to create a unique index on a field. (See Day 10.) This feature keeps you from inserting duplicate key field values into the database.

You should notice several things when choosing a key field. As we mentioned, Oracle provides a ROWID field that is incremented for each row that is added, which makes this field by default always a unique key. ROWID fields make excellent key fields for several reasons. First, it is much faster to join on an integer value than on an 80-character string. Such joins result in smaller database sizes over time if you store an integer value in every primary and foreign key as opposed to a long CHAR value. Another advantage is that you can use ROWID fields to see how a table is organized. Also, using CHAR values leaves you open to a number of data entry problems. For instance, what would happen if one person entered 111 First Street, another entered 111 1st Street, and yet another entered 111 First St.? With today's graphical user environments, the correct string could be entered into a list box. When a user makes a selection from the list box, the code would convert this string to a unique ID and save this ID to the database.

Now you can create the tables you used earlier today. You will use these tables for the rest of today, so you will want to fill them with some data. Use the INSERT command covered yesterday to load the tables with the data in Tables 9.3, 9.4, and 9.5.

INPUT/OUTPUT

```
SQL>   create database PAYMENTS;

Statement processed.

SQL>   create table BILLS (
   2    NAME CHAR(30) NOT NULL,
   3    AMOUNT NUMBER,
   4    ACCOUNT_ID NUMBER NOT NULL);

Table created.

SQL>   create table BANK_ACCOUNTS (
   2    ACCOUNT_ID NUMBER NOT NULL,
   3    TYPE CHAR(30),
   4    BALANCE NUMBER,
   5    BANK CHAR(30));

Table created.

SQL>   create table COMPANY (
   2    NAME CHAR(30) NOT NULL,
   3    ADDRESS CHAR(50),
   4    CITY CHAR(30),
   5    STATE CHAR(2));

Table created.
```

Table 9.3. Sample data for the BILLS table.

Name	Amount	Account_ID
Phone Company	125	1
Power Company	75	1
Record Club	25	2
Software Company	250	1
Cable TV Company	35	3

Table 9.4. Sample data for the BANK_ACCOUNTS table.

Account_ID	Type	Balance	Band
1	Checking	500	First Federal
2	Money Market	1200	First Investor's
3	Checking	90	Credit Union

Table 9.5. Sample data for the COMPANY table.

Name	Address	City	State
Phone Company	111 1st Street	Atlanta	GA
Power Company	222 2nd Street	Jacksonville	FL
Record Club	333 3rd Avenue	Los Angeles	CA
Software Company	444 4th Drive	San Francisco	CA
Cable TV Company	555 5th Drive	Austin	TX

Table Storage and Sizing

Most major RDBMSs have default settings for table sizes and table locations. If you do not specify table size and location, then the table will take the defaults. The defaults may be very undesirable, especially for large tables. The default sizes and locations will vary among the implementations. Here is an example of a CREATE TABLE statement with a storage clause (from Oracle).

INPUT
```
SQL>   CREATE TABLE TABLENAME
  2    (COLUMN1    CHAR    NOT NULL,
  3     COLUMN2    NUMBER,
  4     COLUMN3    DATE)
  5     TABLESPACE TABLESPACE NAME
  6     STORAGE
  7     INITIAL SIZE,
```

```
8      NEXT SIZE,
9      MINEXTENTS value,
10     MAXEXTENTS value,
11     PCTINCREASE value);
```

OUTPUT Table created.

ANALYSIS In Oracle you can specify a tablespace in which you want the table to reside. A decision is usually made according to the space available, often by the database administrator (DBA). INITIAL SIZE is the size for the initial extent of the table (the initial allocated space). NEXT SIZE is the value for any additional extents the table may take through growth. MINEXTENTS and MAXEXTENTS identify the minimum and maximum extents allowed for the table, and PCTINCREASE identifies the percentage the next extent will be increased each time the table grows, or takes another extent.

Creating a Table from an Existing Table

The most common way to create a table is with the CREATE TABLE command. However, some database management systems provide an alternative method of creating tables, using the format and data of an existing table. This method is useful when you want to select the data out of a table for temporary modification. It can also be useful when you have to create a table similar to the existing table and fill it with similar data. (You won't have to reenter all this information.) The syntax for Oracle follows.

SYNTAX

```
CREATE TABLE NEW_TABLE(FIELD1, FIELD2, FIELD3)
AS (SELECT FIELD1, FIELD2, FIELD3
   FROM OLD_TABLE <WHERE...>
```

This syntax allows you to create a new table with the same data types as those of the fields that are selected from the old table. It also allows you to rename the fields in the new table by giving them new names.

```
SQL>  CREATE TABLE NEW_BILLS(NAME, AMOUNT, ACCOUNT_ID)
   2  AS (SELECT * FROM BILLS WHERE AMOUNT < 50);

Table created.
```

ANALYSIS The preceding statement creates a new table (NEW_BILLS) with all the records from the BILLS table that have an AMOUNT less than 50.

Some database systems also allow you to use the following syntax:

SYNTAX

```
INSERT NEW_TABLE
SELECT <field1, field2... ¦ *> from OLD_TABLE
<WHERE...>
```

The preceding syntax would create a new table with the exact field structure and data found in the old table. Using SQL Server's Transact-SQL language in the following example illustrates this technique.

```
INPUT NEW_BILLS
1> select * from BILLS where AMOUNT < 50
2> go
```

(The GO statement in SQL Server processes the SQL statements in the command buffer. It is equivalent to the semicolon (;) used in Oracle7.)

The ALTER TABLE Statement

Many times your database design does not account for everything it should. Also, requirements for applications and databases are always subject to change. The ALTER TABLE statement enables the database administrator or designer to change the structure of a table after it has been created.

The ALTER TABLE command enables you to do two things:

☐ Add a column to an existing table

☐ Modify a column that already exists

The syntax for the ALTER TABLE statement is as follows:

```
ALTER TABLE table_name
    <ADD column_name data_type; |
    MODIFY column_name data_type;>
```

The following command changes the NAME field of the BILLS table to hold 40 characters:

```
SQL>  ALTER TABLE BILLS
  2     MODIFY NAME CHAR(40);

Table altered.
```

> **NOTE**
>
> You can increase or decrease the length of columns; however, you can not decrease a column's length if the current size of one of its values is greater than the value you want to assign to the column length.

Here's a statement to add a new column to the NEW_BILLS table:

```
SQL>  ALTER TABLE NEW_BILLS
  2     ADD COMMENTS CHAR(80);

Table altered.
```

ANALYSIS This statement would add a new column named COMMENTS capable of holding 80 characters. The field would be added to the right of all the existing fields.

Several restrictions apply to using the ALTER TABLE statement. You cannot use it to add or delete fields from a database. It can change a column from NOT NULL to NULL, but not necessarily the other way around. A column specification can be changed from NULL to NOT NULL only if the column does not contain any NULL values. To change a column from NOT NULL to NULL, use the following syntax:

```
ALTER TABLE table_name  MODIFY (column_name data_type NULL);
```

To change a column from NULL to NOT NULL, you might have to take several steps:

1. Determine whether the column has any NULL values.
2. Deal with any NULL values that you find. (Delete those records, update the column's value, and so on.)
3. Issue the ALTER TABLE command.

> **NOTE**
>
> Some database management systems allow the use of the MODIFY clause; others do not. Still others have added other clauses to the ALTER TABLE statement. In Oracle, you can even alter the table's storage parameters. Check the documentation of the system you are using to determine the implementation of the ALTER TABLE statement.

The DROP TABLE Statement

SQL provides a command to completely remove a table from a database. The DROP TABLE command deletes a table along with all its associated views and indexes. (See Day 10 for details.) After this command has been issued, there is no turning back. The most common use of the DROP TABLE statement is when you have created a table for temporary use. When you have completed all operations on the table that you planned to do, issue the DROP TABLE statement with the following syntax:

```
DROP TABLE table_name;
```

Here's how to drop the NEW_BILLS table:

```
SQL> DROP TABLE NEW_BILLS;

Table dropped.
```

Notice the absence of system prompts. This command did not ask Are you sure? (Y/N). After the DROP TABLE command is issued, the table is permanently deleted.

WARNING

If you issue

```
SQL> DROP TABLE NEW_BILLS;
```

you could be dropping the incorrect table. When dropping tables, you should *always* use the owner or schema name. The recommended syntax is

```
SQL> DROP TABLE OWNER.NEW_BILLS;
```

We are stressing this syntax because we once had to repair a production database from which the wrong table had been dropped. The table was not properly identified with the schema name. Restoring the database was an eight-hour job, and we had to work until well past midnight.

The DROP DATABASE Statement

Some database management systems also provide the DROP DATABASE statement, which is identical in usage to the DROP TABLE statement. The syntax for this statement is as follows:

```
DROP DATABASE database_name
```

Don't drop the BILLS database now because you will use it for the rest of today, as well as on Day 10.

NOTE

The various relational database implementations require you to take different steps to drop a database. After the database is dropped, you will need to clean up the operating system files that compose the database.

Exercise 9.2

Create a database with one table in it. Issue the DROP TABLE command and the issue the DROP DATABASE command. Does your database system allow you to do this? Single-file based systems, such as Microsoft Access, do not support this command. The database is contained in a single file. To create a database, you must use the menu options provided in the product itself. To delete a database, simply delete the file from the hard drive.

Summary

Day 9 covers the major features of SQL's Data Manipulation Language (DML). In particular, you learned five new statements: CREATE DATABASE, CREATE TABLE, ALTER TABLE, DROP TABLE, and DROP DATABASE. Today's lesson also discusses the importance of creating a good database design.

A data dictionary is one of the most important pieces of documentation you can create when designing a database. This dictionary should include a complete description of all objects in the database: tables, fields, views, indexes, stored procedures, triggers, and so forth. A complete data dictionary also contains a brief comment explaining the purpose behind each item in the database. You should update the data dictionary whenever you make changes to the database.

Before using any of the data manipulation statements, it is also important to create a good database design. Break down the required information into logical groups and try to identify a primary key field that other groups (or tables) can use to reference this logical group. Use foreign key fields to point to the primary or foreign key fields in other tables.

You learned that the CREATE DATABASE statement is not a standard element within database systems. This variation is primarily due to the many different ways vendors store their databases on disk. Each implementation enables a different set of features and options, which results in a completely different CREATE DATABASE statement. Simply issuing CREATE DATABASE database_name creates a default database with a default size on most systems. The DROP DATABASE statement permanently removes that database.

The CREATE TABLE statement creates a new table. With this command, you can create the fields you need and identify their data types. Some database management systems also allow you to specify other attributes for the field, such as whether it can allow NULL values or whether that field should be unique throughout the table. The ALTER TABLE statement can alter the structure of an existing table. The DROP TABLE statement can delete a table from a database.

Q&A

Q Why does the CREATE DATABASE statement vary so much from one system to another?

A CREATE DATABASE varies because the actual process of creating a database varies from one database system to another. Small PC-based databases usually rely on files that are created within some type of application program. To distribute the database on a large server, related database files are simply distributed over several disk drives. When your code accesses these databases, there is no database process running on the computer, just your application accessing the files directly. More powerful database systems must take into account disk space management as well as support features such as security, transaction control, and stored procedures embedded within the database itself. When your application program accesses a database, a database server manages your requests (along with many others' requests) and returns data to you through a sometimes complex layer of middleware. These topics are discussed more in Week 3. For now, learn all you can about how your particular database management system creates and manages databases.

Q Can I create a table temporarily and then automatically drop it when I am done with it?

A Yes. Many database management systems support the concept of a temporary table. This type of table is created for temporary usage and is automatically deleted when your user's process ends or when you issue the DROP TABLE command. The use of temporary tables is discussed on Day 14, "Dynamic Uses of SQL."

Q Can I remove columns with the ALTER TABLE statement?

A No. The ALTER TABLE command can be used only to add or modify columns within a table. To remove columns, create a new table with the desired format and then select the records from the old table into the new table.

Workshop

The Workshop provides quiz questions to help solidify your understanding of the material covered, as well as exercises to provide you with experience in using what you have learned. Try to answer the quiz and exercise questions before checking the answers in Appendix F, "Answers to Quizzes and Exercises."

Quiz

1. True or False: The ALTER DATABASE statement is often used to modify an existing table's structure.

2. True or False: The DROP TABLE command is functionally equivalent to the DELETE FROM <table_name> command.

3. True or False: To add a new table to a database, use the CREATE TABLE command.

4. What is wrong with the following statement?

```
INPUT    CREATE TABLE new_table (
         ID NUMBER,
         FIELD1 char(40),
         FIELD2 char(80),
         ID char(40);
```

5. What is wrong with the following statement?

```
ALTER DATABASE BILLS (
COMPANY char(80));
```
INPUT

6. When a table is created, who is the owner?

7. If data in a character column has varying lengths, what is the best choice for the data type?

8. Can you have duplicate table names?

Exercises

1. Add two tables to the BILLS database named BANK and ACCOUNT_TYPE using any format you like. The BANK table should contain information about the BANK field used in the BANK_ACCOUNTS table in the examples. The ACCOUNT_TYPE table should contain information about the ACCOUNT_TYPE field in the BANK_ACCOUNTS table also. Try to reduce the data as much as possible.

2. With the five tables that you have created—BILLS, BANK_ACCOUNTS, COMPANY, BANK, and ACCOUNT_TYPE—change the table structure so that instead of using CHAR fields as keys, you use integer ID fields as keys.

3. Using your knowledge of SQL joins (see Day 6, "Joining Tables"), write several queries to join the tables in the BILLS database.

Day 10

Creating Views and Indexes

Objectives

Today we begin to cover topics that may be new even to programmers or database users who have already had some exposure to SQL. Days 1 through 8 covered nearly all the introductory material you need to get started using SQL and relational databases. Day 9, "Creating and Manipulating Tables," was devoted to a discussion of database design, table creation, and other data manipulation commands. The common feature of the objects discussed so far—databases, tables, records, and fields—is that they are all physical objects located on a hard disk. Today the focus shifts to two features of SQL that enable you to view or present data in a different format than it appears on the disk. These two features are the view and the index. By the end of today, you will know the following:

☐ How to distinguish between indexes and views

☐ How to create views

☐ How to create indexes

☐ How to modify data using views

☐ What indexes do

A view is often referred to as a *virtual table*. Views are created by using the CREATE VIEW statement. After the view has been created, you can use the following SQL commands to refer to that view:

☐ SELECT

☐ INSERT

☐ INPUT

☐ UPDATE

☐ DELETE

An index is another way of presenting data differently than it appears on the disk. Special types of indexes reorder the record's physical location within a table. Indexes can be created on a column within a table or on a combination of columns within a table. When an index is used, the data is presented to the user in a sorted order, which you can control with the CREATE INDEX statement. You can usually gain substantial performance improvements by indexing on the correct fields, particularly fields that are being joined between tables.

NOTE

Views and indexes are two totally different objects, but they have one thing in common: They are both associated with a table in the database. Although each object's association with a table is unique, they both enhance a table, thus unveiling powerful features such as presorted data and predefined queries.

NOTE

We used Personal Oracle7 to generate today's examples. Please see the documentation for your specific SQL implementation for any minor differences in syntax.

Using Views

You can use views, or virtual tables, to encapsulate complex queries. After a view on a set of data has been created, you can treat that view as another table. However, special restrictions are placed on modifying the data within views. When data in a table changes, what you see when you query the view also changes. Views do not take up physical space in the database as tables do.

The syntax for the CREATE VIEW statement is

```
CREATE VIEW <view_name> [(column1, column2...)] AS
SELECT <table_name column_names>
FROM <table_name>
```

As usual, this syntax may not be clear at first glance, but today's material contains many examples that illustrate the uses and advantages of views. This command tells SQL to create a view (with the name of your choice) that comprises columns (with the names of your choice if you like). An SQL SELECT statement determines the fields in these columns and their data types. Yes, this is the same SELECT statement that you have used repeatedly for the last nine days.

Before you can do anything useful with views, you need to populate the BILLS database with a little more data. Don't worry if you got excited and took advantage of your newfound knowledge of the DROP DATABASE command. You can simply re-create it. (See Tables 10.1, 10.2, and 10.3 for sample data.)

INPUT/
OUTPUT

```
SQL> create database BILLS;

Statement processed.

SQL> create table BILLS (
  2    NAME CHAR(30) NOT NULL,
  3    AMOUNT NUMBER,
  4    ACCOUNT_ID NUMBER NOT NULL);

Table created.

SQL> create table BANK_ACCOUNTS (
  2    ACCOUNT_ID NUMBER NOT NULL,
  3    TYPE CHAR(30),
  4    BALANCE NUMBER,
  5    BANK CHAR(30));

Table created.

SQL> create table COMPANY (
  2    NAME CHAR(30) NOT NULL,
  3    ADDRESS CHAR(50),
  4    CITY CHAR(30),
  5    STATE CHAR(2));

Table created.
```

Table 10.1. Sample data for the BILLS table.

Name	Amount	Account_ID
Phone Company	125	1
Power Company	75	1
Record Club	25	2
Software Company	250	1
Cable TV Company	35	3
Joe's Car Palace	350	5
S.C. Student Loan	200	6
Florida Water Company	20	1
U-O-Us Insurance Company	125	5
Debtor's Credit Card	35	4

Table 10.2. Sample data for the BANK_ACCOUNTS table.

Account_ID	Type	Balance	Bank
1	Checking	500	First Federal
2	Money Market	1200	First Investor's
3	Checking	90	Credit Union
4	Savings	400	First Federal
5	Checking	2500	Second Mutual
6	Business	4500	Fidelity

Table 10.3. Sample data for the COMPANY table.

Name	Address	City	State
Phone Company	111 1st Street	Atlanta	GA
Power Company	222 2nd Street	Jacksonville	FL
Record Club	333 3rd Avenue	Los Angeles	CA
Software Company	444 4th Drive	San Francisco	CA
Cable TV Company	555 5th Drive	Austin	TX
Joe's Car Palace	1000 Govt. Blvd	Miami	FL
S.C. Student Loan	25 College Blvd	Columbia	SC

10

Name	Address	City	State
Florida Water Company	1883 Hwy 87	Navarre	FL
U-O-Us Insurance Company	295 Beltline Hwy	Macon	GA
Debtor's Credit Card	115 2nd Avenue	Newark	NJ

Now that you have successfully used the CREATE DATABASE, CREATE TABLE, and INSERT commands to input all this information, you are ready for an in-depth discussion of the view.

A Simple View

Let's begin with the simplest of all views. Suppose, for some unknown reason, you want to make a view on the BILLS table that looks identical to the table but has a different name. (We call it DEBTS.) Here's the statement:

INPUT

```
SQL> CREATE VIEW DEBTS AS
        SELECT * FROM BILLS;
```

To confirm that this operation did what it should, you can treat the view just like a table:

INPUT/ OUTPUT

```
SQL> SELECT * FROM DEBTS;

NAME                        AMOUNT  ACCOUNT_ID
Phone Company               125     1
Power Company               75      1
Record Club                 25      2
Software Company            250     1
Cable TV Company            35      3
Joe's Car Palace            350     5
S.C. Student Loan           200     6
Florida Water Company       20      1
U-O-Us Insurance Company    125     5
Debtor's Credit Card        35      4

10 rows selected.
```

You can even create new views from existing views. Be careful when creating views of views. Although this practice is acceptable, it complicates maintenance. Suppose you have a view three levels down from a table, such as a view of a view of a view of a table. What do you think will happen if the first view on the table is dropped? The other two views will still exist, but they will be useless because they get part of their information from the first view. Remember, after the view has been created, it functions as a virtual table.

```
SQL> CREATE VIEW CREDITCARD_DEBTS AS
  2    SELECT * FROM DEBTS
  3    WHERE ACCOUNT_ID = 4;
SQL> SELECT * FROM CREDITCARD_DEBTS;

NAME                    AMOUNT    ACCOUNT_ID
Debtor's Credit Card       35    4

1 row selected.
```

The CREATE VIEW also enables you to select individual columns from a table and place them in a view. The following example selects the NAME and STATE fields from the COMPANY table.

```
SQL> CREATE VIEW COMPANY_INFO (NAME, STATE) AS
  2    SELECT * FROM COMPANY;
SQL> SELECT * FROM COMPANY_INFO;

NAME                       STATE
Phone Company               GA
Power Oompany               FI
Record Club                 CA
Software Company            CA
Cable TV Company            TX
Joe's Car Palace            FL
S.C. Student Loan           SC
Florida Water Company       FL
U-O-Us Insurance Company    GA
Debtor's Credit Card        NJ

10 rows selected.
```

NOTE

Users may create views to query specific data. Say you have a table with 50 columns and hundreds of thousands of rows, but you need to see data in only 2 columns. You can create a view on these two columns, and then by querying from the view, you should see a remarkable difference in the amount of time it takes for your query results to be returned.

Renaming Columns

Views simplify the representation of data. In addition to naming the view, the SQL syntax for the CREATE VIEW statement enables you to rename selected columns. Consider the preceding example a little more closely. What if you wanted to combine the ADDRESS, CITY, and STATE fields from the COMPANY table to print them on an envelope? The following example illustrates this. This example uses the SQL + operator to combine the address fields into one long address by combining spaces and commas with the character data.

INPUT
```
SQL> CREATE VIEW ENVELOPE (COMPANY, MAILING_ADDRESS) AS
  2    SELECT NAME, ADDRESS + " " + CITY + ", " + STATE
  3    FROM COMPANY;
SQL> SELECT * FROM ENVELOPE;
```

OUTPUT
```
COMPANY                         MAILING_ADDRESS
Phone Company                   111 1st Street Atlanta, GA
Power Company                   222 2nd Street Jacksonville, FL
Record Club                     333 3rd Avenue Los Angeles, CA
Software Company                444 4th Drive San Francisco, CA
Cable TV Company                555 5th Drive Austin, TX
Joe's Car Palace                1000 Govt. Blvd Miami, FL
S.C. Student Loan               25 College Blvd. Columbia, SC
Florida Water Company           1883 Hwy. 87 Navarre, FL
U-O-Us Insurance Company        295 Beltline Hwy. Macon, GA
Debtor's Credit Card            115 2nd Avenue Newark, NJ

10 rows selected.
```

ANALYSIS The SQL syntax requires you to supply a virtual field name whenever the view's virtual field is created using a calculation or SQL function. This procedure makes sense because you wouldn't want a view's column name to be COUNT(*) or AVG(PAYMENT).

NOTE

> Check your implementation for the use of the + operator.

SQL View Processing

Views can represent data within tables in a more convenient fashion than what actually exists in the database's table structure. Views can also be extremely convenient when performing several complex queries in a series (such as within a stored procedure or application program). To solidify your understanding of the view and the SELECT statement, the next section examines the way in which SQL processes a query against a view. Suppose you have a query that occurs often, for example, you routinely join the BILLS table with the BANK_ACCOUNTS table to retrieve information on your payments.

INPUT
```
SQL> SELECT BILLS.NAME, BILLS.AMOUNT, BANK_ACCOUNTS.BALANCE,
  2    BANK_ACCOUNTS.BANK FROM BILLS, BANK_ACCOUNTS
  3    WHERE BILLS.ACCOUNT_ID = BANK_ACCOUNTS.ACCOUNT_ID;
```

OUTPUT

BILLS.NAME	BILLS.AMOUNT	BANK_ACCOUNTS.BALANCE	BANK_ACCOUNTS.BANK
Phone Company	125	500	First Federal
Power Company	75	500	First Federal
Record Club	25	1200	First Investor's
Software Company	250	500	First Federal
Cable TV Company	35	90	Credit Union
Joe's Car Palace	350	2500	Second Mutual

10

```
S.C. Student Loan          200      4500            Fidelity
Florida Water Company       20       500            First Federal
U-O-Us Insurance Company   125      2500            Second Mutual
```

    9 rows selected.

You could convert this process into a view using the following statement:

```
SQL> CREATE VIEW BILLS_DUE (NAME, AMOUNT, ACCT_BALANCE, BANK) AS
  2    SELECT BILLS.NAME, BILLS.AMOUNT, BANK_ACCOUNTS.BALANCE,
  3    BANK_ACCOUNTS.BANK FROM BILLS, BANK_ACCOUNTS
  4    WHERE BILLS.ACCOUNT_ID = BANK_ACCOUNTS.ACCOUNT_ID;
```

    View created.

If you queried the BILLS_DUE view using some condition, the statement would look like this:

```
SQL> SELECT * FROM BILLS_DUE
  2    WHERE ACCT_BALANCE > 500;
```

```
NAME                       AMOUNT     ACCT_BALANCE     BANK
Record Club                  25         1200           First Investor's
Joe's Car Palace            350         2500           Second Mutual
S.C. Student Loan           200         4500           Fidelity
U-O-Us Insurance Company    125         2500           Second Mutual
```

    4 rows selected.

ANALYSIS SQL uses several steps to process the preceding statement. Because BILLS_DUE is a view, not an actual table, SQL first looks for a table named BILLS_DUE and finds nothing. The SQL processor will probably (depending on what database system you are using) find out from a system table that BILLS_DUE is a view. It will then use the view's plan to construct the following query:

```
SQL> SELECT BILLS.NAME, BILLS.AMOUNT, BANK_ACCOUNTS.BALANCE,
  2    BANK_ACCOUNTS.BANK FROM BILLS, BANK_ACCOUNTS
  3    WHERE BILLS.ACCOUNT_ID = BANK_ACCOUNTS.ACCOUNT_ID
  4    AND BANK_ACCOUNTS.BALANCE > 500;
```

Example 10.1

Construct a view that shows all states to which the bills are being sent. Also display the total amount of money and the total number of bills being sent to each state.

First of all, you know that the CREATE VIEW part of the statement will look like this:

```
CREATE VIEW EXAMPLE (STATE, TOTAL_BILLS, TOTAL_AMOUNT) AS...
```

Now you must determine what the SELECT query will look like. You know that you want to select the STATE field first using the SELECT DISTINCT syntax based on the requirement to show the states to which bills are being sent. For example:

INPUT

```
SQL> SELECT DISTINCT STATE FROM COMPANY;
```

OUTPUT

```
STATE
GA
FL
CA
TX
SC
NJ

6 rows selected.
```

In addition to selecting the STATE field, you need to total the number of payments sent to that STATE. Therefore, you need to join the BILLS table and the COMPANY table.

INPUT/OUTPUT

```
SQL> SELECT DISTINCT COMPANY.STATE, COUNT(BILLS.*) FROM BILLS, COMPANY
  2    GROUP BY COMPANY.STATE
  3    HAVING BILLS.NAME = COMPANY.NAME;

STATE       COUNT(BILLS.*)
GA          2
FL          3
CA          2
TX          1
SC          1
NJ          1

6 rows selected.
```

Now that you have successfully returned two-thirds of the desired result, you can add the final required return value. Use the SUM function to total the amount of money sent to each state.

INPUT/OUTPUT

```
SQL> SELECT DISTINCT COMPANY.STATE, COUNT(BILLS.NAME), SUM(BILLS.AMOUNT)
  2    FROM BILLS, COMPANY
  3    GROUP BY COMPANY.STATE
  4    HAVING BILLS.NAME = COMPANY.NAME;

STATE       COUNT(BILLS.*)      SUM(BILLS.AMOUNT)
GA          2                   250
FL          3                   445
CA          2                   275
TX          1                   35
SC          1                   200
NJ          1                   35

6 rows selected.
```

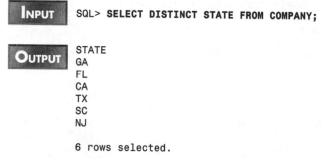

10

As the final step, you can combine this SELECT statement with the CREATE VIEW statement you
created at the beginning of this project:

```
SQL> CREATE VIEW EXAMPLE (STATE, TOTAL_BILLS, TOTAL_AMOUNT) AS
  2    SELECT DISTINCT COMPANY.STATE, COUNT(BILLS.NAME),➡
        SUM(BILLS.AMOUNT)
  3    FROM BILLS, COMPANY
  4    GROUP BY COMPANY.STATE
  5    HAVING BILLS.NAME = COMPANY.NAME;

View created.
```

INPUT/OUTPUT

```
SQL> SELECT * FROM EXAMPLE;

STATE       TOTAL_BILLS      TOTAL_AMOUNT
GA          2                250
FL          3                445
CA          2                275
TX          1                35
SC          1                200
NJ          1                35

6 rows selected.
```

ANALYSIS The preceding example shows you how to plan the CREATE VIEW statement and the
SELECT statements. This code tests the SELECT statements to see whether they will
generate the proper results and then combines the statements to create the view.

Example 10.2

Assume that your creditors charge a 10 percent service charge for all late payments, and
unfortunately you are late on everything this month. You want to see this late charge along
with the type of accounts the payments are coming from.

This join is straightforward. (You don't need to use anything like COUNT or SUM.) However,
you will discover one of the primary benefits of using views. You can add the 10 percent
service charge and present it as a field within the view. From that point on, you can select
records from the view and already have the total amount calculated for you. The statement
would look like this:

INPUT

```
SQL> CREATE VIEW LATE_PAYMENT (NAME, NEW_TOTAL, ACCOUNT_TYPE) AS
  2    SELECT BILLS.NAME, BILLS.AMOUNT * 1.10, BANK_ACCOUNTS.TYPE
  3    FROM BILLS, BANK_ACCOUNTS
  4    WHERE BILLS.ACCOUNT_ID = BANK_ACCOUNTS.ACCOUNT_ID;
```

OUTPUT View created.

INPUT/
OUTPUT

```
SQL> SELECT * FROM LATE_PAYMENT;

NAME                         NEW_TOTAL     ACCOUNT_TYPE
Phone Company                137.50        Checking
Power Company                82.50         Checking
Record Club                  27.50         Money Market
Software Company             275           Checking
Cable TV Company             38.50         Checking
Joe's Car Palace             385           Checking
S.C. Student Loan            220           Business
Florida Water Company        22            Checking
U-O-Us Insurance Company     137.50        Business
Debtor's Credit Card         38.50         Savings

10 rows selected.
```

Restrictions on Using SELECT

SQL places certain restrictions on using the SELECT statement to formulate a view. The following two rules apply when using the SELECT statement:

☐ You cannot use the UNION operator.

☐ You cannot use the ORDER BY clause. However, you can use the GROUP BY clause in a view to perform the same functions as the ORDER BY clause.

Modifying Data in a View

As you have learned, by creating a view on one or more physical tables within a database, you can create a virtual table for use throughout an SQL script or a database application. After the view has been created using the CREATE VIEW...SELECT statement, you can update, insert, or delete view data using the UPDATE, INSERT, and DELETE commands you learned about on Day 8, "Manipulating Data."

We discuss the limitations on modifying a view's data in greater detail later. The next group of examples illustrates how to manipulate data that is in a view.

To continue on the work you did in Example 10.2, update the BILLS table to reflect that unfortunate 10 percent late charge.

INPUT/
OUTPUT

```
SQL> CREATE VIEW LATE_PAYMENT AS
  2  SELECT * FROM BILLS;

View created.

SQL> UPDATE LATE_PAYMENT
  2  SET AMOUNT = AMOUNT * 1.10;

1 row updated.
```

```
SQL> SELECT * FROM LATE_PAYMENT;

NAME                           NEW_TOTAL        ACCOUNT_ID
Phone Company                  137.50           1
Power Company                  82.50            1
Record Club                    27.50            2
Software Company               275              1
Cable TV Company               38.50            3
Joe's Car Palace               385              5
S.C. Student Loan              220              6
Florida Water Company          22               1
U-O-Us Insurance Company       137.50           5
Debtor's Credit Card           38.50            4

10 rows selected.
```

To verify that the UPDATE actually updated the underlying table, BILLS, query the BILLS table:

**INPUT/
OUTPUT**

```
SQL> SELECT * FROM BILLS;

NAME                           NEW_TOTAL        ACCOUNT_ID
Phone Company                  137.50           1
Power Company                  82.50            1
Record Club                    27.50            2
Software Company               275              1
Cable TV Company               38.50            3
Joe's Car Palace               385              5
S.C. Student Loan              220              6
Florida Water Company          22               1
U-O-Us Insurance Company       137.50           5
Debtor's Credit Card           38.50            4

10 rows selected.
```

Now delete a row from the view:

**INPUT/
OUTPUT**

```
SQL> DELETE FROM LATE_PAYMENT
  2   WHERE ACCOUNT_ID = 4;

1 row deleted.

SQL> SELECT * FROM LATE_PAYMENT;

NAME                           NEW_TOTAL        ACCOUNT_ID
Phone Company                  137.50           1
Power Company                  82.50            1
Record Club                    27.50            2
Software Company               275              1
Cable TV Company               38.50            3
Joe's Car Palace               385              5
S.C. Student Loan              220              6
Florida Water Company          22               1
U-O-Us Insurance Company       137.50           5

9 rows selected.
```

The final step is to test the UPDATE function. For all bills that have a NEW_TOTAL greater than 100, add an additional 10.

INPUT/OUTPUT

```
SQL> UPDATE LATE_PAYMENT
  2  SET NEW_TOTAL = NEW_TOTAL + 10
  3  WHERE NEW_TOTAL > 100;

9 rows updated.

SQL> SELECT * FROM LATE_PAYMENT;

NAME                          NEW_TOTAL      ACCOUNT_ID
Phone Company                 147.50         1
Power Company                 82.50          1
Record Club                   27.50          2
Software Company              285            1
Cable TV Company              38.50          3
Joe's Car Palace              395            5
S.C. Student Loan             230            6
Florida Water Company         22             1
U-O-Us Insurance Company      147.50         5

9 rows selected.
```

Problems with Modifying Data Using Views

Because what you see through a view can be some set of a group of tables, modifying the data in the underlying tables is not always as straightforward as the previous examples. Following is a list of the most common restrictions you will encounter while working with views:

☐ You cannot use DELETE statements on multiple table views.

☐ You cannot use the INSERT statement unless all NOT NULL columns used in the underlying table are included in the view. This restriction applies because the SQL processor does not know which values to insert into the NOT NULL columns.

☐ If you do insert or update records through a join view, all records that are updated must belong to the same physical table.

☐ If you use the DISTINCT clause to create a view, you cannot update or insert records within that view.

☐ You cannot update a virtual column (a column that is the result of an expression or function).

Common Applications of Views

Here are a few of the tasks that views can perform:

☐ Providing user security functions

☐ Converting between units

☐ Creating a new virtual table format

☐ Simplifying the construction of complex queries

Views and Security

Although a complete discussion of database security appears in Day 12, "Database Security," we briefly touch on the topic now to explain how you can use views in performing security functions.

All relational database systems in use today include a full suite of built-in security features. Users of the database system are generally divided into groups based on their use of the database. Common group types are database administrators, database developers, data entry personnel, and public users. These groups of users have varying degrees of privileges when using the database. The database administrator will probably have complete control of the system, including UPDATE, INSERT, DELETE, and ALTER database privileges. The public group may be granted only SELECT privileges—and perhaps may be allowed to SELECT only from certain tables within certain databases.

Views are commonly used in this situation to control the information that the database user has access to. For instance, if you wanted users to have access only to the NAME field of the BILLS table, you could simply create a view called BILLS_NAME:

```
SQL>  CREATE VIEW BILLS_NAME AS
   2     SELECT NAME FROM BILLS;

View created.
```

Someone with system administrator-level privileges could grant the public group SELECT privileges on the BILLS_NAME view. This group would not have any privileges on the underlying BILLS table. As you might guess, SQL has provided data security statements for your use also. Keep in mind that views are very useful for implementing database security.

Using Views to Convert Units

Views are also useful in situations in which you need to present the user with data that is different from the data that actually exists within the database. For instance, if the AMOUNT field is actually stored in U.S. dollars and you don't want Canadian users to have to continually do mental calculations to see the AMOUNT total in Canadian dollars, you could create a simple view called CANADIAN_BILLS:

```
SQL>  CREATE VIEW CANADIAN_BILLS (NAME, CAN_AMOUNT) AS
   2     SELECT NAME, AMOUNT / 1.10
   3     FROM BILLS;

View Created.

SQL> SELECT * FROM CANADIAN_BILLS;

NAME                              CAN_AMOUNT
Phone Company                     125
Power Company                     75
Record Club                       25
```

10

```
Software Company              250
Cable TV Company              35
Joe's Car Palace              350
S.C. Student Loan             200
Florida Water Company         20
U-O-Us Insurance Company      125

9 rows selected.
```

ANALYSIS When converting units like this, keep in mind the possible problems inherent in modifying the underlying data in a table when a calculation (such as the preceding example) was used to create one of the columns of the view. As always, you should consult your database system's documentation to determine exactly how the system implements the CREATE VIEW command.

Simplifying Complex Queries Using Views

Views are also useful in situations that require you to perform a sequence of queries to arrive at a result. The following example illustrates the use of a view in this situation.

To give the name of all banks that sent bills to the state of Texas with an amount less than $50, you would break the problem into two separate problems:

- [ ] Retrieve all bills that were sent to Texas
- [ ] Retrieve all bills less than $50

Let's solve this problem using two separate views: BILLS_1 and BILLS_2:

INPUT/ OUTPUT
```
SQL> CREATE TABLE BILLS1 AS
  2  SELECT * FROM BILLS
  3  WHERE AMOUNT < 50;

Table created.

SQL> CREATE TABLE BILLS2 (NAME, AMOUNT, ACCOUNT_ID) AS
  2  SELECT BILLS.* FROM BILLS, COMPANY
  3  WHERE BILLS.NAME = COMPANY.NAME AND COMPANY.STATE = "TX";

Table created.
```

ANALYSIS Because you want to find all bills sent to Texas *and* all bills that were less than $50, you can now use the SQL IN clause to find which bills in BILLS1 were sent to Texas. Use this information to create a new view called BILLS3:

INPUT/ OUTPUT
```
SQL> CREATE VIEW BILLS3 AS
  2  SELECT * FROM BILLS2 WHERE NAME IN
  3  (SELECT * FROM BILLS1);

View created.
```

Now combine the preceding query with the BANK_ACCOUNTS table to satisfy the original requirements of this example:

```
SQL> CREATE VIEW BANKS_IN_TEXAS (BANK) AS
   2  SELECT BANK_ACCOUNTS.BANK
   3  FROM BANK_ACCOUNTS, BILLS3
   4  WHERE BILLS3.ACCOUNT_ID = BANK_ACCOUNTS.ACCOUNT_ID;

View created.

SQL> SELECT * FROM BANK_IN_TEXAS;

BANK
Credit Union

1 row selected.
```

As you can see, after the queries were broken down into separate views, the final query was rather simple. Also, you can reuse the individual views as often as necessary.

The DROP VIEW **Statement**

In common with every other SQL CREATE... command, CREATE VIEW has a corresponding DROP... command. The syntax is as follows:

```
SQL> DROP VIEW view_name;
```

The only thing to remember when using the DROP VIEW command is that all other views that reference that view are now invalid. Some database systems even drop all views that used the view you dropped. Using Personal Oracle7, if you drop the view BILLS1, the final query would produce the following error:

```
SQL> DROP VIEW BILLS1;

View dropped.

SQL> SELECT * FROM BANKS_IN_TEXAS;
*
ERROR at line 1:
ORA-04063: view "PERKINS.BANKS_IN_TEXAS" has errors
```

NOTE

> A view can be dropped without any of the actual tables being modified, which explains why we often refer to views as virtual tables. (The same logic can be applied to the technology of virtual reality.)

10

Using Indexes

Another way to present data in a different format than it physically exists on the disk is to use an index. In addition, indexes can also reorder the data stored on the disk (something views cannot do).

Indexes are used in an SQL database for three primary reasons:

☐ To enforce referential integrity constraints by using the UNIQUE keyword

☐ To facilitate the ordering of data based on the contents of the index's field or fields

☐ To optimize the execution speed of queries

What Are Indexes?

Data can be retrieved from a database using two methods. The first method, often called the Sequential Access Method, requires SQL to go through each record looking for a match. This search method is inefficient, but it is the only way for SQL to locate the correct record. Think back to the days when libraries had massive card catalog filing systems. Suppose the librarian removed the alphabetical index cards, tossed the cards into the air, then placed them back into the filing cabinets. When you wanted to look up this book's shelf location, you would probably start at the very beginning, then go through one card at a time until you found the information you wanted. (Chances are, you would stop searching as soon as you found any book on this topic!)

Now suppose the librarian sorted the book titles alphabetically. You could quickly access this book's information by using your knowledge of the alphabet to move through the catalog.

Imagine the flexibility if the librarian was diligent enough to not only sort the books by title but also create another catalog sorted by author's name and another sorted by topic. This process would provide you, the library user, with a great deal of flexibility in retrieving information. Also, you would be able to retrieve your information in a fraction of the time it originally would have taken.

Adding indexes to your database enables SQL to use the Direct Access Method. SQL uses a treelike structure to store and retrieve the index's data. Pointers to a group of data are stored at the top of the tree. These groups are called *nodes*. Each node contains pointers to other nodes. The nodes pointing to the left contain values that are less than its parent node. The pointers to the right point to values greater than the parent node.

The database system starts its search at the top node and simply follows the pointers until it is successful.

10

NOTE

> The result of a query against the unindexed table is commonly referred to as a *full-table scan*. A full-table scan is the process used by the database server to search every row of a table until all rows are returned with the given condition(s). This operation is comparable to searching for a book in the library by starting at the first book on the first shelf and scanning every book until you find the one you want. On the other hand, to find the book quickly, you would probably look in the (computerized) card catalog. Similarly, an index enables the database server to point to specific rows of data quickly within a table.

Fortunately, you are not required to actually implement the tree structure yourself, just as you are not required to write the implementation for saving and reading in tables or databases. The basic SQL syntax to create an index is as follows:

INPUT/OUTPUT

```
SQL>    CREATE INDEX index_name
  2       ON table_name(column_name1, [column_name2], ...);
```

```
Index created.
```

As you have seen many times before, the syntax for CREATE INDEX can vary widely among database systems. For instance, the CREATE INDEX statement under Oracle7 looks like this:

SYNTAX

```
CREATE INDEX [schema.]index
ON { [schema.]table (column [!!under!!ASC¦DESC]
    [, column [!!under!!ASC¦DESC]] ...)
    ¦ CLUSTER [schema.]cluster }
[INITRANS integer] [MAXTRANS integer]
[TABLESPACE tablespace]
[STORAGE storage_clause]
[PCTFREE integer]
[NOSORT]
```

The syntax for CREATE INDEX using Sybase SQL Server is as follows:

SYNTAX

```
create [unique] [clustered ¦ nonclustered]
      index index_name
on [[database.]owner.]table_name (column_name
    [, column_name]...)
[with {fillfactor = x, ignore_dup_key, sorted_data,
      [ignore_dup_row ¦ allow_dup_row]}]
[on segment_name]
```

Informix SQL implements the command like this:

SYNTAX

```
CREATE [UNIQUE ¦ DISTINCT] [CLUSTER] INDEX index_name
ON table_name (column_name [ASC ¦ DESC],
                column_name [ASC ¦ DESC]...)
```

Notice that all of these implementations have several things in common, starting with the basic statement

```
CREATE INDEX index_name ON table_name (column_name, ...)
```

SQL Server and Oracle allow you to create a clustered index, which is discussed later. Oracle and Informix allow you to designate whether the column name should be sorted in ascending or descending order. We hate to sound like a broken record, but, once again, you should definitely consult your database management system's documentation when using the CREATE INDEX command.

For instance, to create an index on the ACCOUNT_ID field of the BILLS table, the CREATE INDEX statement would look like this:

INPUT

```
SQL> SELECT * FROM BILLS;
```

OUTPUT

```
NAME                           AMOUNT    ACCOUNT_ID
Phone Company                  125       1
Power Company                  75        1
Record Club                    25        2
Software Company               250       1
Cable TV Company               35        3
Joe's Car Palace               350       5
S.C. Student Loan              200       6
Florida Water Company          20        1
U-O-Us Insurance Company       125       5
Debtor's Credit Card           35        4

10 rows selected.
```

INPUT/ OUTPUT

```
SQL> CREATE INDEX ID_INDEX ON BILLS( ACCOUNT_ID );

Index created.

SQL> SELECT * FROM BILLS;

NAME                           AMOUNT    ACCOUNT_ID
Phone Company                  125       1
Power Company                  75        1
Software Company               250       1
Florida Water Company          20        1
Record Club                    25        2
Cable TV Company               35        3
Debtor's Credit Card           35        4
Joe's Car Palace               350       5
U-O-Us Insurance Company       125       5
S.C. Student Loan              200       6

10 rows selected.
```

The BILLS table is sorted by the ACCOUNT_ID field until the index is dropped using the DROP INDEX statement. As usual, the DROP INDEX statement is very straightforward:

```
SQL> DROP INDEX index_name;
```

Here's what happens when the index is dropped:

INPUT/
OUTPUT

```
SQL> DROP INDEX ID_INDEX;

Index dropped.

SQL> SELECT * FROM BILLS;

NAME                         AMOUNT      ACCOUNT_ID
Phone Company                125         1
Power Company                75          1
Record Club                  25          2
Software Company             250         1
Cable TV Company             35          3
Joe's Car Palace             350         5
S.C. Student Loan            200         6
Florida Water Company        20          1
U-O-Us Insurance Company     125         5
Debtor's Credit Card         35          4

10 rows selected.
```

ANALYSIS

Now the BILLS table is in its original form. Using the simplest form of the CREATE INDEX statement did not physically change the way the table was stored.

You may be wondering why database systems even provide indexes if they also enable you to use the ORDER BY clause.

INPUT/
OUTPUT

```
SQL> SELECT * FROM BILLS ORDER BY ACCOUNT_ID;

NAME                         AMOUNT      ACCOUNT_ID
Phone Company                125         1
Power Company                75          1
Software Company             250         1
Florida Water Company        20          1
Record Club                  25          2
Cable TV Company             35          3
Debtor's Credit Card         35          4
Joe's Car Palace             350         5
U-O-Us Insurance Company     125         5
S.C. Student Loan            200         6

10 rows selected.
```

ANALYSIS

This SELECT statement and the ID_INDEX on the BILLS table generate the same result. The difference is that an ORDER BY clause re-sorts and orders the data each time you execute the corresponding SQL statement. When using an index, the database system creates a physical index object (using the tree structure explained earlier) and reuses the same index each time you query the table.

10

WARNING

When a table is dropped, all indexes associated with the table are dropped as well.

Indexing Tips

Listed here are several tips to keep in mind when using indexes:

- [ ] For small tables, using indexes does not result in any performance improvement.
- [ ] Indexes produce the greatest improvement when the columns you have indexed on contain a wide variety of data or many NULL values.
- [ ] Indexes can optimize your queries when those queries are returning a small amount of data (a good rule of thumb is less than 25 percent of the data). If you are returning more data most of the time, indexes simply add overhead.
- [ ] Indexes can improve the speed of data retrieval. However, they slow data updates. Keep this in mind when doing many updates in a row with an index. For very large updates, you might consider dropping the index before you perform the update. When the update is complete, simply rebuild your index. On one particular update, we were able to save the programmers 18 hours by dropping the index and re-creating it after the data load.
- [ ] Indexes take up space within your database. If you are using a database management system that enables you to manage the disk space taken up your database, factor in the size of indexes when planning your database's size.
- [ ] Always index on fields that are used in joins between tables. This technique can greatly increase the speed of a join.
- [ ] Most database systems do not allow you to create an index on a view. If your database system allows it, use the technique clause with the SELECT statement that builds the view to order the data within the view. (Unfortunately, many systems don't enable the ORDER BY clause with the CREATE VIEW statement either.)
- [ ] Do not index on fields that are updated or modified regularly. The overhead required to constantly update the index will offset any performance gain you hope to acquire.
- [ ] Do not store indexes and tables on the same physical drive. Separating these objects will eliminate drive contention and result in faster queries.

Indexing on More Than One Field

SQL also enables you to index on more than one field. This type of index is a *composite index*. The following code illustrates a simple composite index. Note that even though two fields are being combined, only one physical index is created (called ID_CMPD_INDEX).

```
SQL> CREATE INDEX ID_CMPD_INDEX ON BILLS( ACCOUNT_ID, AMOUNT );

Index created.

SQL> SELECT * FROM BILLS;

NAME                            AMOUNT          ACCOUNT_ID
Florida Water Company              20                   1
Power Company                      75                   1
Phone Company                     125                   1
Software Company                  250                   1
Record Club                        25                   2
Cable TV Company                   35                   3
Debtor's Credit Card               35                   4
U-O-Us Insurance Company          125                   5
Joe's Car Palace                  350                   5
S.C. Student Loan                 200                   6

10 rows selected.

SQL> DROP INDEX ID_CMPD_INDEX;

Index dropped.
```

ANALYSIS You can achieve performance gains by selecting the column with the most unique values. For instance, every value in the NAME field of the BILLS table is unique. When using a compound index, place the most selective field first in the column list. That is, place the field that you expect to select most often at the beginning of the list. (The order in which the column names appear in the CREATE INDEX statement does not have to be the same as their order within the table.) Assume you are routinely using a statement such as the following:

```
SQL> SELECT * FROM BILLS WHERE NAME = "Cable TV Company";
```

To achieve performance gains, you must create an index using the NAME field as the leading column. Here are two examples:

```
SQL> CREATE INDEX NAME_INDEX ON BILLS(NAME, AMOUNT);
```

or

```
SQL> CREATE INDEX NAME_INDEX ON BILLS(NAME);
```

The NAME field is the left-most column for both of these indexes, so the preceding query would be optimized to search on the NAME field.

Composite indexes are also used to combine two or more columns that by themselves may have low selectivity. For an example of *selectivity,* examine the BANK_ACCOUNTS table:

```
ACCOUNT_ID      TYPE            BALANCE     BANK
1               Checking        500         First Federal
2               Money Market    1200        First Investor's
3               Checking        90          Credit Union
```

```
4               Savings       400       First Federal
5               Checking      2500      Second Mutual
6               Business      4500      Fidelity
```

Notice that out of six records, the value Checking appears in three of them. This column has a lower selectivity than the ACCOUNT_ID field. Notice that every value of the ACCOUNT_ID field is unique. To improve the selectivity of your index, you could combine the TYPE and ACCOUNT_ID fields in a new index. This step would create a unique index value (which, of course, is the highest selectivity you can get).

NOTE

> An index containing multiple columns is often referred to as a *composite index*. Performance issues may sway your decision on whether to use a single-column or composite index. In Oracle, for example, you may decide to use a single-column index if most of your queries involve one particular column as part of a condition; on the other hand, you would probably create a composite index if the columns in that index are often used together as conditions for a query. Check your specific implementation on guidance when creating multiple-column indexes.

10

Using the UNIQUE Keyword with CREATE INDEX

Composite indexes are often used with the UNIQUE keyword to prevent multiple records from appearing with the same data. Suppose you wanted to force the BILLS table to have the following built-in "rule": Each bill paid to a company must come from a different bank account. You would create a UNIQUE index on the NAME and ACCOUNT_ID fields. Unfortunately, Oracle7 does not support the UNIQUE syntax. Instead, it implements the UNIQUE feature using the UNIQUE integrity constraint. The following example demonstrates the UNIQUE keyword with CREATE INDEX using Sybase's Transact-SQL language.

INPUT

```
1> create unique index unique_id_name
2> on BILLS(ACCOUNT_ID, NAME)
3> go
1> select * from BILLS
2> go
```

OUTPUT

```
NAME                         AMOUNT       ACCOUNT_ID
Florida Water Company        20           1
Power Company                75           1
Phone Company                125          1
Software Company             250          1
Record Club                  25           2
Cable TV Company             35           3
Debtor's Credit Card         35           4
U-O-Us Insurance Company     125          5
```

```
Joe's Car Palace                350      5
S.C. Student Loan               200      6
```

Now try to insert a record into the BILLS table that duplicates data that already exists.

```
1> insert BILLS (NAME, AMOUNT, ACCOUNT_ID)
2> values("Power Company", 125, 1)
3> go
```

You should have received an error message telling you that the INSERT command was not allowed. This type of error message can be trapped within an application program, and a message could tell the user he or she inserted invalid data.

Example 10.3

Create an index on the BILLS table that will sort the AMOUNT field in descending order.

```
SQL> CREATE INDEX DESC_AMOUNT
     ON  BILLS(AMOUNT DESC);

Index created.
```

This is the first time you have used the DESC operator, which tells SQL to sort the index in descending order. (By default a number field is sorted in ascending order.) Now you can examine your handiwork:

```
SQL> SELECT * FROM BILLS;
```

NAME	AMOUNT	ACCOUNT_ID
Joe's Car Palace	350	5
Software Company	250	1
S.C. Student Loan	200	6
Phone Company	125	1
U-O-Us Insurance Company	125	5
Power Company	75	1
Cable TV Company	35	3
Debtor's Credit Card	35	4
Record Club	25	2
Florida Water Company	20	1

```
10 rows selected.
```

This example created an index using the DESC operator on the column amount. Notice in the output that the amount is ordered from largest to smallest.

Indexes and Joins

When using complicated joins in queries, your SELECT statement can take a long time. With large tables, this amount of time can approach several seconds (as compared to the milliseconds you are used to waiting). This type of performance in a client/server environment with many users becomes extremely frustrating to the users of your application. Creating an index on fields that are frequently used in joins can optimize the performance of your query considerably. However, if too many indexes are created, they can slow down

10

the performance of your system, rather than speed it up. We recommend that you experiment with using indexes on several large tables (on the order of thousands of records). This type of experimentation leads to a better understanding of optimizing SQL statements.

NOTE

> Most implementations have a mechanism for gathering the elapsed time of a query; Oracle refers to this feature as *timing*. Check your implementation for specific information.

The following example creates an index on the ACCOUNT_ID fields in the BILLS and BANK_ACCOUNTS tables:

INPUT/ OUTPUT

```
SQL> CREATE INDEX BILLS_INDEX ON BILLS(ACCOUNT_ID);

Index created.

SQL> CREATE INDEX BILLS_INDEX2 ON BANK_ACCOUNTS(ACCOUNT_ID);

Index created.

SQL> SELECT BILLS.NAME NAME, BILLS.AMOUNT AMOUNT, BANK_ACCOUNTS.BALANCE
  2  ACCOUNT_BALANCE
  3  FROM BILLS, BANK_ACCOUNTS
  4  WHERE BILLS.ACCOUNT_ID = BANK_ACCOUNTS.ACCOUNT_ID;

NAME                        AMOUNT      ACCOUNT_BALANCE
Phone Company               125         500
Power Company               75          500
Software Company            250         500
Florida Water Company       20          500
Record Club                 25          1200
Cable TV Company            35          90
Debtor's Credit Card        35          400
Joe's Car Palace            350         2500
U-O-Us Insurance Company    125         2500
S.C. Student Loan           200         4500

10 rows selected.
```

ANALYSIS This example first created an index for the ACCOUNT_ID on both tables in the associated query. By creating indexes for ACCOUNT_ID on each table, the join can more quickly access specific rows of data. As a rule, you should index the column(s) of a table that are unique or that you plan to join tables with in queries.

Using Clusters

Although we originally said that indexes can be used to present a view of a table that is different from the existing physical arrangement, this statement is not entirely accurate. A special type of index supported by many database systems allows the database manager or developer to *cluster* data. When a clustered index is used, the physical arrangement of the data within a table is modified. Using a clustered index usually results in faster data retrieval than using a traditional, nonclustered index. However, many database systems (such as Sybase SQL Server) allow only one clustered index per table. The field used to create the clustered index is usually the primary key field. Using Sybase Transact-SQL, you could create a clustered, unique index on the ACCOUNT_ID field of the BANK_ACCOUNTS table using the following syntax:

```
create unique clustered index id_index
on BANK_ACCOUNTS(ACCOUNT_ID)
 go
```

Oracle treats the concept of clusters differently. When using the Oracle relational database, a cluster is a database object like a database or table. A cluster is used to store tables with common fields so that their access speed is improved.

Here is the syntax to create a cluster using Oracle7:

```
CREATE CLUSTER [schema.]cluster
(column datatype [,column datatype] ... )
[PCTUSED integer] [PCTFREE integer]
[SIZE integer [K¦M] ]
[INITRANS integer] [MAXTRANS integer]
[TABLESPACE tablespace]
[STORAGE storage_clause]
[!!under!!INDEX
¦ [HASH IS column] HASHKEYS integer]
```

You should then create an index within the cluster based on the tables that will be added to it. Then you can add the tables. You should add tables only to clusters that are frequently joined. Do not add tables to clusters that are accessed individually through a simple SELECT statement.

Obviously, clusters are a very vendor-specific feature of SQL. We will not go into more detail here on their use or on the syntax that creates them. However, consult your database vendor's documentation to determine whether your database management system supports these useful objects.

Summary

Views are virtual tables. Views are simply a way of presenting data in a format that is different from the way it actually exists in the database. The syntax of the CREATE VIEW statement uses a standard SELECT statement to create the view (with some exceptions). You can treat a view as a regular table and perform inserts, updates, deletes, and selects on it. We briefly discussed the use of database security and how views are commonly used to implement this security. Database security is covered in greater detail on Day 12.

The basic syntax used to create a view is

```
CREATE VIEW view_name AS
SELECT field_name(s) FROM table_name(s);
```

Here are the most common uses of views:

- [ ] To perform user security functions
- [ ] To convert units
- [ ] To create a new virtual table format
- [ ] To simplify the construction of complex queries

Indexes are also database design and SQL programming tools. Indexes are physical database objects stored by your database management system that can be used to retrieve data already sorted from the database. In addition, thanks to the way indexes are mapped out, using indexes and properly formed queries can yield significant performance improvements.

The basic syntax used to create an index looks like this:

```
CREATE INDEX index_name
ON table_name(field_name(s));
```

Some database systems include very useful additional options such as the UNIQUE and CLUSTERED keywords.

Q&A

Q If the data within my table is already in sorted order, why should I use an index on that table?

A An index still gives you a performance benefit by looking quickly through key values in a tree. The index can locate records faster than a direct access search through each record within your database. Remember—the SQL query processor doesn't necessarily know that your data is in sorted order.

Q Can I create an index that contains fields from multiple tables?

A No, you cannot. However, Oracle7, for instance, allows you to create a cluster. You can place tables within a cluster and create cluster indexes on fields that are common to the tables. This implementation is the exception, not the rule, so be sure to study your documentation on this topic in more detail.

10

Workshop

The Workshop provides quiz questions to help solidify your understanding of the material covered, as well as exercises to provide you with experience in using what you have learned. Try to answer the quiz and exercise questions before checking the answers in Appendix F, "Answers to Quizzes and Exercises."

Quiz

1. What will happen if a unique index is created on a nonunique field?

2. Are the following statements true or false?

   Both views and indexes take up space in the database and therefore must be factored in the planning of the database size.

   If someone updates a table on which a view has been created, the view must have an identical update performed on it to see the same data.

   If you have the disk space and you really want to get your queries smoking, the more indexes the better.

3. Is the following CREATE statement correct?

   ```
   SQL> create view credit_debts as
        (select all from debts
        where account_id = 4);
   ```

4. Is the following CREATE statement correct?

   ```
   SQL> create unique view debts as
        select * from debts_tbl;
   ```

5. Is the following CREATE statement correct?

   ```
   SQL> drop * from view debts;
   ```

6. Is the following CREATE statement correct?

   ```
   SQL> create index id_index on bills
        (account_id);
   ```

Exercises

1. Examine the database system you are using. Does it support views? What options are you allowed to use when creating a view? Write a simple SQL statement that will create a view using the appropriate syntax. Perform some traditional operations such as SELECT or DELETE and then DROP the view.

2. Examine the database system you are using to determine how it supports indexes. You will undoubtedly have a wide range of options. Try out some of these options on a table that exists within your database. In particular, determine whether you are allowed to create UNIQUE or CLUSTERED indexes on a table within your database.

3. If possible, locate a table that has several thousand records. Use a stopwatch or clock to time various operations against the database. Add some indexes and see whether you can notice a performance improvement. Try to follow the tips given to you today.

10

Day **11**

Controlling Transactions

You have spent the last 10 days learning virtually everything that you can do with data within a relational database. For example, you know how to use the SQL SELECT statement to retrieve data from one or more tables based on a number of conditions supplied by the user. You have also had a chance to use data modification statements such as INSERT, UPDATE, and DELETE. As of today, you have become an intermediate-level SQL and database user. If required, you could build a database with its associated tables, each of which would contain several fields of different data types. Using proper design techniques, you could leverage the information contained within this database into a powerful application.

Objectives

If you are a casual user of SQL who occasionally needs to retrieve data from a database, the topics of the first 10 days provide most of the information you will need. However, if you intend to (or are currently required to) develop a professional application using any type of relational database, the advanced topics covered over the next four days—transaction control, security, embedded SQL programming, and database procedures—will help you a great deal. We begin with transaction control. By the end of the day, you will know the following:

- [ ] The basics of transaction control
- [ ] How to finalize and or cancel a transaction
- [ ] Some of the differences between Sybase and Oracle transactions

NOTE

> We used both Personal Oracle7 and Sybase's SQL Server to generate today's examples. Please see the documentation for your specific SQL implementation for any minor differences in syntax.

Transaction Control

Transaction control, or transaction management, refers to the capability of a relational database management system to perform database transactions. Transactions are units of work that must be done in a logical order and successfully as a group or not at all. The term *unit of work* means that a transaction has a beginning and an end. If anything goes wrong during the transaction, the entire unit of work can be canceled if desired. If everything looks good, the entire unit of work can be saved to the database.

In the coming months or years you will probably be implementing applications for multiple users to use across a network. Client/server environments are designed specifically for this purpose. Traditionally, a server (in this case, a database server) supports multiple network connections to it. As often happens with technology, this newfound flexibility adds a new degree of complexity to the environment. Consider the banking application described in the next few paragraphs.

The Banking Application

You are employed by First Federal Financial Bank to set up an application that handles checking account transactions that consist of debits and credits to customers' checking accounts. You have set up a nice database, which has been tested and verified to work correctly. After calling up your application, you verify that when you take $20 out of the account, $20 actually disappears from the database. When you add $50.25 to the checking account, this deposit shows up as expected. You proudly announce to your bosses that the system is ready to go, and several computers are set up in a local branch to begin work.

Within minutes, you notice a situation that you did not anticipate: As one teller is depositing a check, another teller is withdrawing money from the same account. Within minutes, many depositors' balances are incorrect because multiple users are updating tables simultaneously. Unfortunately, these multiple updates are overwriting each other. Shortly thereafter, your application is pulled offline for an overhaul. We will work through this problem with a database called CHECKING. Within this database are two tables, shown in Tables 11.1 and 11.2.

Table 11.1. The CUSTOMERS table.

Name	Address	City	State	Zip	Customer_ID
Bill Turner	725 N. Deal Parkway	Washington	DC	20085	1
John Keith	1220 Via De Luna Dr.	Jacksonville	FL	33581	2
Mary Rosenberg	482 Wannamaker Avenue	Williamsburg	VA	23478	3
David Blanken	405 N. Davis Highway	Greenville	SC	29652	4
Rebecca Little	7753 Woods Lane	Houston	TX	38764	5

Table 11.2. The BALANCES table.

Average_Bal	Curr_Bal	Account_ID
1298.53	854.22	1
5427.22	6015.96	2
211.25	190.01	3
73.79	25.87	4
1285.90	1473.75	5
1234.56	1543.67	6
345.25	348.03	7

Assume now that your application program performs a SELECT operation and retrieves the following data for Bill Turner:

```
NAME:  Bill Turner
ADDRESS:  725 N. Deal Parkway
CITY:  Washington
STATE:  DC
ZIP:  20085
CUSTOMER_ID:  1
```

While this information is being retrieved, another user with a connection to this database updates Bill Turner's address information:

INPUT

```
SQL> UPDATE CUSTOMERS SET Address = "11741 Kingstowne Road"
        WHERE Name =   "Bill Turner";
```

As you can see, the information you retrieved earlier could be invalid if the update occurred during the middle of your SELECT. If your application fired off a letter to be sent to Mr. Bill Turner, the address it used would be wrong. Obviously, if the letter has already been sent, you won't be able to change the address. However, if you had used a transaction, this data change could have been detected, and all your other operations could have been rolled back.

Beginning a Transaction

Transactions are quite simple to implement. You will examine the syntax used to perform transactions using the Oracle RDBMS SQL syntax as well as the Sybase SQL Server SQL syntax.

All database systems that support transactions must have a way to explicitly tell the system that a transaction is beginning. (Remember that a transaction is a logical grouping of work that has a beginning and an end.) Using Personal Oracle7, the syntax looks like this:

SYNTAX

```
SET TRANSACTION {READ ONLY ¦ USE ROLLBACK SEGMENT segment}
```

The SQL standard specifies that each database's SQL implementation must support statement-level read consistency; that is, data must stay consistent while one statement is executing. However, in many situations data must remain valid across a single unit of work, not just within a single statement. Oracle enables the user to specify when the transaction will begin by using the SET TRANSACTION statement. If you wanted to examine Bill Turner's information and make sure that the data was not changed, you could do the following:

INPUT

```
SQL> SET TRANSACTION READ ONLY;
SQL> SELECT * FROM CUSTOMERS
        WHERE NAME = 'Bill Turner';

---Do Other Operations---

SQL> COMMIT;
```

We discuss the COMMIT statement later today. The SET TRANSACTION READ ONLY option enables you to effectively lock a set of records until the transaction ends. You can use the READ ONLY option with the following commands:

```
SELECT

LOCK TABLE

SET ROLE
```

```
ALTER SESSION

ALTER SYSTEM
```

The option USE ROLLBACK SEGMENT tells Oracle which database segment to use for rollback storage space. This option is an Oracle extension to standard SQL syntax. Consult your Oracle documentation for more information on using segments to maintain your database.

SQL Server's Transact-SQL language implements the BEGIN TRANSACTION command with the following syntax:

SYNTAX

```
begin {transaction | tran} [transaction_name]
```

This implementation is a little different from the Oracle implementation. (Sybase does not allow you to specify the READ ONLY option.) However, Sybase does allow you to give a transaction a name, as long as that transaction is the outermost of a set of nested transactions.

The following group of statements illustrates the use of nested transactions using Sybase's Transact-SQL language:

INPUT

```
1> begin transaction new_account
2> insert CUSTOMERS values ("Izetta Parsons", "1285 Pineapple Highway",
➥"Greenville", "AL"  32854, 6)
3> if exists(select * from CUSTOMERS where Name = "Izetta Parsons")
4> begin
5> begin transaction
6> insert BALANCES values(1250.76, 1431.26, 8)
7> end
8> else
9> rollback transaction
10> if exists(select * from BALANCES where Account_ID = 8)
11> begin
12> begin transaction
13> insert ACCOUNTS values(8, 6)
14> end
15> else
16> rollback transaction
17> if exists (select * from ACCOUNTS where Account_ID = 8 and
➥Customer_ID = 6)
18> commit transaction
19> else
20> rollback transaction
21> go
```

For now, don't worry about the ROLLBACK TRANSACTION and COMMIT TRANSACTION statements. The important aspect of this example is the nested transaction—or a transaction within a transaction.

Notice that the original transaction (new_account) begins on line 1. After the first insert, you check to make sure the INSERT was executed properly. Another transaction begins on line 5. This transaction within a transaction is termed a *nested transaction*.

Other databases support the AUTOCOMMIT option. This option can be used with the SET command. For example:

```
SET AUTOCOMMIT [ON ¦ OFF]
```

By default, the SET AUTOCOMMIT ON command is executed at startup. It tells SQL to automatically commit all statements you execute. If you do not want these commands to be automatically executed, set the AUTOCOMMIT option to off:

```
SET AUTOCOMMIT OFF
```

> **NOTE**
>
> Check your database system's documentation to determine how you would begin a transaction.

Finishing a Transaction

The Oracle syntax to end a transaction is as follows:

```
COMMIT [WORK]
[ COMMENT 'text'
¦ FORCE 'text' [, integer] ] ;
```

Here is the same command using Sybase syntax:

```
COMMIT (TRANSACTION ¦ TRAN ¦ WORK) (TRANSACTION_NAME)
```

The COMMIT command saves all changes made during a transaction. Executing a COMMIT statement before beginning a transaction ensures that no errors were made and no previous transactions are left hanging.

The following example verifies that the COMMIT command can be used by itself without receiving an error back from the database system.

INPUT
```
SQL> COMMIT;
SQL> SET TRANSACTION READ ONLY;
SQL> SELECT * FROM CUSTOMERS
     WHERE NAME = 'Bill Turner';

---Do Other Operations---

SQL> COMMIT;
```

An Oracle SQL use of the COMMIT statement would look like this:

INPUT
```
SQL> SET TRANSACTION;
SQL> INSERT INTO CUSTOMERS VALUES
     ("John MacDowell", "2000 Lake Lunge Road", "Chicago", "IL", 42854, 7);
SQL> COMMIT;
SQL> SELECT * FROM CUSTOMERS;
```

The CUSTOMERS **table.**

Name	Address	City	State	Zip	Customer_ID
Bill Turner	725 N. Deal Parkway	Washington	DC	20085	1
John Keith	1220 Via De Luna Dr.	Jacksonville	FL	33581	2
Mary Rosenberg	482 Wannamaker Avenue	Williamsburg	VA	23478	3
David Blanken	405 N. Davis Highway	Greenville	SC	29652	4
Rebecca Little	7753 Woods Lane	Houston	TX	38764	5
Izetta Parsons	1285 Pineapple Highway	Greenville	AL	32854	6
John MacDowell	2000 Lake Lunge Road	Chicago	IL	42854	7

A Sybase SQL use of the COMMIT statement would look like this:

INPUT

```
1> begin transaction
2> insert into CUSTOMERS values
   ("John MacDowell", "2000 Lake Lunge Road", "Chicago", "IL", 42854, 7)
3> commit transaction
4> go
1> select * from CUSTOMERS
2> go
```

The CUSTOMERS **table.**

Name	Address	City	State	Zip	Customer_ID
Bill Turner	725 N. Deal Parkway	Washington	DC	20085	1
John Keith	1220 Via De Luna Dr.	Jacksonville	FL	33581	2
Mary Rosenberg	482 Wannamaker Avenue	Williamsburg	VA	23478	3
David Blanken	405 N. Davis Highway	Greenville	SC	29652	4
Rebecca Little	7753 Woods Lane	Houston	TX	38764	5
Izetta Parsons	1285 Pineapple Highway	Greenville	AL	32854	6
John MacDowell	2000 Lake Lunge Road	Chicago	IL	42854	7

The preceding statements accomplish the same thing as they do using the Oracle7 syntax. However, by putting the COMMIT command soon after the transaction begins, you ensure that the new transaction will execute correctly.

NOTE   The COMMIT WORK command performs the same operation as the COMMIT command (or Sybase's COMMIT TRANSACTION command). It is provided simply to comply with ANSI SQL syntax.

Remember that every COMMIT command must correspond with a previously executed SET TRANSACTION or BEGIN TRANSACTION command. Note the errors you receive with the following statements:

Oracle SQL:

INPUT
```
SQL> INSERT INTO BALANCES values (18765.42, 19073.06, 8);
SQL> COMMIT WORK;
```

Sybase SQL:

INPUT
```
1> insert into BALANCES values (18765.42, 19073.06, 8)
2> commit work
```

Canceling the Transaction

While a transaction is in progress, some type of error checking is usually performed to determine whether it is executing successfully. You can undo your transaction even after successful completion by issuing the ROLLBACK statement, but it must be issued before a COMMIT. The ROLLBACK statement must be executed from within a transaction. The ROLLBACK statement rolls the transaction back to its beginning; in other words, the state of the database is returned to what it was at the transaction's beginning. The syntax for this command using Oracle7 is the following:

```
ROLLBACK [WORK]
[ TO [SAVEPOINT] savepoint
¦ FORCE 'text' ]
```

As you can see, this command makes use of a transaction savepoint. We discuss this technique later today.

Sybase Transact-SQL's ROLLBACK statement looks very similar to the COMMIT command:

```
rollback {transaction ¦ tran ¦ work}
  [transaction_name ¦ savepoint_name]
```

An Oracle SQL sequence of commands might look like this:

INPUT
```
SQL> SET TRANSACTION;
SQL> INSERT INTO CUSTOMERS VALUES
        ("Bubba MacDowell", "2222 Blue Lake Way", "Austin", "TX", 39874, 8);
SQL> ROLLBACK;
SQL> SELECT * FROM CUSTOMERS;
```

The CUSTOMERS table.

Name	Address	City	State	Zip	Customer_ID
Bill Turner	725 N. Deal Parkway	Washington	DC	20085	1
John Keith	1220 Via De Luna Dr.	Jacksonville	FL	33581	2

Name	Address	City	State	Zip	Customer_ID
Mary Rosenberg	482 Wannamaker Avenue	Williamsburg	VA	23478	3
David Blanken	405 N. Davis Highway	Greenville	SC	29652	4
Rebecca Little	7753 Woods Lane	Houston	TX	38764	5
Izetta Parsons	1285 Pineapple Highway	Greenville	AL	32854	6
John MacDowell	2000 Lake Lunge Road	Chicago	IL	42854	7

A Sybase SQL sequence of commands might look like this:

```
1> begin transaction
2> insert into CUSTOMERS values
   ("Bubba MacDowell", "2222 Blue Lake Way", "Austin", "TX", 39874, 8)
3> rollback transaction
4> go
1> SELECT * FROM CUSTOMERS
2> go
```

INPUT

The CUSTOMERS table.

Name	Address	City	State	Zip	Customer_ID
Bill Turner	725 N. Deal Parkway	Washington	DC	20085	1
John Keith	1220 Via De Luna Dr.	Jacksonville	FL	33581	2
Mary Rosenberg	482 Wannamaker Avenue	Williamsburg	VA	23478	3
David Blanken	405 N. Davis Highway	Greenville	SC	29652	4
Rebecca Little	7753 Woods Lane	Houston	TX	38764	5
Izetta Parsons	1285 Pineapple Highway	Greenville	AL	32854	6
John MacDowell	2000 Lake Lunge Road	Chicago	IL	42854	7

As you can see, the new record was not added because the ROLLBACK statement rolled the insert back.

Suppose you are writing an application for a graphical user interface, such as Microsoft Windows. You have a dialog box that queries a database and allows the user to change values. If the user chooses OK, the database saves the changes. If the user chooses Cancel, the changes are canceled. Obviously, this situation gives you an opportunity to use a transaction.

NOTE

The following code listing uses Oracle SQL syntax; notice the SQL> prompt and line numbers. The subsequent listing uses Sybase SQL syntax, which lacks the SQL> prompt.

When the dialog box is loaded, these SQL statements are executed:

INPUT/
OUTPUT

```
SQL> SET TRANSACTION;
SQL> SELECT CUSTOMERS.NAME, BALANCES.CURR_BAL, BALANCES.ACCOUNT_ID
   2 FROM CUSTOMERS, BALANCES
   3 WHERE CUSTOMERS.NAME = "Rebecca Little"
   4 AND CUSTOMERS.CUSTOMER_ID = BALANCES.ACCOUNT_ID;
```

The dialog box allows the user to change the current account balance, so you need to store this value back to the database.

When the user selects OK, the update will run.

INPUT

```
SQL> UPDATE BALANCES SET CURR_BAL = 'new-value' WHERE ACCOUNT_ID = 6;
SQL> COMMIT;
```

When the user selects Cancel, the ROLLBACK statement is issued.

INPUT

```
SQL> ROLLBACK;
```

When the dialog box is loaded using Sybase SQL, these SQL statements are executed:

INPUT

```
1> begin transaction
2> select CUSTOMERS.Name, BALANCES.Curr_Bal, BALANCES.Account_ID
3> from CUSTOMERS, BALANCES
4> where CUSTOMERS.Name = "Rebecca Little"
5> and CUSTOMERS.Customer_ID = BALANCES.Account_ID
6> go
```

The dialog box allows the user to change the current account balance, so you can store this value back to the database.

Here again, when the OK button is selected, the update will run.

INPUT

```
1> update BALANCES set Curr_BAL = 'new-value' WHERE Account_ID = 6
2> commit transaction
3> go
```

When the user selects Cancel, the ROLLBACK statement is issued.

INPUT

```
1> rollback transaction
2> go
```

The ROLLBACK statement cancels the entire transaction. When you are nesting transactions, the ROLLBACK statement completely cancels all the transactions, rolling them back to the beginning of the outermost transaction.

If no transaction is currently active, issuing the ROLLBACK statement or the COMMIT command has no effect on the database system. (Think of them as dead commands with no purpose.)

After the COMMIT statement has been executed, all actions with the transaction are executed. At this point it is too late to roll back the transaction.

Using Transaction Savepoints

Rolling back a transaction cancels the entire transaction. But suppose you want to "semicommit" your transaction midway through its statements. Both Sybase and Oracle SQL allow you to save the transaction with a *savepoint*. From that point on, if a ROLLBACK is issued, the transaction is rolled back to the savepoint. All statements that were executed up to the point of the savepoint are saved. The syntax for creating a savepoint using Oracle SQL is as follows:

```
SAVEPOINT savepoint_name;
```

Sybase SQL Server's syntax to create a savepoint is the following:

```
save transaction savepoint_name
```

This following example uses Oracle SQL syntax.

INPUT
```
SQL> SET TRANSACTION;
SQL> UPDATE BALANCES SET CURR_BAL = 25000 WHERE ACCOUNT_ID = 5;
SQL> SAVEPOINT save_it;
SQL> DELETE FROM BALANCES WHERE ACCOUNT_ID = 5;
SQL> ROLLBACK TO SAVEPOINT save_it;
SQL> COMMIT;
SQL> SELECT * FROM BALANCES;
```

The BALANCES table.

Average_Bal	Curr_Bal	Account_ID
1298.53	854.22	1
5427.22	6015.96	2
211.25	190.01	3
73.79	25.87	4
1285.90	25000.00	5
1234.56	1543.67	6
345.25	348.03	7
1250.76	1431.26	8

This example uses Sybase SQL syntax:

INPUT
```
1> begin transaction
2> update BALANCES set Curr_Bal = 25000 where Account_ID = 5
3> save transaction save_it
4> delete from BALANCES where Account_ID = 5
5> rollback transaction save_it
6> commit transaction
7> go
1> select * from BALANCES
2> go
```

The BALANCES table.

Average_Bal	Curr_Bal	Account_ID
1298.53	854.22	1
5427.22	6015.96	2
211.25	190.01	3
73.79	25.87	4
1285.90	25000.00	5
1234.56	1543.67	6
345.25	348.03	7
1250.76	1431.26	8

The previous examples created a savepoint called SAVE_IT. An update was made to the database that changed the value of the CURR_BAL column of the BALANCES table. You then saved this change as a savepoint. Following this save, you executed a DELETE statement, but you rolled the transaction back to the savepoint immediately thereafter. Then you executed COMMIT TRANSACTION, which committed all commands up to the savepoint. Had you executed a ROLLBACK TRANSACTION after the ROLLBACK TRANSACTION savepoint_name command, the entire transaction would have been rolled back and no changes would have been made.

This example uses Oracle SQL syntax:

```
SQL> SET TRANSACTION;
SQL> UPDATE BALANCES SET CURR_BAL = 25000 WHERE ACCOUNT_ID = 5;
SQL> SAVEPOINT save_it;
SQL> DELETE FROM BALANCES WHERE ACCOUNT_ID = 5;
SQL> ROLLBACK TO SAVEPOINT save_it;
SQL> ROLLBACK;
SQL> SELECT * FROM BALANCES;
```

INPUT

The BALANCES table.

Average_Bal	Curr_Bal	Account_ID
1298.53	854.22	1
5427.22	6015.96	2
211.25	190.01	3
73.79	25.87	4
1285.90	1473.75	5
1234.56	1543.67	6
345.25	348.03	7
1250.76	1431.26	8

This example uses Sybase SQL syntax:

INPUT

```
1> begin transaction
2> update BALANCES set Curr_Bal = 25000 where Account_ID = 5
3> save transaction save_it
4> delete from BALANCES where Account_ID = 5
5> rollback transaction save_it
6> rollback transaction
7> go
1> select * from BALANCES
2> go
```

The BALANCES table.

Average_Bal	Curr_Bal	Account_ID
1298.53	854.22	1
5427.22	6015.96	2
211.25	190.01	3
73.79	25.87	4
1285.90	1473.75	5
1234.56	1543.67	6
345.25	348.03	7
1250.76	1431.26	8

Summary

A transaction can be defined as an organized unit of work. A transaction usually performs a series of operations that depend on previously executed operations. If one of these operations is not executed properly or if data is changed for some reason, the rest of the work in a transaction should be canceled. Otherwise, if all statements are executed correctly, the transaction's work should be saved.

The process of canceling a transaction is called a *rollback*. The process of saving the work of a correctly executed transaction is called a *commit*. SQL syntax supports these two processes through syntax similar to the following two statements:

```
BEGIN TRANSACTION
      statement 1
      statement 2
      statement 3
ROLLBACK TRANSACTION
```

or

```
BEGIN TRANSACTION
       statement 1
       statement 2
       statement 3
COMMIT TRANSACTION
```

Q&A

Q If I have a group of transactions and one transaction is unsuccessful, will the rest of the transactions process?

A No. The entire group must run successfully.

Q After issuing the COMMIT command, I discovered that I made a mistake. How can I correct the error?

A Use the DELETE, INSERT, and UPDATE commands.

Q Must I issue the COMMIT command after every transaction?

A No. But it is safer to do so to ensure that no errors were made and no previous transactions are left hanging.

Workshop

The Workshop provides quiz questions to help solidify your understanding of the material covered, as well as exercises to provide you with experience in using what you have learned. Try to answer the quiz and exercise questions before checking the answers in Appendix F, "Answers to Quizzes and Exercises."

Quiz

1. When nesting transactions, does issuing a ROLLBACK TRANSACTION command cancel the current transaction and roll back the batch of statements into the upper-level transaction? Why or why not?

2. Can savepoints be used to "save off" portions of a transaction? Why or why not?

3. Can a COMMIT command be used by itself or must it be embedded?

4. If you issue the COMMIT command and then discover a mistake, can you still use the ROLLBACK command?

5. Will using a savepoint in the middle of a transaction save all that happened before it automatically?

Exercises

1. Use Personal Oracle7 syntax and correct the syntax (if necessary) for the following:

```
SQL> START TRANSACTION
     INSERT INTO CUSTOMERS VALUES
     ('SMITH', 'JOHN')
SQL> COMMIT;
```

2. Use Personal Oracle7 syntax and correct the syntax (if necessary) for the following:

```
SQL> SET TRANSACTION;
     UPDATE BALANCES SET CURR_BAL = 25000;
SQL> COMMIT;
```

3. Use Personal Oracle7 syntax and correct the syntax (if necessary) for the following:

```
SQL> SET TRANSACTION;
     INSERT INTO BALANCES VALUES
     ('567.34', '230.00', '8');
SQL> ROLLBACK;
```

11

Day **12**

Database Security

Today we discuss database security. We specifically look at various SQL statements and constructs that enable you to administer and effectively manage a relational database. Like many other topics you have studied thus far, how a database management system implements security varies widely among products. We focus on the popular database product Oracle7 to introduce this topic. By the end of the day, you will understand and be able to do the following:

- ☐ Create users
- ☐ Change passwords
- ☐ Create roles
- ☐ Use views for security purposes
- ☐ Use synonyms in place of views

Wanted: Database Administrator

Security is an often-overlooked aspect of database design. Most computer professionals enter the computer world with some knowledge of computer programming or hardware, and they tend to concentrate on those areas. For instance, if your boss asked you to work on a brand-new project that obviously required some type of relational database design, what would be your first step? After choosing some type of hardware and software baseline, you would probably begin by designing the basic database for the project. This phase would gradually be split up among several people—one of them a graphical user interface designer, another a low-level component builder. Perhaps you, after reading this book, might be asked to code the SQL queries to provide the guts of the application. Along with this task comes the responsibility of actually administering and maintaining the database.

Many times, little thought or planning goes into the actual production phase of the application. What happens when many users are allowed to use the application across a wide area network (WAN)? With today's powerful personal computer software and with technologies such as Microsoft's Open Database Connectivity (ODBC), any user with access to your network can find a way to get at your database. (We won't even bring up the complexities involved when your company decides to hook your LAN to the Internet or some other wide-ranging computer network!) Are you prepared to face this situation?

Fortunately for you, software manufacturers provide most of the tools you need to handle this security problem. Every new release of a network operating system faces more stringent security requirements than its predecessors. In addition, most major database vendors build some degree of security into their products, which exists independently of your operating system or network security. Implementation of these security features varies widely from product to product.

Popular Database Products and Security

As you know by now, many relational database systems are vying for your business. Every vendor wants you for short- and long-term reasons. During the development phase of a project, you might purchase a small number of product licenses for testing, development, and so forth. However, the total number of licenses required for your production database can reach the hundreds or even thousands. In addition, when you decide to use a particular database product, the chances are good that you will stay with that product for years to come. Here are some points to keep in mind when you examine these products:

☐ Microsoft FoxPro database management system is a powerful database system that is used primarily in single-user environments. FoxPro uses a limited subset of SQL. No security measures are provided with the system. It also uses an Xbase file format, with each file containing one table. Indexes are stored in separate files.

☐ Microsoft Access relational database management system implements more of SQL. Access is still intended for use on the PC platform, although it does contain a rudimentary security system. The product enables you to build queries and store them within the database. In addition, the entire database and all its objects exist within one file.

12

☐ Oracle7 relational database management system supports nearly the full SQL standard. In addition, Oracle has added its own extension to SQL, called PL*SQL. It contains full security features, including the capability to create roles and assign permissions and privileges on objects in the database.

☐ Sybase SQL Server is similar in power and features to the Oracle product. SQL Server also provides a wide range of security features and has its own extensions to the SQL language, called Transact-SQL.

The purpose behind describing these products is to illustrate that not all software is suitable for every application. If you are in a business environment, your options may be limited. Factors such as cost and performance are extremely important. However, without adequate security measures, any savings your database creates can be easily offset by security problems.

How Does a Database Become Secure?

Up to this point you haven't worried much about the "security" of the databases you have created. Has it occurred to you that you might not want other users to come in and tamper with the database information you have so carefully entered? What would your reaction be if you logged on to the server one morning and discovered that the database you had slaved over had been dropped (remember how silent the DROP DATABASE command is)? We examine in some detail how one popular database management system (Personal Oracle7) enables you to set up a secure database. You will be able to apply most of this information to other database management systems, so make sure you read this information even if Oracle is not your system of choice.

 TIP

> Keep the following questions in mind as you plan your security system:
>
> ☐ Who gets the DBA role?
>
> ☐ How many users will need access to the database?
>
> ☐ Which users will need which privileges and which roles?
>
> ☐ How will you remove users who no longer need access to the database?

12

Personal Oracle7 and Security

Oracle7 implements security by using three constructs:

☐ Users

☐ Roles

☐ Privileges

Creating Users

Users are account names that are allowed to log on to the Oracle database. The SQL syntax used to create a new user follows.

```
CREATE USER user
IDENTIFIED {BY password ¦ EXTERNALLY}
[DEFAULT TABLESPACE tablespace]
[TEMPORARY TABLESPACE tablespace]
[QUOTA {integer [K¦M] ¦ UNLIMITED} ON tablespace]
[PROFILE profile]
```

If the BY password option is chosen, the system prompts the user to enter a password each time he or she logs on. As an example, create a username for yourself:

INPUT/ OUTPUT

```
SQL> CREATE USER Bryan IDENTIFIED BY CUTIGER;

User created.
```

Each time I log on with my username Bryan, I am prompted to enter my password: CUTIGER.

If the EXTERNALLY option is chosen, Oracle relies on your computer system logon name and password. When you log on to your system, you have essentially logged on to Oracle.

NOTE

> Some implementations allow you to use the external, or operating system, password as a default when using SQL (IDENTIFIED externally). However, we recommend that you force the user to enter a password by utilizing the IDENTIFIED BY clause (IDENTIFIED BY password).

As you can see from looking at the rest of the CREATE USER syntax, Oracle also allows you to set up default tablespaces and quotas. You can learn more about these topics by examining the Oracle documentation.

As with every other CREATE command you have learned about in this book, there is also an ALTER USER command. It looks like this:

```
ALTER USER user
[IDENTIFIED {BY password ¦ EXTERNALLY}]
[DEFAULT TABLESPACE tablespace]
[TEMPORARY TABLESPACE tablespace]
[QUOTA {integer [K¦M] ¦ UNLIMITED} ON tablespace]
[PROFILE profile]
[DEFAULT ROLE { role [, role] ...
    ¦ ALL [EXCEPT role [, role] ...] ¦ NONE}]
```

You can use this command to change all the user's options, including the password and profile. For example, to change the user Bryan's password, you type this:

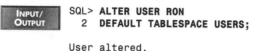

```
SQL> ALTER USER Bryan
  2  IDENTIFIED BY ROSEBUD;
```

User altered.

To change the default tablespace, type this:

```
SQL> ALTER USER RON
  2  DEFAULT TABLESPACE USERS;
```

User altered.

To remove a user, simply issue the DROP USER command, which removes the user's entry in the system database. Here's the syntax for this command:

```
DROP USER user_name [CASCADE];
```

If the CASCADE option is used, all objects owned by username are dropped along with the user's account. If CASCADE is not used and the user denoted by user_name still owns objects, that user is not dropped. This feature is somewhat confusing, but it is useful if you ever want to drop users.

Creating Roles

A *role* is a privilege or set of privileges that allows a user to perform certain functions in the database. To grant a role to a user, use the following syntax:

```
GRANT role TO user [WITH ADMIN OPTION];
```

If WITH ADMIN OPTION is used, that user can then grant roles to other users. Isn't power exhilarating?

To remove a role, use the REVOKE command:

```
REVOKE role FROM user;
```

When you log on to the system using the account you created earlier, you have exhausted the limits of your permissions. You can log on, but that is about all you can do. Oracle lets you register as one of three roles:

- ☐ Connect
- ☐ Resource
- ☐ DBA (or database administrator)

These three roles have varying degrees of privileges.

NOTE

If you have the appropriate privileges, you can create your own role, grant privileges to your role, and then grant your role to a user for further security.

The Connect Role

The Connect role can be thought of as the entry-level role. A user who has been granted Connect role access can be granted various privileges that allow him or her to do something with a database.

INPUT/
OUTPUT

```
SQL> GRANT CONNECT TO Bryan;

Grant succeeded.
```

The Connect role enables the user to select, insert, update, and delete records from tables belonging to other users (after the appropriate permissions have been granted). The user can also create tables, views, sequences, clusters, and synonyms.

The Resource Role

The Resource role gives the user more access to Oracle databases. In addition to the permissions that can be granted to the Connect role, Resource roles can also be granted permission to create procedures, triggers, and indexes.

INPUT/
OUTPUT

```
SQL> GRANT RESOURCE TO Bryan;

Grant succeeded.
```

The DBA Role

The DBA role includes all privileges. Users with this role are able to do essentially anything they want to the database system. You should keep the number of users with this role to a minimum to ensure system integrity.

INPUT/
OUTPUT

```
SQL> GRANT DBA TO Bryan;

Grant succeeded.
```

After the three preceding steps, user Bryan was granted the Connect, Resource, and DBA roles. This is somewhat redundant because the DBA role encompasses the other two roles, so you can drop them now:

INPUT/
OUTPUT

```
SQL> REVOKE CONNECT FROM Bryan;

Revoke succeeded.

SQL> REVOKE RESOURCE FROM Bryan;

Revoke succeeded.
```

Bryan can do everything he needs to do with the DBA role.

User Privileges

After you decide which roles to grant your users, your next step is deciding which permissions these users will have on database objects. (Oracle7 calls these permissions *privileges.*) The types of privileges vary, depending on what role you have been granted. If you actually create an object, you can grant privileges on that object to other users as long as their role permits access to that privilege. Oracle defines two types of privileges that can be granted to users: system privileges and object privileges. (See Tables 12.1 and 12.2.)

System privileges apply systemwide. The syntax used to grant a system privilege is as follows:

```
GRANT system_privilege TO {user_name ¦ role ¦ PUBLIC}
[WITH ADMIN OPTION];
```

WITH ADMIN OPTION enables the grantee to grant this privilege to someone else.

User Access to Views

The following command permits all users of the system to have CREATE VIEW access within their own schema.

INPUT

```
SQL> GRANT CREATE VIEW
  2  TO PUBLIC;
```

OUTPUT

```
Grant succeeded.
```

ANALYSIS The public keyword means that everyone has CREATE VIEW privileges. Obviously, these system privileges enable the grantee to have a lot of access to nearly all the system settings. System privileges should be granted only to special users or to users who have a need to use these privileges. Table 12.1 shows the system privileges you will find in the help files included with Personal Oracle7.

WARNING

Use caution when granting privileges to public. Granting public gives all users with access to the database privileges you may not want them to have.

12

Table 12.1. System privileges in Oracle7.

System Privilege	Operations Permitted
ALTER ANY INDEX	Allows the grantees to alter any index in any schema.
ALTER ANY PROCEDURE	Allows the grantees to alter any stored procedure, function, or package in any schema.
ALTER ANY ROLE	Allows the grantees to alter any role in the database.
ALTER ANY TABLE	Allows the grantees to alter any table or view in the schema.
ALTER ANY TRIGGER	Allows the grantees to enable, disable, or compile any database trigger in any schema.

continues

Table 12.1. continued

System Privilege	Operations Permitted
ALTER DATABASE	Allows the grantees to alter the database.
ALTER USER	Allows the grantees to alter any user. This privilege authorizes the grantee to change another user's password or authentication method, assign quotas on any tablespace, set default and temporary tablespaces, and assign a profile and default roles.
CREATE ANY INDEX	Allows the grantees to create an index on any table in any schema.
CREATE ANY PROCEDURE	Allows the grantees to create stored procedures, functions, and packages in any schema.
ONCATE ANY TABLE	Allows the grantees to create tables in any schema. The owner of the schema containing the table must have space quota on the tablespace to contain the table.
CREATE ANY TRIGGER	Allows the grantees to create a database trigger in any schema associated with a table in any schema.
CREATE ANY VIEW	Allows the grantees to create views in any schema.
CREATE PROCEDURE	Allows the grantees to create stored procedures, functions, and packages in their own schema.
CREATE PROFILE	Allows the grantees to create profiles.
CREATE ROLE	Allows the grantees to create roles.
CREATE SYNONYM	Allows the grantees to create synonyms in their own schemas.
CREATE TABLE	Allows the grantees to create tables in their own schemas. To create a table, the grantees must also have space quota on the tablespace to contain the table.
CREATE TRIGGER	Allows the grantees to create a database trigger in their own schemas.
CREATE USER	Allows the grantees to create users. This privilege also allows the creator to assign quotas on any tablespace, set default and temporary tablespaces, and assign a profile as part of a CREATE USER statement.
CREATE VIEW	Allows the grantees to create views in their own schemas.
DELETE ANY TABLE	Allows the grantees to delete rows from tables or views in any schema or truncate tables in any schema.
DROP ANY INDEX	Allows the grantees to drop indexes in any schema.

System Privilege	Operations Permitted
DROP ANY PROCEDURE	Allows the grantees to drop stored procedures, functions, or packages in any schema.
DROP ANY ROLE	Allows the grantees to drop roles.
DROP ANY SYNONYM	Allows the grantees to drop private synonyms in any schema.
DROP ANY TABLE	Allows the grantees to drop tables in any schema.
DROP ANY TRIGGER	Allows the grantees to drop database triggers in any schema.
DROP ANY VIEW	Allows the grantees to drop views in any schema.
DROP USER	Allows the grantees to drop users.
EXECUTE ANY PROCEDURE	Allows the grantees to execute procedures or functions (standalone or packaged) or reference public package variables in any schema.
GRANT ANY PRIVILEGE	Allows the grantees to grant any system privilege.
GRANT ANY ROLE	Allows the grantees to grant any role in the database.
INSERT ANY TABLE	Allows the grantees to insert rows into tables and views in any schema.
LOCK ANY TABLE	Allows the grantees to lock tables and views in any schema.
SELECT ANY SEQUENCE	Allows the grantees to reference sequences in any schema.
SELECT ANY TABLE	Allows the grantees to query tables, views, or snapshots in any schema.
UPDATE ANY ROWS	Allows the grantees to update rows in tables.

Object privileges are privileges that can be used against specific database objects. Table 12.2 lists the object privileges in Oracle7.

Table 12.2. Object privileges enabled under Oracle7.

ALL
ALTER
DELETE
EXECUTE
INDEX
INSERT
REFERENCES
SELECT
UPDATE

12

You can use the following form of the GRANT statement to give other users access to your tables:

```
GRANT {object_priv ¦ ALL [PRIVILEGES]} [ (column
[, column]...) ]
[, {object_priv ¦ ALL [PRIVILEGES]} [ (column
[, column] ...) ] ] ...
ON [schema.]object
TO {user ¦ role ¦ PUBLIC} [, {user ¦ role ¦ PUBLIC}] ...
[WITH GRANT OPTION]
```

To remove the object privileges you have granted to someone, use the REVOKE command with the following syntax:

```
REVOKE {object_priv ¦ ALL [PRIVILEGES]}
[, {object_priv ¦ ALL [PRIVILEGES]} ]
ON [schema.]object
FROM {user ¦ role ¦ PUBLIC} [, {user ¦ role ¦ PUBLIC}]
[CASCADE CONSTRAINTS]
```

From Creating a Table to Granting Roles

Create a table named SALARIES with the following structure:

INPUT

```
NAME, CHAR(30)
SALARY, NUMBER
AGE, NUMBER

SQL> CREATE TABLE SALARIES (
  2    NAME CHAR(30),
  3    SALARY NUMBER,
  4    AGE NUMBER);
```

OUTPUT   Table created.

Now, create two users—Jack and Jill:

**INPUT/
OUTPUT**

```
SQL> create user Jack identified by Jack;

User created.

SQL> create user Jill identified by Jill;

User created.

SQL> grant connect to Jack;

Grant succeeded.

SQL> grant resource to Jill;

Grant succeeded.
```

ANALYSIS So far, you have created two users and granted each a different role. Therefore, they will have different capabilities when working with the database. First create the SALARIES table with the following information:

INPUT/ OUTPUT
```
SQL> SELECT * FROM SALARIES;

NAME                                 SALARY      AGE
-----------------------------------  ----------  ----------
JACK                                  35000        29
JILL                                  48000        42
JOHN                                  61000        55
```

ANALYSIS You could then grant various privileges to this table based on some arbitrary reasons for this example. We are assuming that you currently have DBA privileges and can grant any system privilege. Even if you do not have DBA privileges, you can still grant object privileges on the SALARIES table because you own it (assuming you just created it).

Because Jack belongs only to the Connect role, you want him to have only SELECT privileges.

INPUT/ OUTPUT
```
SQL> GRANT SELECT ON SALARIES TO JACK;

Grant succeeded.
```

Because Jill belongs to the Resource role, you allow her to select and insert some data into the table. To liven things up a bit, allow Jill to update values only in the SALARY field of the SALARIES table.

INPUT/ OUTPUT
```
SQL> GRANT SELECT, UPDATE(SALARY) ON SALARIES TO Jill;

Grant succeeded.
```

Now that this table and these users have been created, you need to look at how a user accesses a table that was created by another user. Both Jack and Jill have been granted SELECT access on the SALARIES table. However, if Jack tries to access the SALARIES table, he will be told that it does not exist because Oracle requires the username or schema that owns the table to precede the table name.

Qualifying a Table

Make a note of the username you used to create the SALARIES table (mine was Bryan). For Jack to select data out of the SALARIES table, he must address the SALARIES table with that username.

INPUT
```
SQL> SELECT * FROM SALARIES;
SELECT * FROM SALARIES
              *
```

OUTPUT
```
ERROR at line 1:
ORA-00942: table or view does not exist
```

Here Jack was warned that the table did not exist. Now use the owner's username to identify the table:

```
SQL> SELECT *
  2  FROM Bryan.SALARIES;

NAME                            SALARY       AGE
------------------------------- ---------- ----------
JACK                             35000        29
JILL                             48000        42
JOHN                             61000        55
```

You can see that now the query worked. Now test out Jill's access privileges. First log out of Jack's logon and log on again as Jill (using the password Jill).

```
SQL> SELECT *
  2  FROM Bryan.SALARIES;

NAME                            SALARY       AGE
------------------------------- ---------- ----------
JACK                             35000        29
JILL                             48000        42
JOHN                             61000        55
```

That worked just fine. Now try to insert a new record into the table.

```
SQL> INSERT INTO Bryan.SALARIES
  2  VALUES('JOE',85000,38);
INSERT INTO Bryan.SALARIES
            *
ERROR at line 1:
ORA-01031: insufficient privileges
```

This operation did not work because Jill does not have INSERT privileges on the SALARIES table.

```
SQL> UPDATE Bryan.SALARIES
  2  SET AGE = 42
  3  WHERE NAME = 'JOHN';
UPDATE Bryan.SALARIES
       *
ERROR at line 1:
ORA-01031: insufficient privileges
```

Once again, Jill tried to go around the privileges that she had been given. Naturally, Oracle caught this error and corrected her quickly.

```
SQL> UPDATE Bryan.SALARIES
  2  SET SALARY = 35000
  3  WHERE NAME = 'JOHN';

1 row updated.

SQL> SELECT *
  2  FROM Bryan.SALARIES;
```

```
NAME                                 SALARY        AGE
- - - - - - - - - - - - - - - - -    - - - - - -   - - - - - - - -
JACK                                 35000         29
JILL                                 48000         42
JOHN                                 35000         55
```

ANALYSIS You can see now that the update works as long as Jill abides by the privileges she has been given.

Using Views for Security Purposes

As we mentioned on Day 10, "Creating Views and Indexes," views are virtual tables that you can use to present a view of data that is different from the way it physically exists in the database. Today you will learn more about how to use views to implement security measures. First, however, we explain how views can simplify SQL statements.

Earlier you learned that when a user must access a table or database object that another user owns, that object must be referenced with a username. As you can imagine, this procedure can get wordy if you have to write writing several SQL queries in a row. More important, novice users would be required to determine the owner of a table before they could select the contents of a table, which is not something you want all your users to do. One simple solution is shown in the following paragraph.

A Solution to Qualifying a Table or View

Assume that you are logged on as Jack, your friend from earlier examples. You learned that for Jack to look at the contents of the SALARIES table, he must use the following statement:

INPUT
```
SQL> SELECT *
  2  FROM Bryan.SALARIES;
```

OUTPUT
```
NAME                                 SALARY        AGE
- - - - - - - - - - - - - - - -      - - - - - -   - - - - - - - -
JACK                                 35000         29
JILL                                 48000         42
JOHN                                 35000         55
```

If you were to create a view named SALARY_VIEW, a user could simply select from that view.

INPUT/OUTPUT
```
SQL> CREATE VIEW SALARY_VIEW
  2  AS SELECT *
  3  FROM Bryan.SALARIES;

View created.

SQL> SELECT * FROM SALARY_VIEW;
```

```
NAME                                 SALARY        AGE
- - - - - - - - - - - - - - - - -    - - - - - -   - - - - - - - -
JACK                                 35000         29
JILL                                 48000         42
JOHN                                 35000         55
```

12

ANALYSIS The preceding query returned the same values as the records returned from
Bryan.SALARIES.

Using Synonyms in Place of Views

SQL also provides an object known as a *synonym*. A synonym provides an alias for a table to
simplify or minimize keystrokes when using a table in an SQL statement. There are two types
of synonyms: private and public. Any user with the resource role can create a private
synonym. On the other hand, only a user with the DBA role can create a public synonym.

The syntax for a public synonym follows.

 SYNTAX

```
CREATE [PUBLIC] SYNONYM [schema.]synonym
FOR [schema.]object[@dblink]
```

In the preceding example, you could have issued the following command to achieve the same
results:

 **INPUT/
OUTPUT**

```
SQL> CREATE PUBLIC SYNONYM SALARY FOR SALARIES

Synonym created.
```

Then log back on to Jack and type this:

**INPUT/
OUTPUT**

```
SQL> SELECT * FROM SALARY;

NAME                             SALARY      AGE
------------------------------- --------- ---------
JACK                               35000       29
JILL                               48000       42
JOHN                               35000       55
```

Using Views to Solve Security Problems

Suppose you changed your mind about Jack and Jill and decided that neither of them should
be able to look at the SALARIES table completely. You can use views to change this situation
and allow them to examine only their own information.

**INPUT/
OUTPUT**

```
SQL> CREATE VIEW JACK_SALARY AS
  2  SELECT * FROM BRYAN.SALARIES
  3  WHERE NAME = 'JACK';

View created.
```

**INPUT/
OUTPUT**

```
SQL> CREATE VIEW JILL_SALARY AS
  2  SELECT * FROM BRYAN.SALARIES
  3  WHERE NAME = 'JILL';

View created.
```

**INPUT/
OUTPUT**

```
SQL> GRANT SELECT ON JACK_SALARY
  2  TO JACK;

Grant succeeded.
```

**INPUT/
OUTPUT**

```
SQL> GRANT SELECT ON JILL_SALARY
  2  TO JILL;
```

Grant succeeded.

**INPUT/
OUTPUT**

```
SQL> REVOKE SELECT ON SALARIES FROM JACK;
```

Revoke succeeded.

**INPUT/
OUTPUT**

```
SQL> REVOKE SELECT ON SALARIES FROM JILL;
```

Revoke succeeded.

Now log on as Jack and test out the view you created for him.

**INPUT/
OUTPUT**

```
SQL> SELECT * FROM Bryan.JACK_SALARY;

NAME         SALARY      AGE
----------  ----------  ----
Jack         35000       29
```

**INPUT/
OUTPUT**

```
SQL> SELECT * FROM PERKINS.SALARIES;
SELECT * FROM PERKINS.SALARIES
                      *
ERROR at line 1:
ORA-00942: table or view does not exist
```

Log out of Jack's account and test Jill's.

**INPUT/
OUTPUT**

```
SQL> SELECT * FROM Bryan.JILL_SALARY;

NAME              SALARY          AGE
----------------  -------------  ----
Jill              48000           42
```

ANALYSIS   You can see that access to the SALARIES table was completely controlled using views. SQL enables you to create these views as you like and then assign permissions to other users. This technique allows a great deal of flexibility.

SYNTAX   The syntax to drop a synonym is

```
SQL> drop [public] synonym synonym_name;
```

NOTE   By now, you should understand the importance of keeping to a minimum the number of people with DBA roles. A user with this access level can have complete access to all commands and operations within the database. Note, however, that with Oracle and Sybase you must have DBA-level access (or SA-level in Sybase) to import or export data on the database.

12

Using the WITH GRANT OPTION **Clause**

What do you think would happen if Jill attempted to pass her UPDATE privilege on to Jack? At first glance you might think that Jill, because she was entrusted with the UPDATE privilege, should be able to pass it on to other users who are allowed that privilege. However, using the GRANT statement as you did earlier, Jill cannot pass her privileges on to others:

```
SQL> GRANT SELECT, UPDATE(SALARY) ON Bryan.SALARIES TO Jill;
```

Here is the syntax for the GRANT statement that was introduced earlier today:

```
GRANT {object_priv ¦ ALL [PRIVILEGES]} [ (column
[, column]...) ]
[, {object_priv ¦ ALL [PRIVILEGES]} [ (column
[, column] ...) ] ] ...
ON [schema.]object
TO {user ¦ role ¦ PUBLIC} [, {user ¦ role ¦ PUBLIC}] ...
[WITH GRANT OPTION]
```

What you are looking for is the WITH GRANT OPTION clause at the end of the GRANT statement. When object privileges are granted and WITH GRANT OPTION is used, these privileges can be passed on to others. So if you want to allow Jill to pass on this privilege to Jack, you would do the following:

INPUT
```
SQL> GRANT SELECT, UPDATE(SALARY)
  2  ON Bryan.SALARIES TO JILL
  3  WITH GRANT OPTION;
```

OUTPUT   Grant succeeded.

Jill could then log on and issue the following command:

**INPUT/
OUTPUT**
```
SQL> GRANT SELECT, UPDATE(SALARY)
  2  ON Bryan.SALARIES TO JACK;
```

```
Grant succeeded.
```

Summary

Security is an often-overlooked topic that can cause many problems if not properly thought out and administered. Fortunately, SQL provides several useful commands for implementing security on a database.

Users are originally created using the CREATE USER command, which sets up a username and password for a user. After the user account has been set up, this user must be assigned to a role in order to accomplish any work. The three roles available within Oracle7 are Connect, Resource, and DBA. Each role has different levels of access to the database, with Connect being the simplest and DBA having access to everything.

The GRANT command gives a permission or privilege to a user. The REVOKE command can take that permission or privilege away from the user. The two types of privileges are object privileges and system privileges. The system privileges should be monitored closely and should not be granted to inexperienced users. Giving inexperienced users access to commands allows them to (inadvertently perhaps) destroy data or databases you have painstakingly set up. Object privileges can be granted to give users access to individual objects existing in the owner's database schema.

All these techniques and SQL statements provide the SQL user with a broad range of tools to use when setting up system security. Although we focused on the security features of Oracle7, you can apply much of this information to the database system at your site. Just remember that no matter what product you are using, it is important to enforce some level of database security.

Q&A

Q I understand the need for security, but doesn't Oracle carry it a bit too far?

A No, especially in larger applications where there are multiple users. Because different users will be doing different types of work in the database, you'll want to limit what users can and can't do. Users should have only the necessary roles and privileges they need to do their work.

Q It appears that there is a security problem when the DBA that created my ID also knows the password. Is this true?

A Yes it is true. The DBA creates the IDs and passwords. Therefore, users should use the ALTER USER command to change their ID and password immediately after receiving them.

Workshop

The Workshop provides quiz questions to help solidify your understanding of the material covered, as well as exercises to provide you with experience in using what you have learned. Try to answer the quiz and exercise questions before checking the answers in Appendix F, "Answers to Quizzes and Exercises."

Quiz

1. What is wrong with the following statement?

   ```
   SQL> GRANT CONNECTION TO DAVID;
   ```

2. True or False (and why): Dropping a user will cause all objects owned by that user to be dropped as well.

3. What would happen if you created a table and granted select privileges on the table to public?

4. Is the following SQL statement correct?

```
SQL> create user RON
     identified by RON;
```

5. Is the following SQL statement correct?

```
SQL> alter RON
     identified by RON;
```

6. Is the following SQL statement correct?

```
SQL> grant connect, resource to RON;
```

7. If you own a table, who can select from that table?

Exercise

1. Experiment with your database system's security by creating a table and then by creating a user. Give this user various privileges and then take them away.

Day 13

Advanced SQL Topics

Objectives

Over the course of the past 12 days, you have examined every major topic used to write powerful queries to retrieve data from a database. You have also briefly explored aspects of database design and database security. Today's purpose is to cover advanced SQL topics, which include the following:

- ☐ Temporary tables
- ☐ Cursors
- ☐ Stored procedures
- ☐ Triggers
- ☐ Embedded SQL

NOTE

Today's examples use Oracle7's PL/SQL and Microsoft/Sybase SQL Server's Transact-SQL implementations. We made an effort to give examples using both flavors of SQL wherever possible. You do not need to own a copy of either the Oracle7 or the SQL Server database product. Feel free to choose your database product based on your requirements. (If you are reading this to gain enough knowledge to begin a project for your job, chances are you won't have a choice.)

NOTE

Although you can apply most of the examples within this book to any popular database management system, this statement does not hold for all the material covered today. Many vendors still do not support temporary tables, stored procedures, and triggers. Check your documentation to determine which of these features are included with your favorite database system.

Temporary Tables

The first advanced topic we discuss is the use of temporary tables, which are simply tables that exist temporarily within a database and are automatically dropped when the user logs out or their database connection ends. Transact-SQL creates these temporary tables in the `tempdb` database. This database is created when you install SQL Server. Two types of syntax are used to create a temporary table.

```
SYNTAX 1:
create table #table_name (
field1 datatype,
.
.
.
fieldn datatype)
```

Syntax 1 creates a table in the `tempdb` database. This table is created with a unique name consisting of a combination of the table name used in the CREATE TABLE command and a date-time stamp. A temporary table is available only to its creator. Fifty users could simultaneously issue the following commands:

```
1> create table #albums (
2> artist char(30),
3> album_name char(50),
4> media_type int)
5> go
```

The pound sign (#) before the table's name is the identifier that SQL Server uses to flag a temporary table. Each of the 50 users would essentially receive a private table for his or her own use. Each user could update, insert, and delete records from this table without worrying about other users invalidating the table's data. This table could be dropped as usual by issuing the following command:

```
1> drop table #albums
2> go
```

The table could also be dropped automatically when the user who created it logs out of the SQL Server. If you created this statement using some type of dynamic SQL connection (such as SQL Server's DB-Library), the table will be deleted when that dynamic SQL connection is closed.

Syntax 2 shows another way to create a temporary table on an SQL Server. This syntax produces a different result than the syntax used in syntax 1, so pay careful attention to the syntactical differences.

```
SYNTAX 2:
create table tempdb..tablename (
field1 datatype,
.
.
.
fieldn datatype)
```

Creating a temporary table using the format of syntax 2 still results in a table being created in the `tempdb` database. This table's name has the same format as the name for the table created using syntax 1. The difference is that this table is not dropped when the user's connection to the database ends. Instead, the user must actually issue a DROP TABLE command to remove this table from the `tempdb` database.

> **TIP** Another way to get rid of a table that was created using the `create table tempdb..tablename` syntax is to shut down and restart the SQL Server. This method removes all temporary tables from the `tempdb` database.

13

Examples 13.1 and 13.2 illustrate the fact that temporary tables are indeed temporary, using the two different forms of syntax. Following these two examples, Example 13.3 illustrates a common usage of temporary tables: to temporarily store data returned from a query. This data can then be used with other queries.

You need to create a database to use these examples. The database MUSIC is created with the following tables:

- ☐ ARTISTS
- ☐ MEDIA
- ☐ RECORDINGS

Use the following SQL statements to create these tables:

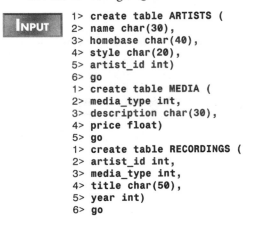

```
1> create table ARTISTS (
2> name char(30),
3> homebase char(40),
4> style char(20),
5> artist_id int)
6> go
1> create table MEDIA (
2> media_type int,
3> description char(30),
4> price float)
5> go
1> create table RECORDINGS (
2> artist_id int,
3> media_type int,
4> title char(50),
5> year int)
6> go
```

NOTE

Tables 13.1, 13.2, and 13.3 show some sample data for these tables.

Table 13.1. The ARTISTS table.

Name	Homebase	Style	Artist_ID
Soul Asylum	Minneapolis	Rock	1
Maurice Ravel	France	Classical	2
Dave Matthews Band	Charlottesville	Rock	3
Vince Gill	Nashville	Country	4
Oingo Boingo	Los Angeles	Pop	5
Crowded House	New Zealand	Pop	6
Mary Chapin-Carpenter	Nashville	Country	7
Edward MacDowell	U.S.A.	Classical	8

13

Table 13.2. The MEDIA table.

Media_Type	Description	Price
1	Record	4.99
2	Tape	9.99
3	CD	13.99
4	CD-ROM	29.99
5	DAT	19.99

Table 13.3. The RECORDINGS table.

Artist_Id	Media_Type	Title	Year
1	2	Hang Time	1988
1	3	Made to Be Broken	1986
2	3	Bolero	1990
3	5	Under the Table and Dreaming	1994
4	3	When Love Finds You	1994
5	2	Boingo	1987
5	1	Dead Man's Party	1984
6	2	Woodface	1990
6	3	Together Alone	1993
7	5	Come On, Come On	1992
7	3	Stones in the Road	1994
8	5	Second Piano Concerto	1985

Example 13.1

You can create a temporary table in the tempdb database. After inserting a dummy record into this table, log out. After logging back into SQL Server, try to select the dummy record out of the temporary table. Note the results:

```
1> create table #albums (
2> artist char(30),
3> album_name char(50),
4> media_type int)
5> go
1> insert #albums values ("The Replacements", "Pleased To Meet Me", 1)
2> go
```

13

Now log out of the SQL Server connection using the EXIT (or QUIT) command. After logging back in and switching to the database you last used, try the following command:

INPUT
```
1> select * from #albums
2> go
```

ANALYSIS This table does not exist in the current database.

Example 13.2

Now create the table with syntax 2:

INPUT
```
1> create table tempdb..albums (
2> artist char(30),
3> album_name char(50),
4> media_type int)
5> go
1> insert #albums values ("The Replacements", "Pleased To Meet Me", 1)
2> go
```

After logging out and logging back in, switch to the database you were using when create table tempdb..albums() was issued; then issue the following command:

INPUT
```
1> select * from #albums
2> go
```

This time, you get the following results:

OUTPUT

artist	album_name	media_type
The Replacements	Pleased To Meet Me	1

Example 13.3

This example shows a common usage of temporary tables: to store the results of complex queries for use in later queries.

INPUT
```
1> create table #temp_info (
2> name char(30),
3> homebase char(40),
4> style char(20),
5> artist_id int)
6> insert #temp_info
7> select * from ARTISTS where homebase = "Nashville"
8> select RECORDINGS.* from RECORDINGS, ARTISTS
9> where RECORDINGS.artist_id = #temp_info.artist_id
10> go
```

The preceding batch of commands selects out the recording information for all the artists whose home base is Nashville.

13

The following command is another way to write the set of SQL statements used in Example 13.3:

```
1> select ARTISTS.* from ARTISTS, RECORDINGS where ARTISTS.homebase =
➥"Nashville"
2> go
```

Cursors

A database cursor is similar to the cursor on a word processor screen. As you press the Down Arrow key, the cursor scrolls down through the text one line at a time. Pressing the Up Arrow key scrolls your cursor up one line at a time. Hitting other keys such as Page Up and Page Down results in a leap of several lines in either direction. Database cursors operate in the same way.

Database cursors enable you to select a group of data, scroll through the group of records (often called a recordset), and examine each individual line of data as the cursor points to it. You can use a combination of local variables and a cursor to individually examine each record and perform any external operation needed before moving on to the next record.

One other common use of cursors is to save a query's results for later use. A cursor's result set is created from the result set of a SELECT query. If your application or procedure requires the repeated use of a set of records, it is faster to create a cursor once and reuse it several times than to repeatedly query the database. (And you have the added advantage of being able to scroll through the query's result set with a cursor.)

Follow these steps to create, use, and close a database cursor:

1. Create the cursor.
2. Open the cursor for use within the procedure or application.
3. Fetch a record's data one row at a time until you have reached the end of the cursor's records.
4. Close the cursor when you are finished with it.
5. Deallocate the cursor to completely discard it.

Creating a Cursor

To create a cursor using Transact-SQL, issue the following syntax:

```
declare cursor_name cursor
    for select_statement
    [for {read only ¦ update [of column_name_list]}]
```

The Oracle7 SQL syntax used to create a cursor looks like this:

```
DECLARE cursor_name CURSOR
       FOR {SELECT command ¦ statement_name ¦ block_name}
```

By executing the DECLARE cursor_name CURSOR statement, you have defined the cursor result set that will be used for all your cursor operations. A cursor has two important parts: the cursor result set and the cursor position.

The following statement creates a cursor based on the ARTISTS table:

```
1> create Artists_Cursor cursor
2> for select * from ARTISTS
3> go
```

You now have a simple cursor object named Artists_Cursor that contains all the records in the ARTISTS table. But first you must open the cursor.

Opening a Cursor

The simple command to open a cursor for use is

```
open cursor_name
```

Executing the following statement opens Artists_Cursor for use:

```
1> open Artists_Cursor
2> go
```

Now you can use the cursor to scroll through the result set.

Scrolling a Cursor

To scroll through the cursor's result set, Transact-SQL provides the following FETCH command.

```
fetch cursor_name [into fetch_target_list]
```

Oracle SQL provides the following syntax:

```
FETCH cursor_name {INTO : host_variable
      [[INDICATOR] : indicator_variable]
        [,    : host_variable
        [[INDICATOR] : indicator_variable] ]...
      ¦ USING DESCRIPTOR descriptor }
```

Each time the FETCH command is executed, the cursor pointer advances through the result set one row at a time. If desired, data from each row can be fetched into the fetch_target_list variables.

NOTE

> Transact-SQL enables the programmer to advance more than one row at a time by using the following command: `set cursor rows number for cursor_name`. This command cannot be used with the INTO clause, however. It is useful only to jump forward a known number of rows instead of repeatedly executing the FETCH statement.

The following statements fetch the data from the `Artists_Cursor` result set and return the data to the program variables:

INPUT

```
1> declare @name char(30)
2> declare @homebase char(40)
3> declare @style char(20)
4> declare @artist_id int
5> fetch Artists_Cursor into @name, @homebase, @style, @artist_id
6> print @name
7> print @homebase
8> print @style
9> print char(@artist_id)
10> go
```

You can use the WHILE loop (see Day 12, "Database Security") to loop through the entire result set. But how do you know when you have reached the end of the records?

Testing a Cursor's Status

Transact-SQL enables you to check the status of the cursor at any time through the maintenance of two global variables: @@sqlstatus and @@rowcount.

The @@sqlstatus variable returns status information concerning the last executed FETCH statement. (The Transact-SQL documentation states that no command other than the FETCH statement can modify the @@sqlstatus variable.) This variable contains one of three values. The following table appears in the Transact-SQL reference manuals:

Status	Meaning
0	Successful completion of the FETCH statement.
1	The FETCH statement resulted in an error.
2	There is no more data in the result set.

The @@rowcount variable contains the number of rows returned from the cursor's result set up to the previous fetch. You can use this number to determine the number of records in a cursor's result set.

13

The following code extends the statements executed during the discussion of the FETCH statement. You now use the WHILE loop with the @@sqlstatus variable to scroll the cursor:

```
1> declare @name char(30)
2> declare @homebase char(40)
3> declare @style char(20)
4> declare @artist_id int
5> fetch Artists_Cursor into @name, @homebase, @style, @artist_id
6> while (@@sqlstatus = 0)
7> begin
8>      print @name
9>      print @homebase
10>     print @style
11>     print char(@artist_id)
12>     fetch Artists_Cursor into @name, @homebase, @style, @artist_id
13> end
14> go
```

ANALYSIS Now you have a fully functioning cursor! The only step left is to close the cursor.

Closing a Cursor

Closing a cursor is a very simple matter. The statement to close a cursor is as follows:

```
close cursor_name
```

This cursor still exists; however, it must be reopened. Closing a cursor essentially closes out its result set, not its entire existence. When you are completely finished with a cursor, the DEALLOCATE command frees the memory associated with a cursor and frees the cursor name for reuse. The DEALLOCATE statement syntax is as follows:

```
deallocate cursor cursor_name
```

Example 13.4 illustrates the complete process of creating a cursor, using it, and then closing it, using Transact-SQL.

Example 13.4

```
1> declare @name char(30)
2> declare @homebase char(40)
3> declare @style char(20)
4> declare @artist_id int
5> create Artists_Cursor cursor
6> for select * from ARTISTS
7> open Artists_Cursor
8> fetch Artists_Cursor into @name, @homebase, @style, @artist_id
9> while (@@sqlstatus = 0)
10> begin
11>      print @name
12>      print @homebase
13>     print @style
14>     print char(@artist_id)
15>     fetch Artists_Cursor into @name, @homebase, @style, @artist_id
```

13

```
16> end
17> close Artists_Cursor
18> deallocate cursor Artists_Cursor
19> go
```

NOTE

The following is sample data only.

OUTPUT

```
Soul Asylum              Minneapolis         Rock        1
Maurice Ravel            France              Classical   2
Dave Matthews Band       Charlottesville     Rock        3
Vince Gill               Nashville           Country     4
Oingo Boingo             Los Angeles         Pop         5
Crowded House            New Zealand         Pop         6
Mary Chapin-Carpenter    Nashville           Country     7
Edward MacDowell         U.S.A.              Classical   8
```

The Scope of Cursors

Unlike tables, indexes, and other objects such as triggers and stored procedures, cursors do not exist as database objects after they are created. Instead, cursors have a limited scope of use.

WARNING

Remember, however, that memory remains allocated for the cursor, even though its name may no longer exist. Before going outside the cursor's scope, the cursor should always be closed and deallocated.

A cursor can be created within three regions:

☐ In a session—A session begins when a user logs on. If the user logged on to an SQL Server and then created a cursor, then cursor_name would exist until the user logged off. The user would not be able to reuse cursor_name during the current session.

☐ Stored procedure—A cursor created inside a stored procedure is good only during the execution of the stored procedure. As soon as the stored procedure exits, cursor_name is no longer valid.

☐ Trigger—A cursor created inside a trigger has the same restrictions as one created inside a stored procedure.

13

Creating and Using Stored Procedures

The concept of stored procedures is an important one for the professional database programmer to master. Stored procedures are functions that contain potentially large groupings of SQL statements. These functions are called and executed just as C, FORTRAN, or Visual Basic functions would be called. A stored procedure should encapsulate a logical set of commands that are often executed (such as a complex set of queries, updates, or inserts). Stored procedures enable the programmer to simply call the stored procedure as a function instead of repeatedly executing the statements inside the stored procedure. However, stored procedures have additional advantages.

Sybase, Inc., pioneered stored procedures with its SQL Server product in the late 1980s. These procedures are created and then stored as part of a database, just as tables and indexes are stored inside a database. Transact SQL permits both input and output parameters to stored procedure calls. This mechanism enables you to create the stored procedures in a generic fashion so that variables can be passed to them.

One of the biggest advantages to stored procedures lies in the design of their execution. When executing a large batch of SQL statements to a database server over a network, your application is in constant communication with the server, which can create an extremely heavy load on the network very quickly. As multiple users become engaged in this communication, the performance of the network and the database server becomes increasingly slower. The use of stored procedures enables the programmer to greatly reduce this communication load.

After the stored procedure is executed, the SQL statements run sequentially on the database server. Some message or data is returned to the user's computer only when the procedure is finished. This approach improves performance and offers other benefits as well. Stored procedures are actually compiled by database engines the first time they are used. The compiled map is stored on the server with the procedure. Therefore, you do not have to optimize SQL statements each time you execute them, which also improves performance.

Use the following syntax to create a stored procedure using Transact-SQL:

▼ **SYNTAX**

```
create procedure procedure_name
    [[(]@parameter_name
        datatype [(length) ¦ (precision [, scale])
        [= default][output]
    [, @parameter_name
        datatype [(length) ¦ (precision [, scale])
        [= default][output]]...[)]]
    [with recompile]
    as SQL_statements
```

This EXECUTE command executes the procedure:

SYNTAX

```
execute [@return_status = ]
    procedure_name
    [[@parameter_name =] value ¦
        [@parameter_name =] @variable [output]...]]
    [with recompile]
```

Example 13.5

This example creates a simple procedure using the contents of Example 13.4.

INPUT

```
1> create procedure Print_Artists_Name
2> as
3> declare @name char(30)
4> declare @homebase char(40)
5> declare @style char(20)
6> declare @artist_id int
7> create Artists_Cursor cursor
8> for select * from ARTISTS
9> open Artists_Cursor
10> fetch Artists_Cursor into @name, @homebase, @style, @artist_id
11> while (@@sqlstatus = 0)
12> begin
13>     print @name
14>     fetch Artists_Cursor into @name, @homebase, @style, @artist_id
15> end
16> close Artists_Cursor
17> deallocate cursor Artists_Cursor
18> go
```

You can now execute the `Print_Artists_Name` procedure using the EXECUTE statement:

INPUT

```
1> execute Print_Artists_Name
2> go
```

OUTPUT

```
Soul Asylum
Maurice Ravel
Dave Matthews Band
Vince Gill
Oingo Boingo
Crowded House
Mary Chapin-Carpenter
Edward MacDowell
```

ANALYSIS Example 13.5 was a small stored procedure; however, a stored procedure can contain many statements, which means you do not have to execute each statement individually.

Using Stored Procedure Parameters

Example 13.5 was an important first step because it showed the use of the simplest CREATE PROCEDURE statement. However, by looking at the syntax given here, you can see that there is more to the CREATE PROCEDURE statement than was demonstrated in Example 13.5. Stored procedures also accept parameters as input to their SQL statements. In addition, data can be returned from a stored procedure through the use of output parameters.

Input parameter names must begin with the @ symbol, and these parameters must be a valid Transact-SQL data type. Output parameter names must also begin with the @ symbol. In addition, the OUTPUT keyword must follow the output parameter names. (You must also give this OUTPUT keyword when executing the stored procedure.)

13

Example 13.6 demonstrates the use of input parameters to a stored procedure.

Example 13.6

The following stored procedure selects the names of all artists whose media type is a CD:

INPUT

```
1> create procedure Match_Names_To_Media @description char(30)
2> as
3>     select ARTISTS.name from ARTISTS, MEDIA, RECORDINGS
4>     where MEDIA.description = @description and
5>     MEDIA.media_type = RECORDINGS.media_type and
6>     RECORDINGS.artist_id = ARTISTS.artist_id
7> go
1> execute Match_Names_To_Media "CD"
2> go
```

Executing this statement would return the following set of records:

OUTPUT

```
NAME
Soul Asylum
Maurice Ravel
Vince Gill
Crowded House
Mary Chapin-Carpenter
```

Example 13.7

This example demonstrates the use of output parameters. This function takes the artist's homebase as input and returns the artist's name as output:

INPUT

```
1> create procedure Match_Homebase_To_Name @homebase char(40), @name
➥char(30) output
2> as
3>         select @name = name from ARTISTS where homebase = @homebase
4> go
1> declare @return_name char(30)
2> execute Match_Homebase_To_Name "Los Angeles", @return_name = @name
➥output
3> print @name
4> go
```

OUTPUT   Oingo Boingo

Removing a Stored Procedure

By now, you can probably make an educated guess as to how to get rid of a stored procedure. If you guessed the DROP command, you are absolutely correct. The following statement removes a stored procedure from a database:

SYNTAX

```
drop procedure procedure_name
```

The DROP command is used frequently: Before a stored procedure can be re-created, the old procedure with its name must be dropped. From personal experience, there are few instances in which a procedure is created and then never modified. Many times, in fact, errors occur somewhere within the statements that make up the procedure. We recommend that you create your stored procedures using an SQL script file containing all your statements. You can run this script file through your database server to execute your desired statements and rebuild your procedures. This technique enables you to use common text editors such as vi or Windows Notepad to create and save your SQL scripts. When running these scripts, however, you need to remember to always drop the procedure, table, and so forth from the database before creating a new one. If you forget the DROP command, errors will result.

The following syntax is often used in SQL Server script files before creating a database object:

SYNTAX ▼

```
if exists (select * from sysobjects where name = "procedure_name")
begin
        drop procedure procedure_name
end
go
create procedure procedure_name
as
.
.
.
```

These commands check the SYSOBJECTS table (where database object information is stored in SQL Server) to see whether the object exists. If it does, it is dropped before the new one is created. Creating script files and following the preceding steps saves you a large amount of time (and many potential errors) in the long run.

Nesting Stored Procedures

Stored procedure calls can also be nested for increased programming modularity. A stored procedure can call another stored procedure, which can then call another stored procedure, and so on. Nesting stored procedures is an excellent idea for several reasons:

☐ Nesting stored procedures reduces your most complex queries to a functional level. (Instead of executing 12 queries in a row, you could perhaps reduce these 12 queries to three stored procedure calls, depending on the situation.)

☐ Nesting stored procedures improves performance. The query optimizer optimizes smaller, more concise groups of queries more effectively than one large group of statements.

When nesting stored procedures, any variables or database objects created in one stored procedure are visible to all the stored procedures it calls. Any local variables or temporary objects (such as temporary tables) are deleted at the end of the stored procedure that created these elements.

When preparing large SQL script files, you might run into table or database object referencing problems. You must create the nested stored procedures before you can call them. However, the calling procedure may create temporary tables or cursors that are then used in

13

the called stored procedures. These called stored procedures are unaware of these temporary tables or cursors, which are created later in the script file. The easiest way around this problem is to create the temporary objects before all the stored procedures are created; then drop the temporary items (in the script file) before they are created again in the stored procedure. Are you confused yet? Example 13.8 should help you understand this process.

Example 13.8

INPUT

```
1> create procedure Example13_8b
2> as
3>     select * from #temp_table
4> go
1> create procedure Example13_8a
2> as
3>     create #temp_table (
4>     data char(20),
5>     numbers int)
6>     execute Example13_8b
7>     drop table #temp_table
8> go
```

ANALYSIS

As you can see, procedure Example13_8b uses the #temp_table. However, the #temp_table is not created until later (in procedure Example13_8a). This results in a procedure creation error. In fact, because Example13_8b was not created (owing to the missing table #temp_table), procedure Example13_8a is not created either (because Example13_8b was not created).

The following code fixes this problem by creating the #temp_table before the first procedure is created. #temp_table is then dropped before the creation of the second procedure:

INPUT

```
1> create #temp_table (
2> data char(20),
3> numbers int)
4> go
1> create procedure Example13_8b
2> as
3>     select * from #temp_table
4> go
1> drop table #temp_table
2> go
1> create procedure Example13_8a
2> as
3>     create #temp_table (
4>     data char(20),
5>     numbers int)
6>     execute Example13_8b
7>     drop table #temp_table
8> go
```

13

Designing and Using Triggers

A trigger is essentially a special type of stored procedure that can be executed in response to one of three conditions:

☐ An UPDATE

☐ An INSERT

☐ A DELETE

The Transact-SQL syntax to create a trigger looks like this:

SYNTAX

```
create trigger trigger_name
  on table_name
  for {insert, update, delete}
  as SQL_Statements
```

The Oracle7 SQL syntax used to create a trigger follows.

SYNTAX

```
CREATE [OR REPLACE] TRIGGER [schema.]trigger_name
  {BEFORE ¦ AFTER}
  {DELETE ¦ INSERT ¦ UPDATE [OF column[, column]...]}
[OR {DELETE ¦ INSERT ¦ UPDATE [OF column [, column] ...]}]...
  ON [schema.]table
[[REFERENCING { OLD [AS] old [NEW [AS] new]
     ¦ NEW [AS] new [OLD [AS] old]}]
FOR EACH ROW
[WHEN (condition)] ]
pl/sql statements...
```

Triggers are most useful to enforce referential integrity, as mentioned on Day 9, "Creating and Maintaining Tables," when you learned how to create tables. Referential integrity enforces rules used to ensure that data remains valid across multiple tables. Suppose a user entered the following command:

INPUT
```
1> insert RECORDINGS values (12, "The Cross of Changes", 3, 1994)
2> go
```

ANALYSIS This perfectly valid SQL statement inserts a new record in the RECORDINGS table. However, a quick check of the ARTISTS table shows that there is no Artist_ID = 12. A user with INSERT privileges in the RECORDINGS table can completely destroy your referential integrity.

13

NOTE

Although many database systems can enforce referential integrity through the use of constraints in the CREATE TABLE statement, triggers provide a great deal more flexibility. Constraints return system error messages to the user, and (as you probably know by now) these error

> messages are not always helpful. On the other hand, triggers can print error messages, call other stored procedures, or try to rectify a problem if necessary.

Triggers and Transactions

The actions executed within a trigger are implicitly executed as part of a transaction. Here's the broad sequence of events:

1. A BEGIN TRANSACTION statement is implicitly issued (for tables with triggers).

2. The insert, update, or delete operation occurs.

3. The trigger is called and its statements are executed.

4. The trigger either rolls back the transaction or the transaction is implicitly committed.

Example 13.9

This example illustrates the solution to the RECORDINGS table update problem mentioned earlier.

INPUT

```
1> create trigger check_artists
2> on RECORDINGS
3> for insert, update as
4>     if not exists (select * from ARTISTS, RECORDINGS
5>     where ARTISTS.artist_id = RECORDINGS.artist_id)
6>     begin
7>         print "Illegal Artist_ID!"
8>         rollback transaction
9>     end
10> go
```

ANALYSIS A similar problem could exist for deletes from the RECORDINGS table. Suppose that when you delete an artist's only record from the RECORDINGS table, you also want to delete the artist from the ARTISTS table. If the records have already been deleted when the trigger is fired, how do you know which Artist_ID should be deleted? There are two methods to solve this problem:

- ☐ Delete all the artists from the ARTISTS table who no longer have any recordings in the RECORDINGS table. (See Example 13.10a.)

- ☐ Examine the deleted logical table. Transact-SQL maintains two tables: DELETED and INSERTED. These tables, which maintain the most recent changes to the actual table, have the same structure as the table on which the trigger is created. Therefore, you could retrieve the artist IDs from the DELETED table and then delete these IDs from the ARTISTS table. (See Example 13.10b.)

Example 13.10a

```
1> create trigger delete_artists
2> on RECORDINGS
3> for delete as
4> begin
5>      delete from ARTISTS where artist_id not in
6>      (select artist_id from RECORDINGS)
7> end
8> go
```

Example 13.10b

```
1> create trigger delete_artists
2> on RECORDINGS
3> for delete as
4> begin
5>      delete ARTISTS from ARTISTS, deleted
6>      where ARTIST.artist_id  = deleted.artist_id
7> end
8> go
```

Restrictions on Using Triggers

You must observe the following restrictions when you use triggers:

☐ Triggers cannot be created on temporary tables.

☐ Triggers must be created on tables in the current database.

☐ Triggers cannot be created on views.

☐ When a table is dropped, all triggers associated with that table are automatically dropped with it.

Nested Triggers

Triggers can also be nested. Say that you have created a trigger to fire on a delete, for instance. If this trigger itself then deletes a record, the database server can be set to fire another trigger. This approach would, of course, result in a loop, ending only when all the records in the table were deleted (or some internal trigger conditions were met). Nesting behavior is not the default, however. The environment must be set to enable this type of functionality. Consult your database server's documentation for more information on this topic.

13

Using SELECT Commands with UPDATE and DELETE

Here are some complex SQL statements using UPDATE and DELETE:

```
SQL> UPPDATE EMPLOYEE_TBL
     SET LAST_NAME = 'SMITH'
     WHERE EXISTS (SELECT EMPLOYEE_ID
     FROM PAYROLL_TBL
     WHERE EMPLOYEE_ID = 2);
```

OUTPUT

```
1 row updated.
```

 ANALYSIS

The EMPLOYEE table had an incorrect employee name. We updated the EMPLOYEE table only if the payroll table had the correct ID.

 INPUT/ OUTPUT

```
SQL> UPDATE EMPLOYEE_TABLE
     SET HOURLY_PAY = 'HOURLY_PAY * 1.1
     WHERE EMPLOYEE_ID = (SELECT EMPLOYEE_ID
     FROM PAYROLL_TBL
     WHERE EMPLOYEE_ID = '222222222');
```

```
1 row updated.
```

 ANALYSIS

We increased the employee's hourly rate by 10 percent.

 INPUT/ OUTPUT

```
SQL> DELETE FROM EMPLOYEE_TBL
     WHERE EMPLOYEE_ID = (SELECT EMPLOYEE_ID
     FROM PAYROLL_TBL
     WHERE EMPLOYEE_ID = '222222222';
```

```
1 row deleted.
```

ANALYSIS Here we deleted an employee with the ID of 222222222.

Testing SELECT Statements Before Implementation

 SYNTAX

If you are creating a report (using SQL*PLUS for an example) and the report is rather large, you may want to check spacing, columns, and titles before running the program and wasting a lot of time. A simple way of checking is to add where rownum < 3 to your SQL statement:

```
SQL> select *
     from employee_tbl
     where rownum < 5;
```

ANALYSIS

You get the first four rows in the table from which you can check the spelling and spacing to see if it suits you. Otherwise, your report may return hundreds or thousands of rows before you discover a misspelling or incorrect spacing.

TIP

A major part of your job—probably 50 percent—is to figure out what your customer really wants and needs. Good communication skills and a knowledge of the particular business that you work for will complement your programming skills. For example, suppose you are the programmer at a car dealership. The used car manager wants to know how many vehicles he has for an upcoming inventory. You think (to yourself): Go count them. Well, he asked for how many vehicles he has; but you know that for an inventory the manager really wants to know how many types (cars, trucks), models, model year, and so on. Should you give him what he asked for and waste your time, or should you give him what he needs?

Embedded SQL

This book uses the term *embedded SQL* to refer to the larger topic of writing actual program code using SQL—that is, writing stored procedures embedded in the database that can be called by an application program to perform some task. Some database systems come with complete tool kits that enable you to build simple screens and menu objects using a combination of a proprietary programming language and SQL. The SQL code is embedded within this code.

On the other hand, *embedded SQL* commonly refers to what is technically known as Static SQL.

Static and Dynamic SQL

Static SQL means embedding SQL statements directly within programming code. This code cannot be modified at runtime. In fact, most implementations of Static SQL require the use of a precompiler that fixes your SQL statement at runtime. Both Oracle and Informix have developed Static SQL packages for their database systems. These products contain precompilers for use with several languages, including the following:

- [ ] C
- [ ] Pascal
- [ ] Ada
- [ ] COBOL
- [ ] FORTRAN

Some advantages of Static SQL are

- [ ] Improved runtime speed
- [ ] Compile-time error checking

13

The disadvantages of Static SQL are that

☐ It is inflexible.

☐ It requires more code (because queries cannot be formulated at runtime).

☐ Static SQL code is not portable to other database systems (a factor that you should always consider).

If you print out a copy of this code, the SQL statements appear next to the C language code (or whatever language you are using). Program variables are bound to database fields using a precompiler command. See Example 13.11 for a simple example of Static SQL code.

Dynamic SQL, on the other hand, enables the programmer to build an SQL statement at runtime and pass this statement off to the database engine. The engine then returns data into program variables, which are also bound at runtime. This topic is discussed thoroughly on Day 12.

Example 13.11

This example illustrates the use of Static SQL in a C function. Please note that the syntax used here does not comply with the ANSI standard. This Static SQL syntax does not actually comply with any commercial product, although the syntax used is similar to that of most commercial products.

INPUT

```
BOOL Print_Employee_Info (void)
{
int Age = 0;
char Name[41] = "\0";
char Address[81] = "\0";
/* Now Bind Each Field We Will Select To a Program Variable */
#SQL BIND(AGE, Age)
#SQL BIND(NAME, Name);
#SQL BIND(ADDRESS, Address);
/* The above statements "bind" fields from the database to variables
➥from the program.
 After we query the database, we will scroll the records returned
and then print them to the screen */

#SQL SELECT AGE, NAME, ADDRESS FROM EMPLOYEES;

#SQL FIRST_RECORD
if (Age == NULL)
{
    return FALSE;
}
while (Age != NULL)
{
    printf("AGE = %d\n, Age);
    printf("NAME = %s\n, Name);
    printf("ADDRESS = %s\n", Address);
    #SQL NEXT_RECORD
}
return TRUE;
}
```

13

ANALYSIS After you type in your code and save the file, the code usually runs through some type of precompiler. This precompiler converts the lines that begin with the #SQL precompiler directive to actual C code, which is then compiled with the rest of your program to accomplish the task at hand.

If you have never seen or written a C program, don't worry about the syntax used in Example 13.11. (As was stated earlier, the Static SQL syntax is only pseudocode. Consult the Static SQL documentation for your product's actual syntax.)

Programming with SQL

So far, we have discussed two uses for programming with SQL. The first, which was the focus of the first 12 days of this book, used SQL to write queries and modify data. The second is the capability to embed SQL statements within third- or fourth-generation language code. Obviously, the first use for SQL is essential if you want to understand the language and database programming in general. We have already discussed the drawbacks to using embedded or Static SQL as opposed to Dynamic SQL. Day 18, "PL/SQL: An Introduction," and Day 19 "Transact-SQL: An Introduction," cover two extensions to SQL that you can use instead of embedded SQL to perform the same types of functions discussed in this section.

Summary

The popularity of programming environments such as Visual Basic, Delphi, and PowerBuilder gives database programmers many tools that are great for executing queries and updating data with a database. However, as you become increasingly involved with databases, you will discover the advantages of using the tools and topics discussed today. Unfortunately, concepts such as cursors, triggers, and stored procedures are recent database innovations and have a low degree of standardization across products. However, the basic theory of usage behind all these features is the same in all database management systems.

Temporary tables are tables that exist during a user's session. These tables typically exist in a special database (named tempdb under SQL Server) and are often identified with a unique date-time stamp as well as a name. Temporary tables can store a result set from a query for later usage by other queries. Performance can erode, however, if many users are creating and using temporary tables all at once, owing to the large amount of activity occurring in the tempdb database.

Cursors can store a result set in order to scroll through this result set one record at a time (or several records at a time if desired). The FETCH statement is used with a cursor to retrieve an individual record's data and also to scroll the cursor to the next record. Various system variables can be monitored to determine whether the end of the records has been reached.

13

Stored procedures are database objects that can combine multiple SQL statements into one function. Stored procedures can accept and return parameter values as well as call other stored procedures. These procedures are executed on the database server and are stored in compiled form in the database. Using stored procedures, rather than executing standalone queries, improves performance.

Triggers are special stored procedures that are executed when a table undergoes an INSERT, a DELETE, or an UPDATE operation. Triggers often enforce referential integrity and can also call other stored procedures.

Embedded SQL is the use of SQL in the code of an actual program. Embedded SQL consists of both Static and Dynamic SQL statements. Static SQL statements cannot be modified at runtime; Dynamic SQL statements are subject to change.

Q&A

Q If I create a temporary table, can any other users use my table?

A No, the temporary table is available only to its creator.

Q Why must I close and deallocate a cursor?

A Memory is still allocated for the cursor, even though its name may no longer exist.

Workshop

The Workshop provides quiz questions to help solidify your understanding of the material covered, as well as exercises to provide you with experience in using what you have learned. Try to answer the quiz and exercise questions before checking the answers in Appendix F, "Answers to Quizzes and Exercises."

Quiz

1. True or False: Microsoft Visual C++ allows programmers to call the ODBC API directly.
2. True or False: The ODBC API can be called directly only from a C program.
3. True or False: Dynamic SQL requires the use of a precompiler.
4. What does the # in front of a temporary table signify?
5. What must be done after closing a cursor to return memory?
6. Are triggers used with the SELECT statement?
7. If you have a trigger on a table and the table is dropped, does the trigger still exist?

Exercises

1. Create a sample database application. (We used a music collection to illustrate these points today.) Break this application into logical data groupings.

2. List the queries you think will be required to complete this application.

3. List the various rules you want to maintain in the database.

4. Create a database schema for the various groups of data you described in step 1.

5. Convert the queries in step 2 to stored procedures.

6. Convert the rules in step 3 to triggers.

7. Combine steps 4, 5, and 6 into a large script file that can be used to build the database and all its associated procedures.

8. Insert some sample data. (This step can also be a part of the script file in step 7.)

9. Execute the procedures you have created to test their functionality.

13

Day 14

Dynamic Uses of SQL

Objectives

The purpose of today's lesson is to show you where to start to apply what you have learned so far. Today's lesson covers, in very broad strokes, practical applications of SQL. We focus on applications in the Microsoft Windows environment, but the principles involved are just as applicable to other software platforms. Today you will learn the following:

- [ ] How various commercial products—Personal Oracle7, open database connectivity (ODBC), InterBase ISQL, Microsoft's Visual C++, and Borland's Delphi relate to SQL

- [ ] How to set up your environment for SQL

- [ ] How to create a database using Oracle7, Microsoft Query, and InterBase ISQL

- [ ] How to use SQL inside applications written in Visual C++ and Delphi

After reading this material, you will know where to start applying your new SQL skills.

A Quick Trip

This section examines several commercial products in the context of the Microsoft Windows operating system and briefly describes how they relate to SQL. The principles, if not the products themselves, apply across various software platforms.

ODBC

One of the underlying technologies in the Windows operating system is ODBC, which enables Windows-based programs to access a database through a driver. Rather than having a custom interface to each database, something you might very well have to write yourself, you can connect to the database of your choice through a driver. The concept of ODBC is very similar to the concept of Windows printer drivers, which enables you to write your program without regard for the printer. Individual differences, which DOS programming forced you to address, are conveniently handled by the printer driver. The result is that you spend your time working on the tasks peculiar to your program, not on writing printer drivers.

ODBC applies this idea to databases. The visual part of ODBC resides in the control panel in Windows 3.1, 3.11, and Windows 95 and in its own program group in Windows NT.

We cover ODBC in more detail when we discuss creating the database later today.

Personal Oracle7

Personal Oracle7 is the popular database's latest incursion into the personal PC market. Don't be put off by the number of programs that Oracle7 installs—we built all the examples used in the first several days using only the Oracle Database Manager and SQL*Plus 3.3. SQL*Plus is shown in Figure 14.1.

Figure 14.1.

*Oracle7's SQL*Plus.*

```
================= Oracle SQL*Plus =================
 File   Edit   Search   Options   Help
SQL> SELECT *
  2  FROM BIKES;

NAME              FRAMESIZE COMPOSITION      MILERIDDEN TYPE
----------------- --------- --------------- ---------- ----------
TREK 2300              22.5 CARBON FIBER          3500 RACING
BURLEY                  22  STEEL                 2000 TANDEM
GIANT                   19  STEEL                 1500 COMMUTER
FUJI                    20  STEEL                  500 TOURING
SPECIALIZED             16  STEEL                  100 MOUNTAIN
CANNONDALE            22.5  ALUMINUM              3000 RACING

6 rows selected.
```

INTERBASE SQL (ISQL)

The tool used in the other examples is Borland's ISQL. It is essentially the same as Oracle7 except that Oracle7 is character oriented and ISQL is more Windows-like.

14

An ISQL screen is shown in Figure 14.2. You type your query in the top edit box, and the result appears in the lower box. The Previous and Next buttons scroll you through the list of all the queries you make during a session.

Figure 14.2.

InterBase's Interactive SQL.

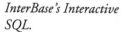

An ISQL screen image showing:

InterBase Interactive SQL

File   Edit   Session   View   Extract   Help

SQL Statement:
```
SELECT *
FROM CUSTOMER
```
Run
Previous
Next

ISQL Output: Save Result
```
SELECT *
FROM CUSTOMER

NAME        ADDRESS     STATE  ZIP        PHONE        REMARKS
=========   ==========  =====  =========  ==========   =========

TRUE WHEEL  550 HUSKER  NE        58702    555-4545     NONE
BIKE SPEC   CPT SHRIVE  LA        45670    555-1234     NONE
LE SHOPPE   HOMETOWN    KS        54678    555-1278     NONE
AAA BIKE    10 OLDTOWN  NE        56784    555-3421     JOHN-MGR
JACKS BIKE  24 EGLIN    FL        34567    555-2314     NONE
```

Database: TYSSQL   Local Server

Visual C++

Dozens of books have been written about Visual C++. For the examples in this book, we used version 1.52. The procedures we used are applicable to the 32-bit version, C++ 2.0. It is used here because of its simple interface with ODBC. It is not the only compiler with the capability to connect to ODBC. If you use a different compiler, this section provides a good point of departure.

Visual C++ installs quite a few tools. We use only two: the compiler and the resource editor.

Delphi

The last tool we examine is Borland's Delphi, which is the subject of many new books. Delphi provides a scalable interface to various databases.

Delphi has two programs that we use: the InterBase Server (Ibmgr) and the Windows ISQL (Wisql).

Setting Up

Enough with the introductions—let's get to work. After you install your SQL engine or your ODBC-compatible compiler, you must do a certain amount of stage setting before the stars

14

can do their stuff. With both Oracle7 and InterBase, you need to log on and create an account for yourself. The procedures are essentially the same. The hardest part is sorting through the hard copy and online documentation for the default passwords. Both systems have a default system administrator account. (See Figure 14.3.)

Figure 14.3.

InterBase Security manager screen.

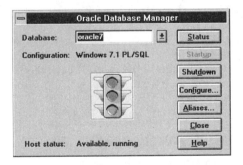

After logging on and creating an account, you are ready to create the database.

Creating the Database

This step is where all your SQL training starts to pay off. First, you have to start up the database you want to use. Figure 14.4 shows Oracle7's stoplight visual metaphor.

Figure 14.4.

Oracle7 Database Manager.

After you get the green light, you can open up the SQL*Plus 3.3 tool shown in Figure 14.5.

Figure 14.5.

*Oracle SQL*Plus.*

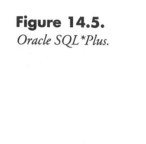

At this point you can create your tables and enter your data using the CREATE and INSERT keywords. Another common way of creating tables and entering data is with a script file. A script file is usually a text file with the SQL commands typed out in the proper order. Look at this excerpt from a script file delivered with Oracle7:

```
------------------------------------------------------------
-- Script to build seed database for Personal Oracle
------------------------------------------------------------
-- NTES
      Called from buildall.sql
-- MODIFICATIONS
.,    rs  13/04/04    Oammant, clean up, resize, for production

------------------------------------------------------------
startup nomount pfile=%rdbms71%\init.ora
--   Create database for Windows RDBMS
create database oracle
      controlfile reuse
      logfile '%oracle_home%\dbs\wdblog1.ora' size 400K reuse,
              '%oracle_home%\dbs\wdblog2.ora' size 400K reuse
      datafile '%oracle_home%\dbs\wdbsys.ora' size 10M reuse
      character set WE8ISO8859P1;
```

The syntax varies slightly with the implementation of SQL and the database you are using, so be sure to check your documentation. Select File | Open to load this script into your SQL engine.

Borland's InterBase loads data in a similar way. The following excerpt is from one of the files to insert data:

```
/*
 *  Add countries.
 */
INSERT INTO country (country, currency) VALUES ('USA',         'Dollar');
INSERT INTO country (country, currency) VALUES ('England',     'Pound');
INSERT INTO country (country, currency) VALUES ('Canada',      'CdnDlr');
INSERT INTO country (country, currency) VALUES ('Switzerland', 'SFranc');
INSERT INTO country (country, currency) VALUES ('Japan',       'Yen');
```

14

```
INSERT INTO country (country, currency) VALUES ('Italy',       'Lira');
INSERT INTO country (country, currency) VALUES ('France',      'FFranc');
INSERT INTO country (country, currency) VALUES ('Germany',     'D-Mark');
INSERT INTO country (country, currency) VALUES ('Australia',   'ADollar');
INSERT INTO country (country, currency) VALUES ('Hong Kong',   'HKDollar');
INSERT INTO country (country, currency) VALUES ('Netherlands', 'Guilder');
INSERT INTO country (country, currency) VALUES ('Belgium',     'BFranc');
INSERT INTO country (country, currency) VALUES ('Austria',     'Schilling');
INSERT INTO country (country, currency) VALUES ('Fiji',        'fdollar');
```

ANALYSIS This example inserts a country name and the type currency used in that country into the COUNTRY table. (Refer to Day 8, "Manipulating Data," for an introduction to the INSERT command.)

There is nothing magic here. Programmers *always* find ways to save keystrokes. If you are playing along at home, enter the following tables:

INPUT
```
/* Table: CUSTOMER, Owner: PERKINS */
CREATE TABLE CUSTOMER (NAME CHAR(10),
        ADDRESS CHAR(10),
        STATE CHAR(2),
        ZIP CHAR(10),
        PHONE CHAR(11),
        REMARKS CHAR(10));
```

INPUT
```
/* Table: ORDERS, Owner: PERKINS */
CREATE TABLE ORDERS (ORDEREDON DATE,
        NAME CHAR(10),
        PARTNUM INTEGER,
        QUANTITY INTEGER,
        REMARKS CHAR(10));
```

INPUT
```
/* Table: PART, Owner: PERKINS */
CREATE TABLE PART (PARTNUM INTEGER,
        DESCRIPTION CHAR(20),
        PRICE NUMERIC(9, 2));
```

Now fill these tables with the following data:

INPUT/ OUTPUT
```
SELECT * FROM CUSTOMER

NAME        ADDRESS     STATE  ZIP     PHONE     REMARKS
==========  ==========  ====== ======  ========  ==========

TRUE WHEEL  550 HUSKER  NE     58702   555-4545  NONE
BIKE SPEC   CPT SHRIVE  LA     45678   555-1234  NONE
LE SHOPPE   HOMETOWN    KS     54678   555-1278  NONE
AAA BIKE    10 OLDTOWN  NE     56784   555-3421  JOHN-MGR
JACKS BIKE  24 EGLIN    FL     34567   555-2314  NONE
```

INPUT/ OUTPUT `SELECT * FROM ORDERS`

```
ORDEREDON NAME          PARTNUM    QUANTITY REMARKS
=========== ==========  =========== =========== =======
15-MAY-1996 TRUE WHEEL       23          6 PAID
19-MAY-1996 TRUE WHEEL       76          3 PAID
 2-SEP-1996 TRUE WHEEL       10          1 PAID
30-JUN-1996 TRUE WHEEL       42          8 PAID
30-JUN-1996 BIKE SPEC        54         10 PAID
30-MAY-1996 BIKE SPEC        10          2 PAID
30-MAY-1996 BIKE SPEC        23          8 PAID
17-JAN-1996 BIKE SPEC        76         11 PAID
17-JAN-1996 LE SHOPPE        76          5 PAID
 1-JUN-1996 LE SHOPPE        10          3 PAID
 1-JUN-1996 AAA BIKE         10          1 PAID
 1-JUL-1996 AAA BIKE         76          4 PAID
 1-JUL-1996 AAA BIKE         46         14 PAID
11-JUL-1996 JACKS BIKE       76         14 PAID
```

SELECT * FROM PART

```
PARTNUM DESCRIPTION                PRICE
=========== ====================== ===========

     54 PEDALS                    54.25
     42 SEATS                     24.50
     46 TIRES                     15.25
     23 MOUNTAIN BIKE            350.45
     76 ROAD BIKE                630.00
     10 TANDEM                  1200.00
```

After you enter this data, the next step is to create an ODBC connection. Open the Control Panel (if you are in Win 3.1, 3.11, or Windows 95) and double-click the ODBC icon.

NOTE

Several flavors of SQL engines load ODBC. Visual C++, Delphi, and Oracle7 load ODBC as part of their setup. Fortunately, ODBC is becoming as common as printer drivers.

The initial ODBC screen is shown in Figure 14.6.

Figure 14.6.

ODBC's Data Sources selection.

Data Sources

Data Sources (Driver):

CARD [Microsoft Text Driver (*.txt; *.csv)]
CFPS [Microsoft Access Driver (*.mdb)]
InterBase [Borland Interbase]
MNEMONIC [Microsoft Access Driver (*.mdb)]
Oracle7 [Oracle71]
PROTRACK [Microsoft Access Driver (*.mdb)]
RS_Btrieve [Btrieve Data [file.ddf]]
RS_dBASE [dBase Files (*.dbf)]
RS_Excel [Excel Files (*.xls)]
RS_FoxPro [FoxPro Files (*.dbf)]

Close
Help
Setup...
Delete
Add...
Drivers...

Options...

14

This screen shows the current ODBC connections. You want to create a new connection. Assuming you used InterBase and called the new database TYSSQL (give yourself 10 bonus points if you know what TYSSQL stands for), press the Add button and select the InterBase Driver, as shown in Figure 14.7.

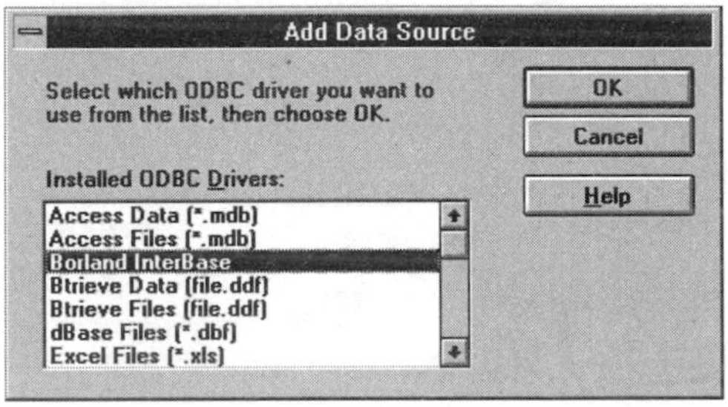

Figure 14.7.

Driver selection.

From this selection you move to the setup screen. Fill it in as shown in Figure 14.8.

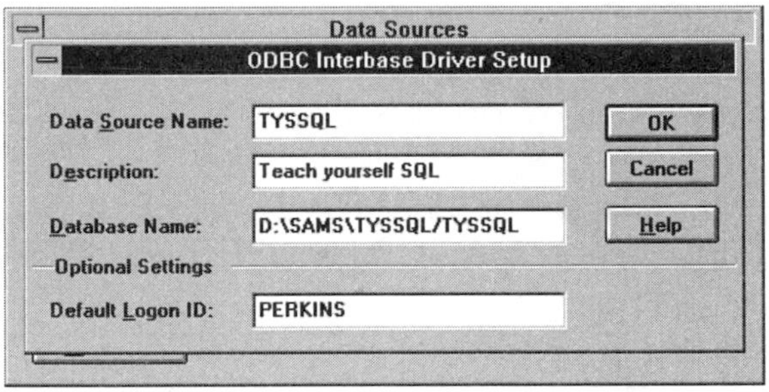

Figure 14.8.

Driver setup.

You can use your own name or something short and easy to type, depending on the account you set up for yourself. The only tricky bit here, at least for us, was figuring out what InterBase wanted as a database name. Those of you coming from a PC or small database background will have to get used to some odd-looking pathnames. These pathnames tell the SQL engine where to look for the database in the galaxy of computers that could be connected via LANs.

Using Microsoft Query to Perform a Join

Now that you have made an ODBC connection, we need to make a slight detour to a rather useful tool called Microsoft Query. This program is loaded along with Visual C++. We have used it to solve enough database and coding problems to pay for the cost of the compiler several times over. Query normally installs itself in its own program group. Find it and open it. It should look like Figure 14.9.

Figure 14.9.
Microsoft Query.

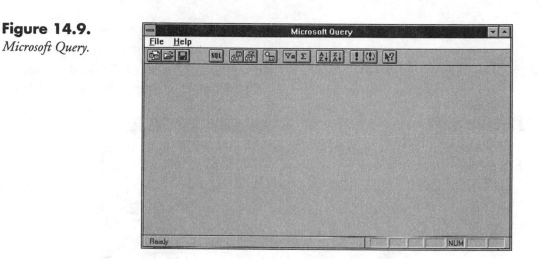

Select File | New Query. Your TYSSQL ODBC link does not appear, so click the Other button to bring up the ODBC Data Sources dialog box, shown in Figure 14.10, and select TYSSQL.

Figure 14.10.
Data Sources dialog box.

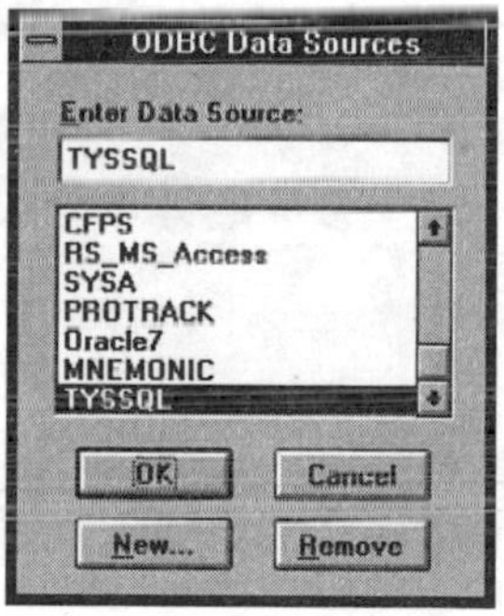

Click OK to return to the Select Data Source dialog box. Select TYSSQL and click Use, as shown in Figure 14.11.

Figure 14.11.
Select Data Source dialog box.

14

Again, small database users aren't accustomed to logging on. Nevertheless, type your password to move through the screen.

The Add Tables dialog box, shown in Figure 14.12, presents the tables associated with the database to which you are connected. Select PART, ORDERS, and CUSTOMER, and click Close.

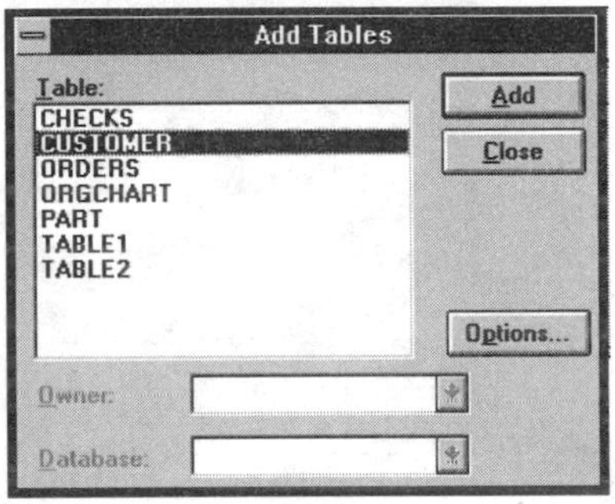

Figure 14.12.

Selecting tables in Query.

Your screen should look like Figure 14.13. Double-click ADDRESS and NAME from the CUSTOMER table. Then double-click ORDEREDON and PARTNUM from ORDERS.

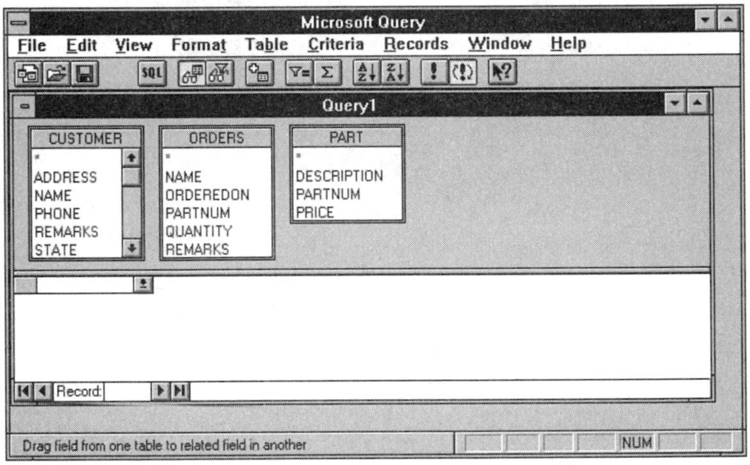

Figure 14.13.

Visual representation of a table in Query.

Now for some magic! Click the button marked SQL in the toolbar. Your screen should now look like Figure 14.14.

Figure 14.14.

The query that Query built.

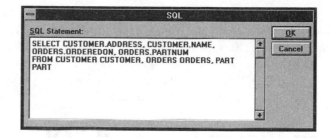

This tool has two functions. The first is to check the ODBC connection. If it works here, it should work in the program. This step can help you determine whether a problem is in the database or in the program. The second use is to generate and check queries. Add the following line to the SQL box and click OK:

```
WHERE CUSTOMER.NAME = ORDERS.NAME AND PART.PARTNUM = ORDERS.PARTNUM
```

Figure 14.15 shows the remarkable result.

Figure 14.15.

Query's graphic representation of a join.

ADDRESS	NAME	ORDEREDO	PARTNUM
10 OLDTOWN	AAA BIKE	1996-06-01	10
10 OLDTOWN	AAA BIKE	1996-07-01	46
10 OLDTOWN	AAA BIKE	1996-07-01	76
CPT SHRIVE	BIKE SPEC	1996-05-30	10
CPT SHRIVE	BIKE SPEC	1996-05-30	23
CPT SHRIVE	BIKE SPEC	1996-06-30	54
CPT SHRIVE	BIKE SPEC	1996-01-17	76
24 EGLIN	JACKS BIKE	1996-07-11	76
HOMETOWN	LE SHOPPE	1996-06-01	10
HOMETOWN	LE SHOPPE	1996-01-17	76
550 HUSKER	TRUE WHEEL	1996-09-02	10
550 HUSKER	TRUE WHEEL	1996-05-15	23
550 HUSKER	TRUE WHEEL	1996-06-30	42
550 HUSKER	TRUE WHEEL	1996-05-19	76

You have just performed a join! Not only that, but the fields you joined on have been graphically connected in the table diagrams (note the zigzag lines between NAME and PARTNUM).

14

Query is an important tool to have in your SQL arsenal on the Windows software platform. It enables you examine and manipulate tables and queries. You can also use it to create tables and manipulate data. If you work in Windows with ODBC and SQL, either buy this tool yourself or have your company or client buy it for you. It is not as interesting as a network version of DOOM, but it will save you time and money. Now that you have established an ODBC link, you can use it in a program.

Using Visual C++ and SQL

NOTE   The source code for this example is located in Appendix B, "Source Code Listings for the C++ Program Used on Day 14."

Call up Visual C++ and select AppWizard, as shown in Figure 14.16. The name and subdirectory for your project do not have to be identical.

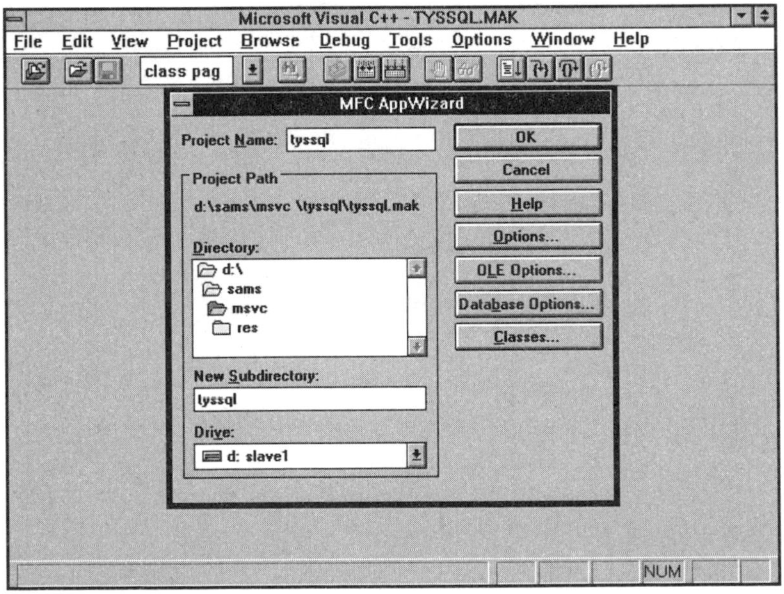

Figure 14.16.
Initial project setup.

![Screenshot of Microsoft Visual C++ - TYSSQL.MAK showing the MFC AppWizard dialog. Menu bar: File Edit View Project Browse Debug Tools Options Window Help. The dialog contains: Project Name: tyssql; Project Path: d:\sams\msvc \tyssql\tyssql.mak; Directory: d:\ sams msvc res; New Subdirectory: tyssql; Drive: d: slave1. Buttons: OK, Cancel, Help, Options..., OLE Options..., Database Options..., Classes...]

Click the Options button and fill out the screen as shown in Figure 14.17.

14

Figure 14.17.

The Options dialog box.

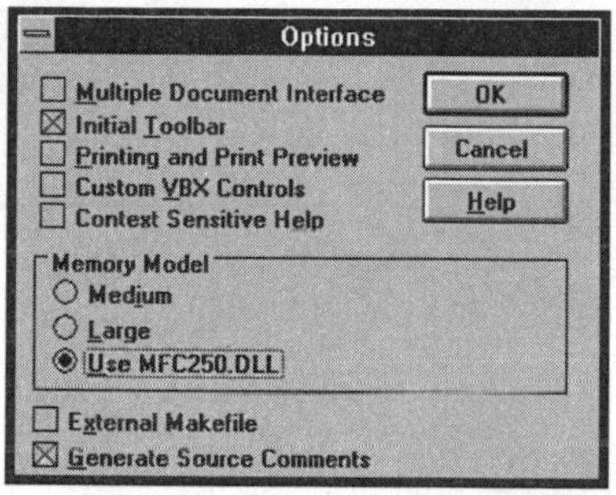

Options

☐ Multiple Document Interface
☒ Initial Toolbar
☐ Printing and Print Preview
☐ Custom VBX Controls
☐ Context Sensitive Help

Memory Model
○ Medium
○ Large
◉ Use MFC250.DLL

☐ External Makefile
☒ Generate Source Comments

OK
Cancel
Help

Click OK and then choose Database Options. Select Database Support, No File Support as shown in Figure 14.18.

Figure 14.18.

The Database Options dialog box.

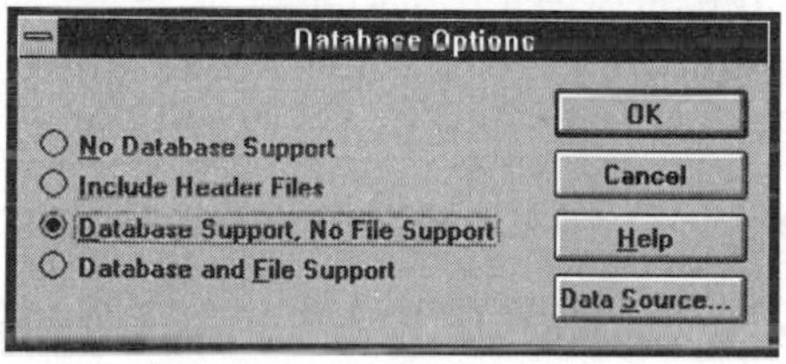

Database Options

○ No Database Support
○ Include Header Files
◉ Database Support, No File Support
○ Database and File Support

OK
Cancel
Help
Data Source...

Click the Data Source button and make the choices shown in Figure 14.19.

Figure 14.19.

Selecting a data source.

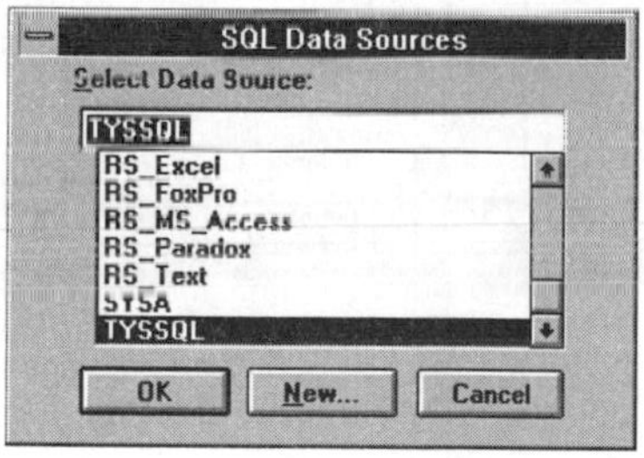

SQL Data Sources

Select Data Source:

TYSSQL

RS_Excel
RS_FoxPro
RS_MS_Access
RS_Paradox
RS_Text
SYSA
TYSSQL

OK   New...   Cancel

Then select the CUSTOMER table from the Select a Table dialog box, shown in Figure 14.20.

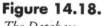

Figure 14.20.

Selecting a table.

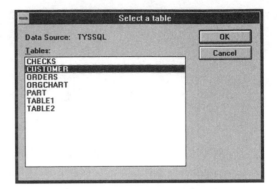

Now you have selected the CUSTOMER table from the TYSSQL database. Go back to the AppWizard basic screen by clicking OK twice. Then click OK again to display the new application information (see Figure 14.21), showing the specifications of a new skeleton application.

Figure 14.21.

AppWizard's new application information.

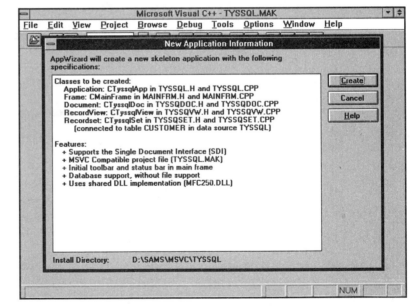

After the program is generated, you need to use the resource editor to design your main screen. Select Tools | App Studio to launch App Studio. The form you design will be simple—just enough to show some of the columns in your table as you scroll through the rows. Your finished form should look something like Figure 14.22.

Figure 14.22.
Finished form in App Studio.

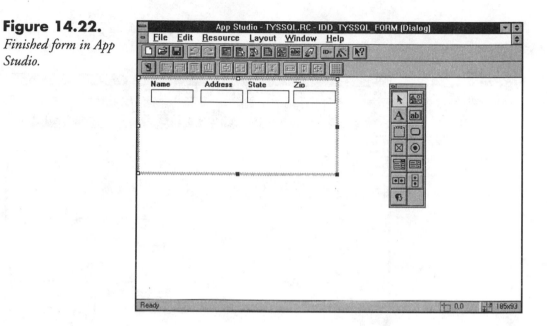

For simplicity we named the edit boxes IDC_NAME, IDC_ADDRESS, IDC_STATE, and IDC_ZIP, although you can name them whatever you choose. Press Ctrl+W to send the Class Wizard page to the Member Variables and set the variables according to Figure 14.23.

Figure 14.23.
Adding member variables in Class Wizard.

NOTE

The program was nice enough to provide links to the table to which you are connected. Links are one of the benefits of working through Microsoft's wizards or Borland's experts.

14

Save your work; then press Alt+Tab to return to the compiler and compile the program. If all went well, your output should look like Figure 14.24. If it doesn't, retrace your steps and try again.

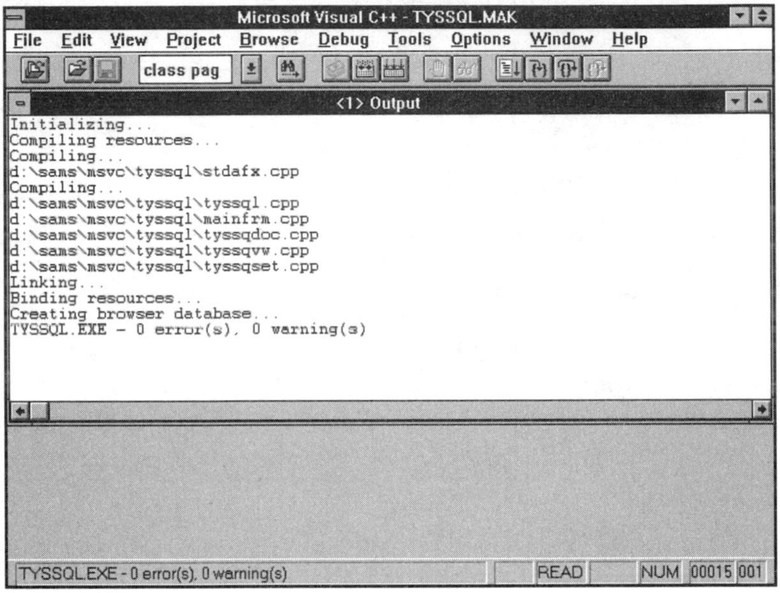

Figure 14.24.

A clean compile for the test program.

Now run your program. It should appear, after that pesky logon screen, and look like Figure 14.25.

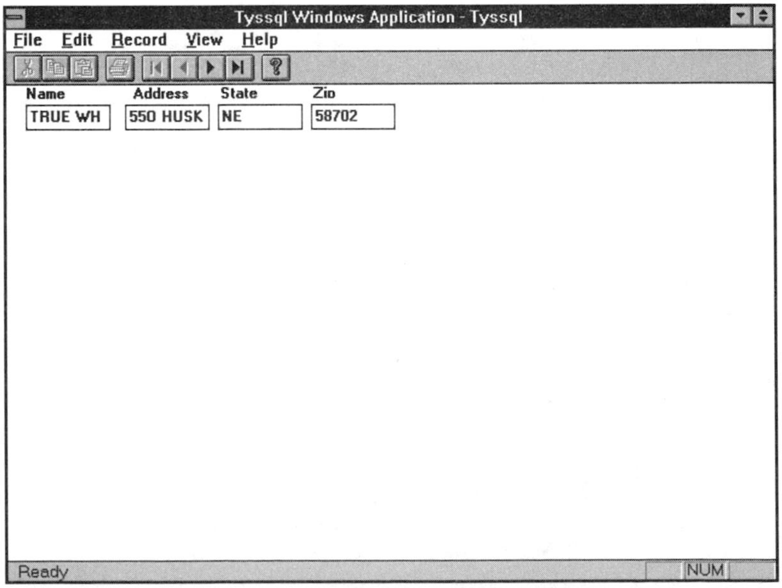

Figure 14.25.

The test program.

An impressive program, considering that you have written zero lines of code so far. Use the arrow keys on the toolbar to move back and forth in the database. Notice that the order of the data is the same as its input order. It is not alphabetical (unless you typed it in that way). How can you change the order?

Your connection to the database is encapsulated in a class called CtyssqlSet, which the AppWizard created for you. Look at the header file (tyssqset.h):

```
// tyssqset.h : interface of the CTyssqlSet class
//
/////////////////////////////////////////////////////////////////////////
class CTyssqlSet : public CRecordset
{
DECLARE_DYNAMIC(CTyssqlSet)
public:
CTyssqlSet(CDatabase* pDatabase = NULL);
// Field/Param Data
//{{AFX_FIELD(CTyssqlSet, CRecordset)
Cstring     m_NAME;
Cstring     m_ADDRESS;
Cstring     m_STATE;
Cstring     m_ZIP;
Cstring     m_PHONE;
Cstring     m_REMARKS;
//}}AFX_FIELD
// Implementation
protected:
virtual CString GetDefaultConnect();// Default connection string
virtual CString GetDefaultSQL();// default SQL for Recordset
virtual void DoFieldExchange(CFieldExchange* pFX);// RFX support
};
```

ANALYSIS Note that member variables have been constructed for all the columns in the table. Also notice the functions GetDefaultConnect and GetDefaultSQL; here's their implementations from tyssqset.opp:

```
CString CTyssqlSet::GetDefaultConnect()
{
return ODBC;DSN=TYSSQL;";
}
CString CTyssqlSet::GetDefaultSQL()
{
return "CUSTOMER";
}
```

GetDefaultConnect makes the ODBC connection. You shouldn't change it. However, GetDefaultSQL enables you to do some interesting things. Change it to this:

```
return "SELECT * FROM CUSTOMER ORDER BY NAME";
```

Recompile, and magically your table is sorted by name, as shown in Figure 14.26.

14

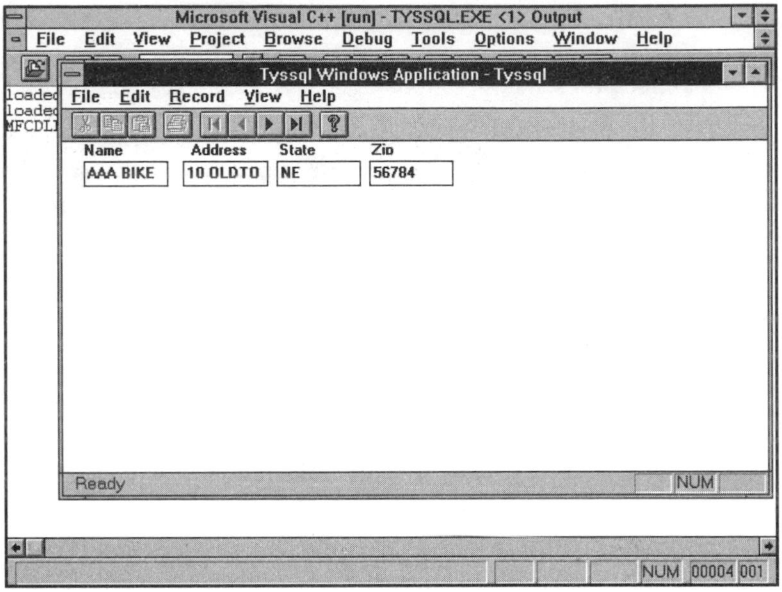

Figure 14.26.

Database order changed by SQL.

Without going into a tutorial on the Microsoft Foundation Class, let us just say that you can manipulate CRecordSet and Cdatabase objects, join and drop tables, update and insert rows, and generally have all the fun possible in SQL. You have looked as far over the edge as you can, and we have pointed the way to integrate SQL into C++ applications. Topics suggested for further study are CRecordSet and Cdatabase (both in the C++ books online that should come as part of the C++ software), ODBC API (the subject of several books), and the APIs provided by Oracle and Sybase (which are both similar to the ODBC API).

Using Delphi and SQL

Another important database tool on the Windows software platform is Delphi. The splash that comes up as the program is loading has a picture of the Oracle at Delphi, surrounded by the letters *SQL*. In the C++ example you rewrote one line of code. Using Delphi, you will join two tables without writing a single line of code!

NOTE

The code for this program is located in Appendix C, "Source Code Listings for the Delphi Program Used on Day 14."

Double-click Delphi's icon to get it started. At rest the program looks like Figure 14.27.

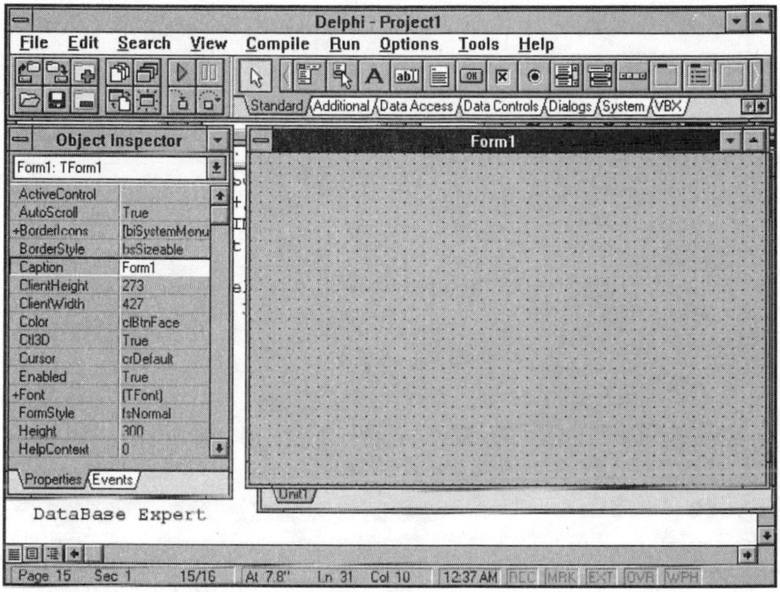

Figure 14.27.

The Delphi program-ming environment.

Delphi requires you to register any ODBC connections you are going to use in your programming. Select BDE (Borland Database Environment) from the Tools menu and then fill out the dialog box shown in Figure 14.28.

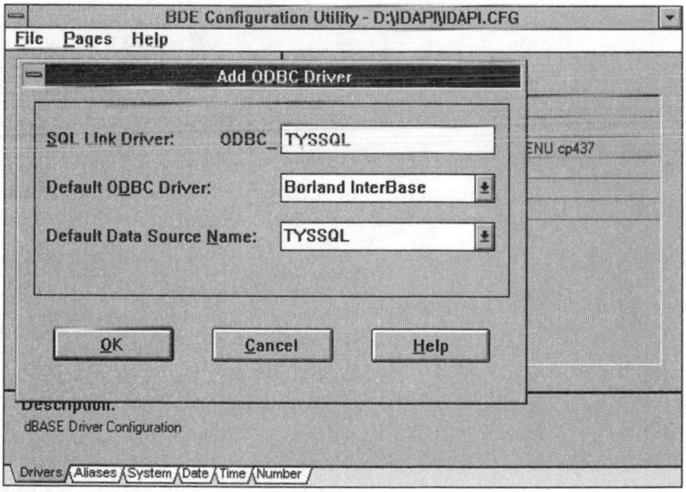

Figure 14.28.

Registering your connections.

Click the Aliases tab shown at the bottom of Figure 14.28 and assign the name TYSSQL, as shown in Figure 14.29.

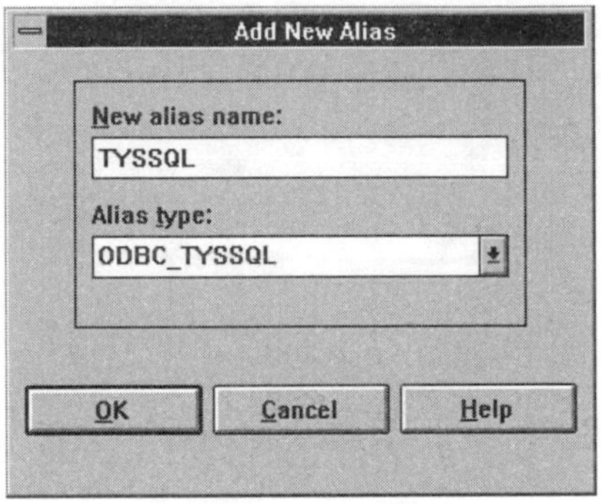

Figure 14.29.

Adding a new alias.

Select File | New Form to make the following selections. Start by choosing the Database Form from the Experts tab, as shown in Figure 14.30.

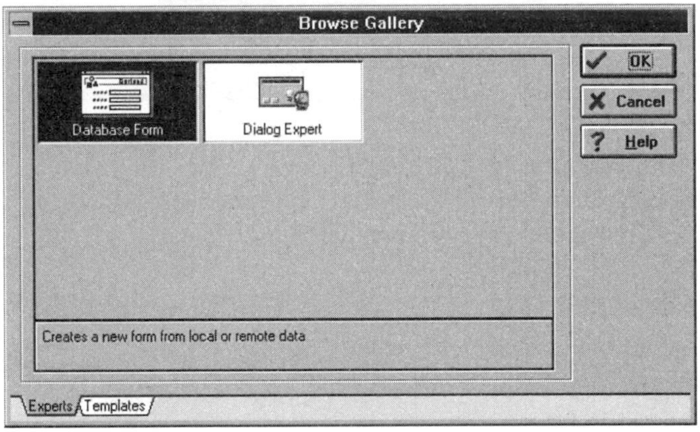

Figure 14.30.

The Experts page in the Browse gallery.

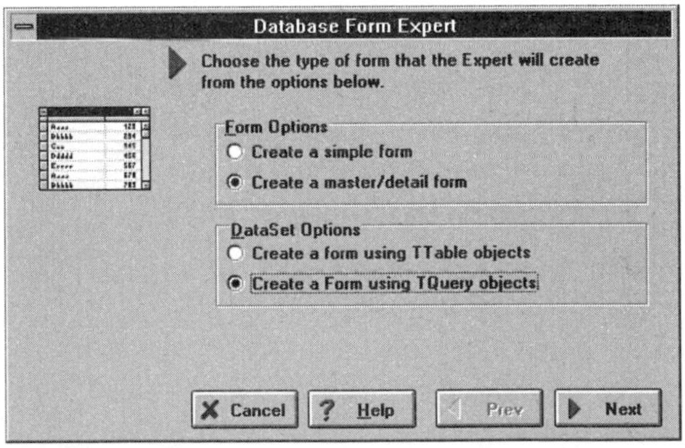

Figure 14.31.

The Database Form Expert dialog box.

Then choose the master/detail form and TQuery objects, as shown in Figure 14.31.

NOTE Delphi enables you to work with either a query or a table. If you need flexibility, we recommend the TQuery object. If you need the whole table without modification, use the TTable object.

Now select the TYSSQL data source you set up earlier, as shown in Figure 14.32.

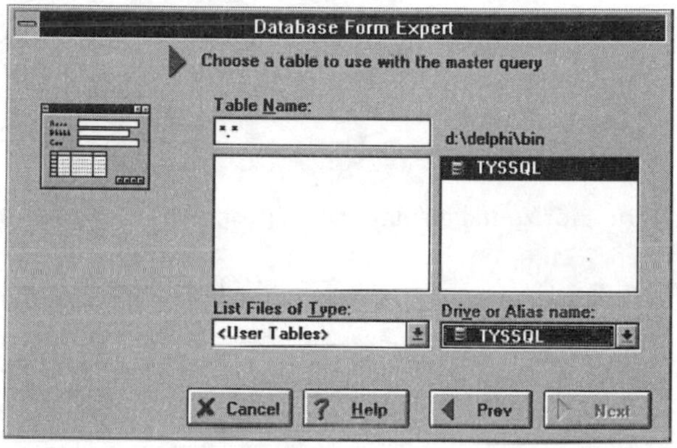

Figure 14.32.

Choosing a data source.

Choose the PART table as the master, as shown in Figure 14.33.

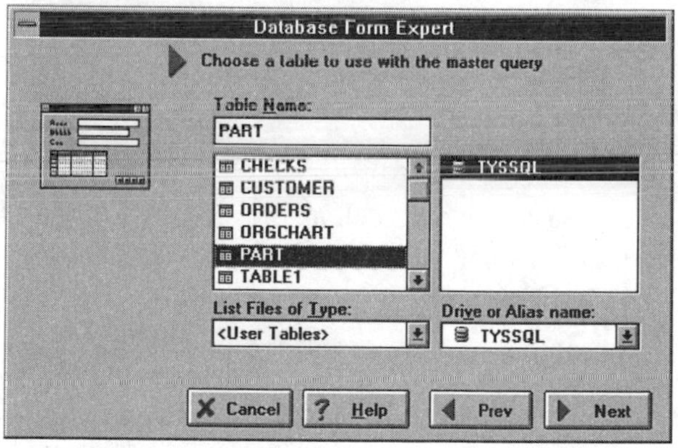

Figure 14.33.

Choosing a table.

Choose all its fields, as shown in Figure 14.34.

14

Figure 14.34.
Adding all the fields.

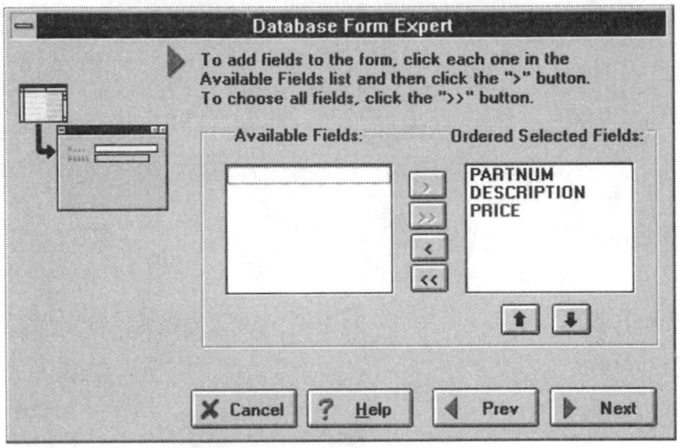

Pick the Horizontal display mode, as shown in Figure 14.35.

Figure 14.35.
Display mode selection.

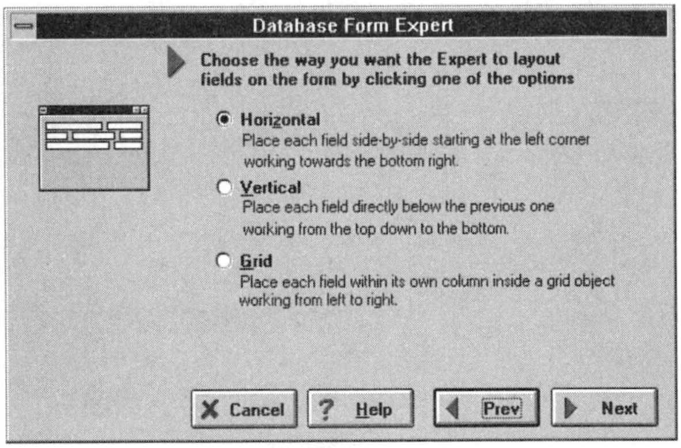

Then choose ORDERS, select all its fields, and select Grid for its display mode, as shown in Figures 14.36, 14.37, and 14.38.

Figure 14.36.
Choosing the table for the detail part of the form.

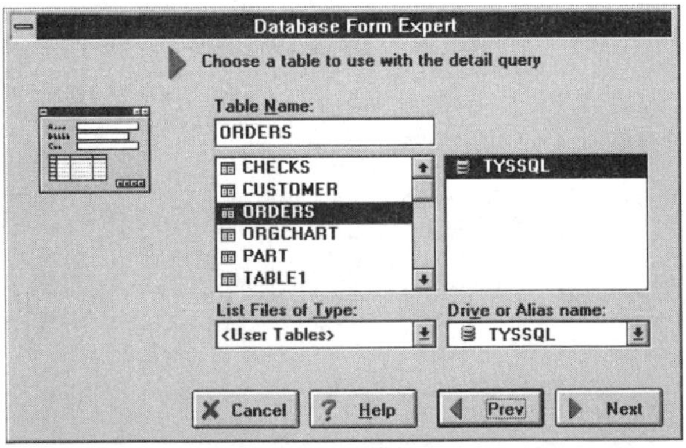

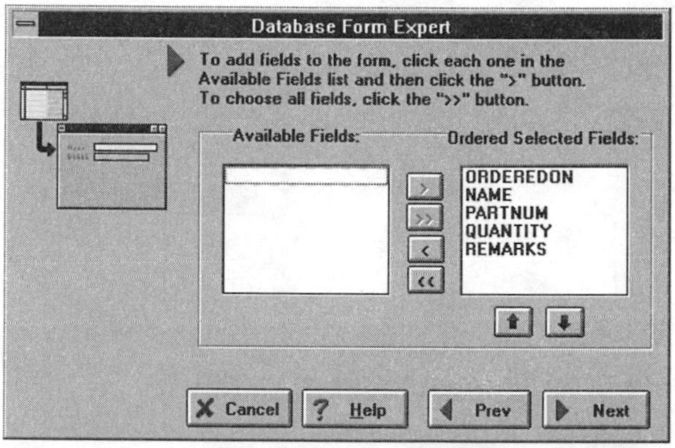

Figure 14.37.
Selecting all the fields.

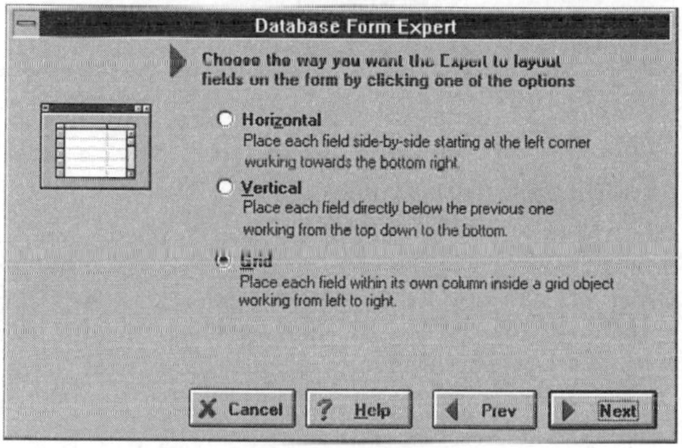

Figure 14.38.
*Selecting the orienta
tion.*

Now the software enables you to make a join. Make the join on PARTNUM, as shown in Figure 14.39.

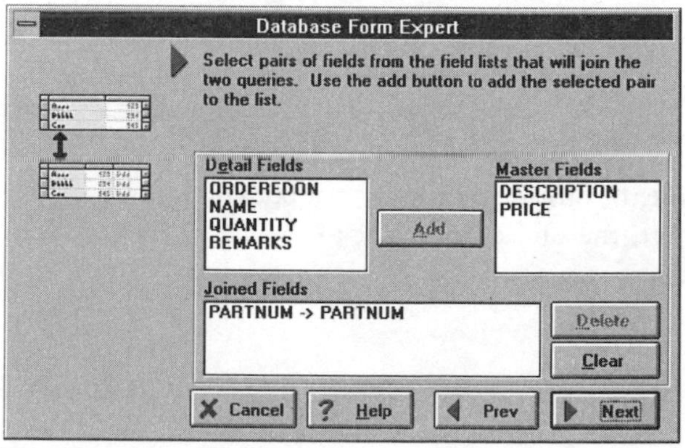

Figure 14.39.
Making the join.

14

Now go ahead and generate the form. The result looks like Figure 14.40.

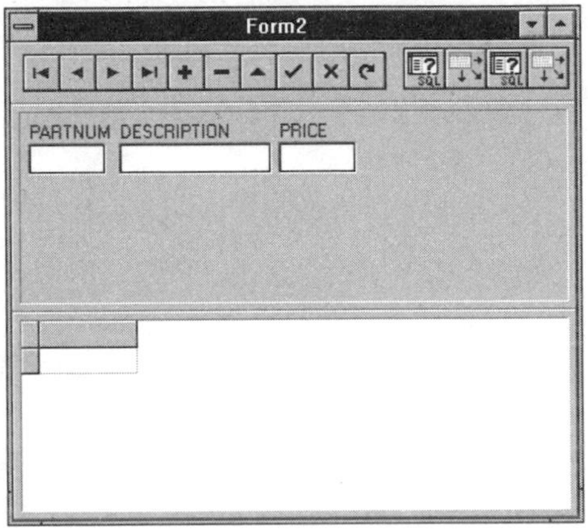

Figure 14.40.
The finished form.

Compile and run the program. As you select different parts, the order for them should appear in the lower table, as shown in Figure 14.41.

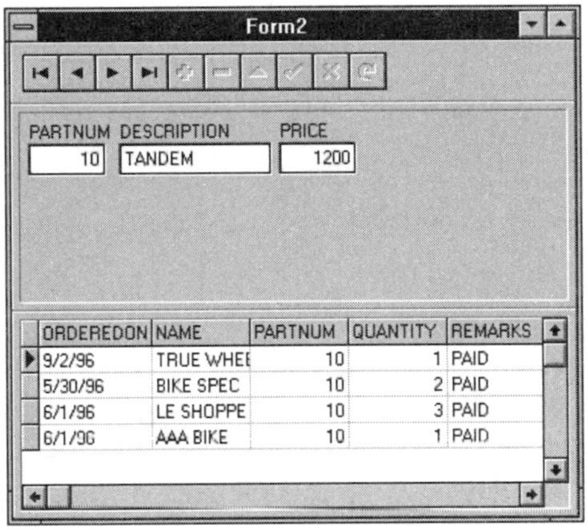

Figure 14.41.
The finished program.

Close the project and click one or both of the query objects on the form. When you click an object, the Object Inspector to the left of the screen in Figure 14.42 shows the various properties.

Figure 14.42.

The query in the TQuery object.

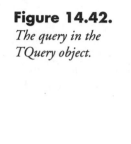

Try experimenting with the query to see what happens. Just think what you can do when you start writing code!

Summary

Today you learned where to start applying SQL using the ordinary, everyday stuff you find lying on your hard drive. The best way to build on what you have learned is to go out and query. Query as much as you can.

Q&A

Q What is the difference between the ODBC API and the Oracle and Sybase APIs?

A On a function-by-function level, Oracle and Sybase are remarkably similar, which is not a coincidence. Multiple corporate teamings and divorces have led to libraries that were derived from somewhat of a common base. ODBC's API is more generic—it isn't specific to any database. If you need to do something specific to a database or tune the performance of a specific database, you might consider using that database's API library in your code.

Q With all the available products, how do I know what to use?

A In a business environment, product selection is usually a compromise between management and "techies." Management looks at the cost of a product; techies will look at the features and how the product can make their lives easier. In the best of all programming worlds, that compromise will get your job done quickly and efficiently.

14

Workshop

The Workshop provides quiz questions to help solidify your understanding of the material covered, as well as exercises to provide you with experience in using what you have learned. Try to answer the quiz and exercise questions before checking the answers in Appendix F, "Answers to Quizzes and Exercises."

Quiz

1. In which object does Microsoft Visual C++ place its SQL?
2. In which object does Delphi place its SQL?
3. What is ODBC?
4. What does Delphi do?

Exercises

1. Change the sort order in the C++ example from ascending to descending on the State field.
2. Go out, find an application that needs SQL, and use it.

WEEK 2

In Review

Week 1 spent a great deal of time introducing a very important topic: the SELECT statement. Week 2 branched out into various topics that collectively form a thorough introduction to the Structured Query Language (SQL).

Day 8 introduced data manipulation language (DML) statements, which are SQL statements that you can use to modify the data within a database. The three commands most commonly used are INSERT, DELETE, and UPDATE. Day 9 described how to design and build a database and introduced the commands CREATE DATABASE and CREATE TABLE. A table can be created with any number of fields, each of which can be a database-vendor-defined data type. The ALTER DATABASE command can change the physical size or location of a database. The DROP DATABASE and DROP TABLE statements, respectively, remove a database or remove a table within a database.

Day 10 explained two ways to display data: the view and the index. A view is a virtual table created from the output of a SELECT statement. An index orders the records within a table based on the contents of a field or fields.

Day 11 covered transaction management, which was your first taste of programming with SQL. Transactions start with the BEGIN TRANSACTION statement. The COMMIT TRANSACTION saves the work of a transaction. The ROLLBACK TRANSACTION command cancels the work of a transaction.

Day 12 focused on database security. Although the implementation of database security varies widely among database products, most implementations use the GRANT and REVOKE commands. The GRANT command grants permissions to a user. The REVOKE command removes these permissions.

Day 13 focused on developing application programs using SQL. Static SQL typically involves the use of a precompiler and is static at runtime. Dynamic SQL is very flexible and has become very popular in the last few years. Sample programs used Dynamic SQL with the Visual C++ and Delphi development toolkits.

Day 14 covered advanced aspects of SQL. Cursors can scroll through a set of records. Stored procedures are database objects that execute several SQL statements in a row. Stored procedures can accept and return values. Triggers are a special type of stored procedure that are executed when records are inserted, updated, or deleted within a table.

WEEK

3

At A Glance

Applying Your Knowledge of SQL

Welcome to Week 3. So far you have learned the fundamentals of SQL and already know enough to apply what you have learned to some real-life situations. This week builds on the foundation established in Weeks 1 and 2. Day 15 shows you how to streamline SQL statements for improved performance. Day 16 talks about the data dictionary, or system catalog, of a relational database and shows you how to retrieve valuable information. Day 17 extends the concept of using the data dictionary to generate SQL as output from another SQL statement. You will learn the benefits of this technique and discover how generating SQL can improve your efficiency on the job. Day 18 covers Oracle's PL/SQL, or Oracle procedural language. PL/SQL is one of the many extensions to standard SQL. Another extension is Sybase's and Microsoft

Server's Transact-SQL, which is covered on Day 19. Day 20 returns to Oracle to cover SQL*Plus, which allows you to use advanced commands to communicate with the database. SQL*Plus also enables you to format query-generated reports in an attractive manner. You can use SQL*Plus in collaboration with PL/SQL. Day 21 examines errors and logical mistakes that relational database users frequently encounter. We provide brief descriptions of the errors, solutions, and tips on avoiding errors.

Day **15**

Streamlining SQL Statements for Improved Performance

Streamlining SQL statements is as much a part of application performance as database designing and tuning. No matter how fine-tuned the database or how sound the database structure, you will not receive timely query results that are acceptable to you, or even worse, the customer, if you don't follow some basic guidelines. Trust us, if the customer is not satisfied, then you can bet your boss won't be satisfied cither.

Objectives

You already know about the major components of the relational database language of SQL and how to communicate with the database; now it's time to apply your knowledge to real-life performance concerns. The objective of Day 15 is to recommend methods for improving the performance of, or streamlining, an SQL statement. By the end of today, you should

☐ Understand the concept of streamlining your SQL code

☐ Understand the differences between batch loads and transactional processing and their effects on database performance

☐ Be able to manipulate the conditions in your query to expedite data retrieval

☐ Be familiar with some underlying elements that affect the tuning of the entire database

Here's an analogy to help you understand the phrase *streamline an SQL statement*. The objective of competitive swimmers is to complete an event in as little time as possible without being disqualified. The swimmers must have an acceptable technique, be able to torpedo themselves through the water, and use all their physical resources as effectively as possible. With each stroke and breath they take, competitive swimmers remain *streamlined* and move through the water with very little resistance.

Look at your SQL query the same way. You should always know exactly what you want to accomplish and then strive to follow the path of least resistance. The more time you spend planning, the less time you'll have to spend revising later. Your goal should always be to retrieve accurate data and to do so in as little time as possible. An end user waiting on a slow query is like a hungry diner impatiently awaiting a tardy meal. Although you can write most queries in several ways, the arrangement of the components within the query is the factor that makes the difference of seconds, minutes, and sometimes hours when you execute the query. *Streamlining SQL* is the process of finding the optimal arrangement of the elements within your query.

In addition to streamlining your SQL statement, you should also consider several other factors when trying to improve general database performance, for example, concurrent user transactions that occur within a database, indexing of tables, and deep-down database tuning.

Note

Today's examples use Personal Oracle7 and tools that are available with the Oracle7.3 relational database management system. The concepts discussed today are not restricted to Oracle; they may be applied to other relational database management systems.

Make Your SQL Statements Readable

Even though readability doesn't affect the actual performance of SQL statements, good programming practice calls for readable code. Readability is especially important if you have multiple conditions in the WHERE clause. Anyone reading the clause should be able to determine whether the tables are being joined properly and should be able to understand the order of the conditions.

Try to read this statement:

```
SQL> SELECT EMPLOYEE_TBL.EMPLOYEE_ID, EMPLOYEE_TBL.NAME,
     ➥EMPLOYEE_PAY_TBL.SALARY,EMPLOYEE_PAY_TBL.HIRE_DATE
  2  FROM EMPLOYEE_TBL, EMPLOYEE_PAY_TBL
  3  WHERE EMPLOYEE_TBL.EMPLOYEE_ID = EMPLOYEE_PAY_TBL.EMPLOYEE_ID AND
  4  EMPLOYEE_PAY_TBL.SALARY > 30000 OR (EMPLOYEE_PAY_TBL.SALARY BETWEEN 25000
  5  AND 30000 AND EMPLOYEE_PAY_TBL.HIRE_DATE < SYSDATE - 365);
```

Here's the same query reformatted to enhance readability:

```
SQL> SELECT E.EMPLOYEE_ID, E.NAME, P.SALARY, P.HIRE_DATE
  2  FROM EMPLOYEE_TBL E,
  3         EMPLOYEE_PAY_TBL P
  4  WHERE E.EMPLOYEE_ID = P.EMPLOYEE_ID
  5    AND P.SALARY > 30000
  6     OR (P.SALARY BETWEEN 25000 AND 30000
  7    AND P.HIRE_DATE < SYSDATE - 365);
```

NOTE

> Notice the use of table aliases in the preceding query. EMPLOYEE_TBL in line 2 has been assigned the alias E, and EMPLOYEE_PAY_TBL in line 3 has been assigned the alias P. You can see that in lines 4, 5, 6, and 7, the E and P stand for the full table names. Aliases require much less typing than spelling out the full table name, and even more important, queries that use aliases are more organized and easier to read than queries that are cluttered with unnecessarily long full table names.

The two queries are identical, but the second one is obviously much easier to read. It is very *structured;* that is, the logical components of the query have been separated by carriage returns and consistent spacing. You can quickly see what is being selected (the SELECT clause), what tables are being accessed (the FROM clause), and what conditions need to be met (the WHERE clause).

The Full-Table Scan

A full-table scan occurs when the database server reads every record in a table in order to execute an SQL statement. Full-table scans are normally an issue when dealing with queries or the SELECT statement. However, a full-table scan can also come into play when dealing with updates and deletes. A full-table scan occurs when the columns in the WHERE clause do not have an index associated with them. A full-table scan is like reading a book from cover to cover, trying to find a keyword. Most often, you will opt to use the index.

You can avoid a full-table scan by creating an index on columns that are used as conditions in the WHERE clause of an SQL statement. Indexes provide a direct path to the data the same way an index in a book refers the reader to a page number. Adding an index speeds up data access.

Although programmers usually frown upon full-table scans, they are sometimes appropriate. For example:

☐ You are selecting most of the rows from a table.

☐ You are updating every row in a table.

☐ The tables are small.

In the first two cases an index would be inefficient because the database server would have to refer to the index, read the table, refer to the index again, read the table again, and so on. On the other hand, indexes are most efficient when the data you are accessing is a small percentage, usually no more than 10 to 15 percent, of the total data contained within the table.

In addition, indexes are best used on large tables. You should always consider table size when you are designing tables and indexes. Properly indexing tables involves familiarity with the data, knowing which columns will be referenced most, and may require experimentation to see which indexes work best.

NOTE

When speaking of a "large table," *large* is a relative term. A table that is extremely large to one individual may be minute to another. The size of a table is relative to the size of other tables in the database, to the disk space available, to the number of disks available, and simple common sense. Obviously, a 2GB table is large, whereas a 16KB table is small. In a database environment where the average table size is 100MB, a 500MB table may be considered massive.

Adding a New Index

You will often find situations in which an SQL statement is running for an unreasonable amount of time, although the performance of other statements seems to be acceptable; for example, when conditions for data retrieval change or when table structures change.

We have also seen this type of slowdown when a new screen or window has been added to a front-end application. One of the first things to do when you begin to troubleshoot is to find out whether the target table has an index. In most of the cases we have seen, the target table has an index, but one of the new conditions in the WHERE clause may lack an index. Looking at the WHERE clause of the SQL statement, we have asked, Should we add another index? The answer may be yes if:

- ☐ The most restrictive condition(s) returns less than 10 percent of the rows in a table.
- ☐ The most restrictive condition(s) will be used often in an SQL statement.
- ☐ Condition(s) on columns with an index will return unique values.
- ☐ Columns are often referenced in the ORDER BY and GROUP BY clauses.

Composite indexes may also be used. A *composite index* is an index on two or more columns in a table. These indexes can be more efficient than single-column indexes if the indexed columns are often used together as conditions in the WHERE clause of an SQL statement. If the indexed columns are used separately as well as together, especially in other queries, single-column indexes may be more appropriate. Use your judgment and run tests on your data to see which type of index best suits your database.

Arrangement of Elements in a Query

The best arrangement of elements within your query, particularly in the WHERE clause, really depends on the order of the processing steps in a specific implementation. The arrangement of conditions depends on the columns that are indexed, as well as on which condition will retrieve the fewest records.

You do not have to use a column that is indexed in the WHERE clause, but it is obviously more beneficial to do so. Try to narrow down the results of the SQL statement by using an index that returns the fewest number of rows. The condition that returns the fewest records in a table is said to be the *most restrictive condition*. As a general statement, you should place the most restrictive conditions last in the WHERE clause. (Oracle's query optimizer reads a WHERE clause from the bottom up, so in a sense, you would be placing the most restrictive condition first.)

When the optimizer reads the most restrictive condition first, it is able to narrow down the first set of results before proceeding to the next condition. The next condition, instead of looking at the whole table, should look at the subset that was selected by the most selective condition. Ultimately, data is retrieved faster. The most selective condition may be unclear in complex queries with multiple conditions, subqueries, calculations, and several combinations of the AND, OR, and LIKE.

TIP   Always check your database documentation to see how SQL statements are processed in your implementation.

The following test is one of many we have run to measure the difference of elapsed time between two uniquely arranged queries with the same content. These examples use Oracle7.3 relational database management system. Remember, the optimizer in this implementation reads the WHERE clause from the bottom up.

Before creating the SELECT statement, we selected distinct row counts on each condition that we planned to use. Here are the values selected for each condition:

Condition	Distinct Values
calc_ytd = '-2109490.8'	13,000 +
dt_stmp = '01-SEP-96'	15
output_cd = '001'	13
activity_cd = 'IN'	10
status_cd = 'A'	4
function_cd = '060'	6

NOTE

The most restrictive condition is also the condition with the most distinct values.

The next example places the most restrictive conditions first in the WHERE clause:

INPUT
```
SQL> SET TIMING ON
  2  SELECT COUNT(*)
  3  FROM FACT_TABLE
  4  WHERE CALC_YTD = '-2109490.8'
  5    AND DT_STMP = '01-SEP-96'
  6    AND OUTPUT_CD = '001'
  7    AND ACTIVITY_CD = 'IN'
  8    AND STATUS_CD = 'A'
  9    AND FUNCTION_CD = '060';
```

OUTPUT
```
COUNT(*)
--------
       8
1 row selected.
Elapsed:  00:00:15.37
```

This example places the most restrictive conditions last in the WHERE clause:

INPUT/OUTPUT
```
SQL> SET TIMING ON
  2  SELECT COUNT(*)
  3  FROM FACT_TABLE
  4  WHERE FUNCTION_CD = '060'
  5    AND STATUS_CD = 'A'
  6    AND ACTIVITY_CD = 'IN'
  7    AND OUTPUT_CD = '001'
```

```
8      AND DT_STMP = '01-SEP-96'
9      AND CALC_YTD = '-2109490.8';

COUNT(*)
--------
       8
1 row selected.
Elapsed:  00:00:01.80
```

ANALYSIS Notice the difference in elapsed time. Simply changing the order of conditions according to the given table statistics, the second query ran almost 14 seconds faster than the first one. Imagine the difference on a poorly structured query that runs for three hours!

Procedures

For queries that are executed on a regular basis, try to use procedures. A *procedure* is a potentially large group of SQL statements. (Refer to Day 13, "Advanced SQL Topics.")

Procedures are compiled by the database engine and then executed. Unlike an SQL statement, the database engine need not optimize the procedure before it is executed. Procedures, as opposed to numerous individual queries, may be easier for the user to maintain and more efficient for the database.

Avoiding OR

Avoid using the logical operator OR in a query if possible. OR inevitably slows down nearly any query against a table of substantial size. We find that IN is generally much quicker than OR. This advice certainly doesn't agree with documentation stating that optimizers convert IN arguments to OR conditions. Nevertheless, here is an example of a query using multiple ORs:

INPUT
```
SQL> SELECT *
  2  FROM FACT_TABLE
  3  WHERE STATUS_CD = 'A'
  4      OR STATUS_CD = 'B'
  5      OR STATUS_CD = 'C'
  6      OR STATUS_CD = 'D'
  7      OR STATUS_CD = 'E'
  8      OR STATUS_CD = 'F'
  9  ORDER BY STATUS_CD;
```

Here is the same query using SUBSTR and IN:

INPUT
```
SQL> SELECT *
  2  FROM FACT_TABLE
  3  WHERE STATUS_CD IN ('A','B','C','D','E','F')
  4  ORDER BY STATUS_CD;
```

ANALYSIS Try testing something similar for yourself. Although books are excellent sources for standards and direction, you will find it is often useful to come to your own conclusions on certain things, such as performance.

Here is another example using SUBSTR and IN. Notice that the first query combines LIKE with OR.

INPUT

```
SQL> SELECT *
  2  FROM FACT_TABLE
  3  WHERE PROD_CD LIKE 'AB%'
  4     OR PROD_CD LIKE 'AC%'
  5     OR PROD_CD LIKE 'BB%'
  6     OR PROD_CD LIKE 'BC%'
  7     OR PROD_CD LIKE 'CC%'
  8  ORDER BY PROD_CD;

SQL> SELECT *
  2  FROM FACT_TABLE
  3  WHERE SUBSTR(PROD_CD,1,2) IN ('AB','AC','BB','BC','CC')
  4  ORDER BY PROD_CD;
```

ANALYSIS The second example not only avoids the OR but also eliminates the combination of the OR and LIKE operators. You may want to try this example to see what the real-time performance difference is for your data.

OLAP Versus OLTP

When tuning a database, you must first determine what the database is being used for. An online analytical processing (OLAP) database is a system whose function is to provide query capabilities to the end user for statistical and general informational purposes. The data retrieved in this type of environment is often used for statistical reports that aid in the corporate decision-making process. These types of systems are also referred to as decision support systems (DSS). An online transactional processing (OLTP) database is a system whose main function is to provide an environment for end-user input and may also involve queries against day-to-day information. OLTP systems are used to manipulate information within the database on a daily basis. Data warehouses and DSSs get their data from online transactional databases and sometimes from other OLAP systems.

OLTP Tuning

A transactional database is a delicate system that is heavily accessed in the form of transactions and queries against day-to-day information. However, an OLTP does not usually require a vast sort area, at least not to the extent to which it is required in an OLAP environment. Most OLTP transactions are quick and do not involve much sorting.

One of the biggest issues in a transactional database is rollback segments. The amount and size of rollback segments heavily depend on how many users are concurrently accessing the database, as well as the amount of work in each transaction. The best approach is to have several rollback segments in a transactional environment.

Another concern in a transactional environment is the integrity of the *transaction logs,* which are written to after each transaction. These logs exist for the sole purpose of recovery. Therefore, each SQL implementation needs a way to back up the logs for use in a "point in time recovery." SQL Server uses dump devices; Oracle uses a database mode known as ARCHIVELOG mode. Transaction logs also involve a performance consideration because backing up logs requires additional overhead.

OLAP Tuning

Tuning OLAP systems, such as a data warehouse or decision support system, is much different from tuning a transaction database. Normally, more space is needed for sorting.

Because the purpose of this type of system is to retrieve useful decision-making data, you can expect many complex queries, which normally involve grouping and sorting of data. Compared to a transactional database, OLAP systems typically take more space for the sort area but less space for the rollback area.

Most transactions in an OLAP system take place as part of a batch process. Instead of having several rollback areas for user input, you may resort to one large rollback area for the loads, which can be taken offline during daily activity to reduce overhead.

Batch Loads Versus Transactional Processing

A major factor in the performance of a database and SQL statements is the type of processing that takes place within a database. One type of processing is OLTP, discussed earlier today. When we talk about transactional processing, we are going to refer to two types: user input and batch loads.

Regular user input usually consists of SQL statements such as INSERT, UPDATE, and DELETE. These types of transactions are often performed by the end user, or the customer. End users are normally using a front-end application such as PowerBuilder to interface with the database, and therefore they seldom issue visible SQL statements. Nevertheless, the SQL code has already been generated for the user by the front-end application.

Your main focus when optimizing the performance of a database should be the end-user transactions. After all, "no customer" equates to "no database," which in turn means that you are out of a job. Always try to keep your customers happy, even though their expectations of system/database performance may sometimes be unreasonable. One consideration with end-user input is the number of concurrent users. The more concurrent database users you have, the greater the possibilities of performance degradation.

What is a batch load? A *batch load* performs heaps of transactions against the database at once. For example, suppose you are archiving last year's data into a massive history table. You may need to insert thousands, or even millions, of rows of data into your history table. You probably wouldn't want to do this task manually, so you are likely to create a batch job or script to automate the process. (Numerous techniques are available for loading data in a batch.) Batch loads are notorious for taxing system and database resources. These database resources may include table access, system catalog access, the database rollback segment, and sort area space; system resources may include available CPU and shared memory. Many other factors are involved, depending on your operating system and database server.

Both end-user transactions and batch loads are necessary for most databases to be successful, but your system could experience serious performance problems if these two types of processing lock horns. Therefore, you should know the difference between them and keep them segregated as much as possible. For example, you would not want to load massive amounts of data into the database when user activity is high. The database response may already be slow because of the number of concurrent users. Always try to run batch loads when user activity is at a minimum. Many shops reserve times in the evenings or early morning to load data in batch to avoid interfering with daily processing.

You should always plan the timing for massive batch loads, being careful to avoid scheduling them when the database is expected to be available for normal use. Figure 15.1 depicts heavy batch updates running concurrently with several user processes, all contending for system resources.

As you can see, many processes are contending for system resources. The heavy batch updates

Figure 15.1.

System resource contention.

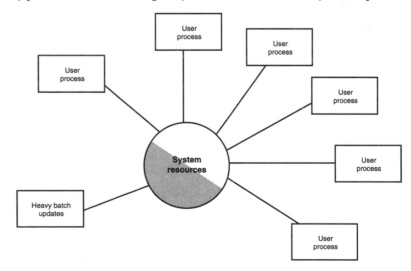

that are being done throw a monkey wrench into the equation. Instead of the system resources being dispersed somewhat evenly among the users, the batch updates appear to be hogging them. This situation is just the beginning of resource contention. As the batch transactions proceed, the user processes may eventually be forced out of the picture. This condition is not a good way of doing business. Even if the system has only one user, significant contention for that user could occur.

Another problem with batch processes is that the process may hold locks on a table that a user is trying to access. If there is a lock on a table, the user will be refused access until the lock is freed by the batch process, which could be hours. Batch processes should take place when system resources are at their best if possible. Don't make the users' transactions compete with batch. Nobody wins that game.

Optimizing Data Loads by Dropping Indexes

One way to expedite batch updates is by dropping indexes. Imagine the history table with many thousands of rows. That history table is also likely to have one or more indexes. When you think of an index, you normally think of faster table access, but in the case of batch loads, you can benefit by dropping the index(es).

When you load data into a table with an index, you can usually expect a great deal of index use, especially if you are updating a high percentage of rows in the table. Look at it this way. If you are studying a book and highlighting key points for future reference, you may find it quicker to browse through the book from beginning to end rather than using the index to locate your key points. (Using the index would be efficient if you were highlighting only a small portion of the book.)

To maximize the efficiency of batch loads/updates that affect a high percentage of rows in a table, you can take these three basic steps to disable an index:

1. Drop the appropriate index(es).
2. Load/update the table's data.
3. Rebuild the table's index.

A Frequent COMMIT Keeps the DBA Away

When performing batch transactions, you must know how often to perform a "commit." As you learned on Day 11, "Controlling Transactions," a COMMIT statement finalizes a transaction. A COMMIT saves a transaction or writes any changes to the applicable table(s). Behind the scenes, however, much more is going on. Some areas in the database are reserved to store completed transactions before the changes are actually written to the target table. Oracle calls these areas *rollback segments*. When you issue a COMMIT statement, transactions associated with your SQL session in the rollback segment are updated in the target table. After the update takes place, the contents of the rollback segment are removed. A ROLLBACK command, on the other hand, clears the contents of the rollback segment without updating the target table.

As you can guess, if you never issue a COMMIT or ROLLBACK command, transactions keep building within the rollback segments. Subsequently, if the data you are loading is greater in size than the available space in the rollback segments, the database will essentially come to a halt and ban further transactional activity. Not issuing COMMIT commands is a common programming pitfall; regular COMMITs help to ensure stable performance of the entire database system.

The management of rollback segments is a complex and vital database administrator (DBA) responsibility because transactions dynamically affect the rollback segments, and in turn, affect the overall performance of the database as well as individual SQL statements. So when you are loading large amounts of data, be sure to issue the COMMIT command on a regular basis. Check with your DBA for advice on how often to commit during batch transactions. (See Figure 15.2.)

Figure 15.2.
The rollback area.

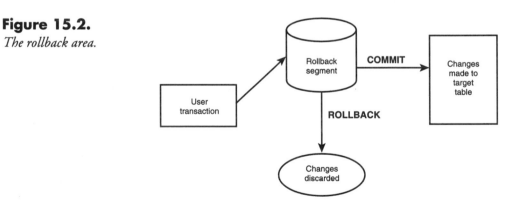

As you can see in Figure 15.2, when a user performs a transaction, the changes are retained in the rollback area.

Rebuilding Tables and Indexes in a Dynamic Environment

The term *dynamic database environment* refers to a large database that is in a constant state of change. The changes that we are referring to are frequent batch updates and continual daily transactional processing. Dynamic databases usually entail heavy OLTP systems, but can also refer to DSSs or data warehouses, depending upon the volume and frequency of data loads.

The result of constant high-volume changes to a database is growth, which in turn yields fragmentation. Fragmentation can easily get out of hand if growth is not managed properly. Oracle allocates an initial extent to tables when they are created. When data is loaded and fills the table's initial extent, a next extent, which is also allocated when the table is created, is taken.

Sizing tables and indexes is essentially a DBA function and can drastically affect SQL statement performance. The first step in growth management is to be proactive. Allow room for tables to grow from day one, within reason. Also plan to defragment the database on a regular basis, even if doing so means developing a weekly routine. Here are the basic conceptual steps involved in defragmenting tables and indexes in a relational database management system:

1. Get a good backup of the table(s) and/or index(es).
2. Drop the table(s) and/or index(es).
3. Rebuild the table(s) and/or index(es) with new space allocation.
4. Restore the data into the newly built table(s).
5. Re-create the index(es) if necessary.
6. Reestablish user/role permissions on the table if necessary.
7. Save the backup of your table until you are absolutely sure that the new table was built successfully. If you choose to discard the backup of the original table, you should first make a backup of the new table after the data has been fully restored.

WARNING

> Never get rid of the backup of your table until you are sure that the new table was built successfully.

The following example demonstrates a practical use of a mailing list table in an Oracle database environment.

INPUT

```
CREATE TABLE MAILING_TBL_BKUP AS
SELECT * FROM MAILING_TBL;
```

OUTPUT

```
Table Created.
```

```
drop table mailing_tbl;
```

Table Dropped.

```
CREATE TABLE MAILING_TBL
    (
    INDIVIDUAL_ID           VARCHAR2(12)      NOT NULL,
    INDIVIDUAL_NAME     VARCHAR2(30)     NOT NULL,
    ADDRESS             VARCHAR(40)     NOT NULL,
    CITY            VARCHAR(25)     NOT NULL,
    STATE           VARCHAR(2)      NOT NULL,
    ZIP_CODE        VARCHAR(9)      NOT NULL,
    )
    TABLESPACE TABLESPACE_NAME
    STORAGE    (    INITIAL           NEW_SIZE,
            NEXT         NEW_SIZE      );
```

Table created.

```
INSERT INTO MAILING_TBL
select * from mailing_tbl_bkup;
```

93,451 rows inserted.

```
CREATE INDEX MAILING_IDX ON MAILING TABLE
    (
    INDIVIDUAL_ID
    )
    TABLESPACE TABLESPACE_NAME
    STORAGE    (    INITIAL           NEW_SIZE,
            NEXT         NEW_SIZE      );
```

Index Created.

```
grant select on mailing_tbl to public;
```

Grant Succeeded.

```
drop table mailing_tbl_bkup;
```

Table Dropped.

ANALYSIS Rebuilding tables and indexes that have grown enables you to optimize storage, which improves overall performance. Remember to drop the backup table only after you have verified that the new table has been created successfully. Also keep in mind that you can achieve the same results with other methods. Check the options that are available to you in your database documentation.

Tuning the Database

Tuning a database is the process of fine-tuning the database server's performance. As a newcomer to SQL, you probably will not be exposed to database tuning unless you are a new DBA or a DBA moving into a relational database environment. Whether you will be managing a database or using SQL in applications or programming, you will benefit by knowing something about the database-tuning process. The key to the success of any database is for all parties to work together. Some general tips for tuning a database follow.

☐ Minimize the overall size required for the database.

It's good to allow room for growth when designing a database, but don't go overboard. Don't tie up resources that you may need to accommodate database growth.

☐ Experiment with the user process's time-slice variable.

This variable controls the amount of time the database server's scheduler allocates to each user's process.

☐ Optimize the network packet size used by applications.

The larger the amount of data sent over the network, the larger the network packet size should be. Consult your database and network documentation for more details.

☐ Store transaction logs on separate hard disks.

For each transaction that takes place, the server must write the changes to the transaction logs. If you store these log files on the same disk as you store data, you could create a performance bottleneck. (See Figure 15.3.)

☐ Stripe extremely large tables across multiple disks.

If concurrent users are accessing a large table that is spread over multiple disks, there is much less chance of having to wait for system resources. (See Figure 15.3.)

☐ Store database sort area, system catalog area, and rollback areas on separate hard disks.

These are all areas in the database that most users access frequently. By spreading these areas over multiple disk drives, you are maximizing the use of system resources. (See Figure 15.3.)

☐ Add CPUs.

This system administrator function can drastically improve database performance. Adding CPUs can speed up data processing for obvious reasons. If you have multiple CPUs on a machine, then you may be able to implement parallel processing strategies. See your database documentation for more information on parallel processing, if it is available with your implementation.

☐ Add memory.

Generally, the more the better.

☐ Store tables and indexes on separate hard disks.

You should store indexes and their related tables on separate disk drives whenever possible. This arrangement enables the table to be read at the same time the index is being referenced on another disk. The capability to store objects on multiple disks may depend on how many disks are connected to a controller. (See Figure 15.3.)

Figure 15.3 shows a simple example of how you might segregate the major areas of your database.

Figure 15.3.

Using available disks to enhance performance.

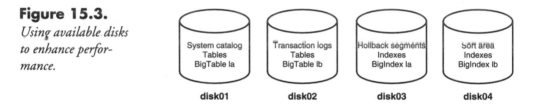

The scenario in Figure 15.3 uses four devices: disk01 through disk04. The objective when spreading your heavy database areas and objects is to keep areas of high use away from each another.

☐ Disk01—The system catalog stores information about tables, indexes, users, statistics, database files, sizing, growth information, and other pertinent data that is often accessed by a high percentage of transactions.

☐ Disk02—Transaction logs are updated every time a change is made to a table (insert, update, or delete). Transaction logs are a grand factor in an online transactional database. They are not of great concern in a read-only environment, such as a data warehouse or DSS.

☐ Disk03—Rollback segments are also significant in a transactional environment. However, if there is little transactional activity (insert, update, delete), rollback segments will not be heavily used.

☐ Disk04— The database's sort area, on the other hand, is used as a temporary area for SQL statement processing when sorting data, as in a GROUP BY or ORDER BY clause. Sort areas are typically an issue in a data warehouse or DSS. However, the use of sort areas should also be considered in a transactional environment.

TIP

> Also note how the application tables and indexes have been placed on each disk. Tables and indexes should be spread as much as possible.

Notice that in Figure 15.3 the tables and indexes are stored on different devices. You can also see how a "Big Table" or index may be *striped* across two or more devices. This technique splits the table into smaller segments that can be accessed simultaneously. Striping a table or index across multiple devices is a way to control fragmentation. In this scenario, tables may be read while their corresponding indexes are being referenced, which increases the speed of overall data access.

This example is really quite simple. Depending on the function, size, and system-related issues of your database, you may find a similar method for optimizing system resources that works better. In a perfect world where money is no obstacle, the best configuration is to have a separate disk for each major database entity, including large tables and indexes.

NOTE

> The DBA and system administrator should work together to balance database space allocation and optimize the memory that is available on the server.

Tuning a database very much depends on the specific database system you are using. Obviously, tuning a database entails much more than just preparing queries and letting them fly. On the other hand, you won't get much reward for tuning a database when the application SQL is not fine-tuned itself. Professionals who tune databases for a living often specialize on one database product and learn as much as they possibly can about its features and idiosyncrasies. Although database tuning is often looked upon as a painful task, it can provide very lucrative employment for the people who truly understand it.

Performance Obstacles

We have already mentioned some of the countless possible pitfalls that can hinder the general performance of a database. These are typically general bottlenecks that involve system-level maintenance, database maintenance, and management of SQL statement processing.

This section summarizes the most common obstacles in system performance and database response time.

☐ Not making use of available devices on the server—A company purchases multiple disk drives for a reason. If you do not use them accordingly by spreading apart the vital database components, you are limiting the performance capabilities. Maximizing the use of system resources is just as important as maximizing the use of the database server capabilities.

☐ Not performing frequent COMMITs—Failing to use periodic COMMITs or ROLLBACKs during heavy batch loads will ultimately result in database bottlenecks.

☐ Allowing batch loads to interfere with daily processing—Running batch loads during times when the database is expected to be available will cause problems for everybody. The batch process will be in a perpetual battle with end users for system resources.

☐ Being careless when creating SQL statements—Carelessly creating complex SQL statements will more than likely contribute to substandard response time.

TIP

> You can use various methods to optimize the structure of an SQL statement, depending upon the steps taken by the database server during SQL statement processing.

☐ Running batch loads with table indexes—You could end up with a batch load that runs all day and all night, as opposed to a batch load that finishes within a few hours. Indexes slow down batch loads that are accessing a high percentage of the rows in a table.

☐ Having too many concurrent users for allocated memory—As the number of concurrent database and system users grows, you may need to allocate more memory for the shared process. See your system administrator.

☐ Creating indexes on columns with few unique values—Indexing on a column such as GENDER, which has only two unique values, is not very efficient. Instead, try to index columns that will return a low percentage of rows in a query.

☐ Creating indexes on small tables—By the time the index is referenced and the data read, a full-table scan could have been accomplished.

☐ Not managing system resources efficiently—Poor management of system resources can result from wasted space during database initialization, table creation, uncontrolled fragmentation, and irregular system/database maintenance.

☐ Not sizing tables and indexes properly—Poor estimates for tables and indexes that grow tremendously in a large database environment can lead to serious fragmentation problems, which if not tended to, will snowball into more serious problems.

Built-In Tuning Tools

Check with your DBA or database vendor to determine what tools are available to you for performance measuring and tuning. You can use performance-tuning tools to identify deficiencies in the data access path; in addition, these tools can sometimes suggest changes to improve the performance of a particular SQL statement.

Oracle has two popular tools for managing SQL statement performance. These tools are explain plan and tkprof. The explain plan tool identifies the access path that will be taken when the SQL statement is executed. tkprof measures the performance by time elapsed during each phase of SQL statement processing. Oracle Corporation also provides other tools that help with SQL statement and database analysis, but the two mentioned here are the most popular. If you want to simply measure the elapsed time of a query in Oracle, you can use the SQL*Plus command SET TIMING ON.

SET TIMING ON and other SET commands are covered in more depth on Day 20, "SQL*Plus."

Sybase's SQL Server has diagnostic tools for SQL statements. These options are in the form of SET commands that you can add to your SQL statements. (These commands are similar to Oracle's SET commands). Some common commands are SET SHOWPLAN ON, SET STATISTIC IO ON, and SET STATISTICS TIME ON. These SET commands display output concerning the steps performed in a query, the number of reads and writes required to perform the query, and general statement-parsing information. SQL Server SET commands are covered on Day 19, "Transact-SQL: An Introduction."

Summary

Two major elements of streamlining, or tuning, directly affect the performance of SQL statements: application tuning and database tuning. Each has its own role, but one cannot be optimally tuned without the other. The first step toward success is for the technical team and system engineers to work together to balance resources and take full advantage of the database features that aid in improving performance. Many of these features are built into the database software provided by the vendor.

Application developers must know the data. The key to an optimal database design is thorough knowledge of the application's data. Developers and production programmers must know when to use indexes, when to add another index, and when to allow batch jobs to run. Always plan batch loads and keep batch processing separate from daily transactional processing.

Databases can be tuned to improve the performance of individual applications that access them. Database administrators must be concerned with the daily operation and performance of the database. In addition to the meticulous tuning that occurs behind the scenes, the DBA can usually offer creative suggestions for accessing data more efficiently, such as manipulating indexes or reconstructing an SQL statement. The DBA should also be familiar with the tools that are readily available with the database software to measure performance and provide suggestions for statement tweaking.

Q&A

Q If I streamline my SQL statement, how much of a gain in performance should I expect?

A Performance gain depends on the size of your tables, whether or not columns in the table are indexed, and other relative factors. In a very large database, a complex query that runs for hours can sometimes be cut to minutes. In the case of transactional processing, streamlining an SQL statement can save important seconds for the end user.

Q How do I coordinate my batch loads or updates?

A Check with the database administrator and, of course, with management when scheduling a batch load or update. If you are a system engineer, you probably will not know everything that is going on within the database.

Q How often should I commit my batch transactions?

A Check with the DBA for advice. The DBA will need to know approximately how much data you are inserting, updating, or deleting. The frequency of COMMIT statements should also take into account other batch loads occurring simultaneously with other database activities.

Q Should I stripe all of my tables?

A Striping offers performance benefits only for large tables and/or for tables that are heavily accessed on a regular basis.

Workshop

The Workshop provides quiz questions to help solidify your understanding of the material covered, as well as exercises to provide you with experience in using what you have learned. Try to answer the quiz and exercise questions before checking the answers in Appendix F, "Answers to Quizzes and Exercises."

Quiz

1. What does *streamline an SQL statement* mean?
2. Should tables and their corresponding indexes reside on the same disk?
3. Why is the arrangement of conditions in an SQL statement important?
4. What happens during a full-table scan?
5. How can you avoid a full-table scan?
6. What are some common hindrances of general performance?

Exercises

1. Make the following SQL statement more readable.

```
SELECT EMPLOYEE.LAST_NAME, EMPLOYEE.FIRST_NAME, EMPLOYEE.MIDDLE_NAME,
EMPLOYEE.ADDRESS, EMPLOYEE.PHONE_NUMBER, PAYROLL.SALARY, PAYROLL.POSITION,
EMPLOYEE.SSN, PAYROLL.START_DATE FROM EMPLOYEE, PAYROLL WHERE
EMPLOYEE.SSN = PAYROLL.SSN AND EMPLOYEE.LAST_NAME LIKE 'S%' AND
PAYROLL.SALARY > 20000;
```

2. Rearrange the conditions in the following query to optimize data retrieval time. Use the following statistics (on the tables in their entirety) to determine the order of the conditions:

   593 individuals have the last name SMITH.

   712 individuals live in INDIANAPOLIS.

   3,492 individuals are MALE.

   1,233 individuals earn a salary >= 30,000.

   5,009 individuals are single.

   Individual_id is the primary key for both tables.

```
SELECT M.INDIVIDUAL_NAME, M.ADDRESS, M.CITY, M.STATE, M.ZIP_CODE,
       S.SEX, S.MARITAL_STATUS, S.SALARY
FROM MAILING_TBL M,
     INDIVIDUAL_STAT_TBL S
WHERE M.NAME LIKE 'SMITH%'
  AND M.CITY = 'INDIANAPOLIS'
  AND S.SEX = 'MALE'
  AND S.SALARY >= 30000
  AND S.MARITAL_STATUS = 'S'
  AND M.INDIVIDUAL_ID = S.INDIVIDUAL_ID;
```

Day 16

Using Views to Retrieve Useful Information from the Data Dictionary

Objectives

Today we discuss the data dictionary, also known as the system catalog. By the end of the day, you should have a solid understanding of the following:

☐ The definition of the data dictionary

☐ The type of information the data dictionary contains

☐ Different types of tables within the data dictionary

☐ Effective ways to retrieve useful information from the data dictionary

Introduction to the Data Dictionary

Every relational database has some form of data dictionary, or system catalog. (We use both terms in today's presentation.) A *data dictionary* is a system area within a database environment that contains information about the ingredients of a database. Data dictionaries include information such as database design, stored SQL code, user statistics, database processes, database growth, and database performance statistics.

The data dictionary has tables that contain database design information, which are populated upon the creation of the database and the execution of Data Definition Language (DDL) commands such as CREATE TABLE. This part of the system catalog stores information about a table's columns and attributes, table-sizing information, table privileges, and table growth. Other objects that are stored within the data dictionary include indexes, triggers, procedures, packages, and views.

User statistics tables report the status of items such as database connectivity information and privileges for individual users. These privileges are divided into two major components: system-level privileges and object-level privileges. The authority to create another user is a system-level privilege, whereas the capability to access a table is an object-level privilege. Roles are also used to enforce security within a database. This information is stored as well.

Day 16 extends what you learned yesterday (Day 15, "Streamlining SQL Statements for Improved Performance"). Data retrieved from the system catalog can be used to monitor database performance and to modify database parameters that will improve database and SQL statement performance.

The data dictionary is one of the most useful tools available with a database. It is a way of keeping a database organized, much like an inventory file in a retail store. It is a mechanism that ensures the integrity of the database. For instance, when you create a table, how does the database server know whether a table with the same name exists? When you create a query to select data from a table, how can it be verified that you have been given the proper privileges to access the table? The data dictionary is the heart of a database, so you need to know how to use it.

Users of the Data Dictionary

End users, system engineers, and database administrators all use the data dictionary, whether they realize it or not. Their access can be either direct or indirect.

End users, often the customers for whom the database was created, access the system catalog indirectly. When a user attempts to log on to the database, the data dictionary is referenced to verify that user's username, password, and privileges to connect to the database. The database is also referenced to see whether the user has the appropriate privileges to access

16

certain data. The most common method for an end user to access the data dictionary is through a front-end application. Many graphical user interface (GUI) tools, which allow a user to easily construct an SQL statement, have been developed. When logging on to the database, the front-end application may immediately perform a select against the data dictionary to define the tables to which the user has access. The front-end application may then build a "local" system catalog for the individual user based on the data retrieved from the data dictionary. The customer can use the local catalog to select the specific tables he or she wishes to query.

System engineers are database users who are responsible for tasks such as database modeling and design, application development, and application management. (Some companies use other titles, such as programmers, programmer analysts, and data modelers, to refer to their system engineers.) System engineers use the data dictionary directly to manage the development process, as well as to maintain existing projects. Access may also be achieved through front-end applications, development tools, and computer assisted software engineering (CASE) tools. Common areas of the system catalog for these users are queries against objects under groups of schemas, queries against application roles and privileges, and queries to gather statistics on schema growth. System engineers may also use the data dictionary to reverse-engineer database objects in a specified schema.

Database administrators (DBAs) are most definitely the largest percentage of direct users of the data dictionary. Unlike the other two groups of users, who occasionally use the system catalog directly, DBAs must explicitly include the use of the data dictionary as part of their daily routine. Access is usually through an SQL query but can also be through administration tools such as Oracle's Server Manager. A DBA uses data dictionary information to manage users and resources and ultimately to achieve a well-tuned database.

As you can see, all database users need to use the data dictionary. Even more important, a relational database cannot exist without some form of a data dictionary.

Contents of the Data Dictionary

This section examines the system catalogs of two RDBMS vendors, Oracle and Sybase. Although both implementations have unique specifications for their data dictionaries, they serve the same function. Don't concern yourself with the different names for the system tables; simply understand the concept of a data dictionary and the data it contains.

Oracle's Data Dictionary

Because every table must have an owner, the owner of the system tables in an Oracle data dictionary is SYS. Oracle's data dictionary tables are divided into three basic categories: user accessible views, DBA views, and dynamic performance tables, which also appear as views. Views that are accessible to a user allow the user to query the data dictionary for information about the individual database account, such as privileges, or a catalog of tables created. The DBA views aid in the everyday duties of a database administrator, allowing the DBA to manage users and objects within the database. The dynamic performance tables in Oracle are also used by the DBA and provide a more in-depth look for monitoring performance of a database. These views provide information such as statistics on processes, the dynamic usage of rollback segments, memory usage, and so on. The dynamic performance tables are all prefixed V$.

Sybase's Data Dictionary

As in Oracle, the owner of the tables in a Sybase data dictionary is SYS. The tables within the data dictionary are divided into two categories: system tables and database tables.

The system tables are contained with the master database only. These tables define objects (such as tables and indexes) that are common through multiple databases. The second set of tables in a Sybase SQL Server data dictionary are the database tables. These tables are related only to objects within each database.

A Look Inside Oracle's Data Dictionary

The examples in this section show you how to retrieve information from the data dictionary and are applicable to most relational database users, that is, system engineer, end user, or DBA. Oracle's data dictionary has a vast array of system tables and views for all types of database users, which is why we have chosen to explore Oracle's data dictionary in more depth.

User Views

User views are data dictionary views that are common to all database users. The only privilege a user needs to query against a user view is the CREATE SESSION system privilege, which should be common to all users.

Who Are You?

Before venturing into the seemingly endless knowledge contained within a database, you should know exactly who you are (in terms of the database) and what you can do. The following two examples show SELECT statements from two tables: one to find out who you are and the other to see who else shares the database.

INPUT
```
SQL> SELECT *
  2  FROM USER_USERS;
```

OUTPUT
```
USERNAME      USER_ID  DEFAULT_TABLESPACE    TEMPORARY TABLESPACE   CREATED
----------    -------  ------------------    -------------------   --------
JSMITH          29     USERS                 TEMP                  14-MAR-97

1 row selected.
```

16

ANALYSIS The USER_USERS view allows you to view how your Oracle ID was set up, when it was set up, and it also shows other user-specific, vital statistics. The default tablespace and the temporary tablespace are also shown. The default tablespace, USERS, is the tablespace that objects will be created under as that user. The temporary tablespace is the designated tablespace to be used during large sorts and group functions for JSMITH.

INPUT/OUTPUT

```
SQL> SELECT *
  2  FROM ALL_USERS;

USERNAME          USER_ID        CREATED
---------------   -------        -----------
SYS                     0        01-JAN-97
SYSTEM                  5        01-JAN-97
SCOTT                   8        01-JAN-97
JSMITH                 10        14-MAR-97
TJONES                 11        15-MAR-97
VJOHNSON               12        15-MAR-97
```

As you can see in the results of the preceding query, you can view all users that exist in the database by using the ALL_USERS view. However, the ALL_USERS view does not provide the same specific information as the previous view (USER_USERS) provided because there is no need for this information at the user level. More specific information may be required at the system level.

What Are Your Privileges?

Now that you know who you are, it would be nice to know what you can do. Several views are collectively able to give you that information. The USER_SYS_PRIVS view and the USER_ROLE_PRIVS view will give you (the user) a good idea of what authority you have.

You can use the USER_SYS_PRIVS view to examine your system privileges. Remember, system privileges are privileges that allow you to do certain things within the database as a whole. These privileges are not specific to any one object or set of objects.

INPUT

```
SQL> SELECT *
  2  FROM USER_SYS_PRIVS;
```

OUTPUT

```
USERNAME        PRIVILEGE               ADM
--------        --------------------    ---
JSMITH          UNLIMITED TABLESPACE    NO
JSMITH          CREATE SESSION          NO

2 rows selected.
```

ANALYSIS JSMITH has been granted two system-level privileges, outside of any granted roles. Notice the second, CREATE SESSION. CREATE SESSION is also contained within an Oracle standard role, CONNECT, which is covered in the next example.

You can use the USER_ROLE_PRIVS view to view information about roles you have been granted within the database. Database roles are very similar to system-level privileges. A role is created much like a user and then granted privileges. After the role has been granted privileges, the role can be granted to a user. Remember that object-level privileges may also be contained within a role.

INPUT/OUTPUT

```
SQL> SELECT *
  2  FROM USER_ROLE_PRIVS;

USERNAME          GRANTED_ROLE        ADM   DEF   OS_
------------      ----------------    ---   ---   --
JSMITH            CONNECT             NO    YES   NO
JSMITH            RESOURCE            NO    YES   NO

2 rows selected.
```

ANALYSIS The USER_ROLE_PRIVS view enables you to see the roles that have been granted to you. As mentioned earlier, CONNECT contains the system privilege CREATE SESSION, as well as other privileges. RESOURCE has a few privileges of its own. You can see that both roles have been granted as the user's default role; the user cannot grant these roles to other users, as noted by the Admin option (ADM); and the roles have not been granted by the operating system. (Refer to Day 12, "Database Security.")

What Do You Have Access To?

Now you might ask, What do I have access to? I know who I am, I know my privileges, but where can I get my data? You can answer that question by looking at various available user views in the data dictionary. This section identifies a few helpful views.

Probably the most basic user view is USER_CATALOG, which is simply a catalog of the tables, views, synonyms, and sequences owned by the current user.

INPUT

```
SQL> SELECT *
  2  FROM USER_CATALOG;
```

OUTPUT

```
TABLE_NAME                          TABLE_TYPE
--------------------------------    ----------
MAGAZINE_TBL                        TABLE
MAG_COUNTER                         SEQUENCE
MAG_VIEW                            VIEW
SPORTS                              TABLE

4 rows selected.
```

ANALYSIS This example provides a quick list of tables and related objects that you own. You can also use a public synonym for USER_CATALOG for simplicity's sake: CAT. That is, try select * from cat;.

Another useful view is ALL_CATALOG, which enables you to see tables owned by other individuals.

INPUT/
OUTPUT

```
SQL> SELECT *
  2  FROM ALL_CATALOG;

OWNER                      TABLE_NAME            TABLE_TYPE
--------------------       ------------------    ----------
SYS                        DUAL                  TABLE
PUBLIC                     DUAL                  SYNONYM
JSMITH                     MAGAZINE_TBL          TABLE
JSMITH                     MAG_COUNTER           SEQUENCE
JSMITH                     MAG_VIEW              VIEW
JSMITH                     SPORTS                TABLE
VJOHNSON                   TEST1                 TABLE
VJOHNSON                   HOBBIES               TABLE
VJOHNSON                   CLASSES               TABLE
VJOHNSON                   STUDENTS              VIEW

10 rows selected.
```

ANALYSIS

More objects than appear in the preceding list will be accessible to you as a user. (The SYSTEM tables alone will add many tables.) We have simply shortened the list. The ALL_CATALOG view is the same as the USER_CATALOG view, but it shows you all tables, views, sequences, and synonyms to which you have access (not just the ones you own).

INPUT

```
SQL> SELECT SUBSTR(OBJECT_TYPE,1,15) OBJECT_TYPE,
  2         SUBSTR(OBJECT_NAME,1,30) OBJECT_NAME,
  3         CREATED,
  4         STATUS
  5  FROM USER_OBJECTS
  6  ORDER BY 1;
```

OUTPUT

```
OBJECT_TYPE       OBJECT_NAME            CREATED      STATUS
--------------    --------------------   -----------  ------
INDEX             MAGAZINE_INX           14-MAR-97    VALID
INDEX             SPORTS_INX             14-MAR-97    VALID
INDEX             HOBBY_INX              14-MAR-97    VALID
TABLE             MAGAZINE_TBL           01-MAR-97    VALID
TABLE             SPORTS                 14-MAR-97    VALID
TABLE             HOBBY_TBL              16-MAR-97    VALID

6 rows selected.
```

ANALYSIS

You can use the USER_OBJECTS view to select general information about a user's owned objects, such as the name, type, date created, date modified, and the status of the object. In the previous query, we are checking the data created and validation of each owned object.

INPUT/
OUTPUT

```
SQL> SELECT TABLE_NAME, INITIAL_EXTENT, NEXT_EXTENT
  2  FROM USER_TABLES;

TABLE_NAME                       INITIAL_EXTENT    NEXT EXTENT
-----------------------------    --------------    -----------
MAGAZINE_TBL                            1048576         540672
SPORTS                                   114688         114688
```

16

ANALYSIS   Much more data is available when selecting from the USER_TABLES view, depending upon what you want to see. Most data consists of storage information.

NOTE

> Notice in the output that the values for initial and next extent are in bytes. In some implementations you can use column formatting to make your output more readable by adding commas. See Day 19, "Transact-SQL: An Introduction," and Day 20, "SQL*Plus."

The ALL_TABLES view is to USER_TABLES as the ALL_CATALOG view is to USER_CATALOG. In other words, ALL_TABLES allows you to see all the tables to which you have access, instead of just the tables you own. The ALL_TABLES view may include tables that exist in another user's catalog.

INPUT/ OUTPUT

```
SQL> SELECT SUBSTR(OWNER,1,15) OWNER,
  2            SUBSTR(TABLE_NAME,1,25) TABLE_NAME,
  3            SUBSTR(TABLESPACE_NAME,1,13) TABLESPACE
  4  FROM ALL_TABLES;

OWNER                   TABLE_NAME                  TABLESPACE
--------------------    --------------------------  ----------
SYS                     DUAL                        SYSTEM
JSMITH                  MAGAZINE_TBL                USERS
SMITH                   SPORTS                      USERS
VJOHNSON                TEST1                       USERS
VJOHNSON                HOBBIES                     USERS
VJOHNSON                CLASSES                     USERS
```

 ANALYSIS   Again, you have selected only the desired information. Many additional columns in ALL_TABLES may also contain useful information.

As a database user, you can monitor the growth of tables and indexes in your catalog by querying the USER_SEGMENTS view. As the name suggests, USER_SEGMENTS gives you information about each segment, such as storage information and extents taken. A segment may consist of a table, index, cluster rollback, temporary, or cache. The following example shows how you might retrieve selected information from the USER_SEGMENTS view.

INPUT/ OUTPUT

```
SQL> SELECT SUBSTR(SEGMENT_NAME,1,30) SEGMENT_NAME,
  2            SUBSTR(SEGMENT_TYPE,1,8) SEG_TYPE,
  3            SUBSTR(TABLESPACE_NAME,1,25) TABLESPACE_NAME,
  4            BYTES, EXTENTS
  5  FROM USER_SEGMENTS
  6  ORDER BY EXTENTS DESC;
```

16

SEGMENT_NAME	SEG_TYPE	TABLESPACE_NAME	BYTES	EXTENTS
MAGAZINE_TBL	TABLE	USERS	4292608	7
SPORTS_INX	INDEX	USERS	573440	4
SPORTS	TABLE	USERS	344064	2
MAGAZINE_INX	INDEX	USERS	1589248	1

4 rows selected.

ANALYSIS The output in the preceding query was sorted by extents in descending order; the segments with the most growth (extents taken) appear first in the results.

Now that you know which tables you have access to, you will want to find out what you can do to each table. Are you limited to query only, or can you update a table? The ALL_TAB_PRIVS view lists all privileges that you have as a database user on each table available to you.

INPUT/OUTPUT
```
SQL> SELECT SUBSTR(TABLE_SCHEMA,1,10) OWNER,
  2         SUBSTR(TABLE_NAME,1,25) TABLE_NAME,
  3         PRIVILEGE
  4  FROM ALL_TAB_PRIVS;
```

OWNER	TABLE_NAME	PRIVILEGE
SYS	DUAL	SELECT
JSMITH	MAGAZINE_TBL	SELECT
JSMITH	MAGAZINE_TBL	INSERT
JSMITH	MAGAZINE_TBL	UPDATE
JSMITH	MAGAZINE_TBL	DELETE
JSMITH	SPORTS	SELECT
JSMITH	SPORTS	INSERT
JSMITH	SPORTS	UPDATE
JSMITH	SPORTS	DELETE
VJOHNSON	TEST1	SELECT
VJOHNSON	TEST1	INSERT
VJOHNSON	TEST1	UPDATE
VJOHNSON	TEST1	DELETE
VJOHNSON	HOBBIES	SELECT
VJOHNSON	CLASSES	SELECT

ANALYSIS As you can see, you can manipulate the data in some tables, whereas you have read-only access (SELECT only) to others.

When you create objects, you usually need to know where to place them in the database unless you allow your target destination to take the default. An Oracle database is broken up into tablespaces, each of which are capable of storing objects. Each tablespace is allocated a certain amount of disk space, according to what is available on the system. Disk space is usually acquired through the system administrator (SA).

The following query is from a view called USER_TABLESPACES, which will list the tablespaces that you have access to, the default initial and next sizes of objects created within them, and their status.

16

```
SQL> SELECT SUBSTR(TABLESPACE_NAME,1,30) TABLESPACE_NAME,
  2              INITIAL_EXTENT,
  3              NEXT_EXTENT,
  4              PCT_INCREASE,
  5              STATUS
  6   FROM USER_TABLESPACES;

TABLESPACE_NAME                  INITIAL_EXTENT NEXT_EXTENT PCT_INCREASE STATUS
-------------------------------- -------------- ----------- ------------ ------
SYSTEM                                    32768       16384            1 ONLINE
RBS                                     2097152     2097152            1 ONLINE
TEMP                                     114688      114688            1 ONLINE
TOOLS                                     32768       16384            1 ONLINE
USERS                                     32768       16384            1 ONLINE

5 rows selected.
```

ANALYSIS This type of query is very useful when you are creating objects, such as tables and indexes, which will require storage. When a table or index is created, if the initial and next storage parameters are not specified in the DDL, the table or index will take the tablespace's default values. The same concept applies to PCT INCREASE, which is an Oracle parameter specifying the percentage of allocated space an object should take when it grows. If a value for PCT INCREASE is not specified when the table or index is created, the database server will allocate the default value that is specified for the corresponding tablespace. Seeing the default values enables you to determine whether you need to use a storage clause in the CREATE statement.

Sometimes, however, you need to know more than which tablespaces you may access, that is, build tables under. For example, you might need to know what your limits are within the tablespaces so that you can better manage the creation and sizing of your objects. The USER_TS_QUOTAS view provides the necessary information. The next query displays a user's space limits for creating objects in the database.

```
SQL> SELECT SUBSTR(TABLESPACE_NAME,1,30) TABLESPACE_NAME,
  2              BYTES, MAX_BYTES
  3   FROM USER_TS_QUOTAS;

TABLESPACE_NAME                       BYTES  MAX_BYTES
-------------------------------- ---------- ----------
SYSTEM                                    0          0
TOOLS                               5242880      16384
USERS                                573440         -1

3 rows selected.
```

ANALYSIS The preceding output is typical of output from an Oracle data dictionary. BYTES identifies the total number of bytes in that tablespace that are associated with the user. MAX BYTES identifies the maximum bytes allotted to the user, or the user's quota, on the tablespace. The first two values in this column are self-explanatory. The -1 in the third row means quota unlimited—that is, no limits are placed on the user for that tablespace.

NOTE The SUBSTR function appears in many of the preceding queries of data dictionary views. You can use many of the functions that you learned about earlier to improve the readablility of the data you retrieve. The use of consistent naming standards in your database may allow you to limit the size of data in your output, as we have done in these examples.

These examples all show how an ordinary database user can extract information from the data dictionary. These views are just a few of the many that exist in Oracle's data dictionary. It is important to check your database implementation to see what is available to you in your data dictionary. Remember, you should use the data dictionary to manage your database activities. Though system catalogs differ by implementation, you need only to understand the concept and know how to retrieve data that is necessary to supplement your job.

System DBA Views

The DBA views that reside within an Oracle data dictionary are usually the primary, or most common, views that a DBA would access. These views are invaluable to the productivity of any DBA. Taking these tables away from a DBA would be like depriving a carpenter of a hammer.

As you may expect, you must have the SELECT_ANY_TABLE system privilege, which is contained in the DBA role, to access the DBA tables. For example, suppose you are JSMITH, who does not have the required privilege to select from the DBA tables.

INPUT
```
SQL> SELECT *
  2  FROM USER_ROLE_PRIVS;
```

OUTPUT

USERNAME	GRANTED_ROLE	ADM	DEF	OS_
JSMITH	CONNECT	NO	YES	NO
JSMITH	RESOURCE	NO	YES	NO

INPUT/OUTPUT
```
SQL> SELECT *
  2  FROM SYS.DBA_ROLES;
FROM SYS.DBA_ROLES;
     *

ERROR at line 2:
ORA-00942: table or view does not exist
```

ANALYSIS When you try to access a table to which you do not have the appropriate privileges, an error is returned stating that the table does not exist. This message can be a little misleading. Virtually, the table does not exist because the user cannot "see" the table. A solution to the problem above would be to grant the role DBA to JSMITH. This role would have to be granted by a DBA, of course.

Database User Information

The USER_USERS and ALL_USERS views give you minimum information about the users. The DBA view called DBA_USERS (owned by SYS) gives you the information on all users if you have the DBA role or SELECT_ANY_TABLE privilege, as shown in the next example.

INPUT
```
SQL> SELECT *
  2  FROM SYS.DBA_USERS;
```

OUTPUT
```
USERNAME                          USER_ID PASSWORD
--------------------------------- ------- -------------------------------
DEFAULT_TABLESPACE                TEMPORARY_TABLESPACE            CREATED
--------------------------------- ------------------------------- --------
PROFILE
---------------------------------
SYS                                     0 4012DA490794C16B
SYSTEM                            TEMP                            06-JUN-96
DEFAULT

JSMITH                                  5 A4A04B17106C10B7
USERS                             TEMP                            06-JUN-96
DEFAULT

2 rows selected.
```

ANALYSIS
When you select all from the DBA_USERS view, you are able to see the vital information on each user. Notice that the password is encrypted. DBA_USERS is the primary view used by a DBA to manage users.

Database Security

Three basic data dictionary views deal with security, although these views can be tied together with other related views for more complete information. These three views deal with database roles, roles granted to users, and system privileges granted to users. The three views introduced in this section are DBA_ROLES, DBA_ROLE_PRIVS, and DBA_SYS_PRIVS. The following sample queries show how to obtain information pertinent to database security.

INPUT
```
SQL> SELECT *
  2  FROM SYS.DBA_ROLES;
```

OUTPUT
```
ROLE                              PASSWORD
--------------------------------- --------
CONNECT                           NO
RESOURCE                          NO
DBA                               NO
EXP_FULL_DATABASE                 NO
IMP_FULL_DATABASE                 NO
END_USER_ROLE                     NO

6 rows selected.
```

ANALYSIS
The view DBA_ROLES lists all the roles that have been created within the database. It gives the role name and whether or not the role has a password.

INPUT/
OUTPUT

```
SQL> SELECT *
  2  FROM SYS.DBA_ROLE_PRIVS
  3  WHERE GRANTEE = 'RJENNINGS';

GRANTEE                          GRANTED_ROLE                     ADM DEF
-------------------------------- -------------------------------- --- ---
RJENNINGS                        CONNECT                          NO  YES
RJENNINGS                        DBA                              NO  YES
RJENNINGS                        RESOURCE                         NO  YES

3 rows selected.
```

ANALYSIS The DBA_ROLE_PRIVS view provides information about database roles that have been granted to users. The first column is the grantee, or user. The second column displays the granted role. Notice that every role granted to the user corresponds to a record in the table. ADM identifies whether the role was granted with the Admin option, meaning that the user is able to grant the matching role to other users. The last column is DEFAULT, stating whether the matching role is a default role for the user.

INPUT/
OUTPUT

```
SQL> SELECT *
  2  FROM SYS.DBA_SYS_PRIVS
  3  WHERE GRANTEE = 'RJENNINGS';

GRANTEE                          PRIVILEGE                        ADM
-------------------------------- -------------------------------- ---
RJENNINGS                        CREATE SESSION                   NO
RJENNINGS                        UNLIMITED TABLESPACE             NO

2 rows selected.
```

ANALYSIS The DBA_SYS_PRIVS view lists all system-level privileges that have been granted to the user. This view is similar to DBA_ROLE_PRIVS. You can include these system privileges in a role by granting system privileges to a role, as you would to a user.

Database Objects

Database objects are another major focus for a DBA. Several views within the data dictionary provide information about objects, such as tables and indexes. These views can contain general information or they can contain detailed information about the objects that reside within the database.

INPUT

```
SQL> SELECT *
  2  FROM SYS.DBA_CATALOG
  3  WHERE ROWNUM < 5;
```

OUTPUT

```
OWNER                            TABLE_NAME                       TABLE_TYPE
-------------------------------- -------------------------------- ----------
SYS                              CDEF$                            TABLE
SYS                              TAB$                             TABLE
SYS                              IND$                             TABLE
SYS                              CLU$                             TABLE

4 rows selected.
```

ANALYSIS The DBA_CATALOG is the same thing as the USER_CATALOG, only the owner of the table is included. In contrast, the USER_CATALOG view deals solely with tables that belonged to the current user. DBA_CATALOG is a view that the DBA can use to take a quick look at all tables.

The following query shows you what type of objects exist in a particular database.

 TIP
> You can use ROWNUM to narrow down the results of your query to a specified number of rows for testing purposes. Oracle calls ROWNUM a *pseudocolumn*. ROWNUM, like ROWID, can be used on any database table or view.

INPUT/OUTPUT
```
SQL> SELECT DISTINCT(OBJECT_TYPE)
  2  FROM SYS.DBA_OBJECTS;

OBJECT_TYPE
------------
CLUSTER
DATABASE LINK
FUNCTION
INDEX
PACKAGE
PACKAGE BODY
PROCEDURE
SEQUENCE
SYNONYM
TABLE
TRIGGER
VIEW

12 rows selected.
```

 ANALYSIS The DISTINCT function in the preceding query lists all unique object types that exist in the database. This query is a good way to find out what types of objects the database designers and developers are using.

The DBA_TABLES view gives specific information about database tables, mostly concerning storage.

INPUT/OUTPUT
```
SQL> SELECT SUBSTR(OWNER,1,8) OWNER,
  2          SUBSTR(TABLE_NAME,1,25) TABLE_NAME,
  3          SUBSTR(TABLESPACE_NAME,1,30) TABLESPACE_NAME
  4  FROM SYS.DBA_TABLES
  5  WHERE OWNER = 'JSMITH';
```

 16

```
OWNER     TABLE_NAME                      TABLESPACE_NAME
--------  ------------------------------  --------------------
JSMITH    MAGAZINE_TBL                    USERS
JSMITH    HOBBY_TBL                       USERS
JSMITH    ADDRESS_TBL                     SYSTEM
JSMITH    CUSTOMER_TBL                    USERS

4 rows selected.
```

ANALYSIS   All tables are in the USERS tablespace except for ADDRESS_TBL, which is in the SYSTEM tablespace. Because the only table you should ever store in the SYSTEM tablespace is the SYSTEM table, the DBA needs to be aware of this situation. It's a good thing you ran this query!

JSMITH should immediately be asked to move his table into another eligible tablespace.

The DBA_SYNONYMS view provides a list of all synonyms that exist in the database. DBA_SYNONYMS gives a list of synonyms for all database users, unlike USER_SYNONYMS, which lists only the current user's private synonyms.

INPUT/ OUTPUT
```
SQL> SELECT SYNONYM_NAME,
  2          SUBSTR(TABLE_OWNER,1,10) TAB_OWNER,
  3          SUBSTR(TABLE_NAME,1,30) TABLE_NAME
  4  FROM SYS.DBA_SYNONYMS
  5  WHERE OWNER = 'JSMITH';

SYNONYM_NAME                      TAB_OWNER   TABLE_NAME
--------------------------------  ----------  ----------
TRIVIA_SYN                        VJOHNSON    TRIVIA_TBL

1 row selected.
```

ANALYSIS   The preceding output shows that JSMITH has a synonym called TRIVIA_SYN on a table called TRIVIA_TBL that is owned by VJOHNSON.

Now suppose that you want to get a list of all tables and their indexes that belong to JSMITH. You would write a query similar to the following, using DBA_INDEXES.

INPUT/ OUTPUT
```
SQL> SELECT SUBSTR(TABLE_OWNER,1,10) TBL_OWNER,
  2          SUBSTR(TABLE_NAME,1,30) TABLE_NAME,
  3          SUBSTR(INDEX_NAME,1,30) INDEX_NAME
  4  FROM SYS.DBA_INDEXES
  5  WHERE OWNER = 'JSMITH'
  6    AND ROWNUM < 5
  7  ORDER BY TABLE_NAME;

TBL_OWNER   TABLE_NAME                      INDEX_NAME
----------  ------------------------------  -----------
JSMITH      ADDRESS_TBL                     ADDR_INX
JSMITH      CUSTOMER_TBL                    CUST_INX
JSMITH      HOBBY_TBL                       HOBBY_PK
JSMITH      MAGAZINE_TBL                    MAGAZINE_INX

4 rows selected.
```

A query such as the previous one is an easy method of listing all indexes that belong to a schema and matching them up with their corresponding table.

```
SQL> SELECT SUBSTR(TABLE_NAME,1,15) TABLE_NAME,
  2         SUBSTR(INDEX_NAME,1,30) INDEX_NAME,
  3         SUBSTR(COLUMN_NAME,1,15) COLUMN_NAME,
  4         COLUMN_POSITION
  5  FROM SYS.DBA_IND_COLUMNS
  6  WHERE TABLE_OWNER = 'JSMITH'
  7    AND ROWNUM < 10
  8  ORDER BY 1,2,3;

TABLE_NAME       INDEX_NAME                     COLUMN_NAME      COLUMN_POSITION
---------------  ------------------------------ ---------------  ---------------
ADDRESS_TBL      ADDR_INX                       PERS_ID                        1
ADDRESS_TBL      ADDR_INX                       NAME                           2
ADDRESS_TBL      ADDR_INX                       CITY                           3
CUSTOMER_TBL     CUST_INX                       CUST_ID                        1
CUSTOMER_TBL     CUST_INX                       CUST_NAME                      2
CUSTOMER_TBL     CUOT_INX                       CUST_ZIP                       3
HOBBY_TBL        HOBBY_PK                       SAKEY                          1
MAGAZINE_TBL     MAGAZINE_INX                   ISSUE_NUM                      1
MAGAZINE_TBL     MAGAZINE_INX                   EDITOR                         2

9 rows selected.
```

Now you have selected each column that is indexed in each table and ordered the results by the order the column appears in the index. You have learned about tables, but what holds tables? Tablespaces are on a higher level than objects such as tables, indexes, and so on. Tablespaces are Oracle's mechanism for allocating space to the database. To allocate space, you must know what tablespaces are currently available. You can perform a select from DBA_TABLESPACES to see a list of all tablespaces and their status, as shown in the next example.

```
SQL> SELECT TABLESPACE_NAME, STATUS
  2  FROM SYS.DBA_TABLESPACES

TABLESPACE_NAME                    STATUS
---------------------------------  ------
SYSTEM                             ONLINE
RBS                                ONLINE
TEMP                               ONLINE
TOOLS                              ONLINE
USERS                              ONLINE
DATA_TS                            ONLINE
INDEX_TS                           ONLINE

7 rows selected.
```

The preceding output tells you that all tablespaces are online, which means that they are available for use. If a tablespace is offline, then the database objects within it (that is, the tables) are not accessible.

16

What is JSMITH's quota on all tablespaces to which he has access? In other words, how much room is available for JSMITH's database objects?

**INPUT/
OUTPUT**

```
SQL> SELECT TABLESPACE_NAME,
  2          BYTES,
  3          MAX_BYTES
  4  FROM SYS.DBA_TS_QUOTAS
  5  WHERE USERNAME = 'JSMITH'

TABLESPACE_NAME                        BYTES  MAX_BYTES
-------------------------------   ----------  ----------
DATA_TS                           134111232          -1
INDEX_TS                          474390528          -1

2 rows selected.
```

16

ANALYSIS   JSMITH has an unlimited quota on both tablespaces to which he has access. In this case the total number of bytes available in the tablespace is available on a first-come first-served basis. For instance, if JSMITH uses all the free space in DATA_TS, then no one else can create objects here.

Database Growth

This section looks at two views that aid in the measurement of database growth: DBA_SEGMENTS and DBA_EXTENTS. DBA_SEGMENTS provides information about each segment, or object in the database such as storage allocation, space used, and extents. Each time a table or index grows and must grab more space as identified by the NEXT EXTENT, the table takes another extent. A table usually becomes fragmented when it grows this way. DBA_EXTENTS provides information about each extent of a segment.

INPUT

```
SQL> SELECT SUBSTR(SEGMENT_NAME,1,30) SEGMENT_NAME,
  2          SUBSTR(SEGMENT_TYPE,1,12) SEGMENT_TYPE,
  3          BYTES,
  4          EXTENTS,
  5  FROM SYS.DBA_SEGMENTS
  6  WHERE OWNER = 'TWILLIAMS'
  7    AND ROWNUM < 5;
```

OUTPUT

```
SEGMENT_NAME                     SEGMENT_TYPE      BYTES    EXTENTS
-------------------------------  ------------  ---------  ----------
INVOICE_TBL                      TABLE            163840          10
COMPLAINT_TBL                    TABLE           4763783           3
HISTORY_TBL                      TABLE         547474996          27
HISTORY_INX                      INDEX         787244534          31

4 rows selected.
```

ANALYSIS   By looking at the output from DBA_SEGMENTS, you can easily identify which tables are experiencing the most growth by referring to the number of extents. Both HISTORY_TBL and HISTORY_INX have grown much more than the other two tables.

Next you can take a look at each extent of one of the tables. You can start with INVOICE_TBL.

```
SQL> SELECT SUBSTR(OWNER,1,10) OWNER,
  2          SUBSTR(SEGMENT_NAME,1,30) SEGMENT_NAME,
  3          EXTENT_ID,
  4          BYTES
  5  FROM SYS.DBA_EXTENTS
  6  WHERE OWNER = 'TWILLIAMS'
  7    AND SEGMENT_NAME = 'INVOICE_TBL'
  8  ORDER BY EXTENT_ID;
```

OWNER	SEGMENT_NAME	EXTENT_ID	BYTES
TWILLIAMS	INVOICE_TBL	0	16384
TWILLIAMS	INVOICE_TBL	1	16384
TWILLIAMS	INVOICE_TBL	2	16384
TWILLIAMS	INVOICE_TBL	3	16384
TWILLIAMS	INVOICE_TBL	4	16384
TWILLIAMS	INVOICE_TBL	5	16384
TWILLIAMS	INVOICE_TBL	6	16384
TWILLIAMS	INVOICE_TBL	7	16384
TWILLIAMS	INVOICE_TBL	8	16384
TWILLIAMS	INVOICE_TBL	9	16384

```
10 rows selected.
```

ANALYSIS This example displays each extent of the table, the extent_id, and the size of the extent in bytes. Each extent is only 16K, and because there are 10 extents, you might want to rebuild the table and increase the size of the initial_extent to optimize space usage. Rebuilding the table will allow all the table's data to fit into a single extent, and therefore, not be fragmented.

Space Allocated

Oracle allocates space to the database by using "data files." Space logically exists within a tablespace, but data files are the physical entities of tablespaces. In other implementations, data is also ultimately contained in data files, though these data files may be referenced by another name. The view called DBA_DATA_FILES enables you to see what is actually allocated to a tablespace.

```
SQL> SELECT SUBSTR(TABLESPACE_NAME,1,25) TABLESPACE_NAME,
  2          SUBSTR(FILE_NAME,1,40) FILE_NAME,
  3          BYTES
  4  FROM SYS.DBA_DATA_FILES;
```

TABLESPACE_NAME	FILE_NAME	BYTES
SYSTEM	/disk01/system0.dbf	41943040
RBS	/disk02/rbs0.dbf	524288000
TEMP	/disk03/temp0.dbf	524288000
TOOLS	/disk04/tools0.dbf	20971520
USERS	/disk05/users0.dbf	20971520
DATA_TS	/disk06/data0.dbf	524288000
INDEX_TS	/disk07/index0.dbf	524288000

```
7 rows selected.
```

ANALYSIS You are now able to see how much space has been allocated for each tablespace that exists in the database. Notice the names of the data files correspond to the tablespace to which they belong.

Space Available

As the following example shows, the DBA_FREE_SPACE view tells you how much free space is available in each tablespace.

INPUT
```
SQL> SELECT TABLESPACE_NAME, SUM(BYTES)
  2  FROM SYS.DBA_FREE_SPACE
  3  GROUP BY TABLESPACE_NAME;
```

OUTPUT
```
TABLESPACE_NAME                 SUM(BYTES)
------------------------------- ----------
SYSTEM                            23543040
RBS                              524288000
TEMP                             524288000
TOOLS                             12871520
USERS                               971520
DATA_TS                             568000
INDEX_TS                           1288000

7 rows selected.
```

ANALYSIS The preceding example lists the total free space for each tablespace. You can also view each segment of free space by simply selecting bytes from DBA_FREE_SPACE instead of SUM(bytes).

Rollback Segments

As areas for rolling back transactions are a crucial part to database performance, you need to know what rollback segments are available. DBA_ROLLBACK_SEGS provides this information.

INPUT
```
SQL> SELECT OWNER,
  2         SEGMENT_NAME
  3  FROM SYS.DBA_ROLLBACK_SEGS;
```

OUTPUT
```
OWNER  SEGMENT_NAME
------ ------------
SYS    SYSTEM
SYS    R0
SYS    R01
SYS    R02
SYS    R03
SYS    R04
SYS    R05

7 rows selected.
```

ANALYSIS This example performs a simple select to list all rollback segments by name. Much more data is available for your evaluation as well.

Dynamic Performance Views

Oracle DBAs frequently access dynamic performance views because they provide greater detail about the internal performance measures than many of the other data dictionary views. (The DBA views contain some of the same information.)

These views involve extensive details, which is implementation-specific. This section simply provides an overview of the type of information a given data dictionary contains.

Session Information

A DESCRIBE command of the V$SESSION views follows. (DESCRIBE is an SQL*Plus command and will be covered on Day 20.) You can see the detail that is contained in the view.

 SQL> **DESCRIBE V$SESSION**

```
Name                             Null?     Type
-------------------------------  -------   ----
SADDR                                      RAW(4)
SID                                        NUMBER
SERIAL#                                    NUMBER
AUDSID                                     NUMBER
PADDR                                      RAW(4)
USER#                                      NUMBER
USERNAME                                   VARCHAR2(30)
COMMAND                                    NUMBER
TADDR                                      VARCHAR2(8)
LOCKWAIT                                   VARCHAR2(8)
STATUS                                     VARCHAR2(8)
SERVER                                     VARCHAR2(9)
SCHEMA#                                    NUMBER
SCHEMANAME                                 VARCHAR2(30)
OSUSER                                     VARCHAR2(15)
PROCESS                                    VARCHAR2(9)
MACHINE                                    VARCHAR2(64)
TERMINAL                                   VARCHAR2(10)
PROGRAM                                    VARCHAR2(48)
TYPE                                       VARCHAR2(10)
SQL_ADDRESS                                RAW(4)
SQL_HASH_VALUE                             NUMBER
PREV_SQL_ADDR                              RAW(4)
PREV_HASH_VALUE                            NUMBER
MODULE                                     VARCHAR2(48)
MODULE_HASH                                NUMBER
ACTION                                     VARCHAR2(32)
ACTION_HASH                                NUMBER
CLIENT_INFO                                VARCHAR2(64)
FIXED_TABLE_SEQUENCE                       NUMBER
ROW_WAIT_OBJ#                              NUMBER
ROW_WAIT_FILE#                            NUMBER
ROW_WAIT_BLOCK#                            NUMBER
ROW_WAIT_ROW#                              NUMBER
LOGON_TIME                                 DATE
LAST_CALL_ET                               NUMBER
```

16

To get information about current database sessions, you could write a SELECT statement similar to the one that follows from V$SESSION.

**INPUT/
OUTPUT**

```
SQL> SELECT USERNAME, COMMAND, STATUS
  2  FROM V$SESSION
  3  WHERE USERNAME IS NOT NULL;

USERNAME                        COMMAND STATUS
------------------------------- ------- --------
TWILLIAMS                             3 ACTIVE
JSMITH                                0 INACTIVE

2 rows selected.
```

ANALYSIS TWILLIAMS is logged on to the database and performing a select from the database, which is represented by command 3.

JSMITH is merely logged on to the database. His session is inactive, and he is not performing any type of commands. Refer to your database documentation to find out how the commands are identified in the data dictionary. Commands include SELECT, INSERT, UPDATE, DELETE, CREATE TABLE, and DROP TABLE.

Performance Statistics

Data concerning performance statistics outside the realm of user sessions is also available in the data dictionary. This type of data is much more implementation specific than the other views discussed today.

Performance statistics include data such as read/write rates, successful hits on tables, use of the system global area, use of memory cache, detailed rollback segment information, detailed transaction log information, and table locks and waits. The well of knowledge is almost bottomless.

The Plan Table

The Plan table is the default table used with Oracle's SQL statement tool, EXPLAIN PLAN. (See Day 15.) This table is created by an Oracle script called UTLXPLAN.SQL, which is copied on to the server when the software is installed. Data is generated by the EXPLAIN PLAN tool, which populates the PLAN table with information about the object being accessed and the steps in the execution plan of an SQL statement.

Summary

Although the details of the data dictionary vary from one implementation to another, the content remains conceptually the same in all relational databases. You must follow the syntax and rules of your database management system, but today's examples should give you the confidence to query your data dictionary and to be creative when doing so.

NOTE

Exploring the data dictionary is an adventure, and you will need to explore in order to learn to use it effectively.

Q&A

Q Why should I use the views and tables in the data dictionary?

A Using the views in the data dictionary is the most accurate way to discover the nature of your database. The tables can tell you what you have access to and what your privileges are. They can also help you monitor various other database events such as user processes and database performance.

Q How is the data dictionary created?

A The data dictionary is created when the database is initialized. Oracle Corporation provides several scripts to run when creating each database. These scripts create all necessary tables and views for that particular database's system catalog.

Q How is the data dictionary updated?

A The data dictionary is updated internally by the RDBMS during daily operations. When you change the structure of a table, the appropriate changes are made to the data dictionary internally. You should *never* attempt to update any tables in the data dictionary yourself. Doing so may cause a corrupt database.

Q How can I find out who did what in a database?

A Normally, tables or views in a system catalog allow you to audit user activity.

Workshop

The Workshop provides quiz questions to help solidify your understanding of the material covered, as well as exercises to provide you with experience in using what you have learned. Try to answer the quiz and exercise questions before checking the answers in Appendix F, "Answers to Quizzes and Exercises."

Quiz

1. In Oracle, how can you find out what tables and views you own?
2. What types of information are stored in the data dictionary?
3. How can you use performance statistics?
4. What are some database objects?

16

Exercise

Suppose you are managing a small to medium-size database. Your job responsibilities include developing and managing the database. Another individual is inserting large amounts of data into a table and receives an error indicating a lack of space. You must determine the cause of the problem. Does the user's tablespace quota need to be increased, or do you need to allocate more space to the tablespace? Prepare a step-by-step list that explains how you will gather the necessary information from the data dictionary. You do not need to list specific table or view names.

16

Day 17

Using SQL to Generate SQL Statements

Objectives

Today you learn the concepts behind generating one or more SQL statements from a query. By the end of the day you should understand the following:

- [ ] The benefits of generating SQL statements from a query
- [ ] How to make the output from a query appear in the form of another SQL statement
- [ ] How to use the data dictionary, database tables, or both to form SQL statements

The Purpose of Using SQL to Generate SQL Statements

Generating SQL from another SQL statement simply means writing an SQL statement whose output forms another SQL statement or command. Until now, all the SQL statements that you have learned to write either do something, such as manipulate the data in a table, one row at a time, or produce some kind of report from a query. Today you learn how to write a query whose output forms another query or SQL statement.

Why you would ever need to produce an SQL statement from a query? Initially, it is a matter of simplicity and efficiency. You may never *need* to produce an SQL statement, but without ever doing so you would be ignoring one of SQL's most powerful features, one that too many people do not realize exists.

Generating SQL is rarely mandatory because you can manually create and issue all SQL statements, although the process can be tedious in certain situations. On the same note generating SQL statements may be necessary when you have a tight deadline. For example, suppose your boss wants to grant access on a new table to all 90 users in the marketing department (and you want to get home for dinner). Because some users of this database do not work in marketing, you cannot simply grant access on the table to public. When you have multiple groups of users with different types of access, you may want to enforce role security, which is a built-in method for controlling user access to data. In this situation you can create an SQL statement that generates GRANT statements to all individuals in the marketing department; that is, it grants each individual the appropriate role(s).

You will find many situations in which it is advantageous to produce an SQL statement as output to another statement. For example, you might need to execute many similar SQL statements as a group or you might need to regenerate DDL from the data dictionary. When producing SQL as output from another statement, you will always get the data for your output from either the data dictionary or the schema tables in the database. Figure 17.1 illustrates this procedure.

As you can see in Figure 17.1, a SELECT statement can be issued to the database, drawing its output results either from the data dictionary or from application tables in the database. Your statement can arrange the retrieved data into one or more SQL statements. For instance, if one row is returned, you will have generated one SQL statement. If 100 rows are returned from your statement, then you will have generated 100 SQL statements. When you successfully generate SQL code from the database, you can run that code against the database, which may perform a series of queries or database actions.

The remainder of the day is devoted to examples that show you how to produce output in the form of SQL statements. Most of your information will come from the data dictionary, so you may want to review yesterday's material. (See Day 16, "Using Views to Retrieve Useful Information from the Data Dictionary.")

Figure 17.1.

The process of generating SQL from the database.

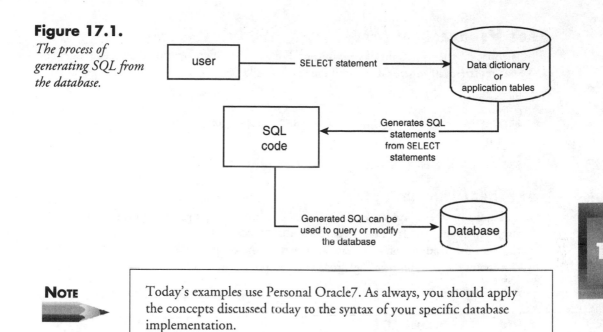

 NOTE
Today's examples use Personal Oracle7. As always, you should apply the concepts discussed today to the syntax of your specific database implementation.

Miscellaneous SQL*Plus Commands

Today's examples use a few new commands. These commands, known as SQL*Plus commands, are specific to Personal Oracle7 and control the format of your output results. (See Day 20, "SQL*Plus.") SQL*Plus commands are issued at the SQL> prompt, or they can be used in a file.

NOTE
Although these commands are specific to Oracle, similar commands are available in other implementations, for example, Transact-SQL. (Also see Day 19, "Transact-SQL: An Introduction.")

set echo on/off

When you set echo on, you will see your SQL statements as they execute. Set echo off means that you do not want to see your SQL statements as they execute—you just want to see the output.

```
SET ECHO [ ON ¦ OFF ]
```

set feedback on/off

Feedback is the row count of your output. For instance, if you executed a SELECT statement that returned 30 rows of data, your feedback would be

```
30 rows selected.
```

SET FEEDBACK ON displays the row count; SET FEEDBACK OFF eliminates the row count from your output.

```
SET FEEDBACK [ ON ¦ OFF ]
```

set heading on/off

The headings being referred to here are the column headings in the output of a SELECT statement, such as LAST_NAME or CUSTOMER_ID. SET HEADING ON, which is the default, displays the column headings of your data as a part of the output. SET HEADING OFF, of course, eliminates the column headings from your output.

```
SET HEADING [ ON ¦ OFF ]
```

spool filename/off

Spooling is the process of directing the results of your query to a file. In order to open a spool file, you enter

```
spool filename
```

To close your spool file, you would type

```
spool off
```

start filename

Most SQL commands that we have covered so far have been issued at the SQL> prompt. Another method for issuing SQL statements is to create and then execute a file. In SQL*Plus the command to execute an SQL file is START FILENAME.

```
START FILENAME
```

ed filename

ED is a Personal Oracle7 command that opens a file (existing or file). When you open a file with ed, you are using a full-screen editor, which is often easier than trying to type a lengthy SQL statement at the SQL> prompt. You will use this command to modify the contents of your spool file. You will find that you use this command often when generating SQL script because you may have to modify the contents of the file for customization. However, you can achieve most customization through SQL*Plus commands.

```
ED FILENAME
```

Counting the Rows in All Tables

The first example shows you how to edit your spool file to remove irrelevant lines in your generated code, thus allowing your SQL statement to run without being tarnished with syntax errors.

NOTE

Take note of the editing technique used in this example because we will not show the step in the rest of today's examples. We assume that you know the basic syntax of SQL statements by now. In addition, you may choose to edit your spool file in various ways.

Start by recalling the function to count all rows in a table: COUNT(*). You already know how to select a count on all rows in a single table. For example:

INPUT

```
SELECT COUNT(*)
FROM TBL1;
```

OUTPUT

```
COUNT(*)
--------
      29
```

That technique is handy, but suppose you want to get a row count on all tables that you own or that are in your schema. For example, here's a list of the tables you own:

**INPUT/
OUTPUT**

```
SELECT * FROM CAT;

TABLE_NAME                          TABLE_TYPE
--------------------------------    -----------
ACCT_PAY                            TABLE
ACCT_REC                            TABLE
CUSTOMERS                           TABLE
EMPLOYEES                           TABLE
HISTORY                             TABLE
INVOICES                            TABLE
ORDERS                              TABLE
PRODUCTS                            TABLE
PROJECTS                            TABLE
VENDORS                             TABLE

10 rows selected.
```

ANALYSIS

If you want to get a row count on all your tables, you could manually issue the COUNT(*) statement on each table. The feedback would be

```
10 rows selected.
```

The following SELECT statement creates more SELECT statements to obtain a row count on all the preceding tables.

```
SQL> SET ECHO OFF
SQL> SET FEEDBACK OFF
SQL> SET HEADING OFF
SQL> SPOOL CNT.SQL
SQL> SELECT 'SELECT COUNT(*) FROM ' || TABLE_NAME || ';'
  2  FROM CAT
  3  /

SELECT COUNT(*) FROM ACCT_PAY;
SELECT COUNT(*) FROM ACCT_REC;
SELECT COUNT(*) FROM CUSTOMERS;
SELECT COUNT(*) FROM EMPLOYEES;
SELECT COUNT(*) FROM HISTORY;
SELECT COUNT(*) FROM INVOICES;
SELECT COUNT(*) FROM ORDERS;
SELECT COUNT(*) FROM PRODUCTS;
SELECT COUNT(*) FROM PROJECTS;
select count(*) FROM VENDORS;
```

ANALYSIS The first action in the preceding example is to use some SQL*Plus commands. Setting echo off, feedback off, and heading off condenses the output to what is actually being selected. Remember, the output is not being used as a report, but rather as an SQL statement that is ready to be executed. The next step is to use the SPOOL command to direct the output to a file, which is specified as cnt.sql. The final step is to issue the SELECT statement, which will produce output in the form of another statement. Notice the use of single quotation marks to select a literal string. The combination of single quotation marks and the concatenation (||) allows you to combine actual data and literal strings to form another SQL statement. This example selects its data from the data dictionary. The command SPOOL OFF closes the spool file.

TIP Always edit your output file before running it to eliminate syntax discrepancies and to further customize the file that you have created.

```
SQL> SPOOL OFF
SQL> ED CNT.SQL
```

OUTPUT
```
SQL> SELECT 'SELECT COUNT(*) FROM '||TABLE_NAME||';'
  2  FROM CAT;

SELECT COUNT(*) FROM ACCT_PAY;
SELECT COUNT(*) FROM ACCT_REC;
SELECT COUNT(*) FROM CUSTOMERS;
SELECT COUNT(*) FROM EMPLOYEES;
SELECT COUNT(*) FROM HISTORY;
SELECT COUNT(*) FROM INVOICES;
SELECT COUNT(*) FROM ORDERS;
SELECT COUNT(*) FROM PRODUCTS;
SELECT COUNT(*) FROM PROJECTS;
SELECT COUNT(*) FROM VENDORS;
SQL> SPOOL OFF
```

ANALYSIS The command SPOOL OFF closes the spool file. Then the ED command edits the file. At this point you are inside the file that you created. You should remove unnecessary lines from the file, such as the SELECT statement, which was used to achieve the results, and the SPOOL OFF at the end of the file.

Here is how your file should look after the edit. Notice that each line is a valid SQL statement.

```
SELECT COUNT(*) FROM ACCT_PAY;
SELECT COUNT(*) FROM ACCT_REC;
SELECT COUNT(*) FROM CUSTOMERS;
SELECT COUNT(*) FROM EMPLOYEES;
SELECT COUNT(*) FROM HISTORY;
SELECT COUNT(*) FROM INVOICES;
SELECT COUNT(*) FROM ORDERS;
SELECT COUNT(*) FROM PRODUCTS;
SELECT COUNT(*) FROM PROJECTS;
SELECT COUNT(*) FROM VENDORS;
```

Now, execute the file:

INPUT/ OUTPUT
```
SQL> SET ECHO ON
SQL> SET HEADING ON
SQL> START CNT.SQL

SQL> SELECT COUNT(*) FROM ACCT_PAY;

  COUNT(*)
---------
        7
SQL> SELECT COUNT(*) FROM ACCT_REC;

  COUNT(*)
---------
        9
SQL> SELECT COUNT(*) FROM CUSTOMERS;

  COUNT(*)
---------
        5
SQL> SELECT COUNT(*) FROM EMPLOYEES;

  COUNT(*)
---------
       10

SQL> SELECT COUNT(*) FROM HISTORY;

  COUNT(*)
---------
       26
SQL> SELECT COUNT(*) FROM INVOICES;

  COUNT(*)
---------
        0
```

17

```
SQL> SELECT COUNT(*) FROM ORDERS;

 COUNT(*)
----------
        0
SQL> SELECT COUNT(*) FROM PRODUCTS;

 COUNT(*)
----------
       10
SQL> SELECT COUNT(*) FROM PROJECTS;

 COUNT(*)
----------
       16
SQL> SELECT COUNT(*) FROM VENDORS;

 COUNT(*)
----------
       22
SQL>
```

ANALYSIS Set echo on enables you to see each statement that was executed. Set heading on displays the column heading COUNT(*) for each SELECT statement. If you had included

set feedback on

then

1 row selected.

would have been displayed after each count. This example executed the SQL script by using the SQL*Plus START command. However, what if you were dealing with 50 tables instead of just 10?

NOTE The proper use of single quotation marks when generating an SQL script is vital. Use these quotations generously and make sure that you are including all elements that will make your generated statement complete. In this example single quotation marks enclose the components of your generated statement (output) that cannot be selected from a table; for example, 'SELECT COUNT(*) FROM' and ';'.

Granting System Privileges to Multiple Users

As a database administrator or an individual responsible for maintaining users, you will often receive requests for user IDs. In addition to having to grant privileges to users that allow them proper database access, you also have to modify users' privileges to accommodate their changing needs. You can get the database to generate the GRANT statements to grant system privileges or roles to many users.

```
SQL> SET ECHO OFF
SQL> SET HEADING OFF
SQL> SET FEEDBACK OFF
SQL> SPOOL GRANTS.SQL
SQL> SELECT 'GRANT CONNECT, RESOURCE TO ' || USERNAME || ';'
  2  FROM SYS.DBA_USERS
  3  WHERE USERNAME NOT IN ('SYS','SYSTEM','SCOTT','RYAN','PO7','DEMO')
  4  /
```

OUTPUT

```
GRANT CONNECT, RESOURCE TO KEVIN;
GRANT CONNECT, RESOURCE TO JOHN;
GRANT CONNECT, RESOURCE TO JUDITH;
GRANT CONNECT, RESOURCE TO STEVE;
GRANT CONNECT, RESOURCE TO RON;
GRANT CONNECT, RESOURCE TO MARY;
GRANT CONNECT, RESOURCE TO DEBRA;
GRANT CONNECT, RESOURCE TO CHRIS;
GRANT CONNECT, RESOURCE TO CAROL;
GRANT CONNECT, RESOURCE TO EDWARD;
GRANT CONNECT, RESOURCE TO BRANDON;
GRANT CONNECT, RESOURCE TO JACOB;
```

INPUT/OUTPUT

```
SQL> spool off

SQL> start grants.sql


SQL> GRANT CONNECT, RESOURCE TO KEVIN;

Grant succeeded.

SQL> GRANT CONNECT, RESOURCE TO JOHN;

Grant succeeded.

SQL> GRANT CONNECT, RESOURCE TO JUDITH;

Grant succeeded.

SQL> GRANT CONNECT, RESOURCE TO STEVE;

Grant succeeded.

SQL> GRANT CONNECT, RESOURCE TO RON;
```

17

```
Grant succeeded.

SQL> GRANT CONNECT, RESOURCE TO MARY;

Grant succeeded.

SQL> GRANT CONNECT, RESOURCE TO DEBRA;

Grant succeeded.

SQL> GRANT CONNECT, RESOURCE TO CHRIS;

Grant succeeded.

SQL> GRANT CONNECT, RESOURCE TO CAROL;

Grant succeeded.

SQL> GRANT CONNECT, RESOURCE TO EDWARD;

Grant succeeded.

SQL> GRANT CONNECT, RESOURCE TO BRANDON;

Grant succeeded.

SQL> GRANT CONNECT, RESOURCE TO JACOB;

Grant succeeded.
```

ANALYSIS In this example you saved many tedious keystrokes by generating GRANT statements using a simple SQL statement, rather than typing each one manually.

NOTE The following examples omit the step in which you edit your output file. You can assume that the files are already edited.

Granting Privileges on Your Tables to Another User

Granting privileges on a table to another user is quite simple, as is selecting a row count on a table. But if you have multiple tables to which you wish to grant access to a role or user, you can make SQL generate a script for you—unless you just love to type.

First, review a simple GRANT to one table:

INPUT SQL> **GRANT SELECT ON HISTORY TO BRANDON;**

OUTPUT   Grant succeeded.

Are you ready for some action? The next statement creates a GRANT statement for each of the
10 tables in your schema.

INPUT/
OUTPUT

```
SQL> SET ECHO OFF
SQL> SET FEEDBACK OFF
SQL> SET HEADING OFF
SQL> SPOOL GRANTS.SQL
SQL> SELECT 'GRANT SELECT ON ' || TABLE_NAME || ' TO BRANDON;'
  2  FROM CAT
  3  /

GRANT SELECT ON ACCT_PAY TO BRANDON;
GRANT SELECT ON ACCT_REC TO BRANDON;
GRANT SELECT ON CUSTOMERS TO BRANDON;
GRANT SELECT ON EMPLOYEES TO BRANDON;
GRANT SELECT ON HISTORY TO BRANDON;
GRANT SELECT ON INVOICES TO BRANDON;
GRANT SELECT ON ORDERS TO BRANDON;
GRANT SELECT ON PRODUCTS TO BRANDON;
GRANT SELECT ON PROJECTS TO BRANDON;
GRANT SELECT ON VENDORS TO BRANDON;
```

ANALYSIS   A GRANT statement has been automatically prepared for each table. BRANDON is
to have Select access on each table.

Now close the output file with the SPOOL command, and assuming that the file has been
edited, the file is ready to run.

INPUT/
OUTPUT

```
SQL> SPOOL OFF

SQL> SET ECHO ON
SQL> SET FEEDBACK ON
SQL> START GRANTS.SQL


SQL> GRANT SELECT ON ACCT_PAY TO BRANDON;

Grant succeeded.

SQL> GRANT SELECT ON ACCT_REC TO BRANDON;

Grant succeeded.

SQL> GRANT SELECT ON CUSTOMERS TO BRANDON;

Grant succeeded.

SQL> GRANT SELECT ON EMPLOYEES TO BRANDON;

Grant succeeded.

SQL> GRANT SELECT ON HISTORY TO BRANDON;
```

17

```
Grant succeeded.

SQL> GRANT SELECT ON INVOICES TO BRANDON;

Grant succeeded.

SQL> GRANT SELECT ON ORDERS TO BRANDON;

Grant succeeded.

SQL> GRANT SELECT ON PRODUCTS TO BRANDON;

Grant succeeded.

SQL> GRANT SELECT ON PROJECTS TO BRANDON;

Grant succeeded.

SQL> GRANT SELECT ON VENDORS TO BRANDON;

Grant succeeded.
```

ANALYSIS   Echo was set on and feedback was set on as well. Setting feedback on displayed the statement Grant succeeded. The Select privilege has been granted to BRANDON on all 10 tables with very little effort. Again, keep in mind that you will often be dealing with many more than 10 tables.

Disabling Table Constraints to Load Data

When loading data into tables, you will sometimes have to disable the constraints on your tables. Suppose that you have truncated your tables and you are loading data into your tables from scratch. More than likely, your tables will have referential integrity constraints, such as foreign keys. Because the database will not let you insert a row of data in a table that references another table (if the referenced column does not exist in the other table), you may have to disable constraints to initially load your data. Of course, after the load is successful, you would want to enable the constraints.

INPUT
```
SQL> SET ECHO OFF
SQL> SET FEEDBACK OFF
SQL> SET HEADING OFF
SQL> SPOOL DISABLE.SQL
SQL> SELECT 'ALTER TABLE ' || TABLE_NAME ||
  2         'DISABLE CONSTRAINT ' || CONSTRAINT_NAME || ';'
  3  FROM SYS.DBA_CONSTRAINTS
  4  WHERE OWNER = 'RYAN'
  5  /
```

OUTPUT
```
ALTER TABLE ACCT_PAY DISABLE CONSTRAINT FK_ACCT_ID;
ALTER TABLE ACCT_REC DISABLE CONSTRAINT FK_ACCT_ID;
ALTER TABLE CUSTOMERS DISABLE CONSTRAINT FK_CUSTOMER_ID;
ALTER TABLE HISTORY DISABLE CONSTRAINT FK_ACCT_ID;
ALTER TABLE INVOICES DISABLE CONSTRAINT FK_ACCT_ID;
ALTER TABLE ORDERS DISABLE CONSTRAINT FK_ACCT_ID;
```

17

ANALYSIS The objective is to generate a series of ALTER TABLE statements that will disable the constraints on all tables owned by RYAN. The semicolon concatenated to the end of what is being selected completes each SQL statement.

INPUT/ OUTPUT
```
SQL> SPOOL OFF

SQL> SET ECHO OFF
SQL> SET FEEDBACK ON
SQL> START DISABLE.SQL


Constraint Disabled.

Constraint Disabled.

Constraint Disabled.

Constraint Disabled.

Constraint Disabled.

Constraint Disabled.
```

ANALYSIS Notice that echo is set to off, which means that you will not see the individual statements. Because feedback is set to on, you can see the results.

```
Constraint Disabled.
```

If both echo and feedback were set to off, nothing would be displayed. There would simply be a pause for as long as it takes to execute the ALTER TABLE statements and then an SQL> prompt would be returned.

Now you can load your data without worrying about receiving errors caused by your constraints. Constraints are good, but they can be barriers during data loads. You may use the same idea to enable the table constraints.

Creating Numerous Synonyms in a Single Bound

Another tedious and exhausting task is creating numerous synonyms, whether they be public or private. Only a DBA can create public synonyms, but any user can create private synonyms.

The following example creates public synonyms for all tables owned by RYAN.

INPUT
```
SQL> SET ECHO OFF
SQL> SET FEEDBACK OFF
SQL> SET HEADING OFF
SQL> SPOOL PUB_SYN.SQL
SQL> SELECT 'CREATE PUBLIC SYNONYM ' || TABLE_NAME || ' FOR ' ||
  2          OWNER || '.' || TABLE_NAME || ';'
  3  FROM SYS.DBA_TABLES
  4  WHERE OWNER = 'RYAN'
  5  /
```

OUTPUT

```
CREATE PUBLIC SYNONYM ACCT_PAY FOR RYAN.ACCT_PAY;
CREATE PUBLIC SYNONYM ACCT_REC FOR RYAN.ACCT_REC;
CREATE PUBLIC SYNONYM CUSTOMERS FOR RYAN.CUSTOMERS;
CREATE PUBLIC SYNONYM EMPLOYEES FOR RYAN.EMPLOYEES;
CREATE PUBLIC SYNONYM HISTORY FOR RYAN.HISTORY;
CREATE PUBLIC SYNONYM INVOICES FOR RYAN.INVOICES;
CREATE PUBLIC SYNONYM ORDERS FOR RYAN.ORDERS;
CREATE PUBLIC SYNONYM PRODUCTS FOR RYAN.PRODUCTS;
CREATE PUBLIC SYNONYM PROJECTS FOR RYAN.PROJECTS;
CREATE PUBLIC SYNONYM VENDORS FOR RYAN.VENDORS;
```

Now run the file.

INPUT/OUTPUT

```
SQL> SPOOL OFF
SQL> ED PUB_SYN.SQL
SQL> SET ECHO ON
SQL> SET FEEDBACK ON
SQL> START PUB_SYN.SQL

SQL> CREATE PUBLIC SYNONYM ACCT_PAY FOR RYAN.ACCT_PAY;

Synonym created.

SQL> CREATE PUBLIC SYNONYM ACCT_REC FOR RYAN.ACCT_REC;

Synonym created.

SQL> CREATE PUBLIC SYNONYM CUSTOMERS FOR RYAN.CUSTOMERS;

Synonym created.

SQL> CREATE PUBLIC SYNONYM EMPLOYEES FOR RYAN.EMPLOYEES;

Synonym created.

SQL> CREATE PUBLIC SYNONYM HISTORY FOR RYAN.HISTORY;

Synonym created.

SQL> CREATE PUBLIC SYNONYM INVOICES FOR RYAN.INVOICES;

Synonym created.

SQL> CREATE PUBLIC SYNONYM ORDERS FOR RYAN.ORDERS;

Synonym created.

SQL> CREATE PUBLIC SYNONYM PRODUCTS FOR RYAN.PRODUCTS;

Synonym created.

SQL> CREATE PUBLIC SYNONYM PROJECTS FOR RYAN.PROJECTS;

Synonym created.

SQL> CREATE PUBLIC SYNONYM VENDORS FOR RYAN.VENDORS;

Synonym created.
```

ANALYSIS Almost instantly, all database users have access to a public synonym for all tables that RYAN owns. Now a user does not need to qualify the table when performing a SELECT operation. (*Qualifying* means identifying the table owner, as in RYAN.VENDORS.)

What if public synonyms do not exist? Suppose that BRANDON has Select access to all tables owned by RYAN and wants to create private synonyms.

INPUT/ OUTPUT

```
SQL> CONNECT BRANDON
ENTER PASSWORD: *******
CONNECTED.

SQL> SET ECHO OFF
SQL> SET FEEDBACK OFF
SQL> SET HEADING OFF
SQL> SPOOL PRIV_SYN.SQL
SQL> SELECT 'CREATE SYNONYM ' || TABLE_NAME || ' FOR ' ||
  2           OWNER || '.' || TABLE_NAME || ';'
  3  FROM ALL_TABLES
  4  /

CREATE SYNONYM DUAL FOR SYS.DUAL;
CREATE SYNONYM AUDIT_ACTIONS FOR SYS.AUDIT_ACTIONS;
CREATE SYNONYM USER_PROFILE FOR SYSTEM.USER_PROFILE;
CREATE SYNONYM CUSTOMERS FOR RYAN.CUSTOMERS;
CREATE SYNONYM ORDERS FOR RYAN.ORDERS;
CREATE SYNONYM PRODUCTS FOR RYAN.PRODUCTS;
CREATE SYNONYM INVOICES FOR RYAN.INVOICES;
CREATE SYNONYM ACCT_REC FOR RYAN.ACCT_REC;
CREATE SYNONYM ACCT_PAY FOR RYAN.ACCT_PAY;
CREATE SYNONYM VENDORS FOR RYAN.VENDORS;
CREATE SYNONYM EMPLOYEES FOR RYAN.EMPLOYEES;
CREATE SYNONYM PROJECTS FOR RYAN.PROJECTS;
CREATE SYNONYM HISTORY FOR RYAN.HISTORY;
```

INPUT/ OUTPUT

```
SQL> SPOOL OFF
SQL>

SQL> SET ECHO OFF
SQL> SET FEEDBACK ON
SQL> START PRIV_SYN.SQL

Synonym created.

Synonym created.

Synonym created.

Synonym created.

Synonym created.

Synonym created.

Synonym created.
```

17

```
Synonym created.

Synonym created.

Synonym created.

Synonym created.

Synonym created.

Synonym created.
```

ANALYSIS With hardly any effort, BRANDON has synonyms for all tables owned by RYAN and no longer needs to qualify the table names.

Creating Views on Your Tables

If you want to create views on a group of tables, you could try something similar to the following example:

INPUT
```
SQL> SET ECHO OFF
SQL> SET FEEDBACK OFF
SQL> SET HEADING OFF
SQL> SPOOL VIEWS.SQL
SQL> SELECT 'CREATE VIEW ' || TABLE_NAME || '_VIEW AS SELECT * FROM ' ||
  2          TABLE_NAME || ';'
  3  FROM CAT
  4  /
```

OUTPUT
```
CREATE VIEW ACCT_PAY_VIEW AS SELECT * FROM ACCT_PAY;
CREATE VIEW ACCT_REC_VIEW AS SELECT * FROM ACCT_REC;
CREATE VIEW CUSTOMERS_VIEW AS SELECT * FROM CUSTOMERS;
CREATE VIEW EMPLOYEES_VIEW AS SELECT * FROM EMPLOYEES;
CREATE VIEW HISTORY_VIEW AS SELECT * FROM HISTORY;
CREATE VIEW INVOICES_VIEW AS SELECT * FROM INVOICES;
CREATE VIEW ORDERS_VIEW AS SELECT * FROM ORDERS;
CREATE VIEW PRODUCTS_VIEW AS SELECT * FROM PRODUCTS;
CREATE VIEW PROJECTS_VIEW AS SELECT * FROM PROJECTS;
CREATE VIEW VENDORS_VIEW AS SELECT * FROM VENDORS;
```

**INPUT/
OUTPUT**
```
SQL> SPOOL OFF
SQL> SET ECHO OFF
SQL> SET FEEDBACK ON
SQL> START VIEWS.SQL
```

```
View Created.

View Created.

View Created.

View Created.

View Created.
```

17

```
View Created.

View Created.

View Created.

View Created.

View Created.
```

ANALYSIS The file `views.sql` was generated by the previous SQL statement. This output file has become another SQL statement file and contains statements to create views on all specified tables. After running `views.sql`, you can see that the views have been created.

Truncating All Tables in a Schema

Truncating tables is an event that occurs in a development environment. To effectively develop and test data load routines and SQL statement performance, data is reloaded frequently. This process identifies and exterminates bugs, and the application being developed or tested is moved into a production environment.

The following example truncates all tables in a specified schema.

INPUT
```
SQL> SET ECHO OFF
SQL> SET FEEDBACK OFF
SQL> SET HEADING OFF
SQL> SPOOL TRUNC.SQL
SQL> SELECT 'TRUNCATE TABLE ' || TABLE_NAME || ';'
  2  FROM ALL_TABLES
  3  WHERE OWNER = 'RYAN'
  4  /
```

OUTPUT
```
TRUNCATE TABLE ACCT_PAY;
TRUNCATE TABLE ACCT_REC;
TRUNCATE TABLE CUSTOMERS;
TRUNCATE TABLE EMPLOYEES;
TRUNCATE TABLE HISTORY;
TRUNCATE TABLE INVOICES;
TRUNCATE TABLE ORDERS;
TRUNCATE TABLE PRODUCTS;
TRUNCATE TABLE PROJECTS;
TRUNCATE TABLE VENDORS;
```

Go ahead and run your script if you dare.

INPUT/ OUTPUT
```
SQL> SPOOL OFF
SQL> SET FEEDBACK ON
SQL> START TRUNC.SQL

Table Truncated.

Table Truncated.
```

```
Table Truncated.

Table Truncated.

Table Truncated.

Table Truncated.

Table Truncated.

Table Truncated.

Table Truncated.

Table Truncated.
```

 ANALYSIS Truncating all tables owned by RYAN removes all the data from those tables. Table truncation is easy. You can use this technique if you plan to repopulate your tables with new data.

 TIP

Before performing an operation such as truncating tables in a schema, you should *always* have a good backup of the tables you plan to truncate, even if you are sure that you will never need the data again. (You will—somebody is sure to ask you to restore the old data.)

Using SQL to Generate Shell Scripts

You can also use SQL to generate other forms of scripts, such as shell scripts. For example, an Oracle RDBMS server may be running in a UNIX environment, which is typically much larger than a PC operating system environment. Therefore, UNIX requires a more organized approach to file management. You can use SQL to easily manage the database files by creating shell scripts.

The following scenario drops tablespaces in a database. Although tablespaces can be dropped using SQL, the actual data files associated with these tablespaces must be removed from the operating system separately.

The first step is to generate an SQL script to drop the tablespaces.

INPUT

```
SQL> SET ECHO OFF
SQL> SET FEEDBACK OFF
SQL> SET HEADING OFF
SQL> SPOOL DROP_TS.SQL
SQL> SELECT 'DROP TABLESPACE ' || TABLESPACE_NAME || ' INCLUDING
    ➥CONTENTS;'
  2  FROM SYS.DBA_TABLESPACES
  3  /
```

17

OUTPUT
```
DROP TABLESPACE SYSTEM INCLUDING CONTENTS;
DROP TABLESPACE RBS INCLUDING CONTENTS;
DROP TABLESPACE TEMP INCLUDING CONTENTS;
DROP TABLESPACE TOOLS INCLUDING CONTENTS;
DROP TABLESPACE USERS INCLUDING CONTENTS;
```

Next you need to generate a shell script to remove the data files from the operating system after the tablespaces have been dropped.

**INPUT/
OUTPUT**
```
SQL> SPOOL OFF
SQL> SPOOL RM_FILES.SH
SQL> SELECT 'RM -F ' ¦¦ FILE_NAME
  2  FROM SYS.DBA_DATA_FILES
  3  /

rm -f /disk01/orasys/db01/system0.dbf
rm -f /disk02/orasys/db01/rbs0.dbf
rm -f /disk03/orasys/db01/temp0.dbf
rm -f /disk04/orasys/db01/tools0.dbf
rm -f /disk05/orasys/db01/users0.dbf
SQL> spool off
SQL>
```

ANALYSIS   Now that you have generated both scripts, you may run the script to drop the tablespaces and then execute the operating system shell script to remove the appropriate data files. You will also find many other ways to manage files and generate non-SQL scripts using SQL.

Reverse Engineering Tables and Indexes

Even though many CASE tools allow you to reverse-engineer tables and indexes, you can always use straight SQL for this purpose. You can retrieve all the information that you need from the data dictionary to rebuild tables and indexes, but doing so effectively is difficult without the use of a procedural language, such as PL/SQL or a shell script.

We usually use embedded SQL within a shell script. Procedural language functions are needed to plug in the appropriate ingredients of syntax, such as commas. The script must be smart enough to know which column is the last one, so as to not place a comma after the last column. The script must also know where to place parentheses and so on. Seek the tools that are available to regenerate objects from the data dictionary, whether you use C, Perl, shell scripts, COBOL, or PL/SQL.

Summary

Generating statements directly from the database spares you the often tedious job of coding SQL statements. Regardless of your job scope, using SQL statement generation techniques frees you to work on other phases of your projects.

What you have learned today is basic, and though these examples use the Oracle database, you can apply the concepts to any relational database. Be sure to check your specific implementation for variations in syntax and data dictionary structure. If you keep an open mind, you will continually find ways to generate SQL scripts, from simple statements to complex high-level system management.

Q&A

Q How do I decide when to issue statements manually and when to write SQL to generate SQL?

A Ask yourself these questions:

☐ How often will I be issuing the statements in question?

☐ Will it take me longer to write the "mother" statement than it would to issue each statement manually?

Q From which tables may I select to generate SQL statements?

A You may select from any tables to which you have access, whether they are tables that you own or tables that reside in the data dictionary. Also keep in mind that you can select from any valid objects in your database, such as views or snapshots.

Q Are there any limits to the statements that I can generate with SQL?

A For the most part any statement that you can write manually can be generated somehow using SQL. Check your implementation for specific options for spooling output to a file and formatting the output the way you want it. Remember that you can always modify the generated statements later because the output is spooled to a file.

Workshop

The Workshop provides quiz questions to help solidify your understanding of the material covered, as well as exercises to provide you with experience in using what you have learned. Try to answer the quiz and exercise questions before checking the answers in Appendix F, "Answers to Quizzes and Exercises."

Quiz

1. From which two sources can you generate SQL scripts?
2. Will the following SQL statement work? Will the generated output work?

```
SQL> SET ECHO OFF
SQL> SET FEEDBACK OFF
SQL> SPOOL CNT.SQL
```

17

```
SQL> SELECT 'COUNT(*) FROM  ' || TABLE_NAME || ';'
  2  FROM CAT
  3  /
```

3. Will the following SQL statement work? Will the generated output work?

```
SQL> SET ECHO OFF
SQL> SET FEEDBACK OFF
SQL> SPOOL GRANT.SQL
SQL> SELECT 'GRANT CONNECT DBA TO ' || USERNAME || ';'
  2  FROM SYS.DBA_USERS
  3  WHERE USERNAME NOT IN ('SYS','SYSTEM','SCOTT')
  4  /
```

4. Will the following SQL statement work? Will the generated output work?

```
SQL> SET ECHO OFF
SQL> SET FEEDBACK OFF
SQL> SELECT 'GRANT CONNECT, DBA TO ' || USERNAME || ';'
  2  FROM SYS.DBA_USERS
  3  WHERE USERNAME NOT IN ('SYS','SYSTEM','SCOTT)
  4  /
```

5. True or False: It is best to set feedback ON when generating SQL.

6. True or False: When generating SQL from SQL, always spool to a list or log file for a record of what happened.

7. True or False: Before generating SQL to truncate tables, you should always make sure you have a good backup of the tables.

8. What is the ED command?

9. What does the SPOOL OFF command do?

Exercises

1. Using the SYS.DBA_USERS view (Personal Oracle7), create an SQL statement that will generate a series of GRANT statements to five new users: John, Kevin, Ryan, Ron, and Chris. Use the column called USERNAME. Grant them Select access to history_tbl.

2. Using the examples in this chapter as guidelines, create some SQL statements that will generate SQL that you can use.

Day 18

PL/SQL: An Introduction

Objectives

PL/SQL is the Oracle technology that enables SQL to act like a procedural language. By the end of today, you should

- ☐ Have a basic understanding of PL/SQL
- ☐ Understand the features that distinguish PL/SQL from standard SQL
- ☐ Have an understanding of the basic elements of a PL/SQL program
- ☐ Be able to write a simple PL/SQL program
- ☐ Understand how errors are handled in PL/SQL programs
- ☐ Be aware of how PL/SQL is used in the real world

Introduction

One way to introduce PL/SQL is to begin by describing standard Structured Query Language, or SQL. SQL is the language that enables relational database users to communicate with the database in a straightforward manner. You can use SQL commands to query the database and modify tables within the database. When you write an SQL statement, you are telling the database what you want to do, not how to do it. The query optimizer decides the most efficient way to execute your statement. If you send a series of SQL statements to the server in standard SQL, the server executes them one at a time in chronological order.

PL/SQL is Oracle's procedural language; it comprises the standard language of SQL and a wide array of commands that enable you to control the execution of SQL statements according to different conditions. PL/SQL can also handle runtime errors. Options such as loops and IF...THEN statements give PL/SQL the power of third-generation programming languages. PL/SQL allows you to write interactive, user-friendly programs that can pass values into variables. You can also use several predefined packages, one of which can display messages to the user.

Day 18 covers these key features of PL/SQL:

- ☐ Programmers can declare variables to be used during statement processing.
- ☐ Programmers can use error-handling routines to prevent programs from aborting unexpectedly.
- ☐ Programmers can write interactive programs that accept input from the user.
- ☐ Programmers can divide functions into logical blocks of code. Modular programming techniques support flexibility during the application development.
- ☐ SQL statements can be processed simultaneously for better overall performance.

Data Types in PL/SQL

Most data types are obviously similar, but each implementation has unique storage and internal-processing requirements. When writing PL/SQL blocks, you will be declaring variables, which must be valid data types. The following subsections briefly describe the data types available in PL/SQL.

In PL/SQL Oracle provides *subtypes* of data types. For example, the data type NUMBER has a subtype called INTEGER. You can use subtypes in your PL/SQL program to make the data types compatible with data types in other programs, such as a COBOL program, particularly if you are embedding PL/SQL code in another program. Subtypes are simply alternative names for Oracle data types and therefore must follow the rules of their associated data type.

NOTE

As in most implementations of SQL, case sensitivity is not a factor in the syntax of a statement. PL/SQL allows either uppercase or lowercase with its commands.

Character String Data Types

Character string data types in PL/SQL, as you might expect, are data types generally defined as having alpha-numeric values. Examples of character strings are names, codes, descriptions, and serial numbers that include characters.

CHAR stores fixed-length character strings. The maximum length of CHAR is 32,767 bytes, although it is hard to imagine a set of fixed-length values in a table being so long.

CHAR (max_length)

Subtype: CHARACTER

VARCHAR2 stores variable-length character strings. You would normally user VARCHAR2 instead of CHAR to store variable-length data, such as an individual's name. The maximum length of VARCHAR2 is also 32,767 bytes.

VARCHAR2 (max_length)

Subtypes: VARCHAR, STRING

LONG also stores variable-length character strings, having a maximum length of 32,760 bytes. LONG is typically used to store lengthy text such as remarks, although VARCHAR2 may be used as well.

Numeric Data Types

NUMBER stores any type of number in an Oracle database.

NUMBER (max_length)

You may specify a NUMBER's data precision with the following syntax:

NUMBER (precision, scale)

Subtypes: DEC, DECIMAL, DOUBLE PRECISION, INTEGER, INT, NUMERIC, REAL, SMALLINT, FLOAT

PLS_INTEGER defines columns that may contained integers with a sign, such as negative numbers.

Binary Data Types

Binary data types store data that is in a binary format, such as graphics or photographs. These data types include RAW and LONGRAW.

The DATE Data Type

DATE is the valid Oracle data type in which to store dates. When you define a column as a DATE, you do not specify a length, as the length of a DATE field is implied. The format of an Oracle date is, for example, 01-OCT-97.

BOOLEAN

BOOLEAN stores the following values: TRUE, FALSE, and NULL. Like DATE, BOOLEAN requires no parameters when defining it as a column's or variable's data type.

ROWID

ROWID is a pseudocolumn that exists in every table in an Oracle database. The ROWID is stored in binary format and identifies each row in a table. Indexes use ROWIDs as pointers to data.

The Structure of a PL/SQL Block

PL/SQL is a block-structured language, meaning that PL/SQL programs are divided and written in logical blocks of code. Within a PL/SQL block of code, processes such as data manipulation or queries can occur. The following parts of a PL/SQL block are discussed in this section:

- ☐ The DECLARE section contains the definitions of variables and other objects such as constants and cursors. This section is an optional part of a PL/SQL block.

- ☐ The PROCEDURE section contains conditional commands and SQL statements and is where the block is controlled. This section is the only mandatory part of a PL/SQL block.

- ☐ The EXCEPTION section tells the PL/SQL block how to handle specified errors and user-defined exceptions. This section is an optional part of a PL/SQL block.

NOTE   A block is a logical unit of PL/SQL code, containing at the least a PROCEDURE section and optionally the DECLARE and EXCEPTION sections.

Here is the basic structure of a PL/SQL block:

```
BEGIN         -- optional, denotes beginning of block
  DECLARE     -- optional, variable definitions
  BEGIN       -- mandatory, denotes beginning of procedure section
  EXCEPTION   -- optional, denotes beginning of exception section
  END         -- mandatory, denotes ending of procedure section
END           -- optional, denotes ending of block
```

Notice that the only mandatory parts of a PL/SQL block are the second BEGIN and the first END, which make up the PROCEDURE section. Of course, you will have statements in between. If you use the first BEGIN, then you must use the second END, and vice versa.

Comments

What would a program be without comments? Programming languages provide commands that allow you to place comments within your code, and PL/SQL is no exception. The comments after each line in the preceding sample block structure describe each command. The accepted comments in PL/SQL are as follows:

```
-- This is a one-line comment.

/* This is a
multiple-line comment.*/
```

NOTE

PL/SQL directly supports Data Manipulation Language (DML) commands and database queries. However, it does not support Data Dictionary Language (DDL) commands. You can generally use PL/SQL to manipulate the data within database structure, but not to manipulate those structures.

The DECLARE Section

18

The DECLARE section of a block of PL/SQL code consists of variables, constants, cursor definitions, and special data types. As a PL/SQL programmer, you can declare all types of variables within your blocks of code. However, you must assign a data type, which must conform to Oracle's rules of that particular data type, to every variable that you define. Variables must also conform to Oracle's object naming standards.

Variable Assignment

Variables are values that are subject to change within a PL/SQL block. PL/SQL variables must be assigned a valid data type upon declaration and can be initialized if necessary. The following example defines a set of variables in the DECLARE portion of a block:

```
DECLARE
  owner char(10);
  tablename char(30);
  bytes number(10);
  today date;
```

ANALYSIS The DECLARE portion of a block cannot be executed by itself. The DECLARE section starts with the DECLARE statement. Then individual variables are defined on separate lines. Notice that each variable declaration ends with a semicolon.

Variables may also be initialized in the DECLARE section. For example:

```
DECLARE
  customer char(30);
  fiscal_year number(2) := '97';
```

You can use the symbol := to initialize, or assign an initial value, to variables in the DECLARE section. You must initialize a variable that is defined as NOT NULL.

```
DECLARE
  customer char(30);
  fiscal_year number(2) NOT NULL := '97';
```

The NOT NULL clause in the definition of fiscal_year resembles a column definition in a CREATE TABLE statement.

Constant Assignment

Constants are defined the same way that variables are, but constant values are static; they do not change. In the previous example, fiscal_year is probably a constant.

NOTE

> You must end each variable declaration with a semicolon.

Cursor Definitions

A cursor is another type of variable in PL/SQL. Usually when you think of a variable, a single value comes to mind. A cursor is a variable that points to a row of data from the results of a query. In a multiple-row result set, you need a way to scroll through each record to analyze the data. A cursor is just that. When the PL/SQL block looks at the results of a query within the block, it uses a cursor to point to each returned row. Here is an example of a cursor being defined in a PL/SQL block:

```
DECLARE
  cursor employee_cursor is
    select * from employees;
```

A cursor is similar to a view. With the use of a loop in the PROCEDURE section, you can scroll a cursor. This technique is covered shortly.

The %TYPE Attribute

%TYPE is a variable attribute that returns the value of a given column of a table. Instead of hard-coding the data type in your PL/SQL block, you can use %TYPE to maintain data type consistency within your blocks of code.

```
DECLARE
  cursor employee_cursor is
    select emp_id, emp_name from employees;
  id_num employees.emp_id%TYPE;
  name employees.emp_name%TYPE;
```

ANALYSIS The variable id_num is declared to have the same data type as emp_id in the EMPLOYEES table. %TYPE declares the variable name to have the same data type as the column emp_name in the EMPLOYEES table.

The %ROWTYPE **Attribute**

Variables are not limited to single values. If you declare a variable that is associated with a defined cursor, you can use the %ROWTYPE attribute to declare the data type of that variable to be the same as each column in one entire row of data from the cursor. In Oracle's lexicon the %ROWTYPE attribute creates a record variable.

INPUT
```
DECLARE
   cursor employee_cursor is
      select emp_id, emp_name from employees;
   employee_record employee_cursor%ROWTYPE;
```

ANALYSIS This example declares a variable called employee_record. The %ROWTYPE attribute defines this variable as having the same data type as an entire row of data in the employee_cursor. Variables declared using the %ROWTYPE attribute are also called *aggregate variables*.

The %ROWCOUNT **Attribute**

The PL/SQL %ROWCOUNT attribute maintains a count of rows that the SQL statements in the particular block have accessed in a cursor.

INPUT
```
DECLARE
   cursor employee_cursor is
      select emp_id, emp_name from employees;
   records_processed := employee_cursor%ROWCOUNT;
```

ANALYSIS In this example the variable records_processed represents the current number of rows that the PL/SQL block has accessed in the employee_cursor.

WARNING

> Beware of naming conflicts with table names when declaring variables. For instance, if you declare a variable that has the same name as a table that you are trying to access with the PL/SQL code, the local variable will take precedence over the table name.

The PROCEDURE **Section**

The PROCEDURE section is the only mandatory part of a PL/SQL block. This part of the block calls variables and uses cursors to manipulate data in the database. The PROCEDURE section is the main part of a block, containing conditional statements and SQL commands.

18

BEGIN...END

In a block, the BEGIN statement denotes the beginning of a procedure. Similarly, the END statement marks the end of a procedure. The following example shows the basic structure of the PROCEDURE section:

```
BEGIN
  open a cursor;
  condition1;
    statement1;
  condition2;
    statement2;
  condition3;
    statement3;
.
.
.
  close the cursor;
END
```

Cursor Control Commands

Now that you have learned how to define cursors in a PL/SQL block, you need to know how to access the defined cursors. This section explains the basic cursor control commands: DECLARE, OPEN, FETCH, and CLOSE.

DECLARE

Earlier today you learned how to define a cursor in the DECLARE section of a block. The DECLARE statement belongs in the list of cursor control commands.

OPEN

Now that you have defined your cursor, how do you use it? You cannot use this book unless you open it. Likewise, you cannot use a cursor until you have opened it with the OPEN command. For example:

```
BEGIN
  open employee_cursor;
  statement1;
  statement2;
  .
  .
  .
END
```

FETCH

FETCH populates a variable with values from a cursor. Here are two examples using FETCH: One populates an aggregate variable, and the other populates individual variables.

```
DECLARE
  cursor employee_cursor is
    select emp_id, emp_name from employees;
  employee_record employee_cursor%ROWTYPE;
```

```
BEGIN
  open employee_cursor;
  loop
    fetch employee_cursor into employee_record;
  end loop;
  close employee_cursor;
END
```

ANALYSIS The preceding example fetches the current row of the cursor into the aggregate variable employee_record. It uses a loop to scroll the cursor. Of course, the block is not actually accomplishing anything.

INPUT
```
DECLARE
  cursor employee_cursor is
    select emp_id, emp_name from employees;
  id_num employees.emp_id%TYPE;
  name employees.emp_name%TYPE;
BEGIN
  open employee_cursor;
  loop
    fetch employee_cursor into id_num, name;
  end loop;
  close employee_cursor;
END
```

ANALYSIS This example fetches the current row of the cursor into the variables id_num and name, which was defined in the DECLARE section.

CLOSE

When you have finished using a cursor in a block, you should close the cursor, as you normally close a book when you have finished reading it. The command you use is CLOSE.

SYNTAX
```
BEGIN
  open employee_cursor;
  statement1;
  statement2;
    .
    .
    .
  close employee_cursor;
END
```

ANALYSIS After a cursor is closed, the result set of the query no longer exists. You must reopen the cursor to access the associated set of data.

Conditional Statements

Now we are getting to the good stuff—the *conditional statements* that give you control over how your SQL statements are processed. The conditional statements in PL/SQL resemble those in most third-generation languages.

IF...THEN

The IF...THEN statement is probably the most familiar conditional statement to most programmers. The IF...THEN statement dictates the performance of certain actions if certain conditions are met. The structure of an IF...THEN statement is as follows:

```
IF condition1 THEN
  statement1;
END IF;
```

If you are checking for two conditions, you can write your statement as follows:

```
IF condition1 THEN
  statement1;
ELSE
  statement2;
END IF;
```

If you are checking for more than two conditions, you can write your statement as follows:

```
IF condition1 THEN
  statement1;
ELSIF condition2 THEN
  statement2;
ELSE
  statement3;
END IF;
```

ANALYSIS The final example states: If condition1 is met, then perform statement1; if condition2 is met, then perform statement2; otherwise, perform statement3. IF...THEN statements may also be nested within other statements and/or loops.

LOOPS

Loops in a PL/SQL block allow statements in the block to be processed continuously for as long as the specified condition exists. There are three types of loops.

LOOP is an infinite loop, most often used to scroll a cursor. To terminate this type of loop, you must specify when to exit. For example, in scrolling a cursor you would exit the loop after the last row in a cursor has been processed:

INPUT
```
BEGIN
open employee_cursor;
LOOP
  FETCH employee_cursor into employee_record;
  EXIT WHEN employee_cursor%NOTFOUND;
  statement1;
     .
     .
     .
END LOOP;
close employee_cursor;
END;
```

18

%NOTFOUND is a cursor attribute that identifies when no more data is found in the cursor. The preceding example exits the loop when no more data is found. If you omit this statement from the loop, then the loop will continue forever.

The WHILE-LOOP executes commands while a specified condition is TRUE. When the condition is no longer true, the loop returns control to the next statement.

INPUT

```
DECLARE
  cursor payment_cursor is
    select cust_id, payment, total_due from payment_table;
  cust_id payment_table.cust_id%TYPE;
  payment payment_table.payment%TYPE;
  total_due payment_table.total_due%TYPE;
BEGIN
  open payment_cursor;
  WHILE payment < total_due LOOP
    FETCH payment_cursor into cust_id, payment, total_due;
    EXIT WHEN payment_cursor%NOTFOUND;
    insert into underpay_table
    values (cust_id, 'STILL OWES');
END LOOP;
  close payment_cursor;
END;
```

ANALYSIS

The preceding example uses the WHILE-LOOP to scroll the cursor and to execute the commands within the loop as long as the condition payment < total_due is met.

You can use the FOR-LOOP in the previous block to implicitly fetch the current row of the cursor into the defined variables.

INPUT

```
DECLARE
  cursor payment_cursor is
    select cust_id, payment, total_due from payment_table;
  cust_id payment_table.cust_id%TYPE;
  payment payment_table.payment%TYPE;
  total_due payment_table.total_due%TYPE;
BEGIN
  open payment_cursor;
  FOR pay_rec IN payment_cursor LOOP
    IF pay_rec.payment < pay_rec.total_due THEN
      insert into underpay_table
      values (pay_rec.cust_id, 'STILL OWES');
    END IF;
  END LOOP;
  close payment_cursor;
END;
```

ANALYSIS

This example uses the FOR-LOOP to scroll the cursor. The FOR-LOOP is performing an implicit FETCH, which is omitted this time. Also, notice that the %NOTFOUND attribute has been omitted. This attribute is implied with the FOR-LOOP; therefore, this and the previous example yield the same basic results.

18

The EXCEPTION Section

The EXCEPTION section is an optional part of any PL/SQL block. If this section is omitted and errors are encountered, the block will be terminated. Some errors that are encountered may not justify the immediate termination of a block, so the EXCEPTION section can be used to handle specified errors or user-defined exceptions in an orderly manner. Exceptions can be user-defined, although many exceptions are predefined by Oracle.

Raising Exceptions

Exceptions are raised in a block by using the command RAISE. Exceptions can be raised explicitly by the programmer, whereas internal database errors are automatically, or implicitly, raised by the database server.

```
BEGIN
  DECLARE
    exception_name EXCEPTION;
  BEGIN
    IF condition THEN
      RAISE exception_name;
    END IF;
  EXCEPTION
    WHEN exception_name THEN
      statement;
  END;
END;
```

ANALYSIS This block shows the fundamentals of explicitly raising an exception. First exception_name is declared using the EXCEPTION statement. In the PROCEDURE section, the exception is raised using RAISE if a given condition is met. The RAISE then references the EXCEPTION section of the block, where the appropriate action is taken.

Handling Exceptions

The preceding example handled an exception in the EXCEPTION section of the block. Errors are easily handled in PL/SQL, and by using exceptions, the PL/SQL block can continue to run with errors or terminate gracefully.

```
EXCEPTION
  WHEN exception1 THEN
    statement1;
  WHEN exception2 THEN
    statement2;
  WHEN OTHERS THEN
    statement3;
```

ANALYSIS This example shows how the EXCEPTION section might look if you have more than one exception. This example expects two exceptions (exception1 and exception2) when running this block. WHEN OTHERS tells statement3 to execute if any other exceptions occur while the block is being processed. WHEN OTHERS gives you control over any errors that may occur within the block.

Executing a PL/SQL Block

PL/SQL statements are normally created using a host editor and are executed like normal SQL script files. PL/SQL uses semicolons to terminate each statement in a block—from variable assignments to data manipulation commands. The forward slash (/) is mainly associated with SQL script files, but PL/SQL also uses the forward slash to terminate a block in a script file. The easiest way to start a PL/SQL block is by issuing the START command, abbreviated as STA or @.

Your PL/SQL script file might look like this:

```
/* This file is called proc1.sql */
BEGIN
  DECLARE
    ...
  BEGIN
    ...
    statements;
    ...
  EXCEPTION
    ...
  END;
END;
/
```

You execute your PL/SQL script file as follows:

```
SQL> start proc1      or
SQL> sta proc1        or
SQL> @proc1
```

NOTE

> PL/SQL script files can be executed using the START command or the character @. PL/SQL script files can also be called within other PL/SQL files, shell scripts, or other programs.

Displaying Output to the User

Particularly when handling exceptions, you may want to display output to keep users informed about what is taking place. You can display output to convey information, and you can display your own customized error messages, which will probably make more sense to the user than an error number. Perhaps you want the user to contact the database administrator if an error occurs during processing, rather than to see the exact message.

PL/SQL does not provide a direct method for displaying output as a part of its syntax, but it does allow you to call a package that serves this function from within the block. The package is called DBMS_OUTPUT.

```
EXCEPTION
  WHEN zero_divide THEN
    DBMS_OUTPUT.put_line('ERROR:  DIVISOR IS ZERO.  SEE YOUR DBA.');
```

 `ZERO_DIVIDE` is an Oracle predefined exception. Most of the common errors that occur during program processing will be predefined as exceptions and are raised implicitly (which means that you don't have to raise the error in the PROCEDURE section of the block).

If this exception is encountered during block processing, the user will see:

 `SQL> @block1`

OUTPUT
```
ERROR:  DIVISOR IS ZERO.  SEE YOUR DBA.
PL/SQL procedure successfully completed.
```

Doesn't that message look friendly than:

INPUT/ OUTPUT
```
SQL> @block1
begin
*

ERROR at line 1:
ORA-01476: divisor is equal to zero
ORA-06512: at line 20
```

Transactional Control in PL/SQL

On Day 11, "Controlling Transactions," we discussed the transactional control commands COMMIT, ROLLBACK, and SAVEPOINT. These commands allow the programmer to control when transactions are actually written to the database, how often, and when they should be undone.

```
BEGIN
  DECLARE
    ...
  BEGIN
    statements...
    IF condition THEN
      COMMIT;
    ELSE
      ROLLBACK;
    END IF;
    ...
  EXCEPTION
    ...
  END;
END;
```

The good thing about PL/SQL is that you can automate the use of transactional control commands instead of constantly monitoring large transactions, which can be very tedious.

Putting Everything Together

So far, you have been introduced to PL/SQL, have become familiar with the supported data types, and are familiar with the major features of a PL/SQL block. You know how to declare local variables, constants, and cursors. You have also seen how to embed SQL in the PROCEDURE section, manipulate cursors, and raise exceptions. When a cursor has been raised, you should have a basic understanding of how to handle it in the EXCEPTION section of the block. Now you are ready to work with some practical examples and create blocks from BEGIN to END. By the end of this section, you should fully understand how the parts of a PL/SQL block interact with each other.

Sample Tables and Data

We will be using two tables to create PL/SQL blocks. PAYMENT_TABLE identifies a customer, how much he or she has paid, and the total amount due. PAY_STATUS_TABLE does not yet contain any data. Data will be inserted into PAY_STATUS_TABLE according to certain conditions in the PAYMENT_TABLE.

INPUT
```
SQL> select *
  2  from payment_table;
```

OUTPUT
```
CUSTOMER  PAYMENT  TOTAL_DUE
--------  -------  ---------
ABC         90.50     150.99
AAA         79.00      79.00
BBB        950.00    1000.00
CCC         27.50      27.50
DDD        350.00     500.95
EEE         67.89      67.89
FFF        555.55     455.55
GGG        122.36     122.36
HHH         26.75       0.00
9 rows selected.
```

INPUT
```
SQL> describe pay_status_table
```

OUTPUT
```
Name                            Null?     Type
------------------------------  --------  ----
CUST_ID                         NOT NULL  CHAR(3)
STATUS                          NOT NULL  VARCHAR2(15)
AMT_OWED                                  NUMBER(8,2)
AMT_CREDIT                                NUMBER(8,2)
```

ANALYSIS DESCRIBE is an Oracle SQL command that displays the structure of a table without having to query the data dictionary. DESCRIBE and other Oracle SQL*Plus commands are covered on Day 20, "SQL*Plus."

A Simple PL/SQL Block

This is how the PL/SQL script (block1.sql) file looks:

INPUT

```
set serveroutput on
BEGIN
  DECLARE
    AmtZero EXCEPTION;
    cCustId payment_table.cust_id%TYPE;
    fPayment payment_table.payment%TYPE;
    fTotalDue payment_table.total_due%TYPE;
    cursor payment_cursor is
      select cust_id, payment, total_due
      from payment_table;
    fOverPaid number(8,2);
    fUnderPaid number(8,2);
  BEGIN
    open payment_cursor;
    loop
      fetch payment_cursor into
        cCustId, fPayment, fTotalDue;
      exit when payment_cursor%NOTFOUND;
      if ( fTotalDue = 0 ) then
        raise AmtZero;
      end if;
      if ( fPayment > fTotalDue ) then
        fOverPaid := fPayment - fTotalDue;
        insert into pay_status_table (cust_id, status, amt_credit)
        values (cCustId, 'Over Paid', fOverPaid);
      elsif ( fPayment < fTotalDue ) then
        fUnderPaid := fTotalDue - fPayment;
        insert into pay_status_table (cust_id, status, amt_owed)
        values (cCustId, 'Still Owes', fUnderPaid);
      else
        insert into pay_status_table
        values (cCustId, 'Paid in Full', null, null);
      end if;
    end loop;
    close payment_cursor;
  EXCEPTION
    when AmtZero then
    DBMS_OUTPUT.put_line('ERROR: amount is Zero. See your supervisor.');
    when OTHERS then
    DBMS_OUTPUT.put_line('ERROR: unknown error. See the DBA');
  END;
END;
/
```

ANALYSIS   The DECLARE section defines six local variables, as well as a cursor called payment_cursor. The PROCEDURE section starts with the second BEGIN statement in which the first step is to open the cursor and start a loop. The FETCH command passes the current values in the cursor into the variables that were defined in the DECLARE section. As long as the loop finds records in the cursor, the statement compares the amount paid by a customer to the total amount due. Overpayments and underpayments are calculated according to the amount paid, and we use those calculated amounts to insert values into the PAY_STATUS_TABLE. The loop terminates, and the cursor closes. The EXCEPTION section handles errors that may occur during processing.

Now start the PL/SQL script file and see what happens.

INPUT

```
SQL> @block1
```

OUTPUT

```
Input truncated to 1 characters
ERROR: amount is Zero. See your supervisor.
PL/SQL procedure successfully completed.
```

Now that you know that an incorrect amount appears in the total due column, you can fix the amount and run the script again.

INPUT/OUTPUT

```
SQL> update payment_table
  2  set total_due = 26.75
  3  where cust_id = 'IIIIII';

1 row updated.

SQL> commit;

Commit complete.

SQL> truncate table pay_status_table;

Table truncated.
```

NOTE

> This example truncates the PAY_STATUS_TABLE to clear the table's contents; the next run of the statement will repopulate the table. You may want to add the TRUNCATE TABLE statement to your PL/SQL block.

INPUT/OUTPUT

```
SQL> @block1

Input truncated to 1 characters
PL/SQL procedure successfully completed.
```

Now you can select from the PAY_STATUS_TABLE and see the payment status of each customer.

INPUT/OUTPUT

```
SQL> select *
  2  from pay_status_table
  3  order by status;

CUSTOMER STATUS          AMT_OWED  AMT_CREDIT
-------- --------------- --------- -----------
FFF      Over Paid                     100.00
AAA      Paid in Full
CCC      Paid in Full
EEE      Paid in Full
```

```
GGG        Paid in Full
HHH        Paid in Full
ABC        Still Owes           60.49
DDD        Still Owes          150.95
BBB        Still Owes           50.00
9 rows selected.
```

ANALYSIS   A row was inserted into PAY_STATUS_TABLE for every row of data that is contained in the PAYMENT_TABLE. If the customer paid more than the amount due, then the difference was input into the amt_credit column. If the customer paid less than the amount owed, then an entry was made in the amt_owed column. If the customer paid in full, then no dollar amount was inserted in either of the two columns.

Another Program

This example uses a table called PAY_TABLE:

INPUT   SQL> **desc pay_table**

OUTPUT
```
Name                            Null?     Type
------------------------------  --------  ----
NAME                            NOT NULL  VARCHAR2(20)
PAY_TYPE                        NOT NULL  VARCHAR2(8)
PAY_RATE                        NOT NULL  NUMBER(8,2)
EFF_DATE                        NOT NULL  DATE
PREV_PAY                                  NUMBER(8,2)
```

First take a look at the data:

INPUT
```
SQL> select *
  2  from pay_table
  3  order by pay_type, pay_rate desc;
```

OUTPUT
```
NAME                     PAY_TYPE  PAY_RATE   EFF_DATE   PREV_PAY
-------------------      --------  ---------  ---------  ---------
SANDRA SAMUELS           HOURLY       12.50   01-JAN-97
ROBERT BOBAY             HOURLY       11.50   15-MAY-96
KEITH JONES              HOURLY       10.00   31-OCT-96
SUSAN WILLIAMS           HOURLY        9.75   01-MAY-97
CHRISSY ZOES             SALARY    50000.00   01-JAN-97
CLODE EVANS              SALARY    42150.00   01-MAR-97
JOHN SMITH               SALARY    35000.00   15-JUN-96
KEVIN TROLLBERG          SALARY    27500.00   15-JUN-96
8 rows selected.
```

Situation: Sales are up. Any individual who has not had a pay increase for six months (180 days) will receive a raise effective today. All eligible hourly employees will receive a 4 percent increase, and eligible salary employees will receive a 5 percent increase.

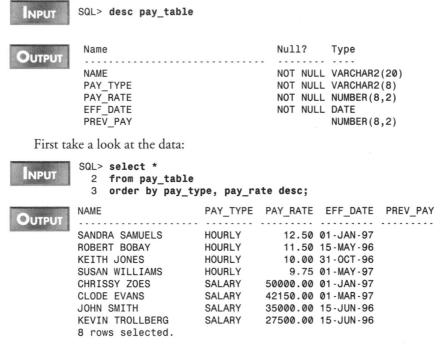

18

Today is:

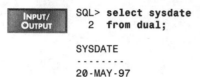

```
SQL> select sysdate
  2  from dual;

SYSDATE
---------
20-MAY-97
```

Before examining the next PL/SQL block, we will perform a manual select from the PAY_TABLE that flags individuals who should receive a raise.

```
SQL> select name, pay_type, pay_rate, eff_date,
  2         'YES' due
  3  from pay_table
  4  where eff_date < sysdate - 180
  5  UNION ALL
  6  select name, pay_type, pay_rate, eff_date,
  7         'No' due
  8  from pay_table
  9  where eff_date >= sysdate - 180
 10  order by 2, 3 desc;
```

NAME	PAY_TYPE	PAY_RATE	EFF_DATE	DUE
SANDRA SAMUELS	HOURLY	12.50	01-JAN-97	No
ROBERT BOBAY	HOURLY	11.50	15-MAY-96	YES
KEITH JONES	HOURLY	10.00	31-OCT-96	YES
SUSAN WILLIAMS	HOURLY	9.75	01-MAY-97	No
CHRISSY ZOES	SALARY	50000.00	01-JAN-97	No
CLODE EVANS	SALARY	42150.00	01-MAR-97	No
JOHN SMITH	SALARY	35000.00	15-JUN-96	YES
KEVIN TROLLBERG	SALARY	27500.00	15-JUN-96	YES

8 rows selected.

The DUE column identifies individuals who should be eligible for a raise. Here's the PL/SQL script:

```
set serveroutput on
BEGIN
  DECLARE
    UnknownPayType exception;
    cursor pay_cursor is
      select name, pay_type, pay_rate, eff_date,
             sysdate, rowid
      from pay_table;
    IndRec pay_cursor%ROWTYPE;
    cOldDate date;
    fNewPay number(8,2);
  BEGIN
    open pay_cursor;
    loop
    fetch pay_cursor into IndRec;
    exit when pay_cursor%NOTFOUND;
    cOldDate := sysdate - 180;
    if (IndRec.pay_type = 'SALARY') then
      fNewPay := IndRec.pay_rate * 1.05;
```

18

```
      elsif (IndRec.pay_type = 'HOURLY') then
        fNewPay := IndRec.pay_rate * 1.04;
            else
              raise UnknownPayType;
            end if;
            if (IndRec.eff_date < cOldDate) then
              update pay_table
              set pay_rate = fNewPay,
                  prev_pay = IndRec.pay_rate,
                  eff_date = IndRec.sysdate
              where rowid = IndRec.rowid;
              commit;
            end if;
            end loop;
            close pay_cursor;
          EXCEPTION
            when UnknownPayType then
              dbms_output.put_line('=======================');
              dbms_output.put_line('ERROR: Aborting program.');
              dbms_output.put_line('Unknown Pay Type for Name');
            when others then
              dbms_output.put_line('ERROR During Processing.  See the DBA.');
          END;
      END;
      /
```

Are you sure that you want to give four employees a pay raise? (The final SELECT statement has four Yes values in the DUE column.) Why not…let's give all four employees a raise. You can apply the appropriate pay increases by executing the PL/SQL script file, named block2.sql:

INPUT/ OUTPUT

```
SQL> @block2

Input truncated to 1 characters
PL/SQL procedure successfully completed.
```

You can do a quick select to verify that the changes have been made to the pay_rate of the appropriate individuals:

INPUT

```
SQL> select *
  2  from pay_table
  3  order by pay_type, pay_rate desc;
```

OUTPUT

```
NAME                 PAY_TYPE  PAY_RATE EFF_DATE  PREV_PAY
-------------------- --------- -------- --------- ----------
SANDRA SAMUELS       HOURLY       12.50 01-JAN-97
ROBERT BOBAY         HOURLY       11.96 20-MAY-97       11.5
KEITH JONES          HOURLY       10.40 20-MAY-97         10
SUSAN WILLIAMS       HOURLY        9.75 01-MAY-97
CHRISSY ZOES         SALARY    50000.00 01-JAN-97
CLODE EVANS          SALARY    42150.00 01-MAR-97
JOHN SMITH           SALARY    36750.00 20-MAY-97      35000
KEVIN TROLLBERG      SALARY    28875.00 20-MAY-97      27500
8 rows selected.
```

18

ANALYSIS Four employees received a pay increase. If you compare this output to the output of the original SELECT statement, you can see the changes. The current pay rate was updated to reflect the pay increase, the original pay rate was inserted into the previous pay column, and the effective date was updated to today's date. No action was taken on those individuals who did not qualify for a pay increase.

Wait—you didn't get a chance to see how the defined exception works. You can test the EXCEPTION section by inserting an invalid PAY_TYPE into PAY_TABLE.

INPUT
```
SQL> insert into pay_table values
  2  ('JEFF JENNINGS','WEEKLY',71.50,'01-JAN-97',NULL);
```

OUTPUT
```
1 row created.
```

The moment of truth:

INPUT/ OUTPUT
```
SQL> @block2

Input truncated to 1 characters
========================
ERROR: Aborting program.
Unknown Pay Type for:  JEFF JENNINGS
PL/SQL procedure successfully completed.
```

ANALYSIS An error message told you that JEFF JENNINGS had a Pay Type with a value other than SALARY or HOURLY. That is, the exception was handled with an error message.

Stored Procedures, Packages, and Triggers

Using PL/SQL, you can create stored objects to eliminate having to constantly enter monotonous code. *Procedures* are simply blocks of code that perform some sort of specific function. Related procedures can be combined and stored together in an object called a *package*. A *trigger* is a database object that is used with other transactions. You might have a trigger on a table called ORDERS that will insert data into a HISTORY table each time the ORDERS table receives data. The basic syntax of these objects follows.

Sample Procedure

SYNTAX
```
PROCEDURE procedure_name IS
   variable1 datatype;
   ...
BEGIN
   statement1;
   ...
EXCEPTION
   when ...
END procedure_name;
```

18

Sample Package

SYNTAX

```
CREATE PACKAGE package_name AS
  PROCEDURE procedure1 (global_variable1 datatype, ...);
  PROCEDURE procedure2 (global_variable1 datatype, ...);
END package_name;
CREATE PACKAGE BODY package_name AS
  PROCEDURE procedure1 (global_variable1 datatype, ...) IS
    BEGIN
      statement1;
      ...
    END procedure1;
  PROCEDURE procedure2 (global_variable1 datatype, ...) IS
    BEGIN
      statement1;
      ...
  END procedure2;
END package_name;
```

Sample Trigger

SYNTAX

```
CREATE TRIGGER trigger_name
  AFTER UPDATE OF column ON table_name
  FOR EACH ROW
BEGIN
  statement1;
  ...
END;
```

The following example uses a trigger to insert a row of data into a transaction table when updating PAY_TABLE. The TRANSACTION table looks like this:

INPUT

```
SQL> describe trans_table
```

OUTPUT

```
Name                                   Null?     Type
----------------------------------    --------  ----
ACTION                                           VARCHAR2(10)
NAME                                             VARCHAR2(20)
PREV_PAY                                         NUMBER(8,2)
CURR_PAY                                         NUMBER(8,2)
EFF_DATE                                         DATE
```

Here's a sample row of data:

INPUT/OUTPUT

```
SQL> select *
  2  from pay_table
  3  where name = 'JEFF JENNINGS';

NAME                 PAY_TYPE  PAY_RATE EFF_DATE  PREV_PAY
-------------------- --------- --------- --------- ----------
JEFF JENNINGS        WEEKLY       71.50 01-JAN-97
```

Now, create a trigger:

```
SQL> CREATE TRIGGER pay_trigger
  2     AFTER update on PAY_TABLE
  3     FOR EACH ROW
  4   BEGIN
  5     insert into trans_table values
  6     ('PAY CHANGE', :new.name, :old.pay_rate,
  7      :new.pay_rate, :new.eff_date);
  8   END;
  9   /

Trigger created.
```

The last step is to perform an update on PAY_TABLE, which should cause the trigger to be executed.

INPUT/OUTPUT

```
SQL> update pay_table
  2   set pay_rate - 15.50,
  3       eff_date = sysdate
  4   where name = 'JEFF JENNINGS';

1 row updated.

SQL> select *
  2   from pay_table
  3   where name = 'JEFF JENNINGS';

NAME                    PAY_TYPE  PAY_RATE EFF_DATE   PREV_PAY
--------------------    --------  -------- --------   --------
JEFF JENNINGS           WEEKLY       15.50 20-MAY-97

SQL> select *
  2   from trans_table;

ACTION      NAME                    PREV_PAY   CURR_PAY EFF_DATE
----------  --------------------    --------   -------- --------
PAY CHANGE  JEFF JENNINGS               71.5       15.5 20-MAY-97
```

ANALYSIS

PREV_PAY is null in PAY_TABLE but PREV_PAY appears in TRANS_TABLE. This approach isn't as confusing as it sounds. PAY_TABLE does not need an entry for PREV_PAY because the PAY_RATE of 71.50 per hour was obviously an erroneous amount. Rather, we inserted the value for PREV_PAY in TRANS_TABLE because the update was a transaction, and the purpose of TRANS_PAY is to keep a record of all transactions against PAY_TABLE.

18

NOTE

If you are familiar with network technologies, you might notice similarities between PL/SQL and Java stored procedures. However, some differences should be noted. PL/SQL is an enhancement of standard SQL, implementing the commands of a procedural language. Java, which is much more advanced than PL/SQL, allows programmers to write more complex programs than are possible with PL/SQL. PL/SQL is based on the database-intensive functionality of SQL; Java is more appropriate for CPU-intensive programs. Most procedural languages, such as PL/SQL, are developed specifically for the appropriate platform. As procedural language technology evolves, a higher level of standardization will be enforced across platforms.

Summary

PL/SQL extends the functionality of standard SQL. The basic components of PL/SQL perform the same types of functions as a third-generation language. The use of local variables supports dynamic code; that is, values within a block may change from time to time according to user input, specified conditions, or the contents of a cursor. PL/SQL uses standard procedural language program control statements. IF...THEN statements and loops enable you to search for specific conditions; you can also use loops to scroll through the contents of a defined cursor.

Errors that occur during the processing of any program are a major concern. PL/SQL enables you to use exceptions to control the behavior of a program that encounters either syntax errors or logical errors. Many exceptions are predefined, such as a divide-by-zero error. Errors can be raised any time during processing according to specified conditions and may be handled any way the PL/SQL programmer desires.

Day 18 also introduces some practical uses of PL/SQL. Database objects such as triggers, stored procedures, and packages can automate many job functions. Today's examples apply some of the concepts that were covered on previous days.

Q&A

Q Does Day 18 cover everything I need to know about PL/SQL?

A Most definitely not. Today's introduction just scratched the surface of one of the greatest concepts of SQL. We have simply tried to highlight some of the major features to give you a basic knowledge of PL/SQL.

Q Can I get by without using PL/SQL?

A Yes, you can get by, but to achieve the results that you would get with PL/SQL, you may have to spend much more time coding in a third-generation language. If you do not have Oracle, check your implementation documentation for procedural features like those of PL/SQL.

Workshop

The Workshop provides quiz questions to help solidify your understanding of the material covered, as well as exercises to provide you with experience in using what you have learned. Try to answer the quiz and exercise questions before checking the answers in Appendix F, "Answers to Quizzes and Exercises."

Quiz

1. How is a database trigger used?
2. Can related procedures be stored together?
3. True or False: Data Manipulation Language can be used in a PL/SQL statement.
4. True or False: Data Definition Language can be used in a PL/SQL statement.
5. Is text output directly a part of the PL/SQL syntax?
6. List the three major parts of a PL/SQL statement.
7. List the commands that are associated with cursor control.

Exercises

1. Declare a variable called HourlyPay in which the maximum accepted value is 99.99/hour.
2. Define a cursor whose content is all the data in the CUSTOMER_TABLE where the CITY is INDIANAPOLIS.
3. Define an exception called UnknownCode.
4. Write a statement that will set the AMT in the AMOUNT_TABLE to 10 if CODE is A, set the AMT to 20 if CODE is B, and raise an exception called UnknownCode if CODE is neither A nor B. The table has one row.

18

Day 19

Transact-SQL: An Introduction

Objectives

Today's material supplements the previous presentations, as Transact-SQL is a supplement to the accepted SQL standard. Today's goals are to

☐ Identify one of the popular extensions to SQL

☐ Outline the major features of Transact-SQL

☐ Provide practical examples to give you an understanding of how Transact-SQL is used

An Overview of Transact-SQL

Day 13, "Advanced SQL Topics," briefly covered static SQL. The examples on Day 13 depicted the use of embedded SQL in third-generation programming languages such as C. With this method of programming, the embedded SQL code does not change and is, therefore, limited. On the other hand, you can write dynamic SQL to perform the same functions as a procedural programming language and allow conditions to be changed within the SQL code.

As we have mentioned during the discussion of virtually every topic in this book, almost every database vendor has added many extensions to the language. Transact-SQL is the Sybase and Microsoft SQL Server database product. Oracle's product is PL/SQL. Each of these languages contains the complete functionality of everything we have discussed so far. In addition, each product contains many extensions to the ANSI SQL standard.

Extensions to ANSI SQL

To illustrate the use of these SQL extensions to create actual programming logic, we are using Sybase and Microsoft SQL Server's Transact-SQL language. It contains most of the constructs found in third-generation languages, as well as some SQL Server–specific features that turn out to be very handy tools for the database programmer. (Other manufacturers' extensions contain many of these features and more.)

Who Uses Transact-SQL?

Everyone reading this book can use Transact-SQL—casual relational database programmers who occasionally write queries as well as developers who write applications and create objects such as triggers and stored procedures.

NOTE

Users of Sybase and Microsoft SQL Server who want to explore the true capabilities of relational database programming must use the Transact-SQL features.

The Basic Components of Transact-SQL

SQL extensions overcome SQL's limits as a procedural language. For example, Transact-SQL enables you to maintain tight control over your database transactions and to write procedural database programs that practically render the programmer exempt from exhausting programming tasks.

Day 19 covers the following key features of Transact-SQL:

☐ A wide range of data types to optimize data storage

☐ Program flow commands such as loops and IF-ELSE statements

☐ Use of variables in SQL statements

19

- [ ] Summarized reports using computations
- [ ] Diagnostic features to analyze SQL statements
- [ ] Many other options to enhance the standard language of SQL

Data Types

On Day 9, "Creating and Maintaining Tables," we discussed data types. When creating tables in SQL, you must specify a specific data type for each column.

> **NOTE**
> Data types vary between implementations of SQL because of the way each database server stores data. For instance, Oracle uses selected data types, whereas Sybase and Microsoft's SQL Server have their own data types.

Sybase and Microsoft's SQL Server support the following data types.

Character Strings

- [ ] char stores fixed-length character strings, such as STATE abbreviations, when you know that the column will always be two characters.

- [ ] varchar stores variable-length character strings, such as an individual's name, where the exact length of a name is not specified, for example, AL RAY to WILLIAM STEPHENSON.

- [ ] text stores strings with nearly unlimited size, such as a remarks column or description of a type of service.

Numeric Data Types

- [ ] int stores integers from -2,147,483,647 to +2,147,483,647.

- [ ] smallint stores integers from -32,768 to 32,767.

- [ ] tinyint stores integers from 0 to 255.

- [ ] float expresses numbers as real floating-point numbers with data precisions. Decimals are allowed with these data types. The values range from +2.23E-308 to +1.79E308.

- [ ] real expresses real numbers with data precisions from +1.18E-38 to +3.40E38.

DATE Data Types

- [ ] datetime values range from Jan 1, 1753 to Dec 31, 9999.

- [ ] smalldatetime values range from Jan 1, 1900 to Jun 6, 2079.

Money Data Types

☐ money stores values up to +922,337,203,685,477.5808.

☐ smallmoney stores values up to +214,748.3647.

Money values are inserted into a table using the dollar sign; for example:

```
insert payment_tbl (customer_id, paydate, pay_amt)
values (012845, "May 1, 1997", $2099.99)
```

Binary Strings

☐ binary stores fixed-length binary strings.

☐ varbinary stores variable-length binary strings.

☐ image stores very large binary strings, for example, photographs and other images.

bit: A Logical Data Type

The data type bit is often used to flag certain rows of data within a table. The value stored within a column whose data type is bit is either a 1 or 0. For example, the value 1 may signify the condition true, whereas 0 denotes a false condition. The following example uses the bit data type to create a table containing individual test scores:

```
create table test_flag
( ind_id int not null,
  test_results int not null,
  result_flag bit not null)
```

 The column result_flag is defined as a bit column, where the bit character represents either a pass or fail, where pass is true and fail is false.

Throughout the rest of the day, pay attention to the data types used when creating tables and writing Transact-SQL code.

NOTE

> The code in today's examples uses both uppercase and lowercase. Although SQL keywords are not case sensitive in most implementations of SQL, always check your implementation.

Accessing the Database with Transact-SQL

All right, enough talk. To actually run the examples today, you will need to build the following database tables in a database named BASEBALL.

The BASEBALL **Database**

The BASEBALL database consists of three tables used to track typical baseball information: the BATTERS table, the PITCHERS table, and the TEAMS table. This database will be used in examples throughout the rest of today.

The BATTERS **TABLE**

```
NAME char(30)
TEAM int
AVERAGE float
HOMERUNS int
RBIS int
```

The table above can be created using the following Transact-SQL statement:

INPUT

```
1> create database BASEBALL on default
2> go
1> use BASEBALL
2> go
1> create table BATTERS (
2> NAME char(30),
3> TEAM int,
4> AVERAGE float,
5> HOMERUNS int,
6> RBIS int)
7> go
```

ANALYSIS Line 1 creates the database. You specify the database BASEBALL and then create the table BATTERS underneath BASEBALL.

Enter the data in Table 19.1 into the BATTERS table.

NOTE The command go that separates each Transact-SQL statement in the preceding example is not part of Transact-SQL. go's purpose is to pass each statement from a front-end application to SQL Server.

Table 19.1. Data for the BATTERS table.

Name	Team	Average	Homeruns	RBIs
Billy Brewster	1	.275	14	46
John Jackson	1	.293	2	29
Phil Hartman	1	.221	13	21
Jim Gehardy	2	.316	29	84
Tom Trawick	2	.258	3	51
Eric Redstone	2	.305	0	28

The PITCHERS Table

The PITCHERS table can be created using the following Transact-SQL statement:

```
1> use BASEBALL
2> go
1> create table PITCHERS (
2> NAME char(30),
3> TEAM int,
4> WON int,
5> LOST int,
6> ERA float)
7> go
```

Enter the data in Table 19.2 into the PITCHERS table.

Table 19.2. Data for the PITCHERS table.

Name	Team	Won	Lost	Era
Tom Madden	1	7	5	3.46
Bill Witter	1	8	2	2.75
Jeff Knox	2	2	8	4.82
Hank Arnold	2	13	1	1.93
Tim Smythe	3	4	2	2.76

The TEAMS Table

The TEAMS table can be created using the following Transact-SQL statement:

```
1> use BASEBALL
2> go
1> create table TEAMS (
2> TEAM_ID int,
3> CITY char(30),
4> NAME char(30),
5> WON int,
6> LOST int,
7> TOTAL_HOME_ATTENDANCE int,
8> AVG_HOME_ATTENDANCE int)
9> go
```

Enter the data in Table 19.3 into the TEAMS table.

Table 19.3. Data for the TEAMS table.

Team_ID	City	Name	Won	Lost	Total_Home_Attendance	Avg_Home_Attendance
1	Portland	Beavers	72	63	1,226,843	19,473
2	Washington	Representatives	50	85	941,228	14,048
3	Tampa	Sharks	99	36	2,028,652	30,278

Declaring Local Variables

Every programming language enables some method for declaring local (or global) variables that can be used to store data. Transact-SQL is no exception. Declaring a variable using Transact-SQL is an extremely simple procedure. The keyword that must be used is the DECLARE keyword. The syntax looks like this:

```
declare @variable_name data_type
```

To declare a character string variable to store players' names, use the following statement:

```
1> declare @name char(30)
2> go
```

Note the @ symbol before the variable's name. This symbol is required and is used by the query processor to identify variables.

Declaring Global Variables

If you delve further into the Transact-SQL documentation, you will notice that the @@ symbol precedes the names of some system-level variables. This syntax denotes SQL Server global variables that store information.

Declaring your own global variables is particularly useful when using stored procedures. SQL Server also maintains several system global variables that contain information that might be useful to the database system user. Table 19.4 contains the complete list of these variables. The source for this list is the Sybase SQL Server System 10 documentation.

Table 19.4. SQL Server global variables.

Variable Name	Purpose
@@char_convert	0 if character set conversion is in effect.
@@client_csid	Client's character set ID.
@@client_csname	Client's character set name.
@@connections	Number of logons since SQL Server was started.
@@cpu_busy	Amount of time, in ticks, the CPU has been busy since SQL Server was started.
@@error	Contains error status.
@@identity	Last value inserted into an identity column.
@@idle	Amount of time, in ticks, that SQL Server has been idle since started.
@@io_busy	Amount of time, in ticks, that SQL Server has spent doing I/O.

continues

Table 19.4. continued

Variable Name	Purpose
@@isolation	Current isolation level of the Transact-SQL program.
@@langid	Defines local language ID.
@@language	Defines the name of the local language.
@@maxcharlen	Maximum length of a character.
@@max_connections	Maximum number of connections that can be made with SQL Server.
@@ncharsize	Average length of a national character.
@@nestlevel	Nesting level of current execution.
@@pack_received	Number of input packets read by SQL Server since it was started.
@@pack_sent	Number of output packets sent by SQL Server since it was started.
@@packet_errors	Number of errors that have occurred since SQL Server was started.
@@procid	ID of the currently executing stored procedure.
@@rowcount	Number of rows affected by the last command.
@@servername	Name of the local SQL Server.
@@spid	Process ID number of the current process.
@@sqlstatus	Contains status information.
@@textsize	Maximum length of text or image data returned with SELECT statement.
@@thresh_hysteresis	Change in free space required to activate a threshold.
@@timeticks	Number of microseconds per tick.
@@total_errors	Number of errors that have occurred while reading or writing.
@@total_read	Number of disk reads since SQL Server was started.
@@total_write	Number of disk writes since SQL Server was started.
@@tranchained	Current transaction mode of the Transact-SQL program.
@@trancount	Nesting level of transactions.
@@transtate	Current state of a transaction after a statement executes.
@@version	Date of the current version of SQL Server.

Using Variables

The DECLARE keyword enables you to declare several variables with a single statement (although this device can sometimes look confusing when you look at your code later). An example of this type of statement appears here:

```
1> declare @batter_name char(30), @team int, @average float
2> go
```

The next section explains how to use variables it to perform useful programming operations.

Using Variables to Store Data

Variables are available only within the current statement block. To execute a block of statements using the Transact-SQL language, the go statement is executed. (Oracle uses the semicolon for the same purpose.) The *scope* of a variable refers to the usage of the variable within the current Transact-SQL statement.

You cannot initialize variables simply by using the = sign. Try the following statement and note that an error will be returned.

INPUT
```
1> declare @name char(30)
2> @name = "Billy Brewster"
3> go
```

You should have received an error informing you of the improper syntax used in line 2. The proper way to initialize a variable is to use the SELECT command. (Yes, the same command you have already mastered.) Repeat the preceding example using the correct syntax:

INPUT
```
1> declare @name char(30)
2> select @name = "Billy Brewster"
3> go
```

This statement was executed correctly, and if you had inserted additional statements before executing the go statement, the @name variable could have been used.

Retrieving Data into Local Variables

Variables often store data that has been retrieved from the database. They can be used with common SQL commands, such as SELECT, INSERT, UPDATE, and DELETE. Example 19.1 illustrates the use of variables in this manner.

Example 19.1

This example retrieves the name of the player in the BASEBALL database who has the highest batting average and plays for the Portland Beavers.

INPUT
```
1> declare @team_id int, @player_name char(30), @max_avg float
2> select @team_id = TEAM_ID from TEAMS where CITY = "Portland"
3> select @max_avg = max(AVERAGE) from BATTERS where TEAM = @team_id
4> select @player_name = NAME from BATTERS where AVERAGE = @max_avg
5> go
```

ANALYSIS This example was broken down into three queries to illustrate the use of variables.

The PRINT Command

One other useful feature of Transact-SQL is the PRINT command that enables you to print output to the display device. This command has the following syntax:

SYNTAX

```
PRINT character_string
```

Although PRINT displays only character strings, Transact-SQL provides a number of useful functions that can convert different data types to strings (and vice versa).

Example 19.2

Example 19.2 repeats Example 19.1 but prints the player's name at the end.

INPUT

```
1> declare @team_id int, @player_name char(30), @max_avg float
2> select @team_id = TEAM_ID from TEAMS where CITY = "Portland"
3> select @max_avg = max(AVERAGE) from BATTERS where TEAM = @team_id
4> select @player_name = NAME from BATTERS where AVERAGE = @max_avg
5> print @player_name
6> go
```

Note that a variable can be used within a WHERE clause (or any other clause) just as if it were a constant value.

Flow Control

Probably the most powerful set of Transact-SQL features involves its capability to control program flow. If you have programmed with other popular languages such as C, COBOL, Pascal, and Visual Basic, then you are probably already familiar with control commands such as IF...THEN statements and loops. This section contains some of the major commands that allow you to enforce program flow control.

BEGIN and END Statements

Transact-SQL uses the BEGIN and END statements to signify the beginning and ending points of blocks of code. Other languages use brackets ({}) or some other operator to signify the beginning and ending points of functional groups of code. These statements are often combined with IF...ELSE statements and WHILE loops. Here is a sample block using BEGIN and END:

SYNTAX

```
BEGIN
  statement1
  statement2
  statement3...
END
```

IF...ELSE Statements

One of the most basic programming constructs is the IF...ELSE statement. Nearly every programming language supports this construct, and it is extremely useful for checking the value of data retrieved from the database. The Transact-SQL syntax for the IF...ELSE statement looks like this:

SYNTAX

```
if (condition)
begin
     (statement block)
end
else if (condition)
begin
     statement block)
end
.
.
.
else
begin
     (statement block)
end
```

Note that for each condition that might be true, a new BEGIN/END block of statements was entered. Also, it is considered good programming practice to indent statement blocks a set amount of spaces and to keep this number of spaces the same throughout your application. This visual convention greatly improves the readability of the program and cuts down on silly errors that are often caused by simply misreading the code.

Example 19.3

Example 19.3 extends Example 19.2 by checking the player's batting average. If the player's average is over .300, the owner wants to give him a raise. Otherwise, the owner could really care less about the player!

Example 19.3 uses the IF...ELSE statement to evaluate conditions within the statement. If the first condition is true, then specified text is printed; alternative text is printed under any other conditions (ELSE).

INPUT

```
1> declare @team_id int, @player_name char(30), @max_avg float
2> select @team_id = TEAM_ID from TEAMS where CITY = "Portland"
3> select @max_avg = max(AVERAGE) from BATTERS where TEAM = @team_id
4> select @player_name = NAME from BATTERS where AVERAGE = @max_avg
5> if (@max_avg > .300)
6> begin
7>      print @player_name
8>      print "Give this guy a raise!"
9> end
10> else
11> begin
12>      print @player_name
13>      print "Come back when you're hitting better!"
14> end
15> go
```

19

Example 19.4

This new IF statement enables you to add some programming logic to the simple BASEBALL database queries. Example 19.4 adds an IF...ELSE IF...ELSE branch to the code in Example 19.3.

INPUT

```
1> declare @team_id int, @player_name char(30), @max_avg float
2> select @team_id = TEAM_ID from TEAMS where CITY = "Portland"
3> select @max_avg = max(AVERAGE) from BATTERS where TEAM = @team_id
4> select @player_name = NAME from BATTERS where AVERAGE = @max_avg
5> if (@max_avg > .300)
6> begin
7>      print @player_name
8>      print "Give this guy a raise!"
9> end
10> else if (@max_avg > .275)
11> begin
12>      print @player_name
13>      print "Not bad.  Here's a bonus!"
14> end
15> else
16> begin
17>       print @player_name
18>       print "Come back when you're hitting better!"
19> end
20> go
```

Transact-SQL also enables you to check for a condition associated with an IF statement. These functions can test for certain conditions or values. If the function returns TRUE, the IF branch is executed. Otherwise, if provided, the ELSE branch is executed, as you saw in the previous example.

The EXISTS Condition

The EXISTS keyword ensures that a value is returned from a SELECT statement. If a value is returned, the IF statement is executed. Example 19.5 illustrates this logic.

Example 19.5

In this example the EXISTS keyword evaluates a condition in the IF. The condition is specified by using a SELECT statement.

INPUT

```
1> if exists (select * from TEAMS where TEAM_ID > 5)
2> begin
3>      print "IT EXISTS!!"
4> end
5> else
6> begin
7>      print "NO ESTA AQUI!"
8> end
```

Testing a Query's Result

The IF statement can also test the result returned from a SELECT query. Example 19.6 implements this feature to check for the maximum batting average among players.

Example 19.6

This example is similar to Example 19.5 in that it uses the SELECT statement to define a condition. This time, however, we are testing the condition with the greater than sign (>).

```
INPUT    1> if (select max(AVG) from BATTERS) > .400
         2> begin
         3>      print "UNBELIEVABLE!!"
         4> end
         5> else
         6>      print "TED WILLIAMS IS GETTING LONELY!"
         7> end
```

We recommend experimenting with your SQL implementation's IF statement. Think of several conditions you would be interested in checking in the BASEBALL (or any other) database. Run some queries making use of the IF statement to familiarize yourself with its use.

The WHILE Loop

Another popular programming construct that Transact-SQL supports is the WHILE loop. This command has the following syntax:

SYNTAX

```
WHILE logical_expression
      statement(s)
```

Example 19.7

The WHILE loop continues to loop through its statements until the logical expression it is checking returns a FALSE. This example uses a simple WHILE loop to increment a local variable (named COUNT).

```
INPUT    1> declare @COUNT int
         2> select @COUNT = 1
         3> while (@COUNT < 10)
         4> begin
         5>      select @COUNT = @COUNT + 1
         6>      print "LOOP AGAIN!"
         7> end
         8> print "LOOP FINISHED!"
```

19

NOTE

Example 19.7 implements a simple FOR loop. Other implementations of SQL, such as Oracle's PL/SQL, actually provide a FOR loop statement. Check your documentation to determine whether the system you are using supports this useful command.

The BREAK Command

You can issue the BREAK command within a WHILE loop to force an immediate exit from the loop. The BREAK command is often used along with an IF test to check some condition. If the condition check succeeds, you can use the BREAK command to exit from the WHILE loop. Commands immediately following the END command are then executed. Example 19.8 illustrates a simple use of the BREAK command. It checks for some arbitrary number (say @COUNT = 8). When this condition is met, it breaks out of the WHILE loop.

Example 19.8

Notice the placement of the BREAK statement after the evaluation of the first condition in the IF.

INPUT

```
1> declare @COUNT int
2> select @COUNT = 1
3> while (@COUNT < 10)
4> begin
5>      select @COUNT = @COUNT + 1
6>      if (@COUNT = 8)
7>      begin
8>          break
9>      end
10>     else
11>     begin
12>         print "LOOP AGAIN!"
13>     end
14> end
15> print "LOOP FINISHED!"
```

ANALYSIS

The BREAK command caused the loop to be exited when the @COUNT variable equaled 8.

The CONTINUE Command

The CONTINUE command is also a special command that can be executed from within a WHILE loop. The CONTINUE command forces the loop to immediately jump back to the beginning, rather than executing the remainder of the loop and then jumping back to the beginning. Like the BREAK command, the CONTINUE command is often used with an IF statement to check for some condition and then force an action, as shown in Example 19.9.

19

Example 19.9

Notice the placement of the CONTINUE statement after the evaluation of the first condition in the IF.

INPUT

```
1> declare @COUNT int
2> select @COUNT = 1
3> while (@COUNT < 10)
4> begin
5>      select @COUNT = @COUNT + 1
6>      if (@COUNT = 8)
7>      begin
8>          continue
9>      end
10>     else
11>     begin
12>         print "LOOP AGAIN!"
13>     end
14> end
15> print "LOOP FINISHED!"
```

ANALYSIS

Example 19.9 is identical to Example 19.8 except that the CONTINUE command replaces the BREAK command. Now instead of exiting the loop when @COUNT = 8, it simply jumps back to the top of the WHILE statement and continues.

Using the WHILE Loop to Scroll Through a Table

SQL Server and many other database systems have a special type of object—the cursor—that enables you to scroll through a table's records one record at a time. (Refer to Day 13.) However, some database systems (including SQL Server pre-System 10) do not support the use of scrollable cursors. Example 19.10 gives you an idea of how to use a WHILE loop to implement a rough cursor-type functionality when that functionality is not automatically supplied.

Example 19.10

You can use the WHILE loop to scroll through tables one record at a time. Transact-SQL stores the rowcount variable that can be set to tell SQL Server to return only one row at a time during a query. If you are using another database product, determine whether your product has a similar setting. By setting rowcount to 1 (its default is 0, which means unlimited), SQL Server returns only one record at a time from a SELECT query. You can use this one record to perform whatever operations you need to perform. By selecting the contents of a table into a temporary table that is deleted at the end of the operation, you can select out one row at a time, deleting that row when you are finished. When all the rows have been selected out of the table, you have gone through every row in the table! (As we said, this is a very rough cursor functionality!) Let's run the example now.

INPUT

```
1> set rowcount 1
2> declare @PLAYER char(30)
3> create table temp_BATTERS (
4> NAME char(30),
5> TEAM int,
6> AVERAGE float,
7> HOMERUNS int,
8> RBIS int)
9> insert temp_BATTERS
10> select * from BATTERS
11> while exists (select * from temp_BATTERS)
12> begin
13>      select @PLAYER = NAME from temp_BATTERS
14>      print @PLAYER
15>      delete from temp_BATTERS where NAME = @PLAYER
16> end
17> print "LOOP IS DONE!"
```

ANALYSIS Note that by setting the rowcount variable, you are simply modifying the number of rows returned from a SELECT. If the WHERE clause of the DELETE command returned five rows, five rows would be deleted! Also note that the rowcount variable can be reset repeatedly. Therefore, from within the loop, you can query the database for some additional information by simply resetting rowcount to 1 before continuing with the loop.

Transact-SQL Wildcard Operators

The concept of using wildcard conditions in SQL was introduced on Day 3, "Expressions, Conditions, and Operators." The LIKE operator enables you to use wildcard conditions in your SQL statements. Transact-SQL extends the flexibility of wildcard conditions. A summary of Transact-SQL's wildcard operators follows.

☐ The underscore character (_) represents any one individual character. For example, _MITH tells the query to look for a five-character string ending with MITH.

☐ The percent sign (%) represents any one or multiple characters. For example, WILL% returns the value WILLIAMS if it exists. WILL% returns the value WILL.

☐ Brackets ([ ]) allow a query to search for characters that are contained within the brackets. For example, [ABC] tells the query to search for strings containing the letters A, B, or C.

☐ The ^ character used within the brackets tells a query to look for any characters that are not listed within the brackets. For example, [^ABC] tells the query to search for strings that do not contain the letters A, B, or C.

Creating Summarized Reports Using
COMPUTE

Transact-SQL also has a mechanism for creating summarized database reports. The command, COMPUTE, has very similar syntax to its counterpart in SQL*Plus. (See Day 20, "SQL*Plus.")

The following query produces a report showing all batters, the number of home runs hit by each batter, and the total number of home runs hit by all batters:

```
select name, homeruns
from batters
compute sum(homeruns)
```

In the previous example, COMPUTE alone performs computations on the report as a whole, whereas COMPUTE BY performs computations on specified groups and the entire report, as the following example shows:

```
COMPUTE FUNCTION(expression) [BY expression]
  where the FUNCTION might include SUM, MAX, MIN, etc. and
  EXPRESSION is usually a column name or alias.
```

Date Conversions

Sybase and Microsoft's SQL Server can insert dates into a table in various formats; they can also extract dates in several different types of formats. This section shows you how to use SQL Server's CONVERT command to manipulate the way a date is displayed.

```
CONVERT (datatype [(length)], expression, format)
```

The following date formats are available with SQL Server when using the CONVERT function:

Format code	Format picture
100	mon dd yyyy hh:miAM/PM
101	mm/dd/yy
102	yy.mm.dd
103	dd/mm/yy
104	dd.mm.yy
105	dd-mm-yy
106	dd mon yy

continues

19

Format code	Format picture
107	mon dd, yy
108	hh:mi:ss
109	mon dd, yyyy hh:mi:ss:mmmAM/PM
110	mm-dd-yy
111	yy/mm/dd
112	yymmdd

INPUT
```
select "PayDate" = convert(char(15), paydate, 107)
from payment_table
where customer_id = 012845
```

OUTPUT
```
PayDate
---------------
May 1, 1997
```

ANALYSIS The preceding example uses the format code 107 with the CONVERT function. According to the date format table, code 107 will display the date in the format mon dd, yy.

SQL Server Diagnostic Tools—SET Commands

Transact-SQL provides a list of SET commands that enable you to turn on various options that help you analyze Transact-SQL statements. Here are some of the popular SET commands:

☐ SET STATISTICS IO ON tells the server to return the number of logical and physical page requests.

☐ SET STATISTICS TIME ON tells the server to display the execution time of an SQL statement.

☐ SET SHOWPLAN ON tells the server to show the execution plan for the designated query.

☐ SET NOEXEC ON tells the server to parse the designated query, but not to execute it.

☐ SET PARSONLY ON tells the server to check for syntax for the designated query, but not to execute it.

Transact-SQL also has the following commands that help to control what is displayed as part of the output from your queries:

☐ SET ROWCOUNT n tells the server to display only the first n records retrieved from a query.

☐ SET NOCOUNT ON tells the server not to report the number of rows returned by a query.

> **NOTE**
>
> If you are concerned with tuning your SQL statements, refer to Day 15, "Streamlining SQL Statements for Improved Performance."

Summary

Day 19 introduces a number of topics that add some teeth to your SQL programming expertise. The basic SQL topics that you learned earlier in this book are extremely important and provide the foundation for all database programming work you undertake. However, these topics are just a foundation. The SQL procedural language concepts explained yesterday and today build on your foundation of SQL. They give you, the database programmer, a great deal of power when accessing data in your relational database.

The Transact-SQL language included with the Microsoft and Sybase SQL Server database products provide many of the programming constructs found in popular third- and fourth-generation languages. Its features include the IF statement, the WHILE loop, and the capability to declare and use local and global variables.

Keep in mind that Day 19 is a brief introduction to the features and techniques of Transact-SQL code. Feel free to dive head first into your documentation and experiment with all the tools that are available to you. For more detailed coverage of Transact-SQL, refer to the Microsoft SQL Server Transact-SQL documentation.

Q&A

Q Does SQL provide a FOR loop?

A Programming constructs such as the FOR loop, the WHILE loop, and the CASE statement are extensions to ANSI SQL. Therefore, the use of these items varies widely among database systems. For instance, Oracle provides the FOR loop, whereas Transact-SQL (SQL Server) does not. Of course, a WHILE loop can increment a variable within the loop, which can simulate the FOR loop.

Q I am developing a Windows (or Macintosh) application in which the user interface consists of Windows GUI elements, such as windows and dialog boxes. Can I use the PRINT statement to issue messages to the user?

A SQL is entirely platform independent. Therefore, issuing the PRINT statement will not pop up a message box. To output messages to the user, your SQL procedures can return predetermined values that indicate success or failure. Then the user can be notified of the status of the queries. (The PRINT command is most useful for debugging because a PRINT statement executed within a stored procedure will not be output to the screen anyway.)

Workshop

The Workshop provides quiz questions to help solidify your understanding of the material covered, as well as exercises to provide you with experience in using what you have learned. Try to answer the quiz and exercise questions before checking the answers in Appendix F, "Answers to Quizzes and Exercises."

Quiz

1. True or False: The use of the word SQL in Oracle's PL/SQL and Microsoft/ Sybase's Transact-SQL implies that these products are fully compliant with the ANSI standard.

2. True or False: Static SQL is less flexible than Dynamic SQL, although the performance of static SQL can be better.

Exercises

1. If you are not using Sybase/Microsoft SQL Server, compare your product's extensions to ANSI SQL to the extensions mentioned today.

2. Write a brief set of statements that will check for the existence of some condition. If this condition is true, perform some operation. Otherwise, perform another operation.

Day 20

SQL*Plus

Objectives

Today you will learn about SQL*Plus, the SQL interface for Oracle's RDBMS. By the end of Day 20, you will understand the following elements of SQL*Plus:

- [ ] How to use the SQL*Plus buffer
- [ ] How to format reports attractively
- [ ] How to manipulate dates
- [ ] How to make interactive queries
- [ ] How to construct advanced reports
- [ ] How to use the powerful DECODE function

Introduction

We are presenting SQL*Plus today because of Oracle's dominance in the relational database market and because of the power and flexibility SQL*Plus offers to the database user. SQL*Plus resembles Transact-SQL (see Day 19,

"Transact-SQL: An Introduction") in many ways. Both implementations comply with the ANSI SQL standard for the most part, which is still the skeleton of any implementation.

SQL*Plus commands can enhance an SQL session and improve the format of queries from the database. SQL*Plus can also format reports, much like a dedicated report writer. SQL*Plus supplements both standard SQL and PL/SQL and helps relational database programmers gather data that is in a desirable format.

The SQL*Plus Buffer

The SQL*Plus buffer is an area that stores commands that are specific to your particular SQL session. These commands include the most recently executed SQL statement and commands that you have used to customize your SQL session, such as formatting commands and variable assignments. This buffer is like a short-term memory. Here are some of the most common SQL buffer commands:

- [ ] LIST line_number—Lists a line from the statement in the buffer and designates it as the current line.
- [ ] CHANGE/old_value/new_value—Changes old_value to new_value on the current line in the buffer.
- [ ] APPEND text—Appends text to the current line in the buffer.
- [ ] DEL— Deletes the current line in the buffer.
- [ ] SAVE newfile—Saves the SQL statement in the buffer to a file.
- [ ] GET filename—Gets an SQL file and places it into the buffer.
- [ ] /—Executes the SQL statement in the buffer.

We begin with a simple SQL statement:

INPUT
```
SQL> select *
  2   from products
  3   where unit_cost > 25;
```

OUTPUT
```
PRO PRODUCT_NAME                      UNIT_COST
--- -------------------------------- ----------
P01 MICKEY MOUSE LAMP                     29.95
P06 SQL COMMAND REFERENCE                 29.99
P07 BLACK LEATHER BRIEFCASE               99.99
```

The LIST command lists the most recently executed SQL statement in the buffer. The output will simply be the displayed statement.

```
SQL> list
  1   select *
  2   from products
  3*  where unit_cost > 25
```

20

Notice that each line is numbered. Line numbers are important in the buffer; they act as pointers that enable you to modify specific lines of your statement using the SQL*PLUS buffer. The SQL*Plus buffer is not a full screen editor; after you hit Enter, you cannot use the cursor to move up a line, as shown in the following example.

```
SQL> select *
  2  from products
  3  where unit_cost > 25
  4  /
```

 NOTE

As with SQL commands, you may issue SQL*Plus commands in either uppercase or lowercase.

 TIP

You can abbreviate most SQL*Plus commands; for example, LIST can be abbreviated as l.

You can move to a specific line from the buffer by placing a line number after the l.

INPUT
```
SQL> l3
```

OUTPUT
```
  3* where unit_cost > 25
```

ANALYSIS Notice the asterisk after the line number 3. This asterisk denotes the current line number. Pay close attention to the placement of the asterisk in today's examples. Whenever a line is marked by the asterisk, you can make changes to that line.

Because you know that your current line is 3, you are free to make changes. The syntax for the CHANGE command is as follows:

SYNTAX
```
CHANGE/old_value/new_value
or
C/old_value/new_value
```

INPUT
```
SQL> c/>/<
```

OUTPUT
```
  3* where unit_cost < 25
```

20

INPUT
```
SQL> 1
```

OUTPUT
```
1  select *
2  from products
3* where unit_cost < 25
```

ANALYSIS The greater than sign (>) has been changed to less than (<) on line 3. Notice after the change was made that the newly modified line was displayed. If you issue the LIST command or 1, you can see the full statement. Now execute the statement:

INPUT
```
SQL> /
```

OUTPUT
```
PRO PRODUCT_NAME                        UNIT_COST
--- ----------------------------------  ---------
P02 NO 2 PENCILS - 20 PACK                   1.99
P03 COFFEE MUG                               6.95
P04 FAR SIDE CALENDAR                        10.5
P05 NATURE CALENDAR                         12.99
```

ANALYSIS The forward slash at the SQL> prompt executes any statement that is in the buffer.

INPUT
```
SQL> 1
```

OUTPUT
```
1  select *
2  from products
3* where unit_cost < 25
```

Now, you can add a line to your statement by typing a new line number at the SQL> prompt and entering text. After you make the addition, get a full statement listing. Here's an example:

INPUT
```
SQL> 4 order by unit_cost
SQL> 1
```

OUTPUT
```
1  select *
2  from products
3  where unit_cost < 25
4* order by unit_cost
```

ANALYSIS Deleting a line is easier than adding a line. Simply type DEL 4 at the SQL> prompt to delete line 4. Now get another statement listing to verify that the line is gone.

INPUT
```
SQL> DEL4
SQL> 1
```

OUTPUT
```
1  select *
2  from products
3* where unit_cost < 25
```

Another way to add one or more lines to your statement is to use the INPUT command. As you can see in the preceding list, the current line number is 3. At the prompt type **input** and then press Enter. Now you can begin typing text. Each time you press Enter, another line will be created. If you press Enter twice, you will obtain another SQL> prompt. Now if you display a statement listing, as in the following example, you can see that line 4 has been added.

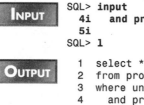

```
SQL> input
   4i    and product_id = 'P01'
   5i
SQL> l
```

```
1  select *
2  from products
3  where unit_cost < 25
4    and product_id = 'P01'
5* order by unit_cost
```

To append text to the current line, issue the APPEND command followed by the text. Compare the output in the preceding example—the current line number is 5—to the following example.

INPUT   `SQL> append  desc`

OUTPUT   `5* order by unit_cost desc`

Now get a full listing of your statement:

INPUT   `SQL> l`

OUTPUT
```
1  select *
2  from products
3  where unit_cost < 25
4    and product_id = 'P01'
5* order by unit_cost desc
```

Suppose you want to wipe the slate clean. You can clear the contents of the SQL*Plus buffer by issuing the command CLEAR BUFFER. As you will see later, you can also use the CLEAR command to clear specific settings from the buffer, such as column formatting information and computes on a report.

INPUT   `SQL> clear buffer`

OUTPUT   `buffer cleared`

INPUT   `SQL> l`

OUTPUT   `No lines in SQL buffer.`

Analysis Obviously, you won't be able to retrieve anything from an empty buffer. You aren't a master yet, but you should be able to maneuver with ease by manipulating your commands in the buffer.

The DESCRIBE Command

The handy DESCRIBE command enables you to view the structure of a table quickly without having to create a query against the data dictionary.

 SYNTAX

```
DESC[RIBE] table_name
```

Take a look at the two tables you will be using throughout the day.

 INPUT SQL> **describe orders**

 OUTPUT

```
Name                                Null?      Type
-----------------------------------  ---------  ----
ORDER_NUM                           NOT NULL   NUMBER(2)
CUSTOMER                            NOT NULL   VARCHAR2(30)
PRODUCT_ID                         NOT NULL   CHAR(3)
PRODUCT_QTY                        NOT NULL   NUMBER(5)
DELIVERY_DATE                                 DATE
```

The following statement uses the abbreviation DESC instead of DESCRIBE:

INPUT SQL> **desc products**

OUTPUT

```
Name                                Null?      Type
-----------------------------------  ---------  ----
PRODUCT_ID                         NOT NULL   VARCHAR2(3)
PRODUCT_NAME                       NOT NULL   VARCHAR2(30)
UNIT_COST                          NOT NULL   NUMBER(8,2)
```

 Analysis DESC displays each column name, which columns must contain data (NULL/NOT NULL), and the data type for each column. If you are writing many queries, you will find that few days go by without using this command. Over a long time, this command can save you many hours of programming time. Without DESCRIBE you would have to search through project documentation or even database manuals containing lists of data dictionary tables to get this information.

The SHOW Command

The SHOW command displays the session's current settings, from formatting commands to who you are. SHOW ALL displays all settings. This discussion covers some of the most common settings.

20

INPUT

SQL> **show all**

OUTPUT

```
appinfo is ON and set to "SQL*Plus"
arraysize 15
autocommit OFF
autoprint OFF
autotrace OFF
blockterminator "." (hex 2e)
btitle OFF and is the 1st few characters of the next SELECT statement
closecursor OFF
colsep " "
cmdsep OFF
compatibility version NATIVE
concat "." (hex 2e)
copycommit 0
copytypecheck is ON
crt ""
define "&" (hex 26)
echo OFF
editfile "afiedt.buf"
embedded OFF
escape OFF
feedback ON for 6 or more rows
flagger OFF
flush ON
heading ON
headsep "¦" (hex 7c)
linesize 100
lno 6
long 80
longchunksize 80
maxdata 60000
newpage 1
null ""
numformat ""
numwidth 9
pagesize 24
pause is OFF
pno 1
recsep WRAP
recsepchar " " (hex 20)
release 703020200
repheader OFF and is NULL
repfooter OFF and is NULL
serveroutput OFF
showmode OFF
spool OFF
sqlcase MIXED
sqlcode 1007
sqlcontinue "> "
sqlnumber ON
sqlprefix "#" (hex 23)
sqlprompt "SQL> "
sqlterminator ";" (hex 3b)
suffix "SQL"
tab ON
```

20

```
termout ON
time OFF
timing OFF
trimout ON
trimspool OFF
ttitle OFF and is the 1st few characters of the next SELECT statement
underline "-" (hex 2d)
user is "RYAN"
verify ON
wrap : lines will be wrapped
```

The SHOW command displays a specific setting entered by the user. Suppose you have access to multiple database user IDs and you want to see how you are logged on. You can issue the following command:

INPUT   `SQL> show user`

OUTPUT   `user is "RYAN"`

To see the current line size of output, you would type:

INPUT   `SQL> show linesize`

OUTPUT   `linesize 100`

File Commands

Various commands enable you to manipulate files in SQL*Plus. These commands include creating a file, editing the file using a full-screen editor as opposed to using the SQL*Plus buffer, and redirecting output to a file. You also need to know how to execute an SQL file after it is created.

The SAVE, GET, and EDIT Commands

The SAVE command saves the contents of the SQL statement in the buffer to a file whose name you specify. For example:

INPUT
```
SQL> select *
  2  from products
  3  where unit_cost < 25

SQL> save query1.sql
```

OUTPUT   `Created file query1.sql`

20

ANALYSIS After a file has been saved, you can use the GET command to list the file. GET is very similar to the LIST command. Just remember that GET deals with statements that have been saved to files, whereas LIST deals with the statement that is stored in the buffer.

INPUT SQL> **get query1**

OUTPUT
```
1  select *
2  from products
3* where unit_cost < 25
```

You can use the EDIT command either to create a new file or to edit an existing file. When issuing this command, you are taken into a full-screen editor, more than likely Notepad in Windows. You will find that it is usually easier to modify a file with EDIT than through the buffer, particularly if you are dealing with a large or complex statement. Figure 20.1 shows an example of the EDIT command.

INPUT SQL> edit query1.**sql**

Figure 20.1.

*Editing a file in SQL*Plus.*

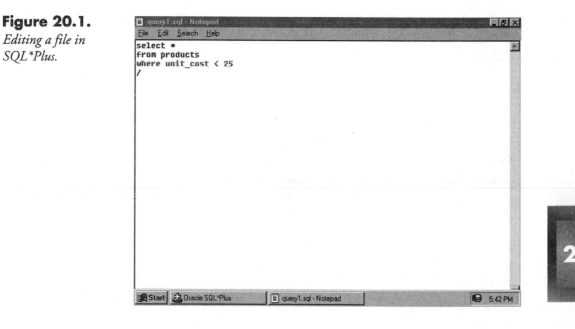

20

Starting a File

Now that you know how to create and edit an SQL file, the command to execute it is simple.
It can take one of the following forms:

```
START filename

or

STA filename

or

@filename
```

TIP

> Commands are not case sensitive.

INPUT

```
SQL> start query1.sql
```

OUTPUT

```
PRO PRODUCT_NAME                    UNIT_COST
--- ------------------------------  ---------
P02 NO 2 PENCILS - 20 PACK               1.99
P03 COFFEE MUG                           6.95
P04 FAR SIDE CALENDAR                    10.5
P05 NATURE CALENDAR                     12.99
```

NOTE

> You do not have to specify the file extension `.sql` to start a file from
> SQL*Plus. The database assumes that the file you are executing has this
> extension. Similarly, when you are creating a file from the SQL> prompt
> or use SAVE, GET, or EDIT, you do not have to include the extension if it
> is `.sql`.

INPUT

```
SQL> @query1
```

OUTPUT

```
PRO PRODUCT_NAME                    UNIT_COST
--- ------------------------------  ---------
P02 NO 2 PENCILS - 20 PACK               1.99
P03 COFFEE MUG                           6.95
P04 FAR SIDE CALENDAR                    10.5
P05 NATURE CALENDAR                     12.99
```

INPUT

```
SQL> run query1
```

20

OUTPUT

```
1  select *
2  from products
3* where unit_cost < 25

PRO PRODUCT_NAME                          UNIT_COST
--- ------------------------------------- ---------
P02 NO 2 PENCILS - 20 PACK                     1.99
P03 COFFEE MUG                                 6.95
P04 FAR SIDE CALENDAR                          10.5
P05 NATURE CALENDAR                           12.99
```

ANALYSIS   Notice that when you use RUN to execute a query, the statement is echoed, or displayed on the screen.

Spooling Query Output

Viewing the output of your query on the screen is very convenient, but what if you want to save the results for future reference or you want to print the file? The SPOOL command allows you to send your output to a specified file. If the file does not exist, it will be created. If the file exists, it will be overwritten, as shown in Figure 20.2.

INPUT

```
SQL> spool prod.lst
SQL> select *
  2  from products;
```

OUTPUT

```
PRO PRODUCT_NAME                          UNIT_COST
--- ------------------------------------- ---------
P01 MICKEY MOUSE LAMP                         29.95
P02 NO 2 PENCILS - 20 PACK                     1.99
P03 COFFEE MUG                                 6.95
P04 FAR 3IDE CALENDAR                          10.5
P05 NATURE CALENDAR                           12.99
P06 SQL COMMAND REFERENCE                      29.99
P07 BLACK LEATHER BRIEFCASE                    99.99

7 rows selected.
```

INPUT

```
SQL> spool off
SQL> edit prod.lst
```

ANALYSIS   The output in Figure 20.2 is an SQL*Plus file. You must use the SPOOL OFF command to stop spooling to a file. When you exit SQL*Plus, SPOOL OFF is automatic. But if you do not exit and you continue to work in SQL*Plus, everything you do will be spooled to your file until you issue the command SPOOL OFF.

20

Figure 20.2.

Spooling your output to a file.

```
prod - Notepad                                                    _ 8 X
File  Edit  Search  Help
SQL> select *
  2  from products;

PRO PRODUCT_NAME                         UNIT_COST
--- ------------------------------       ---------
P01 MICKEY MOUSE LAMP                        29.95
P02 NO 2 PENCILS - 20 PACK                    1.99
P03 COFFEE MUG                                6.95
P04 FAR SIDE CALENDAR                        10.5
P05 NATURE CALENDAR                          12.99
P06 SQL COMMAND REFERENCE                    29.99
P07 BLACK LEATHER BRIEFCASE                  99.99

7 rows selected.

SQL> spool off




Start   Oracle SQL*Plus     Exploring - 3½ Floppy (A:)    prod - Notepad        5:49 PM
```

SET **Commands**

SET commands in Oracle change SQL*Plus session settings. By using these commands, you can customize your SQL working environment and invoke options to make your output results more presentable. You can control many of the SET commands by turning an option on or off.

To see how the SET commands work, perform a simple select:

INPUT

```
SQL> select *
  2  from products;
```

OUTPUT

```
PRO PRODUCT_NAME                         UNIT_COST
--- ------------------------------       ---------
P01 MICKEY MOUSE LAMP                        29.95
P02 NO 2 PENCILS - 20 PACK                    1.99
P03 COFFEE MUG                                6.95
P04 FAR SIDE CALENDAR                        10.5
P05 NATURE CALENDAR                          12.99
P06 SQL COMMAND REFERENCE                    29.99
P07 BLACK LEATHER BRIEFCASE                  99.99

7 rows selected.
```

ANALYSIS   The last line of output

```
7 rows selected.
```

20

is called *feedback,* which is an SQL setting that can be modified. The settings have defaults, and in this case the default for FEEDBACK is on. If you wanted, you could type

```
SET FEEDBACK ON
```

before issuing your select statement. Now suppose that you do not want to see the feedback, as happens to be the case with some reports, particularly summarized reports with computations.

INPUT
```
SQL> set feedback off
SQL> select *
  2  from products;
```

OUTPUT
```
PRO PRODUCT_NAME                      UNIT_COST
--- --------------------------------  ---------
P01 MICKEY MOUSE LAMP                     29.95
P02 NO 2 PENCILS - 20 PACK                 1.99
P03 COFFEE MUG                             6.95
P04 FAR SIDE CALENDAR                      10.5
P05 NATURE CALENDAR                       12.99
P06 SQL COMMAND REFERENCE                 29.99
P07 BLACK LEATHER BRIEFCASE               99.99
```

ANALYSIS SET FEEDBACK OFF turns off the feedback display.

In some cases you may want to suppress the column headings from being displayed on a report. This setting is called HEADING, which can also be set ON or OFF.

INPUT
```
SQL> set heading off
SQL> /
```

OUTPUT
```
P01 MICKEY MOUSE LAMP                     29.95
P02 NO 2 PENCILS - 20 PACK                 1.99
P03 COFFEE MUG                             6.95
P04 FAR SIDE CALENDAR                      10.5
P05 NATURE CALENDAR                       12.99
P06 SQL COMMAND REFERENCE                 29.99
P07 BLACK LEATHER BRIEFCASE               99.99
```

ANALYSIS The column headings have been eliminated from the output. Only the actual data is displayed.

20

You can change a wide array of settings to manipulate how your output is displayed. One option, LINESIZE, allows you to specify the length of each line of your output. A small line size will more than likely cause your output to wrap; increasing the line size may be necessary to suppress wrapping of a line that exceeds the default 80 characters. Unless you are using wide computer paper (11×14), you may want to landscape print your report if you are using a line size greater than 80. The following example shows the use of LINESIZE.

INPUT
```
SQL> set linesize 40
SQL> /
```

OUTPUT
```
P01 MICKEY MOUSE LAMP
    29.95

P02 NO 2 PENCILS - 20 PACK
    1.99

P03 COFFEE MUG
    6.95

P04 FAR SIDE CALENDAR
    10.5

P05 NATURE CALENDAR
    12.99

P06 SQL COMMAND REFERENCE
    29.99

P07 BLACK LEATHER BRIEFCASE
    99.99
```

You can also adjust the size of each page of your output by using the setting PAGESIZE. If you are simply viewing your output on screen, the best setting for PAGESIZE is 23, which eliminates multiple page breaks per screen. In the following example PAGESIZE is set to a low number to show you what happens on each page break.

INPUT
```
SQL> set linesize 80
SQL> set heading on
SQL> set pagesize 7
SQL> /
```

OUTPUT
```
PRO PRODUCT_NAME                     UNIT_COST
-- ------------------------------- --------
P01 MICKEY MOUSE LAMP                   29.95
P02 NO 2 PENCILS - 20 PACK               1.99
P03 COFFEE MUG                           6.95
P04 FAR SIDE CALENDAR                   10.5

PRO PRODUCT_NAME                     UNIT_COST
-- ------------------------------- --------
P05 NATURE CALENDAR                     12.99
P06 SQL COMMAND REFERENCE               29.99
P07 BLACK LEATHER BRIEFCASE             99.99
```

ANALYSIS Using the setting of PAGESIZE 7, the maximum number of lines that may appear on a single page is seven. New column headings will print automatically at the start of each new page.

20

The TIME setting displays the current time as part of your SQL> prompt.

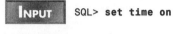 SQL> **set time on**

 08:52:02 SQL>

These were just a few of the SET options, but they are all manipulated in basically the same way. As you saw from the vast list of SET commands in the earlier output from the SHOW ALL statement, you have many options when customizing your SQL*Plus session. Experiment with each option and see what you like best. You will probably keep the default for many options, but you may find yourself changing other options frequently based on different scenarios.

LOGIN.SQL File

When you log out of SQL*Plus, all of your session settings are cleared. When you log back in, your settings will have to be reinitialized if they are not the defaults unless you are using a login.sql file. This file is automatically executed when you sign on to SQL*Plus. This initialization file is similar to the autoexec.bat file on your PC or your .profile in a UNIX Korn Shell environment.

In Personal Oracle7 you can use the EDIT command to create your Login.sql file, as shown in Figure 20.3.

Figure 20.3.

Your Login.sql *file.*

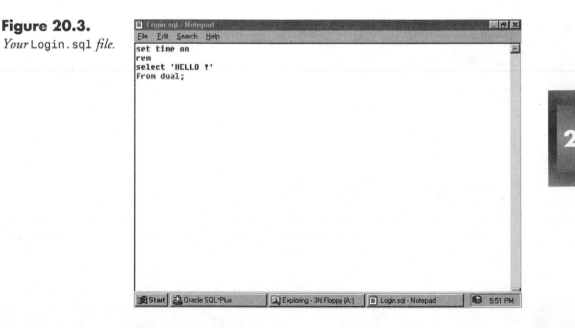

20

When you log on to SQL*Plus, here is what you will see:

```
SQL*Plus: Release 3.3.2.0.2 - Production on Sun May 11 20:37:58 1997

Copyright (c) Oracle Corporation 1979, 1994.  All rights reserved.

Enter password: ****

Connected to:
Personal Oracle7 Release 7.3.2.2.0 - Production Release
With the distributed and replication options
PL/SQL Release 2.3.2.0.0 - Production


'HELLO!
-------
HELLO !

20:38:02 SQL>
```

CLEAR Command

In SQL*Plus, settings are cleared by logging off, or exiting SQL*Plus. Some of your settings may also be cleared by using the CLEAR command, as shown in the following examples.

INPUT

```
SQL> clear col
```

OUTPUT

```
columns cleared
```

INPUT

```
SQL> clear break
```

OUTPUT

```
breaks cleared
```

INPUT

```
SQL> clear compute
```

OUTPUT

```
computes cleared
```

Formatting Your Output

SQL*Plus also has commands that enable you to arrange your output in almost any format. This section covers the basic formatting commands for report titles, column headings and formats, and giving a column a "new value."

TTITLE and BTITLE

TTITLE and BTITLE enable you to create titles on your reports. Previous days covered queries and output, but with SQL*Plus you can convert simple output into presentable reports. The TTITLE command places a title at the top of each page of your output or report. BTITLE places a title at the bottom of each page of your report. Many options are available with each of these commands, but today's presentation covers the essentials. Here is the basic syntax of TTITLE and BTITLE:

```
TTITLE [center¦left¦right] 'text' [&variable] [skip n]
BTITLE [center¦left¦right] 'text' [&variable] [skip n]
```

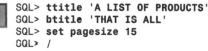

```
SQL> ttitle 'A LIST OF PRODUCTS'
SQL> btitle 'THAT IS ALL'
SQL> set pagesize 15
SQL> /
```

OUTPUT

```
Wed May 07
page     1
                                A LIST OF PRODUCTS

PRO PRODUCT_NAME                        UNIT_COST
--  -------------------------------- ---------
P01 MICKEY MOUSE LAMP                       29.95
P02 NO 2 PENCILS - 20 PACK                   1.99
P03 COFFEE MUG                               6.95
P04 FAR SIDE CALENDAR                       10.5
P05 NATURE CALENDAR                         12.99
P06 SQL COMMAND REFERENCE                   29.99
P07 BLACK LEATHER BRIEFCASE                 99.99

                                THAT IS ALL

7 rows selected.
```

ANALYSIS

The title appears at the top of the page and at the bottom. Many people use the bottom title for signature blocks to verify or make changes to data on the report. Also, in the top title the date and page number are part of the title.

20

Formatting Columns (COLUMN, HEADING, FORMAT)

Formatting columns refers to the columns that are to be displayed or the columns that are listed after the SELECT in an SQL statement. The COLUMN, HEADING, and FORMAT commands rename column headings and control the way the data appears on the report.

The COL[UMN] command is usually used with either the HEADING command or the FORMAT command. COLUMN defines the column that you wish to format. The column that you are defining must appear exactly as it is typed in the SELECT statement. You may use a column alias instead of the full column name to identify a column with this command.

When using the HEADING command, you must use the COLUMN command to identify the column on which to place the heading.

When using the FORMAT command, you must use the COLUMN command to identify the column you wish to format.

The basic syntax for using all three commands follows. Note that the HEADING and FORMAT commands are optional. In the FORMAT syntax, you must use an a if the data has a character format or use 0s and 9s to specify number data types. Decimals may also be used with numeric values. The number to the right of the a is the total width that you wish to allow for the specified column.

SYNTAX

```
COL[UMN] column_name HEA[DING] "new_heading" FOR[MAT] [a1¦99.99]
```

The simple SELECT statement that follows shows the formatting of a column. The specified column is of NUMBER data type, and we want to display the number in a decimal format with a dollar sign.

INPUT

```
SQL> column unit_cost heading "PRICE" format $99.99
SQL> select product_name, unit_cost
  2  from products;
```

OUTPUT

```
PRODUCT_NAME                      PRICE
------------------------------   -------
MICKEY MOUSE LAMP                $29.95
NO 2 PENCILS - 20 PACK            $1.99
COFFEE MUG                        $6.95
FAR SIDE CALENDAR                $10.50
NATURE CALENDAR                  $12.99
SQL COMMAND REFERENCE            $29.99
BLACK LEATHER BRIEFCASE          $99.99

7 rows selected.
```

ANALYSIS Because we used the format 99.99, the maximum number that will be displayed is 99.99.

Now try abbreviating the commands. Here's something neat you can do with the HEADING command:

INPUT

```
SQL> col unit_cost hea "UNIT¦COST" for $09.99
SQL> select product_name, unit_cost
  2  from products;
```

OUTPUT

```
PRODUCT_NAME                   UNIT COST
------------------------------ ---------
MICKEY MOUSE LAMP                $29.95
NO 2 PENCILS - 20 PACK           $01.99
COFFEE MUG                        $06.95
```

20

```
FAR SIDE CALENDAR                 $10.50
NATURE CALENDAR                   $12.99
SQL COMMAND REFERENCE             $29.99
BLACK LEATHER BRIEFCASE           $99.99

7 rows selected.
```

ANALYSIS The pipe sign (¦) in the HEADING command forces the following text of the column heading to be printed on the next line. You may use multiple pipe signs. The technique is handy when the width of your report starts to push the limits of the maximum available line size. The format of the unit cost column is now 09.99. The maximum number displayed is still 99.99, but now a 0 will precede all numbers less than 10. You may prefer this format because it makes the dollar amounts appear uniform.

Report and Group Summaries

What would a report be without summaries and computations? Let's just say that you would have one frustrated programmer. Certain commands in SQL*Plus allow you to break up your report into one or more types of groups and perform summaries or computations on each group. BREAK is a little different from SQL's standard group functions, such as COUNT( ) and SUM( ). These functions are used with report and group summaries to provide a more complete report.

BREAK ON

The BREAK ON command breaks returned rows of data from an SQL statement into one or more groups. If you break on a customer's name, then by default the customer's name will be printed only the first time it is returned and left blank with each row of data with the corresponding name. Here is the very basic syntax of the BREAK ON command:

SYNTAX

```
BRE[AK] [ON column1 ON column2...][SKIP n¦PAGE][DUP¦NODUP]
```

You may also break on REPORT and ROW. Breaking on REPORT performs computations on the report as a whole, whereas breaking on ROW performs computations on each group of rows.

The SKIP option allows you to skip a number of lines or a page on each group. DUP or NODUP suggests whether you want duplicates to be printed in each group. The default is NODUP.

Here is an example:

INPUT

```
SQL> col unit_cost head 'UNIT¦COST' for $09.99
SQL> break on customer
SQL> select o.customer, p.product_name, p.unit_cost
  2  from orders o,
  3       products p
  4  where o.product_id = p.product_id
  5  order by customer;
```

20

```
OUTPUT   CUSTOMER                    PRODUCT_NAME                UNIT COST
         --------------------------  --------------------------  ---------
         JONES and SONS              MICKEY MOUSE LAMP              $29.95
                                     NO 2 PENCILS - 20 PACK        $01.99
                                     COFFEE MUG                    $06.95
         PARAKEET CONSULTING GROUP   MICKEY MOUSE LAMP             $29.95
                                     NO 2 PENCILS - 20 PACK        $01.99
                                     SQL COMMAND REFERENCE         $29.99
                                     BLACK LEATHER BRIEFCASE       $99.99
                                     FAR SIDE CALENDAR             $10.50
         PLEWSKY MOBILE CARWASH      MICKEY MOUSE LAMP             $29.95
                                     BLACK LEATHER BRIEFCASE       $99.99
                                     BLACK LEATHER BRIEFCASE       $99.99
                                     NO 2 PENCILS - 20 PACK        $01.99
                                     NO 2 PENCILS - 20 PACK        $01.99

         13 rows selected.
```

ANALYSIS Each unique customer is printed only once. This report is much easier to read than one in which duplicate customer names are printed. You must order your results in the same order as the column(s) on which you are breaking for the BREAK command to work.

COMPUTE

The COMPUTE command is used with the BREAK ON command. COMPUTE allows you to perform various computations on each group of data and/or on the entire report.

SYNTAX

COMP[UTE] function OF column_or_alias ON column_or_row_or_report

Some of the more popular functions are

☐ AVG—Computes the average value on each group.

☐ COUNT—Computes a count of values on each group.

☐ SUM—Computes a sum of values on each group.

Suppose you want to create a report that lists the information from the PRODUCTS table and computes the average product cost on the report.

INPUT
```
SQL> break on report
SQL> compute avg of unit_cost on report
SQL> select *
  2  from products;
```

OUTPUT
```
PRO PRODUCT_NAME                UNIT_COST
--- --------------------------  ---------
P01 MICKEY MOUSE LAMP               29.95
P02 NO 2 PENCILS - 20 PACK           1.99
P03 COFFEE MUG                       6.95
P04 FAR SIDE CALENDAR               10.50
P05 NATURE CALENDAR                 12.99
P06 SQL COMMAND REFERENCE           29.99
P07 BLACK LEATHER BRIEFCASE         99.99
                                ---------
avg                                 27.48
```

20

ANALYSIS You can obtain the information you want by breaking on REPORT and then computing the avg of the unit_cost on REPORT.

Remember the CLEAR command? Now clear the last compute from the buffer and start again—but this time you want to compute the amount of money spent by each customer. Because you do not want to see the average any longer, you should also clear the computes.

INPUT SQL> **clear compute**

OUTPUT computes cleared

Now clear the last BREAK. (You don't really have to clear the BREAK in this case because you still intend to break on report.)

INPUT SQL> **clear break**

OUTPUT breaks cleared

The next step is to reenter the breaks and computes the way you want them now. You will also have to reformat the column unit_cost to accommodate a larger number because you are computing a sum of the unit_cost on the report. You need to allow room for the grand total that uses the same format as the column on which it is being figured. So you need to add another place to the left of the decimal.

INPUT
```
SQL> col unit_cost hea 'UNIT|COST' for $099.99
SQL> break on report on customer skip 1
SQL> compute sum of unit_cost on customer
SQL> compute sum of unit_cost on report
```

Now list the last SQL statement from the buffer.

INPUT SQL> **l**

OUTPUT
```
1   select o.customer, p.product_name, p.unit_cost
2   from orders o,
3        products p
4   where o.product_id = p.product_id
5*  order by customer
```

ANALYSIS Now that you have verified that this statement is the one you want, you can execute it:

INPUT SQL> **/**

20

```
                                                         UNIT
OUTPUT    CUSTOMER                PRODUCT_NAME             COST
          - - - - - - - - - - -   - - - - - - - - - - - - - - - -  - - - - - -
          JONES and SONS          MICKEY MOUSE LAMP      $029.95
                                  NO 2 PENCILS - 20 PACK $001.99
                                  COFFEE MUG             $006.95
          *****************************                  - - - - - - -
          sum                                            $038.89

          PARAKEET CONSULTING GROUP MICKEY MOUSE LAMP     $029.95
                                  NO 2 PENCILS - 20 PACK $001.99
                                  SQL COMMAND REFERENCE  $029.99
                                  BLACK LEATHER BRIEFCASE $099.99
                                  FAR SIDE CALENDAR      $010.50
          *****************************                  - - - - - - -
          sum                                            $172.42

          PLEWSKY MOBILE CARWASH  MICKEY MOUSE LAMP      $029.95
                                  BLACK LEATHER BRIEFCASE $099.99
                                  BLACK LEATHER BRIEFCASE $099.99
                                  NO 2 PENCILS - 20 PACK $001.99
                                  NO 2 PENCILS - 20 PACK $001.99
          *****************************                  - - - - - - -

                                                         UNIT
          CUSTOMER                PRODUCT_NAME             COST
          - - - - - - - - - - - - - - - -  - - - - - - - - - - - - - - - -  - - - - - -
          sum                                            $233.91


                                                         - - - - - - -
          sum                                            $445.22

          13 rows selected.
```

ANALYSIS This example computed the total amount that each customer spent and also calculated a grand total for all customers.

By now you should understand the basics of formatting columns, grouping data on the report, and performing computations on each group.

Using Variables in SQL*Plus

Without actually getting into a procedural language, you can still define variables in your SQL statement. You can use special options in SQL*Plus (covered in this section) to accept input from the user to pass parameters into your SQL program.

Substitution Variables (&)

An ampersand (&) is the character that calls a value for a variable within an SQL script. If the variable has not previously been defined, the user will be prompted to enter a value.

```
SQL> select *
  2  from &TBL
  3  /

Enter value for tbl: products

The user entered the value "products."

old   2: from &TBL
new   2: from products

PRO PRODUCT_NAME                       UNIT_COST
--- ------------------------------     ---------
P01 MICKEY MOUSE LAMP                      29.95
P02 NO 2 PENCILS - 20 PACK                  1.99
P03 COFFEE MUG                              6.95
P04 FAR SIDE CALENDAR                       10.5
P05 NATURE CALENDAR                        12.99
P06 SQL COMMAND REFERENCE                  29.99
P07 BLACK LEATHER BRIEFCASE                99.99

7 rows selected.
```

ANALYSIS The value products was substituted in the place of &TBL in this "interactive query."

DEFINE

You can use DEFINE to assign values to variables within an SQL script file. If you define your variables within the script, users are not prompted to enter a value for the variable at runtime, as they are if you use the &. The next example issues the same SELECT statement as the preceding example, but this time the value of TBL is defined within the script.

```
SQL> define TBL=products
SQL> select *
  2  from &TBL;

old   2: from &TBL
new   2: from products

PRO PRODUCT_NAME                       UNIT_COST
--- ------------------------------     ---------
P01 MICKEY MOUSE LAMP                      29.95
P02 NO 2 PENCILS - 20 PACK                  1.99
P03 COFFEE MUG                              6.95
P04 FAR SIDE CALENDAR                       10.5
P05 NATURE CALENDAR                        12.99
P06 SQL COMMAND REFERENCE                  29.99
P07 BLACK LEATHER BRIEFCASE                99.99

7 rows selected.
```

20

ANALYSIS Both queries achieved the same result. The next section describes another way to prompt users for script parameters.

ACCEPT

ACCEPT enables the user to enter a value to fill a variable at script runtime. ACCEPT does the same thing as the & with no DEFINE but is a little more controlled. ACCEPT also allows you to issue user-friendly prompts.

The next example starts by clearing the buffer:

 SQL> **clear buffer**

 buffer cleared

Then it uses an INPUT command to enter the new SQL statement into the buffer. If you started to type your statement without issuing the INPUT command first, you would be prompted to enter the value for newtitle first. Alternatively, you could go straight into a new file and write your statement.

```
SQL> input
  1  accept newtitle prompt 'Enter Title for Report: '
  2  ttitle center newtitle
  3  select *
  4  from products
  5
SQL> save prod
```

OUTPUT
```
File "prod.sql" already exists.
Use another name or "SAVE filename REPLACE".
```

ANALYSIS Whoops…the file prod.sql already exists. Let's say that you need the old prod.sql and do not care to overwrite it. You will have to use the replace option to save the statement in the buffer to prod.sql. Notice the use of PROMPT in the preceding statement. PROMPT displays text to the screen that tells the user exactly what to enter.

INPUT SQL> **save prod replace**

OUTPUT Wrote file prod

Now you can use the START command to execute the file.

INPUT
```
SQL> start prod

Enter Title for Report: A LIST OF PRODUCTS
```

OUTPUT
```
                        A LIST OF PRODUCTS

PRO PRODUCT_NAME                    UNIT_COST
--- ------------------------------ ---------
P01 MICKEY MOUSE LAMP                  29.95
P02 NO 2 PENCILS - 20 PACK              1.99
```

```
P03 COFFEE MUG                          6.95
P04 FAR SIDE CALENDAR                   10.5
P05 NATURE CALENDAR                     12.99
P06 SQL COMMAND REFERENCE               29.99
P07 BLACK LEATHER BRIEFCASE             99.99

7 rows selected.
```

ANALYSIS The text that you entered becomes the current title of the report.

The next example shows how you can use substitution variables anywhere in a statement:

INPUT
```
SQL> input
  1  accept prod_id prompt 'Enter PRODUCT ID to Search for: '
  2  select *
  3  from products
  4  where product_id = '&prod_id'
  5
SQL> save prod1
```

OUTPUT Created file prod1

INPUT
```
SQL> start prod1

Enter PRODUCT ID to Search for: P01
```

OUTPUT
```
old   3: where product_id = '&prod_id'
new   3: where product_id = 'P01'

                  A LIST OF PRODUCTS

PRO PRODUCT_NAME                    UNIT_COST
--- ------------------------------ ----------
P01 MICKEY MOUSE LAMP                  29.95
```

ANALYSIS You can use variables to meet many needs—for example, to name the file to which to spool your output or to specify an expression in the ORDER BY clause. One of the ways to use substitution variables is to enter reporting dates in the WHERE clause for transactional quality assurance reports. If your query is designed to retrieve information on one particular individual at a time, you may want to add a substitution variable to be compared with the SSN column of a table.

NEW_VALUE

The NEW_VALUE command passes the value of a selected column into an undefined variable of your choice. The syntax is as follows:

SYNTAX
```
COL[UMN] column_name NEW_VALUE new_name
```

You call the values of variables by using the & character; for example:

&new_name

The COLUMN command must be used with NEW_VALUE.

Notice how the & and COLUMN command are used together in the next SQL*Plus file. The GET command gets the file.

INPUT

```
SQL> get prod1
```

OUTPUT

```
line 5 truncated.
  1   ttitle left 'Report for Product:   &prod_title' skip 2
  2   col product_name new_value prod_title
  3   select product_name, unit_cost
  4   from products
  5*  where product_name = 'COFFEE MUG'
```

INPUT

```
SQL> @prod1
```

OUTPUT

```
Report for Product:   COFFEE MUG

PRODUCT_NAME                      UNIT_COST
-------------------------------- ----------
COFFEE MUG                             6.95
```

ANALYSIS

The value for the column PRODUCT_NAME was passed into the variable prod_title by means of new_value. The value of the variable prod_title was then called in the TTITLE.

For more information on variables in SQL, see Day 18, "PL/SQL: An Introduction," and Day 19.

The DUAL Table

The DUAL table is a dummy table that exists in every Oracle database. This table is composed of one column called DUMMY whose only row of data is the value X. The DUAL table is available to all database users and can be used for general purposes, such as performing arithmetic (where it can serve as a calculator) or manipulating the format of the SYSDATE.

INPUT

```
SQL> desc dual;
```

OUTPUT

```
Name                             Null?    Type
-------------------------------- -------- ----
DUMMY                                     VARCHAR2(1)
```

INPUT
```
SQL> select *
  2  from dual;
```

OUTPUT
```
D
-
X
```

Take a look at a couple of examples using the DUAL table:

INPUT
```
SQL> select sysdate
  2  from dual;
```

OUTPUT
```
SYSDATE
---------
08-MAY-97
```

INPUT
```
SQL> select 2 * 2
  2  from dual;
```

OUTPUT
```
       2*2
  ---------
          4
```

Pretty simple. The first statement selected SYSDATE from the DUAL table and got today's date. The second example shows how to multiply in the DUAL table. Our answer for 2 * 2 is 4.

The DECODE Function

The DECODE function is one of the most powerful commands in SQL*Plus—and perhaps the most powerful. The standard language of SQL lacks procedural functions that are contained in languages such as COBOL and C.

The DECODE statement is similar to an IF...THEN statement in a procedural programming language. Where flexibility is required for complex reporting needs, DECODE is often able to fill the gap between SQL and the functions of a procedural language.

SYNTAX
```
DECODE(column1, value1, output1, value2, output2, output3)
```

The syntax example performs the DECODE function on column1. If column1 has a value of value1, then display output1 instead of the column's current value. If column1 has a value of value2, then display output2 instead of the column's current value. If column1 has a value of anything other than value1 or value2, then display output3 instead of the column's current value.

How about some examples? First, perform a simple select on a new table:

INPUT
```
SQL> select * from states;
```

20

OUTPUT

```
ST
--
IN
FL
KY
IL
OH
CA
NY

7 rows selected.
```

Now use the DECODE command:

INPUT

```
SQL> select decode(state,'IN','INDIANA','OTHER') state
  2  from states;
```

OUTPUT

```
STATE
------
INDIANA
OTHER
OTHER
OTHER
OTHER
OTHER
OTHER

7 rows selected.
```

ANALYSIS   Only one row met the condition where the value of state was IN, so only that one row was displayed as INDIANA. The other states took the default and therefore were displayed as OTHER.

The next example provides output strings for each value in the table. Just in case your table has states that are not in your DECODE list, you should still enter a default value of 'OTHER'.

INPUT

```
SQL> select decode(state,'IN','INDIANA',
  2                       'FL','FLORIDA',
  3                       'KY','KENTUCKY',
  4                       'IL','ILLINOIS',
  5                       'OH','OHIO',
  6                       'CA','CALIFORNIA',
  7                       'NY','NEW YORK','OTHER')
  8  from states;
```

OUTPUT

```
DECODE(STATE)
----------
INDIANA
FLORIDA
KENTUCKY
ILLINOIS
OHIO
CALIFORNIA
NEW YORK

7 rows selected.
```

20

That was too easy. The next example introduces the PAY table. This table shows more of the power that is contained within DECODE.

INPUT

```
SQL> col hour_rate hea "HOURLY¦RATE" for 99.00
SQL> col date_last_raise hea "LAST¦RAISE"
SQL> select name, hour_rate, date_last_raise
  2  from pay;
```

OUTPUT

```
                     HOURLY LAST
NAME                   RATE RAISE
-------------------- ------ ---------
JOHN                  12.60 01-JAN-96
JEFF                   8.50 17-MAR-97
RON                    9.35 01-OCT-96
RYAN                   7.00 15-MAY-96
BRYAN                 11.00 01-JUN-96
MARY                  17.50 01-JAN-96
ELAINE                14.20 01-FEB-97

7 rows selected.
```

Are you ready? It is time to give every individual in the PAY table a pay raise. If the year of an individual's last raise is 1996, calculate a 10 percent raise. If the year of the individual's last raise is 1997, calculate a 20 percent raise. In addition, display the percent raise for each individual in either situation.

INPUT

```
SQL> col new_pay hea 'NEW PAY' for 99.00
SQL> col hour_rate hea 'HOURLY¦RATE' for 99.00
SQL> col date_last_raise hea 'LAST¦RAISE'
SQL> select name, hour_rate, date_last_raise,
  2         decode(substr(date_last_raise,8,2),'96',hour_rate * 1.2,
  3                                             '97',hour_rate * 1.1)
     ►new_pay,
  4         decode(substr(date_last_raise,8,2),'96','20%',
  5                                             '97','10%',null) increase
  6  from pay;
```

OUTPUT

```
                     HOURLY LAST
NAME                   RATE RAISE     NEW PAY INC
-------------------- ------ --------- ------- ---
JOHN                  12.60 01-JAN-96   15.12 20%
JEFF                   8.50 17-MAR-97    9.35 10%
RON                    9.35 01-OCT-96   11.22 20%
RYAN                   7.00 15-MAY-96    8.40 20%
BRYAN                 11.00 01-JUN-96   13.20 20%
MARY                  17.50 01-JAN-96   21.00 20%
ELAINE                14.20 01-FEB-97   15.62 10%

7 rows selected.
```

ANALYSIS

According to the output, everyone will be receiving a 20 percent pay increase except Jeff and Elaine, who have already received one raise this year.

DATE **Conversions**

If you want to add a touch of class to the way dates are displayed, then you can use the TO_CHAR function to change the "date picture." This example starts by obtaining today's date:

INPUT

```
SQL> select sysdate
  2  from dual;
```

OUTPUT

```
SYSDATE
---------
08-MAY-97
```

When converting a date to a character string, you use the TO_CHAR function with the following syntax:

SYNTAX

```
TO_CHAR(sysdate,'date picture')
```

date picture is how you want the date to look. Some of the most common parts of the date picture are as follows:

Month	The current month spelled out.
Mon	The current month abbreviated.
Day	The current day of the week.
mm	The number of the current month.
yy	The last two numbers of the current year.
dd	The current day of the month.
yyyy	The current year.
ddd	The current day of the year since January 1.
hh	The current hour of the day.
mi	The current minute of the hour.
ss	The current seconds of the minute.
a.m.	Displays a.m. or p.m.

The date picture may also contain commas and literal strings as long as the string is enclosed by double quotation marks "".

INPUT

```
SQL> col today for a20
SQL> select to_char(sysdate,'Mon dd, yyyy') today
  2  from dual;
```

OUTPUT

```
TODAY
--------------------
May 08, 1997
```

ANALYSIS Notice how we used the COLUMN command on the alias today.

INPUT

```
SQL> col today hea 'TODAYs JULIAN DATE' for a20
SQL> select to_char(sysdate,'ddd') today
  2  from dual;
```

OUTPUT

```
TODAYs JULIAN DATE
--------------------
128
```

ANALYSIS Some companies prefer to express the Julian date with the two-digit year preceding the three-digit day. Your date picture could also look like this: 'yyddd'.

Assume that you wrote a little script and saved it as day. The next example gets the file, looks at it, and executes it to retrieve various pieces of converted date information.

INPUT

```
SQL> get day
```

OUTPUT

```
line 10 truncated.
  1  set echo on
  2  col day for a10
  3  col today for a25
  4  col year for a25
  5  col time for a15
  6  select to_char(sysdate,'Day') day,
  7         to_char(sysdate,'Mon dd, yyyy') today,
  8         to_char(sysdate,'Year') year,
  9         to_char(sysdate,'hh:mi:ss a.m.') time
 10* from dual
```

Now you can run the script:

INPUT

```
SQL> @day
```

OUTPUT

```
SQL> set echo on
SQL> col day for a10
SQL> col today for a25
SQL> col year for a25
SQL> col time for a15
SQL> select to_char(sysdate,'Day') day,
  2         to_char(sysdate,'Mon dd, yyyy') today,
  3         to_char(sysdate,'Year') year,
  4         to_char(sysdate,'hh:mi:ss a.m.') time
  5  from dual;

DAY        TODAY                     YEAR                       TIME
---------- ------------------------- -------------------------- ------------
Thursday   May 08, 1997              Nineteen Ninety-Seven      04:10:43 p.m.
```

ANALYSIS In this example the entire statement was shown before it ran because ECHO was set to ON. In addition, sysdate was broken into four columns and the date was converted into four formats.

20

The TO_DATE function enables you to convert text into a date format. The syntax is basically the same as TO_CHAR.

SYNTAX

TO_DATE(expression,'date_picture')

Try a couple of examples:

INPUT
```
SQL> select to_date('19970501','yyyymmdd') "NEW DATE"
  2  from dual;
```

OUTPUT
```
NEW DATE
---------
01-MAY-97
```

INPUT
```
SQL> select to_date('05/01/97','mm"/"dd"/"yy') "NEW DATE"
  2  from dual;
```

OUTPUT
```
NEW DATE
---------
01-MAY-97
```

ANALYSIS Notice the use of double quotation marks to represent a literal string.

Running a Series of SQL Files

An SQL script file can include anything that you can type into the SQL buffer at the SQL> prompt, even commands that execute another SQL script. Yes, you can start an SQL script from within another SQL script. Figure 20.4 shows a script file that was created using the EDIT command. The file contains multiple SQL statements as well as commands to run other SQL scripts.

INPUT
```
SQL> edit main.sql
```

OUTPUT
```
SQL> @main
```

ANALYSIS By starting main.sql, you will be executing each SQL command that is contained within the script. Query1 through query5 will also be executed, in that order, as shown in Figure 20.4.

Figure 20.4.

*Running SQL scripts
from within an SQL
script.*

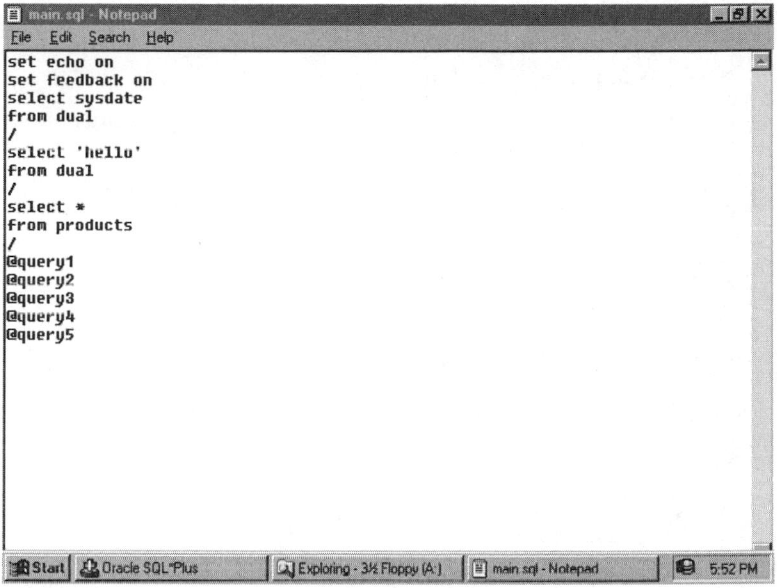

```
🗎 main.sql - Notepad                                              _ 🗗 ✕
File  Edit  Search  Help
set echo on
set feedback on
select sysdate
from dual
/
select 'hello'
from dual
/
select *
from products
/
@query1
@query2
@query3
@query4
@query5




🏁 Start │ 🗄 Oracle SQL*Plus │ 🔍 Exploring - 3½ Floppy (A:) │ 🗎 main.sql - Notepad │ 🖳 5:52 PM
```

Adding Comments to Your SQL Script

SQL*Plus gives you three ways to place comments in your file:

- ☐ -- places a comment on one line at a time.
- ☐ REMARK also places a comment on one line at a time.
- ☐ /* */ places a comment(s) on one or more lines.

Study the following example:

INPUT
```
SQL> input
  1  REMARK this is a comment
  2  -- this is a comment too
  3  REM
  4  -- SET COMMANDS
  5  set echo on
  6  set feedback on
  7  -- SQL STATEMENT
  8  select *
  9  from products
 10
SQL>
```

To see how comments look in an SQL script file, type the following:

```
SQL> edit query10
```

20

Advanced Reports

Now let's have some fun. By taking the concepts that you have learned today, as well as what you learned earlier, you can now create some fancy reports. Suppose that you have a script named report1.sql. Start it, sit back, and observe.

INPUT

```
SQL> @report1
```

OUTPUT

```
SQL> set echo on
SQL> set pagesize 50
SQL> set feedback off
SQL> set newpage 0
SQL> col product_name hea 'PRODUCT¦NAME' for a20 trunc
SQL> col unit_cost hea 'UNIT¦COST' for $99.99
SQL> col product_qty hea 'QTY' for 999
SQL> col total for $99,999.99
SQL> spool report
SQL> compute sum of total on customer
SQL> compute sum of total on report
SQL> break on report on customer skip 1
SQL> select o.customer, p.product_name, p.unit_cost,
  2          o.product_qty, (p.unit_cost * o.product_qty) total
  3  from orders o,
  4          products p
  5  where o.product_id = p.product_id
  6  order by customer
  7  /
```

CUSTOMER	PRODUCT NAME	UNIT COST	QTY	TOTAL
JONES and SONS	MICKEY MOUSE LAMP	$29.95	50	$1,497.50
	NO 2 PENCILS - 20 PA	$1.99	10	$19.90
	COFFEE MUG	$6.95	10	$69.50
******************************				
sum				$1,586.90
PARAKEET CONSULTING GROUP	MICKEY MOUSE LAMP	$29.95	5	$149.75
	NO 2 PENCILS - 20 PA	$1.99	15	$29.85
	SQL COMMAND REFERENC	$29.99	10	$299.90
	BLACK LEATHER BRIEFC	$99.99	1	$99.99
	FAR SIDE CALENDAR	$10.50	22	$231.00
******************************				
sum				$810.49

```
PLEWSKY MOBILE CARWASH     MICKEY MOUSE LAMP    $29.95    1       $29.95
                           BLACK LEATHER BRIEFC $99.99    5      $499.95
                           BLACK LEATHER BRIEFC $99.99    1       $99.99
                           NO 2 PENCILS - 20 PA  $1.99   10       $19.90
                           NO 2 PENCILS - 20 PA  $1.99   10       $19.90
******************************                          ----------
sum                                                       $669.69


                                                       ----------
sum                                                     $3,067.08
SQL> Input truncated to 9 characters
spool off
```

ANALYSIS Several things are taking place in this script. If you look at the actual SQL statement, you can see that it is selecting a data from two tables and performing an arithmetic function as well. The statement joins the two tables in the WHERE clause and is ordered by the customer's name. Those are the basics. In addition, SQL*Plus commands format the data the way we want to see it. These commands break the report into groups, making computations on each group and making a computation on the report as a whole.

Summary

Day 20 explains Oracle's extension to the standard language of SQL. These commands are only a fraction of what is available to you in SQL*Plus. If you use Oracle's products, check your database documentation, take the knowledge that you have learned here, and explore the endless possibilities that lie before you. You will find that you can accomplish almost any reporting task using SQL*Plus rather than by resorting to a procedural programming language. If you are not using Oracle products, use what you have learned today to improve the ways you retrieve data in your implementation. Most major implementations have extensions, or enhancements, to the accepted standard language of SQL.

Q&A

Q Why should I spend valuable time learning SQL*Plus when I can achieve the same results using straight SQL?

A If your requirements for reports are simple, straight SQL is fine. But you can reduce the time you spend on reports by using SQL*Plus. And you can be sure that the person who needs your reports will always want more information.

Q How can I select SYSDATE from the DUAL table if it is not a column?

A You can select SYSDATE from DUAL or any other valid table because SYSDATE is a pseudocolumn.

20

Q **When using the DECODE command, can I use a DECODE within another DECODE?**

A Yes, you can DECODE within a DECODE. In SQL you can perform functions on other functions to achieve the desired results.

Workshop

The Workshop provides quiz questions to help solidify your understanding of the material covered, as well as exercises to provide you with experience in using what you have learned. Try to answer the quiz and exercise questions before checking the answers in Appendix F, "Answers to Quizzes and Exercises."

Quiz

1. Which commands can modify your preferences for an SQL session?
2. Can your SQL script prompt a user for a parameter and execute the SQL statement using the entered parameter?
3. If you are creating a summarized report on entries in a CUSTOMER table, how would you group your data for your report?
4. Are there limitations to what you can have in your LOGIN.SQL file?
5. True or False: The DECODE function is the equivalent of a loop in a procedural programming language.
6. True or False: If you spool the output of your query to an existing file, your output will be appended to that file.

Exercises

1. Using the PRODUCTS table at the beginning of Day 20, write a query that will select all data and compute a count of the records returned on the report without using the SET FEEDBACK ON command.

2. Suppose today is Monday, May 12, 1998. Write a query that will produce the following output:

   `Today is Monday, May 12 1998`

3. Use the following SQL statement for this Exercise:

   ```
   1  select *
   2  from orders
   3  where customer_id = '001'
   4* order by customer_id;
   ```

   Without retyping the statement in the SQL buffer, change the table in the FROM clause to the CUSTOMER table.

   Now append DESC to the ORDER BY clause.

Week 3

Day 21

Common SQL Mistakes/Errors and Resolutions

Objectives

Welcome to Day 21. By the end of today, you will have become familiar with the following:

- [ ] Several typical errors and their resolutions
- [ ] Common logical shortcomings of SQL users
- [ ] Ways to prevent daily setbacks caused by errors

Introduction

Today you will see various common errors that everyone—from novice to pro—makes when using SQL. You will never be able to avoid all errors and/or mistakes, but being familiar with a wide range of errors will help you resolve them in as short a time as possible.

NOTE

We used Personal Oracle7 for our examples. Your particular implementation will be very similar in the type of error, but could differ in the numbering or naming of the error. We ran our SQL statements using SQL*PLUS and set ECHO and FEEDBACK to on to see the statement.

Keep in mind that some mistakes will actually yield error messages, whereas others may just be inadequacies in logic that will inevitably cause more significant errors or problems down the road. With a strict sense of attention to detail, you can avoid most problems, although you will always find yourself stumbling upon errors.

Common Errors

This section describes many common errors that you will receive while executing all types of SQL statements. Most are simple and make you want to kick yourself on the hind side, whereas other seemingly obvious errors are misleading.

Table or View Does Not Exist

When you receive an error stating that the table you are trying to access does not exist, it seems obvious; for example:

INPUT

```
SQL> @tables.sql
```

OUTPUT

```
SQL> spool tables.lst
SQL> set echo on
SQL> set feedback on
SQL> set pagesize 1000
SQL> select owner|| '.' || table_name
  2  from sys.dba_table
  3  where owner = 'SYSTEM'
  4  order by table_name
  5  /
       from sys.dba_table
       *
ERROR at line 2:
ORA-00942: table or view does not exist
 SQL> spool off
 SQL>
```

21

ANALYSIS Notice the asterisk below the word `table`. The correct table name is `sys.dba_tables`. An *s* was omitted from the table name.

But what if you know the table exists and you still receive this error? Sometimes when you receive this error, the table does in fact exist, but there may be a security problem—that is, the table exists, but you do not have access to it. This error can also be the database server's way of saying nicely, "You don't have permission to access this table!"

TIP Before you allow panic to set in, immediately verify whether or not the table exists using a DBA account, if available, or the schema account. You will often find that the table does exist and that the user lacks the appropriate privileges to access it.

Invalid Username or Password

INPUT
```
   SQL*Plus: Release 3.2.3.0.0 - on Sat May 10 11:15:35 1997
Copyright (c) Oracle Corporation 1979, 1994.  All rights reserved.
Enter user-name: rplew
Enter password:
```

OUTPUT
```
ERROR: ORA-01017: invalid username/password; logon denied
Enter user-name:
```

ANALYSIS This error was caused either by entering the incorrect username or the incorrect password. Try again. If unsuccessful, have your password reset. If you are sure that you typed in the correct username and password, then make sure that you are attempting to connect to the correct database if you have access to more than one database.

FROM **Keyword Not Specified**

INPUT
```
SQL> @tblspc.sql
```

OUTPUT
```
SQL> spool tblspc.lst
SQL> set echo on
SQL> set feedback on
SQL> set pagesize 1000
SQL> select substr(tablespace_name,1,15) a,
  2          substrfile_name, 1,45) c, bytes
  3  from sys.dba_data_files
  4  order by tablespace_name;
     substrfile_name, 1,45) c, bytes
        *
ERROR at line 2:
ORA-00923: FROM keyword not found where expected
SQL> spool off
SQL>
```

21

ANALYSIS This error can be misleading. The keyword FROM is there, but you are missing a left parenthesis between substr and file_name on line 2. This error can also be caused by a missing comma between column names in the SELECT statement. If a column in the SELECT statement is not followed by a comma, the query processor automatically looks for the FROM keyword. The previous statement has been corrected as follows:

```
SQL> select substr(tablespace_name,1,15) a,
  2          substr(file_name,1,45) c, bytes
  3  from sys.dba_data_files
  4  order by tablespace_name;
```

Group Function Is Not Allowed Here

  INPUT

```
SQL> select count(last_name), first_name, phone_number
  2  from employee_tbl
  3  group by count(last_name), first_name, phone_number
  4  /
```

OUTPUT

```
    group by count(last_name), first_name, phone_number
                   *
ERROR at line 3:
ORA-00934: group function is not allowed here
SQL>
```

ANALYSIS As with any group function, COUNT may not be used in the GROUP BY clause. You can list only column and nongroup functions, such as SUBSTR, in the GROUP BY clause.

 TIP

> COUNT is a function that is being performed on groups in the query.

The previous statement has been corrected using the proper syntax:

```
SQL> select count(last_name), first_name, phone_number
  2  from employee_tbl
  3  group by last_name, first_name, phone_number;
```

Invalid Column Name

INPUT SQL> @tables.sql

OUTPUT
```
SQL> spool tables.lst
SQL> set echo on
SQL> set feedback on
SQL> set pagesize 1000
SQL> select owner¦¦ '.' ¦¦ tablename
  2  from sys.dba_tables
  3  where owner = 'SYSTEM'
  4  order by table_name
  5  /
    select owner¦¦ '.' ¦¦ tablename
                      *
```

```
ERROR at line 1:
ORA-00904: invalid column name
SQL> spool off
SQL>
```

ANALYSIS In line 1 the column `tablename` is incorrect. The correct column name is `table_name`. The underscore was omitted. To see the correct columns, use the `DESCRIBE` command. This error can also occur when trying to qualify a column in the `SELECT` statement by the wrong table name.

Missing Keyword

INPUT
```
SQL> create view emp_view
  2  select * from employee_tbl
  3  /
```

OUTPUT
```
      select * from employee_tbl
             *
ERROR at line 2:
ORA-00905: missing keyword
SQL>
```

ANALYSIS Here the syntax is incorrect. This error occurs when you omit a mandatory word with any given command syntax. If you are using an optional part of the command, that option may require a certain keyword. The missing keyword in this example is **as**. The statement should look like this:

```
SQL> create view emp_view as
  2  select * from employee_tbl
  3  /
```

Missing Left Parenthesis

INPUT   `SQL> @insert.sql`

OUTPUT
```
SQL> insert into people_tbl values
  2  '303785523', 'SMITH', 'JOHN', 'JAY', 'MALE', '10-JAN-50')
  3  /
     '303785523', 'SMITH', 'JOHN', 'JAY', 'MALE', '10-JAN-50')
     *
ERROR at line 2:
ORA-00906: missing left parenthesis
SQL>
```

ANALYSIS On line 2 a parenthesis does not appear before the Social Security number. The correct syntax should look like this:

```
SQL> insert into people_tbl values
  2  ('303785523', 'SMITH', 'JOHN', 'JAY', 'MALE', '10-JAN-50')
  3  /
```

21

Missing Right Parenthesis

INPUT

```
SQL> @tblspc.sql
```

OUTPUT

```
SQL> spool tblspc.lst
SQL> set echo on
SQL> set feedback on
SQL> set pagesize 1000
SQL> select substr(tablespace_name,1,15 a,
  2         substr(file_name, 1,45) c, bytes
  3  from sys.dba_data_files
  4  order by tablespace_name;
     select substr(tablespace_name,1,15 a,
                                        *
ERROR at line 1:
ORA-00907: missing right parenthesis
SQL> spool off
SQL>
```

ANALYSIS On line 1 the right parenthesis is missing from the substr. The correct syntax looks like this:

```
SQL> select substr(tablespace_name,1,15) a,
  2         substr(file_name,1,45) c, bytes
  3  from sys.dba_data_files
  4  order by tablespace_name;
```

Missing Comma

INPUT

```
SQL> @ezinsert.sql
```

OUTPUT

```
SQL> spool ezinsert.lst
SQL> set echo on
SQL> set feedback on
SQL> insert into office_tbl values
  2  ('303785523' 'SMITH', 'OFFICE OF THE STATE OF INDIANA, ADJUTANT
     ➥GENERAL')
  3  /
     ('303785523' 'SMITH', 'OFFICE OF THE STATE OF INDIANA, ADJUTANT
     ➥GENERAL')
                  *
ERROR at line 2:
ORA-00917: missing comma
SQL> spool off
SQL>
```

ANALYSIS On line 2 a comma is missing between the Social Security number and SMITH.

Column Ambiguously Defined

 INPUT

```
SQL> @employee_tbl
```

OUTPUT

```
SQL> spool employee.lst
SQL> set echo on
SQL> set feedback on
SQL> select p.ssn, name, e.address, e.phone
  2  from employee_tbl e,
  3  payroll_tbl p
  4  where e.ssn =p.ssn;
     select p.ssn, name, e.address, e.phone
            *
ERROR at line 1:
ORA-00918: column ambigously defined
SQL> spool off
SQL>
```

ANALYSIS On line 1 the column name has not been defined. The tables have been given aliases of e and p. Decide which table to pull the name from and define it with the table alias.

SQL Command Not Properly Ended

INPUT

```
SQL> create view emp_tbl as
  2  select * from employee_tbl
  3  order by name
  4  /
```

OUTPUT

```
     order by name
     *
ERROR at line 3:
ORA-00933: SQL command not properly ended
SQL>
```

ANALYSIS Why is the command not properly ended? You know you can use a / to end an SQL statement. Another fooler. An ORDER BY clause cannot be used in a CREATE VIEW statement. Use a GROUP BY instead. Here the query processor is looking for a terminator (semicolon or forward slash) before the ORDER BY clause because the processor assumes the ORDER BY is not part of the CREATE VIEW statement. Because the terminator is not found before the ORDER BY, this error is returned instead of an error pointing to the ORDER BY.

Missing Expression

 INPUT

```
SQL> @tables.sql
```

OUTPUT

```
SQL> spool tables.lst
SQL> set echo on
SQL> set feedback on
SQL> set pagesize 1000
SQL> select owner|| '.' || table,
  2  from sys.dba_tables
  3  where owner = 'SYSTEM'
  4  order by table_name
```

21

```
   5  /
      from sys.dba_tables
      *
ERROR at line 2:
ORA-00936: missing expression
SQL> spool off
SQL>
```

Notice the comma after table on the first line; therefore, the query processor is looking for another column in the SELECT clause. At this point, the processor is not expecting the FROM clause.

Not Enough Arguments for Function

SQL> **@tblspc.sql**

OUTPUT

```
SQL> spool tblspc.lst
SQL> set echo on
SQL> set feedback on
SQL> set pagesize 1000
SQL> select substr(tablespace_name,1,15) a,
   2         decode(substr(file_name,1,45)) c, bytes
   3  from sys.dba_data_files
   4  order by tablespace_name;
      decode(substr(file_name,1,45)) c, bytes
            *
ERROR at line 2:
ORA-00938: not enough arguments for function
SQL> spool off
SQL>
```

ANALYSIS

There are not enough arguments for the DECODE function. Check your implementation for the proper syntax.

Not Enough Values

INPUT

SQL> **@ezinsert.sql**

OUTPUT

```
SQL> spool ezinsert.lst
SQL> set echo on
SQL> set feedback on
SQL> insert into employee_tbl values
   2  ('303785523', 'SMITH', 'JOHN', 'JAY', 'MALE')
   3  /
      insert into employee_tbl values
                  *
ERROR at line 1:
ORA-00947: not enough values
SQL> spool off
SQL>
```

ANALYSIS A column value is missing. Perform a DESCRIBE command on the table to find the missing column. You can insert the specified data only if you list the columns that are to be inserted into, as shown in the next example:

INPUT
```
SQL> spool ezinsert.lst
SQL> set echo on
SQL> set feedback on
SQL> insert into employee_tbl (ssn, last_name, first_name, mid_name,
     ➥sex)
  2  values ('303785523', 'SMITH', 'JOHN', 'JAY', 'MALE')
  3  /
```

Integrity Constraint Violated—Parent Key Not Found

INPUT
```
SQL> insert into payroll_tbl values
  2  ('111111111', 'SMITH', 'JOHN')
  3  /
```

OUTPUT
```
    insert into payroll_tbl values
                *
ERROR at line 1:
ORA-02291: integrity constraint (employee_cons) violated - parent
key not found
SQL>
```

ANALYSIS This error was caused by attempting to insert data into a table without the data existing in the parent table. Check the parent table for correct data. If missing, then you must insert the data into the parent table before attempting to insert data into the child table.

Oracle Not Available

INPUT
```
(sun_su3)/home> sqlplus
SQL*Plus: Release 3.2.3.0.0 - Production on Sat May 10 11:19:50 1997
Copyright (c) Oracle Corporation 1979, 1994.  All rights reserved.
Enter user-name: rplew
Enter password:
```

OUTPUT
```
ERROR: ORA-01034: ORACLE not available
ORA-07318: smsget: open error when opening sgadef.dbf file.
```

ANALYSIS You were trying to sign on to SQL*PLUS. The database is probably down. Check status of the database. Also, make sure that you are trying to connect to the correct database if you have access to multiple databases.

Inserted Value Too Large for Column

INPUT
```
SQL> @ezinsert.sql
```

21

OUTPUT

```
SQL> spool ezinsert.lst
SQL> set echo on
SQL> set feedback on
SQL> insert into office_tbl values
  2  ('303785523', 'SMITH', 'OFFICE OF THE STATE OF INDIANA, ADJUTANT
     ➥GENERAL')
  3  /
     insert into office_tbl values
              *
ERROR at line 1:
ORA-01401: inserted value too large for column
SQL> spool off
SQL>
```

ANALYSIS One of the values being inserted is too large for the column. Use the DESCRIBE command on the table for the correct data length. If necessary, you can perform an ALTER TABLE command on the table to expand the column width.

TNS:listener Could Not Resolve SID Given in Connect Descriptor

INPUT

```
SQLDBA> connect rplew/xxxx@database1
```

OUTPUT

```
ORA-12505: TNS:listener could not resolve SID given in connect
➥descriptor
SQLDBA> disconnect
Disconnected.
SQLDBA>
```

ANALYSIS This error is very common in Oracle databases. The listener referred to in the preceding error is the process that allows requests from a client to communicate with the database on a remote server. Here you were attempting to connect to the database. Either the incorrect database name was typed in or the listener is down. Check the database name and try again. If unsuccessful, notify the database administrator of the problem.

Insufficient Privileges During Grants

INPUT

```
SQL> grant select on people_tbl to ron;
```

OUTPUT

```
grant select on people_tbl to ron
                                 *
ERROR at line 1:
ORA-01749: you may not GRANT/REVOKE privileges to/from yourself
SQL>
```

INPUT

```
SQL> grant select on demo.employee to ron;
```

OUTPUT

```
grant select on demo.employee to ron
                        *
ERROR at line 1:
ORA-01031: insufficient privileges
SQL>
```

21

This error occurs if you are trying to grant privileges on another user's table and you do not have the proper privilege to do so. You must own the table to be able to grant privileges on the table to other users. In Oracle you may be granted a privilege with the Admin option, which means that you can grant the specified privilege on another user's table to another user. Check your implementation for the particular privileges you need to grant a privilege.

Escape Character in Your Statement—Invalid Character

Escape characters are very frustrating when trying to debug a broken SQL statement. This situation can occur if you use the backspace key while you are entering your SQL statement in the buffer or a file. Sometimes the backspace key puts an invalid character in the statement depending upon how your keys are mapped, even though you might not be able see the character.

Cannot Create Operating System File

This error has a number of causes. The most common causes are that the associated disk is full or incorrect permissions have been set on the file system. If the disk is full, you must remove unwanted files. If permissions are incorrect, change them to the correct settings. This error is more of an operating system error, so you may need to get advice from your system administrator.

Common Logical Mistakes

So far today we have covered faults in SQL statements that generate actual error messages. Most of these errors are obvious, and their resolutions leave little to the imagination. The next few mistakes are more (or less) logical, and they may cause problems later—if not immediately.

Using Reserved Words in Your SQL statement

```
SQL> select sysdate DATE
  2  from dual;
```

```
select sysdate DATE
              *
ERROR at line 1:
ORA-00923: FROM keyword not found where expected
```

In this example the query processor is not expecting the word DATE because it is a reserved word. There is no comma after the pseudocolumn SYSDATE; therefore, the next element expected is the FROM clause.

21

```
SQL> select sysdate "DATE"      ·
  2  from dual;
```

```
DATE
--------
15-MAY-97
```

ANALYSIS Notice how the reserved word problem is alleviated by enclosing the word DATE with double quotation marks. Double quotation marks allow you to display the literal string DATE as a column alias.

> **NOTE**   Be sure to check your specific database documentation to get a list of reserved words, as these reserved words will vary between different implementations.

You may or may not have to use double quotation marks when naming a column alias. In the following example you do not have to use double quotation marks because TODAY is not a reserved word. To be sure, check your specific implementation.

```
SQL> select sysdate TODAY
  2  from dual;
```

```
TODAY
--------
15-MAY-97
SQL>
```

The Use of DISTINCT When Selecting Multiple Columns

```
SQL> select distinct(city), distinct(zip)
  2  from address_tbl;
```

```
select distinct(city), distinct(zip)
                               *
ERROR at line 1:
ORA-00936: missing expression
SQL>
```

ANALYSIS A city can have more than one ZIP code. As a rule, you should use the DISTINCT command on only one selected column.

Dropping an Unqualified Table

Whenever dropping a table, *always* use the owner or schema. You can have duplicate table names in the database. If you don't use the owner/schema name, then the wrong table could be dropped.

The *risky* syntax for dropping a table:

```
SQL> drop table people_tbl;
```

The next statement is much safer because it specifies the owner of the table you want to drop.

```
SQL> drop table ron.people_tbl;
```

> Qualifying the table when dropping it is always a safe practice, although sometimes this step may be unnecessary. Never issue the DROP TABLE command without first verifying the user id by which you are connected to the database.

WARNING

The Use of Public Synonyms in a Multischema Database

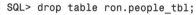

Synonyms make life easier for users; however, public synonyms open tables that you might not want all users to see. Use caution when granting public synonyms especially in a multischema environment.

The Dreaded Cartesian Product

INPUT

```
SQL> select a.ssn, p.last_n
  2  from address_tbl a,
  3       people_tbl p;
```

OUTPUT

```
SSN        LAST_NAME
---------  ---------------
303785523  SMITH
313507927  SMITH
490552223  SMITH
312667771  SMITH
420001690  SMITH
303785523  JONES
313507927  JONES
490552223  JONES
312667771  JONES
420001690  JONES
303785523  OSBORN
313507927  OSBORN
490552223  OSBORN
312667771  OSBORN
420001690  OSBORN
303785523  JONES
313507927  JONES
```

21

```
490552223 JONES
312667771 JONES
420001690 JONES
16 rows selected.
```

This error is caused when you do not join the tables in the WHERE clause. Notice how many rows were selected. Both of the preceding tables have 4 rows; therefore, we wanted 4 rows returned instead of the 16 rows that we received. Without the use of a join in the WHERE clause, each row in the first table is matched up with each row in the second. To calculate the total number of rows returned, you would multiple 4 rows by 4 rows, which yields 16. Unfortunately, most of your tables will contain more than 4 rows of data, with some possibly exceeding thousands or millions of rows. In these cases don't bother doing the multiplication, for your query is sure to become a run-away query.

Failure to Enforce Input Standards

Assuring that input standards are adhered to is commonly known as *quality assurance* (QA). Without frequent checks on the data entered by data entry clerks, you run a very high risk of hosting trash in your database. A good way to keep a handle on quality assurance is to create several QA reports using SQL, run then on a timely basis, and present their output to the data entry manager for appropriate action to correct errors or data inconsistencies.

Failure to Enforce File System Structure Conventions

You can waste a lot of time when you work with file systems that are not standardized. Check your implementation for recommended file system structures.

Allowing Large Tables to Take Default Storage Parameters

Default storage parameters will vary with implementations, but they are usually rather small. When a large or dynamic table is created and forced to take the default storage, serious table fragmentation can occur, which can severely hinder database performance. Good planning before table creation will help to avoid this. The following example uses Oracle's storage parameter options.

INPUT

```
SQL> create table test_tbl
  2  (ssn   number(9) not null,
  3   name  varchar2(30) not null)
  4   storage
  5   (initial extent 100M
  6    next extent     20M
  7    minextents 1
  8    maxextents 121
  9    pctincrease 0};
```

21

Placing Objects in the System Tablespace

The following statement shows a table being created in the SYSTEM tablespace. Although this statement will not return an error, it is likely to cause future problems.

INPUT

```
SQL> create table test_tbl
  2 (ssn   number(9) not null,
  3 name  varchar2(30) not null)
  4 tablespace SYSTEM
  5 storage
  6 (initial extent 100M
  7 next extent     20M
  8 minextents 1
  9 maxextents 121
 10 pctincrease 0};
```

The next example corrects this so-called problem:

INPUT

```
SQL> create table test_tbl
  2 (ssn   number(9) not null,
  3 name  varchar2(30) not null)
  4 tablespace linda_ts
  5 (initial extent 100M
  6  next extent     20M
  7 minextents 1
  8 maxextents 121
  9 pctincrease 0};
```

ANALYSIS In Oracle, the SYSTEM tablespace is typically used to store SYSTEM owned objects, such as those composing the data dictionary. If you happen to place dynamic tables in this tablespace and they grow, you run the risk of corrupting or at least filling up the free space, which in turn will probably cause the database to crash. In this event the database may be forced into an unrecoverable state. Always store application and user tables in separately designated tablespaces.

Failure to Compress Large Backup Files

If you do large exports and do not compress the files, you will probably run out of disk space to store the files. Always compress the export files. If you are storing archived log files on hard disk instead of on tape, these files can be and probably should be compressed to save space.

Failure to Budget System Resources

You should always budget your system resources before you create your database. The result of not budgeting system resources could be a poorly performing database. You should always know whether the database is going to be used for transactions, warehousing, or queries only. The database's function will affect the number and size of rollback segments. The number of database users will inevitably affect the sizing of the USERS and TEMP tablespaces. Do you have enough space to stripe your larger tables? Tables and indexes should be stored on separate devices to reduce disk contention. You should keep the redo logs and the data tablespaces on separate devices to alleviate disk contention. These are just a few of the issues to address when considering system resources.

21

Preventing Problems with Your Data

Your data processing center should have a backup system set up. If your database is small to medium, you can take the extra precaution of using EXPORT to ensure that your data is backed up. You should make a backup of the export file and keep it in another location for further safety. Remember that these files can be large and will require a great deal of space.

Searching for Duplicate Records in Your Database

If your database is perfectly planned, you should not have a problem with duplicate records. You can avoid duplicate records by using constraints, foreign keys, and unique indexes.

Summary

Many different types of errors—literally hundreds—can stand in the way of you and your data. Luckily, most errors/mistakes are not disasters and are easy to remedy. However, some errors/mistakes that happen are very serious. You need to be careful whenever you try to correct an error/mistake, as the error can multiply if you do not dig out the root of the problem. When you do make mistakes, as you definitely will, use them as learning experiences.

TIP

> We prefer to document everything related to database errors, especially uncommon errors that we happen to stumble upon. A file of errors is an invaluable troubleshooting reference.

NOTE

> Day 21 provides you with a sample of some of the most common Personal Oracle7 errors. For a complete list of errors and suggested resolutions, remember to refer to your database documentation.

Q&A

Q You make it sound as if every error has a remedy, so why worry?

A Yes, most errors/mistakes are easy to remedy; but suppose you drop a table in a production environment. You might need hours or days to do a database recovery. The database will be done during this time, and your company will be paying overtime to several people to complete the fix. The boss will not be happy.

Q Any advice on how to avoid errors/mistakes?

A Being human, you will never avoid all errors/mistakes; however, you can avoid many of them through training, concentration, self-confidence, good attitude, and a stress-free work environment.

Workshop

The Workshop provides quiz questions to help solidify your understanding of the material covered, as well as exercises to provide you with experience in using what you have learned. Try to answer the quiz and exercise questions before checking the answers in Appendix F, "Answers to Quizzes and Exercises."

Quiz

1. A user calls and says, "I can't sign on to the database. But everything was working fine yesterday. The error says invalid user/password. Can you help me?" What steps should you take?

2. Why should tables have storage clauses and a tablespace destination?

Exercises

1. Suppose you are logged on to the database as SYSTEM, and you wish to drop a table called HISTORY in your schema. Your regular user id is JSMITH. What is the correct syntax to drop this table?

2. Correct the following error:

```
SQL> select sysdate DATE
  2  from dual;
```

```
select sysdate DATE
              *
ERROR at line 1:
ORA-00923: FROM keyword not found where expected
```

21

WEEK

3

15

16

17

18

19

20

21

In Review

This week should have been very productive. Week 3 shows you the flexibility of SQL, explains how you can apply these features to real-world problems, and introduces some popular extensions to SQL. You should know how to use the tools that are available with your implementation of SQL to make your code more readable. By now you realize that all implementations of SQL share the same general concepts, although the syntax may differ slightly.

You should have a clear understanding of the data dictionary, what data it contains, and how to retrieve useful information from it. If you understand how to generate SQL from another SQL statement, you should be ready to fly to unlimited heights.

What about errors? You will never be immune from syntax errors or logical mistakes, but as you gain experience with SQL, you will learn how to avoid many problems. But then again, errors can be excellent learning opportunities.

APPENDIX A

Glossary of Common SQL Statements

ALTER DATABASE

```
ALTER DATABASE database_name;
```

The ALTER DATABASE command changes the size or settings of a database. Its syntax varies widely among different database systems.

ALTER USER

```
ALTER USER user
```

The ALTER USER statement changes a user's system settings such as password.

BEGIN TRANSACTION

```
1> BEGIN TRANSACTION transaction_name
2> transaction type
3> if exists
4> begin
```

The BEGIN TRANSACTION statement signifies the beginning of a user transaction. A transaction ends when it is either committed (see COMMIT TRANSACTION) or canceled (see ROLLBACK TRANSACTION). A transaction is a logical unit of work.

CLOSE CURSOR

```
close cursor_name
```

The CLOSE cursor_name statement closes the cursor and clears it of data. To completely remove the cursor, use the DEALLOCATE CURSOR statement.

COMMIT TRANSACTION

```
SQL> COMMIT;
```

The COMMIT TRANSACTION statement saves all work begun since the beginning of the transaction (since the BEGIN TRANSACTION statement was executed).

CREATE DATABASE

```
SQL> CREATE DATABASE database_name;
```

CREATE DATABASE database_name creates a new database. Many different options can be supplied, such as the device on which to create the database and the size of the initial database.

CREATE INDEX

```
CREATE INDEX index_name
ON table_name(column_name1, [column_name2], ...);
```

An index can order the contents of a table based on the contents of the indexed field(s).

CREATE PROCEDURE

```
create procedure procedure_name
   [[(|@parameter_name
      datatype [(length) ¦ (precision [, scale])
      [= default][output]
   [, @parameter_name
      datatype [(length) ¦ (precision [, scale])
      [= default][output]]...[)]]
   [with recompile]
   as SQL_statements
```

The CREATE PROCEDURE statement creates a new stored procedure in the database. This stored procedure can consist of SQL statements and can then be executed using the EXECUTE command. Stored procedures support input and output parameters passing and can return an integer value for status checking.

CREATE TABLE

```
CREATE TABLE table_name
(    field1 datatype [ NOT NULL ],
     field2 datatype [ NOT NULL ],
     field3 datatype [ NOT NULL ]...)
```

The CREATE TABLE statement creates a new table within a database. Each optional field is provided with a name and data type for creation within that table.

CREATE TRIGGER

```
create trigger trigger_name
   on table_name
   for {insert, update, delete}
   as SQL_Statements
```

The CREATE TRIGGER statement creates a trigger object in the database that will execute its SQL statements when its corresponding table is modified through an INSERT, UPDATE, or DELETE. Triggers can also call stored procedures to execute complex tasks.

CREATE USER

```
CREATE USER user
```

The CREATE USER statement creates a new user account complete with user ID and password.

CREATE VIEW

```
CREATE VIEW <view_name> [(column1, column2...)] AS
SELECT <table_name column_names>
FROM <table_name>
```

A view is often described as a virtual table. Views are created by using the CREATE VIEW statement. After a view is created, it can be queried and data within the view can be modified.

DEALLOCATE CURSOR

```
deallocate cursor cursor_name
```

The DEALLOCATE CURSOR statement completely removes the cursor from memory and frees the name for use by another cursor. You should always close the cursor with the CLOSE CURSOR statement before deallocating it.

DECLARE CURSOR

```
declare cursor_name cursor
    for select_statement
```

The DECLARE CURSOR statement creates a new cursor from the SELECT statement query. The FETCH statement scrolls the cursor through the data until the variables have been loaded. Then the cursor scrolls to the next record.

DROP DATABASE

```
DROP DATABASE database_name;
```

The DROP DATABASE statement completely deletes a database, including all data and the database's physical structure on disk.

DROP INDEX

```
DROP INDEX index_name;
```

The DROP INDEX statement removes an index from a table.

DROP PROCEDURE

```
drop procedure procedure_name
```

The DROP PROCEDURE statement drops a stored procedure from the database; its function is similar to the DROP TABLE and DROP INDEX statements.

DROP TABLE

```
DROP TABLE table_name;
```

The DROP TABLE statement drops a table from a database.

DROP TRIGGER

```
DROP TRIGGER trigger_name
```

The DROP TRIGGER statement removes a trigger from a database.

DROP VIEW

```
DROP VIEW view_name;
```

The DROP VIEW statement removes a view from a database.

EXECUTE

```
execute [@return_status = ]
  procedure_name
  [[@parameter_name =] value ¦
    [@parameter_name =] @variable [output]...]]
```

The EXECUTE command runs a stored procedure and its associated SQL statements. Parameters can be passed to the stored procedure, and data can be returned in these parameters if the output keyword is used.

FETCH

```
fetch cursor_name [into fetch_target_list]
```

The FETCH command loads the contents of the cursor's data into the provided program variables. After the variables have been loaded, the cursor scrolls to the next record.

FROM

```
FROM <tableref> [, <tableref> ...]
```

FROM specifies which tables are used and/or joined.

GRANT

```
GRANT role TO user
```

or

```
GRANT system_privilege TO {user_name ¦ role ¦ PUBLIC}
```

The GRANT command grants a privilege or role to a user who has been created using the CREATE USER command.

GROUP BY

```
GROUP BY <col> [, <col> ...]
```

The GROUP BY statement groups all the rows with the same column value.

HAVING

```
HAVING <search_cond>
```

HAVING is valid only with GROUP BY and limits the selection of groups to those that satisfy the search condition.

INTERSECT

```
INTERSECT
```

INTERSECT returns all the common elements of two SELECT statements.

ORDER BY

```
ORDER BY <order_list>
```

The ORDER BY statement orders the returned values by the specified column(s).

ROLLBACK TRANSACTION

The ROLLBACK TRANSACTION statement effectively cancels all work done within a transaction (since the BEGIN TRANSACTION statement was executed).

REVOKE

```
REVOKE role FROM user;
```

or

```
REVOKE {object_priv ¦ ALL [PRIVILEGES]}
[, {object_priv ¦ ALL [PRIVILEGES]} ] ...
ON [schema.]object
FROM {user ¦ role ¦ PUBLIC} [, {user ¦ role ¦ PUBLIC}] ...
```

The REVOKE command removes a database privilege from a user, whether it be a system privilege or a role.

SELECT

```
SELECT [DISTINCT ¦ ALL]
```

The SELECT statement is the beginning of each data retrieval statement. The modifier DISTINCT specifies unique values and prevents duplicates. ALL is the default and allows duplicates.

SET TRANSACTION

```
SQL> SET TRANSACTION (READ ONLY ¦ USE ROLLBACK SEGMENT);
```

The SET TRANSACTION enables the user to specify when a transaction should begin. The READ ONLY option locks a set of records until the transaction ends to ensure that the data is not changed.

UNION

```
UNION
```

The UNION statement returns all the elements of two SELECT statements.

WHERE

```
WHERE <search_cond>
```

The WHERE statement limits the rows retrieved to those meeting the search condition.

*

* gets all the columns of a particular table.

APPENDIX

B

Source Code Listings for the C++ Program Used on Day 14

```
// tyssqvw.h : interface of the CTyssqlView class
//
/////////////////////////////////////////////////////////////////////////

class CTyssqlSet;

class CTyssqlView : public CRecordView
{
protected: // create from serialization only
    CTyssqlView();
    DECLARE_DYNCREATE(CTyssqlView)

public:
    //{{AFX_DATA(CTyssqlView)
    enum { IDD = IDD_TYSSQL_FORM };
    CTyssqlSet* m_pSet;
    //}}AFX_DATA

// Attributes
public:
    CTyssqlDoc* GetDocument();

// Operations
public:
    virtual CRecordset* OnGetRecordset();

// Implementation
public:
    virtual ~CTyssqlView();
#ifdef _DEBUG
    virtual void AssertValid() const;
    virtual void Dump(CDumpContext& dc) const;
#endif

protected:
    virtual void DoDataExchange(CDataExchange* pDX);// DDX/DDV support
    virtual void OnInitialUpdate(); // called first time after construct

// Generated message map functions
protected:
    //{{AFX_MSG(CTyssqlView)
        // NOTE - the ClassWizard will add and remove member functions here.
        //    DO NOT EDIT what you see in these blocks of generated code !
    //}}AFX_MSG
    DECLARE_MESSAGE_MAP()
};

#ifndef _DEBUG  // debug version in tyssqvw.cpp
inline CTyssqlDoc* CTyssqlView::GetDocument()
    { return (CTyssqlDoc*)m_pDocument; }
#endif

/////////////////////////////////////////////////////////////////////////

// tyssql.h : main header file for the TYSSQL application
//
```

B

```
#ifndef __AFXWIN_H__
    #error include 'stdafx.h' before including this file for PCH
#endif

#include "resource.h"          // main symbols

/////////////////////////////////////////////////////////////////////////////
// CTyssqlApp:
// See tyssql.cpp for the implementation of this class
//

class CTyssqlApp : public CWinApp
{
public:
    CTyssqlApp();

// Overrides
    virtual BOOL InitInstance();

// Implementation

    //{{AFX_MSG(CTyssqlApp)
    afx_msg void OnAppAbout();
        // NOTE - the ClassWizard will add and remove member functions here.
        //     DO NOT EDIT what you see in these blocks of generated code !
    //}}AFX_MSG
    DECLARE_MESSAGE_MAP()
};


/////////////////////////////////////////////////////////////////////////////
// tyssqset.h : interface of the CTyssqlSet class
//
/////////////////////////////////////////////////////////////////////////////

class CTyssqlSet : public CRecordset
{
DECLARE_DYNAMIC(CTyssqlSet)

public:
    CTyssqlSet(CDatabase* pDatabase = NULL);

// Field/Param Data
    //{{AFX_FIELD(CTyssqlSet, CRecordset)
    CString     m_NAME;
    CString     m_ADDRESS;
    CString     m_STATE;
    CString     m_ZIP;
    CString     m_PHONE;
    CString     m_REMARKS;
    //}}AFX_FIELD

// Implementation
protected:
    virtual CString GetDefaultConnect();     // Default connection string
```

```
    virtual CString GetDefaultSQL();      // default SQL for Recordset
    virtual void DoFieldExchange(CFieldExchange* pFX);     // RFX support
};

// tyssqdoc.h : interface of the CTyssqlDoc class
//
//////////////////////////////////////////////////////////////////////////////

class CTyssqlDoc : public CDocument
{
protected: // create from serialization only
    CTyssqlDoc();
    DECLARE_DYNCREATE(CTyssqlDoc)

// Attributes
public:
    CTyssqlSet m_tyssqlSet;

// Operations
public:

// Implementation
public:
    virtual ~CTyssqlDoc();
#ifdef _DEBUG
    virtual void AssertValid() const;
    virtual void Dump(CDumpContext& dc) const;
#endif

protected:
    virtual BOOL OnNewDocument();

// Generated message map functions
protected:
    //{{AFX_MSG(CTyssqlDoc)
        // NOTE - the ClassWizard will add and remove member functions here.
        //      DO NOT EDIT what you see in these blocks of generated code !
    //}}AFX_MSG
    DECLARE_MESSAGE_MAP()
};

//////////////////////////////////////////////////////////////////////////////
// stdafx.h : include file for standard system include files,
//   or project specific include files that are used frequently, but
//      are changed infrequently
//

#include <afxwin.h>         // MFC core and standard components
#include <afxext.h>         // MFC extensions (including VB)
#include <afxdb.h>          // MFC database classes

//////////////////////////////////////////////////////////////////

//{{NO_DEPENDENCIES}}
// App Studio generated include file.
// Used by TYSSQL.RC
```

```
//
#define IDR_MAINFRAME                   2
#define IDD_ABOUTBOX                    100
#define IDD_TYSSQL_FORM                 101
#define IDP_FAILED_OPEN_DATABASE        103
#define IDC_NAME                        1000
#define IDC_ADDRESS                     1001
#define IDC_STATE                       1002
#define IDC_ZIP                         1003

// Next default values for new objects
//
#ifdef APSTUDIO_INVOKED
#ifndef APSTUDIO_READONLY_SYMBOLS

#define _APS_NEXT_RESOURCE_VALUE        102
#define _APS_NEXT_COMMAND_VALUE         32771
#define _APS_NEXT_CONTROL_VALUE         1004
#define _APS_NEXT_SYMED_VALUE           101
#endif
#endif


/////////////////////////////////////////////////////

// mainfrm.h : interface of the CMainFrame class
//
/////////////////////////////////////////////////////////////////////////////

class CMainFrame : public CFrameWnd
{
protected: // create from serialization only
    CMainFrame();
    DECLARE_DYNCREATE(CMainFrame)

// Attributes
public:

// Operations
public:

// Implementation
public:
    virtual ~CMainFrame();
#ifdef _DEBUG
    virtual void AssertValid() const;
    virtual void Dump(CDumpContext& dc) const;
#endif

protected:  // control bar embedded members
    CStatusBar   m_wndStatusBar;
    CToolBar     m_wndToolBar;

// Generated message map functions
protected:
    //{{AFX_MSG(CMainFrame)
    afx_msg int OnCreate(LPCREATESTRUCT lpCreateStruct);
```

```
        // NOTE - the ClassWizard will add and remove member functions here.
        //    DO NOT EDIT what you see in these blocks of generated code!
    //}}AFX_MSG
    DECLARE_MESSAGE_MAP()
};

////////////////////////////////////////////////////////////////////////////

// tyssqvw.cpp : implementation of the CTyssqlView class
//

#include "stdafx.h"
#include "tyssql.h"

#include "tyssqset.h"
#include "tyssqdoc.h"
#include "tyssqvw.h"

#ifdef _DEBUG
#undef THIS_FILE
static char BASED_CODE THIS_FILE[] = __FILE__;
#endif

////////////////////////////////////////////////////////////////////////////

// CTyssqlView

IMPLEMENT_DYNCREATE(CTyssqlView, CRecordView)

BEGIN_MESSAGE_MAP(CTyssqlView, CRecordView)
    //{{AFX_MSG_MAP(CTyssqlView)
        // NOTE - the ClassWizard will add and remove mapping macros here.
        //    DO NOT EDIT what you see in these blocks of generated code!
    //}}AFX_MSG_MAP
END_MESSAGE_MAP()

////////////////////////////////////////////////////////////////////////////
// CTyssqlView construction/destruction

CTyssqlView::CTyssqlView()
    : CRecordView(CTyssqlView::IDD)
{
    //{{AFX_DATA_INIT(CTyssqlView)
    m_pSet = NULL;
    //}}AFX_DATA_INIT
    // TODO: add construction code here
}

CTyssqlView::~CTyssqlView()
{
}

void CTyssqlView::DoDataExchange(CDataExchange* pDX)
{
    CRecordView::DoDataExchange(pDX);
    //{{AFX_DATA_MAP(CTyssqlView)
```

```
        DDX_FieldText(pDX, IDC_ADDRESS, m_pSet->m_ADDRESS, m_pSet);
        DDX_FieldText(pDX, IDC_NAME, m_pSet->m_NAME, m_pSet);
        DDX_FieldText(pDX, IDC_STATE, m_pSet->m_STATE, m_pSet);
        DDX_FieldText(pDX, IDC_ZIP, m_pSet->m_ZIP, m_pSet);
        //}}AFX_DATA_MAP
}

void CTyssqlView::OnInitialUpdate()
{
    m_pSet = &GetDocument()->m_tyssqlSet;
    CRecordView::OnInitialUpdate();

}

/////////////////////////////////////////////////////////////////////////////
// CTyssqlView diagnostics

#ifdef _DEBUG
void CTyssqlView::AssertValid() const
{
    CRecordView::AssertValid();
}

void CTyssqlView::Dump(CDumpContext& dc) const
{
    CRecordView::Dump(dc);
}

CTyssqlDoc* CTyssqlView::GetDocument() // non-debug version is inline
{
    ASSERT(m_pDocument->IsKindOf(RUNTIME_CLASS(CTyssqlDoc)));
    return (CTyssqlDoc*)m_pDocument;
}
#endif //_DEBUG

/////////////////////////////////////////////////////////////////////////////
// CTyssqlView database support

CRecordset* CTyssqlView::OnGetRecordset()
{
    return m_pSet;
}


/////////////////////////////////////////////////////////////////////////////
// CTyssqlView message handlers


// tyssqset.cpp : implementation of the CTyssqlSet class
//

#include "stdafx.h"
#include "tyssql.h"
#include "tyssqset.h"

/////////////////////////////////////////////////////////////////////////////
```

```
// CTyssqlSet implementation

IMPLEMENT_DYNAMIC(CTyssqlSet, CRecordset)

CTyssqlSet::CTyssqlSet(CDatabase* pdb)
    : CRecordset(pdb)
{
    //{{AFX_FIELD_INIT(CTyssqlSet)
    m_NAME = "";
    m_ADDRESS = "";
    m_STATE = "";
    m_ZIP = "";
    m_PHONE = "";
    m_REMARKS = "";
    m_nFields = 6;
    //}}AFX_FIELD_INIT
}

CString CTyssqlSet::GetDefaultConnect()
{
    return "ODBC;DSN=TYSSQL;";
}

CString CTyssqlSet::GetDefaultSQL()
{
    return "SELECT * FROM CUSTOMER ORDER BY NAME";
}

void CTyssqlSet::DoFieldExchange(CFieldExchange* pFX)
{
    //{{AFX_FIELD_MAP(CTyssqlSet)
    pFX->SetFieldType(CFieldExchange::outputColumn);
    RFX_Text(pFX, "NAME", m_NAME);
    RFX_Text(pFX, "ADDRESS", m_ADDRESS);
    RFX_Text(pFX, "STATE", m_STATE);
    RFX_Text(pFX, "ZIP", m_ZIP);
    RFX_Text(pFX, "PHONE", m_PHONE);
    RFX_Text(pFX, "REMARKS", m_REMARKS);
    //}}AFX_FIELD_MAP
}

// tyssql.cpp : Defines the class behaviors for the application.
//

#include "stdafx.h"
#include "tyssql.h"

#include "mainfrm.h"
#include "tyssqset.h"
#include "tyssqdoc.h"
#include "tyssqvw.h"

#ifdef _DEBUG
#undef THIS_FILE
static char BASED_CODE THIS_FILE[] = __FILE__;
#endif
```

```
/////////////////////////////////////////////////////////////////////
// CTyssqlApp

BEGIN_MESSAGE_MAP(CTyssqlApp, CWinApp)
    //{{AFX_MSG_MAP(CTyssqlApp)
    ON_COMMAND(ID_APP_ABOUT, OnAppAbout)
        // NOTE - the ClassWizard will add and remove mapping macros here.
        //      DO NOT EDIT what you see in these blocks of generated code!
    //}}AFX_MSG_MAP
END_MESSAGE_MAP()

/////////////////////////////////////////////////////////////////////
// CTyssqlApp construction

CTyssqlApp::CTyssqlApp()
{
    // TODO: add construction code here,
    // Place all significant initialization in InitInstance
}

/////////////////////////////////////////////////////////////////////
// The one and only CTyssqlApp object

CTyssqlApp NEAR theApp;

/////////////////////////////////////////////////////////////////////
// CTyssqlApp initialization

BOOL CTyssqlApp::InitInstance()
{
    // Standard initialization
    // If you are not using these features and wish to reduce the size
    //  of your final executable, you should remove from the following
    //  the specific initialization routines you do not need.

    SetDialogBkColor();          // Set dialog background color to gray
    LoadStdProfileSettings();  // Load standard INI file options (including MRU)

    // Register the application's document templates.  Document templates
    //  serve as the connection between documents, frame windows and views.

    CSingleDocTemplate* pDocTemplate;
    pDocTemplate = new CSingleDocTemplate(
        IDR_MAINFRAME,
        RUNTIME_CLASS(CTyssqlDoc),
        RUNTIME_CLASS(CMainFrame),      // main SDI frame window
        RUNTIME_CLASS(CTyssqlView));
    AddDocTemplate(pDocTemplate);

    // create a new (empty) document
    OnFileNew();

    if (m_lpCmdLine[0] != '\0')
    {
        // TODO: add command line processing here
```

```
    }

    return TRUE;
}

//////////////////////////////////////////////////////////////////////////////
// CAboutDlg dialog used for App About

class CAboutDlg : public CDialog
{
public:
    CAboutDlg();

// Dialog Data
    //{{AFX_DATA(CAboutDlg)
    enum { IDD = IDD_ABOUTBOX };
    //}}AFX_DATA

// Implementation
protected:
    virtual void DoDataExchange(CDataExchange* pDX);      // DDX/DDV support
    //{{AFX_MSG(CAboutDlg)
        // No message handlers
    //}}AFX_MSG
    DECLARE_MESSAGE_MAP()
};

CAboutDlg::CAboutDlg() : CDialog(CAboutDlg::IDD)
{
    //{{AFX_DATA_INIT(CAboutDlg)
    //}}AFX_DATA_INIT
}

void CAboutDlg::DoDataExchange(CDataExchange* pDX)
{
    CDialog::DoDataExchange(pDX);
    //{{AFX_DATA_MAP(CAboutDlg)
    //}}AFX_DATA_MAP
}

BEGIN_MESSAGE_MAP(CAboutDlg, CDialog)
    //{{AFX_MSG_MAP(CAboutDlg)
        // No message handlers
    //}}AFX_MSG_MAP
END_MESSAGE_MAP()

// App command to run the dialog
void CTyssqlApp::OnAppAbout()
{
    CAboutDlg aboutDlg;
    aboutDlg.DoModal();
}

//////////////////////////////////////////////////////////////////////////////
// CTyssqlApp commands
```

```
// tyssqdoc.cpp : implementation of the CTyssqlDoc class
//

#include "stdafx.h"
#include "tyssql.h"

#include "tyssqset.h"
#include "tyssqdoc.h"

#ifdef _DEBUG
#undef THIS_FILE
static char BASED_CODE THIS_FILE[] = __FILE__;
#endif

/////////////////////////////////////////////////////////////////////////////
// CTyssqlDoc

IMPLEMENT_DYNCREATE(CTyssqlDoc, CDocument)

BEGIN_MESSAGE_MAP(CTyssqlDoc, CDocument)
    //{{AFX_MSG_MAP(CTyssqlDoc)
        // NOTE - the ClassWizard will add and remove mapping macros here.
        //    DO NOT EDIT what you see in these blocks of generated code!
    //}}AFX_MSG_MAP
END_MESSAGE_MAP()

/////////////////////////////////////////////////////////////////////////////
// CTyssqlDoc construction/destruction

CTyssqlDoc::CTyssqlDoc()
{
    // TODO: add one-time construction code here
}

CTyssqlDoc::~CTyssqlDoc()
{
}

BOOL CTyssqlDoc::OnNewDocument()
{
    if (!CDocument::OnNewDocument())
        return FALSE;

    // TODO: add reinitialization code here
    // (SDI documents will reuse this document)

    return TRUE;
}

/////////////////////////////////////////////////////////////////////////////
// CTyssqlDoc diagnostics

#ifdef _DEBUG
void CTyssqlDoc::AssertValid() const
{
    CDocument::AssertValid();
```

```
}

void CTyssqlDoc::Dump(CDumpContext& dc) const
{
    CDocument::Dump(dc);
}
#endif //_DEBUG

/////////////////////////////////////////////////////////////////////////////
// CTyssqlDoc commands

// stdafx.cpp : source file that includes just the standard includes
//  stdafx.pch will be the pre-compiled header
//  stdafx.obj will contain the pre-compiled type information

#include "stdafx.h"

// mainfrm.cpp : implementation of the CMainFrame class
//

#include "stdafx.h"
#include "tyssql.h"

#include "mainfrm.h"

#ifdef _DEBUG
#undef THIS_FILE
static char BASED_CODE THIS_FILE[] = __FILE__;
#endif

/////////////////////////////////////////////////////////////////////////////
// CMainFrame

IMPLEMENT_DYNCREATE(CMainFrame, CFrameWnd)

BEGIN_MESSAGE_MAP(CMainFrame, CFrameWnd)
    //{{AFX_MSG_MAP(CMainFrame)
        // NOTE - the ClassWizard will add and remove mapping macros here.
        //    DO NOT EDIT what you see in these blocks of generated code !
    ON_WM_CREATE()
    //}}AFX_MSG_MAP
END_MESSAGE_MAP()

/////////////////////////////////////////////////////////////////////////////
// arrays of IDs used to initialize control bars

// toolbar buttons - IDs are command buttons
static UINT BASED_CODE buttons[] =
{
    // same order as in the bitmap 'toolbar.bmp'
    ID_EDIT_CUT,
    ID_EDIT_COPY,
    ID_EDIT_PASTE,
        ID_SEPARATOR,
    ID_FILE_PRINT,
        ID_SEPARATOR,
```

```
        ID_RECORD_FIRST,
        ID_RECORD_PREV,
        ID_RECORD_NEXT,
        ID_RECORD_LAST,
            ID_SEPARATOR,
        ID_APP_ABOUT,
};

static UINT BASED_CODE indicators[] =
{
    ID_SEPARATOR,               // status line indicator
    ID_INDICATOR_CAPS,
    ID_INDICATOR_NUM,
    ID_INDICATOR_SCRL,
};

/////////////////////////////////////////////////////////////////////////////
// CMainFrame construction/destruction

CMainFrame::CMainFrame()
{
    // TODO: add member initialization code here
}

CMainFrame::~CMainFrame()
{
}

int CMainFrame::OnCreate(LPCREATESTRUCT lpCreateStruct)
{
    if (CFrameWnd::OnCreate(lpCreateStruct) == -1)
        return -1;

    if (!m_wndToolBar.Create(this) ||
        !m_wndToolBar.LoadBitmap(IDR_MAINFRAME) ||
        !m_wndToolBar.SetButtons(buttons,
          sizeof(buttons)/sizeof(UINT)))
    {
        TRACE("Failed to create toolbar\n");
        return -1;      // fail to create
    }

    if (!m_wndStatusBar.Create(this) ||
        !m_wndStatusBar.SetIndicators(indicators,
          sizeof(indicators)/sizeof(UINT)))
    {
        TRACE("Failed to create status bar\n");
        return -1;      // fail to create
    }

    return 0;
}

/////////////////////////////////////////////////////////////////////////////
// CMainFrame diagnostics
```

```
#ifdef _DEBUG
void CMainFrame::AssertValid() const
{
    CFrameWnd::AssertValid();
}

void CMainFrame::Dump(CDumpContext& dc) const
{
    CFrameWnd::Dump(dc);
}

#endif //_DEBUG

/////////////////////////////////////////////////////////////////////////////
// CMainFrame message handlers
```

APPENDIX C

Source Code Listings for the Delphi Program Used on Day 14

```
program Tyssql;
uses
  Forms,
  Unit1 in 'UNIT1.PAS' {Form1},
  Unit2 in 'UNIT2.PAS' {Form2};
{$R *.RES}
begin
  Application.CreateForm(TForm2, Form2);
  Application.CreateForm(TForm1, Form1);
  Application.Run;
end.
unit Unit1;
interface
uses
  SysUtils, WinTypes, WinProcs, Messages, Classes, Graphics, Controls,
  Forms, Dialogs;
type
  TForm1 = class(TForm)
  private
    { Private declarations }
  public
    { Public declarations }
  end;
var
  Form1: TForm1;
implementation
{$R *.DFM}
end.
unit Unit2;
interface
uses
  SysUtils, WinTypes, WinProcs, Messages, Classes, Graphics, Controls,
  StdCtrls, Forms, DBCtrls, DB, DBGrids, DBTables, Grids, Mask, ExtCtrls;
type
  TForm2 = class(TForm)
    ScrollBox: TScrollBox;
    Label1: TLabel;
    EditPARTNUM: TDBEdit;
    Label2: TLabel;
    EditDESCRIPTION: TDBEdit;
    Label3: TLabel;
    EditPRICE: TDBEdit;
    DBGrid1: TDBGrid;
    DBNavigator: TDBNavigator;
    Panel1: TPanel;
    DataSource1: TDataSource;
    Panel2: TPanel;
    Panel3: TPanel;
    Query1: TQuery;
    Query2: TQuery;
    DataSource2: TDataSource;
    procedure FormCreate(Sender: TObject);
  private
    { private declarations }
  public
    { public declarations }
  end;
```

```
var
  Form2: TForm2;
implementation
{$R *.DFM}
procedure TForm2.FormCreate(Sender: TObject);
begin
  Query1.Open;
  Query2.Open;
end;
end.
```

APPENDIX

D

Resources

Books

☐ *Developing Sybase Applications*
Imprint: Sams
Author: Daniel J. Worden
ISBN: 0-672-30700-6

☐ *Sybase Developer's Guide*
Imprint: Sams
Author: Daniel J. Worden
ISBN: 0-672-30467-8

☐ *Microsoft SQL Server 6.5 Unleashed, 2E*
Imprint: Sams
Author: David Solomon, Ray Rankins, et al.
ISBN: 0-672-30956-4

☐ *Teach Yourself Delphi in 21 Days*
Imprint: Sams
Author: Andrew Wozniewicz
ISBN: 0-672-30470-8

☐ *Delphi Developer's Guide*
Imprint: Sams
Authors: Steve Teixeira and Xavier Pacheco
ISBN: 0-672-30704-9

☐ *Delphi Programming Unleashed*
Imprint: Sams
Author: Charlie Calvert
ISBN: 0-672-30499-6

☐ *Essential Oracle7.2*
Imprint: Sams
Author: Tom Luers
ISBN: 0-672-30873-8

☐ *Developing Personal Oracle7 for Windows 95 Applications*
Imprint: Sams
Author: David Lockman
ISBN: 0-672-31025-2

☐ *Teach Yourself C++ Programming in 21 Days*
Imprint: Sams
Author: Jesse Liberty
ISBN: 0-672-30541-0

☐ *Teach Yourself Transact-SQL in 21 Days*
Imprint: SAMS
Author: Bennett Wm. McEwan and David Solomon
ISBN: 0-672-31045-7

☐ *Teach Yourself PL/SQL in 21 Days*
Imprint: SAMS
Author: Tom Luers, Timothy Atwood, and Jonathan Gennick
ISBN: 0-672-31123-2

Please check the Information SuperLibrary at www.mcp.com/mcp/ for further information and new releases.

Magazines

☐ *DBMS*
P.O Box 469039
Escondido, CA 92046-9039
800-334-8152

☐ *Oracle Magazine*
500 Oracle Parkway
Box 659510
Redwood Shores, CA 94065-1600
415-506-5304

Internet URLs for the Keyword SQL

☐ http://www.aslaninc.com/
Aslan Computing Inc.: Specializes in SQL databases, Windows development tools, Windows NT networking, and Web services.

☐ http://www.radix.net/~ablaze/
Ablaze Business Systems, Inc.: A leading Microsoft Solution Provider specializing in Visual Basic, MS Server, PowerBuilder, and the Internet.

☐ http://www.fourgen.com/
FourGen: Open systems software supporting Windows, 4GL, UNIX, SQL, and OLE standards.

☐ http://www.indirect.com/www/steelep4/ddi.html
Digital Dreamshop: Providers of innovative client/server applications, computer graphics services, and commercial software programming in Visual Basic, Access, Transact-SQL, C++, and Delphi.

D

☐ `http://www.novalink.com/bachman/index.html`
Bachman Information Systems: Vendor of database design tools for Sybase and Microsoft SQL Server databases and other development tools.

☐ `http://www.everyware.com/`
EveryWare Development Corp.: Developers of Butler SQL, the SQL database server for Macintosh.

☐ `http://www.edb.com/nb/index.html`
Netbase: Netbase provides a low-cost client/server SQL database for UNIX.

☐ `http://www.quadbase.com/quadbase.htm`
Quadbase: Quadbase-SQL is a high-performance, full-featured, industrial-strength SQL relational DBMS.

☐ `http://www.sagus.com/`
Software AG of North America (SAGNA): Develops and markets open, multiplatform product solutions in the areas of distributed computing (ENTIRE), application engineering (NATURAL), SQL querying and reporting (ESPERANT), database management (ADABAS), and data warehousing.

☐ `http://www.nis.net/sqlpower/`
Sql Power Tools: Second-generation tools for SQL developers and database administrators.

☐ `http://world.std.com/~engwiz/`
English Wizard: English Wizard translates plain English into SQL for access to your database.

☐ `http://www.microsoft.com/SQL/`
Microsoft.

☐ `http://www.jcc.com/sql_stnd.html`
SQL Standards: The central source of information about the SQL standards process and its current state.

☐ `http://www.sybase.com/WWW/`
Connecting to Sybase SQL Server via the World Wide Web.

☐ `http://www.ncsa.uiuc.edu/SDG/People/jason/pub/gsql/starthere.html`
GSQL: A Mosaic-SQL gateway.

FTP Sites

☐ `ftp://ftp.cc.gatech.edu/pub/gvu/www/pitkow/gsql-oracle/oracle-backend.html`
   GSQL: Oracle Backend.

Newsgroups

☐ `news:comp.databases.oracle`
   Usenet: The SQL database products of the Oracle Corporation.

☐ `news:comp.databases.sybase`
   Usenet: Implementations of the SQL Server.

D

APPENDIX

E

ASCII Table

Dec X_{10}	Hex X_{16}	Binary X_2	ASCII	Dec X_{10}	Hex X_{16}	Binary X_2	ASCII
000	00	0000 0000	null	026	1A	0001 1010	→
001	01	0000 0001	☺	027	1B	0001 1011	←
002	02	0000 0010	●	028	1C	0001 1100	∟
003	03	0000 0011	♥	029	1D	0001 1101	↔
004	04	0000 0100	♦	030	1E	0001 1110	▲
005	05	0000 0101	♣	031	1F	0001 1111	▼
006	06	0000 0110	♠	032	20	0010 0000	space
007	07	0000 0111	•	033	21	0010 0001	!
008	08	0000 1000	◘	034	22	0010 0010	"
009	09	0000 1001	○	035	23	0010 0011	#
010	0A	0000 1010	◙	036	24	0010 0100	$
011	0B	0000 1011	♂	037	25	0010 0101	%
012	0C	0000 1100	♀	038	26	0010 0110	&
013	0D	0000 1101	♪	039	27	0010 0111	'
014	0E	0000 1110	♫	040	28	0010 1000	(
015	0F	0000 1111	☼	041	29	0010 1001	)
016	10	0001 0000	►	042	2A	0010 1010	*
017	11	0001 0001	◄	043	2B	0010 1011	+
018	12	0001 0010	↕	044	2C	0010 1100	,
019	13	0001 0011	‼	045	2D	0010 1101	-
020	14	0001 0100	¶	046	2E	0010 1110	.
021	15	0001 0101	§	047	2F	0010 1111	/
022	16	0001 0110	▬	048	30	0011 0000	0
023	17	0001 0111	↨	049	31	0011 0001	1
024	18	0001 1000	↑	050	32	0011 0010	2
025	19	0001 1001	↓	051	33	0011 0011	3

Dec X_{10}	Hex X_{16}	Binary X_2	ASCII	Dec X_{10}	Hex X_{16}	Binary X_2	ASCII
052	34	0011 0100	4	078	4E	0100 1110	N
053	35	0011 0101	5	079	4F	0100 1111	O
054	36	0011 0110	6	080	50	0101 0000	P
055	37	0011 0111	7	081	51	0101 0001	Q
056	38	0011 1000	8	082	52	0101 0010	R
057	39	0011 1001	9	083	53	0101 0011	S
058	3A	0011 1010	:	084	54	0101 0100	T
059	3B	0011 1011	;	085	55	0101 0101	U
060	3C	0011 1100	<	086	56	0101 0110	V
061	3D	0011 1101	=	087	57	0101 0111	W
062	3E	0011 1110	>	088	58	0101 1000	X
063	3F	0011 1111	?	089	59	0101 1001	Y
064	40	0100 0000	@	090	5A	0101 1010	Z
065	41	0100 0001	A	091	5B	0101 1011	[
066	42	0100 0010	B	092	5C	0101 1100	\
067	43	0100 0011	C	093	5D	0101 1101	]
068	44	0100 0100	D	094	5E	0101 1110	^
069	45	0100 0101	E	095	5F	0101 1111	–
070	46	0100 0110	F	096	60	0110 0000	`
071	47	0100 0111	G	097	61	0110 0001	a
072	48	0100 1000	H	098	62	0110 0010	b
073	49	0100 1001	I	099	63	0110 0011	c
074	4A	0100 1010	J	100	64	0110 0100	d
075	4B	0100 1011	K	101	65	0110 0101	e
076	4C	0100 1100	L	102	66	0110 0110	f
077	4D	0100 1101	M	103	67	0110 0111	g

E

Dec X_{10}	Hex X_{16}	Binary X_2	ASCII	Dec X_{10}	Hex X_{16}	Binary X_2	ASCII
104	68	0110 1000	h	130	82	1000 0010	é
105	69	0110 1001	i	131	83	1000 0011	â
106	6A	0110 1010	j	132	84	1000 0100	ä
107	6B	0110 1011	k	133	85	1000 0101	à
108	6C	0110 1100	l	134	86	1000 0110	å
109	6D	0110 1101	m	135	87	1000 0111	ç
110	6E	0110 1110	n	136	88	1000 1000	ê
111	6F	0110 1111	o	137	89	1000 1001	ë
112	70	0111 0000	p	138	8A	1000 1010	è
113	71	0111 0001	q	139	8B	1000 1011	ï
114	72	0111 0010	r	140	8C	1000 1100	î
115	73	0111 0011	s	141	8D	1000 1101	ì
116	74	0111 0100	t	142	8E	1000 1110	Ä
117	75	0111 0101	u	143	8F	1000 1111	Å
118	76	0111 0110	v	144	90	1001 0000	É
119	77	0111 0111	w	145	91	1001 0001	æ
120	78	0111 1000	x	146	92	1001 0010	Æ
121	79	0111 1001	y	147	93	1001 0011	ô
122	7A	0111 1010	z	148	94	1001 0100	ö
123	7B	0111 1011	{	149	95	1001 0101	ò
124	7C	0111 1100	¦	150	96	1001 0110	û
125	7D	0111 1101	}	151	97	1001 0111	ù
126	7E	0111 1110	~	152	98	1001 1000	ÿ
127	7F	0111 1111	Δ	153	99	1001 1001	Ö
128	80	1000 0000	Ç	154	9A	1001 1010	Ü
129	81	1000 0001	ü	155	9B	1001 1011	¢

Dec X_{10}	Hex X_{16}	Binary X_2	ASCII	Dec X_{10}	Hex X_{16}	Binary X_2	ASCII
156	9C	1001 1100	£	182	B6	1011 0110	╢
157	9D	1001 1101	¥	183	B7	1011 0111	╖
158	9E	1001 1110	₧	184	B8	1011 1000	╕
159	9F	1001 1111	ƒ	185	B9	1011 1001	╣
160	A0	1010 0000	á	186	BA	1011 1010	║
161	A1	1010 0001	í	187	BB	1011 1011	╗
162	A2	1010 0010	ó	188	BC	1011 1100	╝
163	A3	1010 0011	ú	189	BD	1011 1101	╜
164	A4	1010 0100	ñ	190	BE	1011 1110	╛
165	A5	1010 0101	Ñ	191	BF	1011 1111	┐
166	A6	1010 0110	ª	192	C0	1100 0000	└
167	A7	1010 0111	º	193	C1	1100 0001	┴
168	A8	1010 1000	¿	194	C2	1100 0010	┬
169	A9	1010 1001	⌐	195	C3	1100 0011	├
170	AA	1010 1010	¬	196	C4	1100 0100	─
171	AB	1010 1011	½	197	C5	1100 0101	┼
172	AC	1010 1100	¼	198	C6	1100 0110	╞
173	AD	1010 1101	¡	199	C7	1100 0111	╟
174	AE	1010 1110	«	200	C8	1100 1000	╚
175	AF	1010 1111	»	201	C9	1100 1001	╔
176	B0	1011 0000	░	202	CA	1100 1010	╩
177	B1	1011 0001	▒	203	CB	1100 1011	╦
178	B2	1011 0010	▓	204	CC	1100 1100	╠
179	B3	1011 0011	│	205	CD	1100 1101	═
180	B4	1011 0100	┤	206	CE	1100 1110	╬
181	B5	1011 0101	╡	207	CF	1100 1111	╧

E

Dec X_{10}	Hex X_{16}	Binary X_2	ASCII	Dec X_{10}	Hex X_{16}	Binary X_2	ASCII
208	D0	1101 0000	⊥	234	EA	1110 1010	Ω
209	D1	1101 0001	⊤	235	EB	1110 1011	δ
210	D2	1101 0010	π	236	EC	1110 1100	∞
211	D3	1101 0011	⊔	237	ED	1110 1101	ø
212	D4	1101 0100	⊦	238	EE	1110 1110	∈
213	D5	1101 0101	⊧	239	EF	1110 1111	∩
214	D6	1101 0110	⊓	240	F0	1110 0000	≡
215	D7	1101 0111	⧺	241	F1	1111 0001	±
216	D8	1101 1000	∓	242	F2	1111 0010	≥
217	D9	1101 1001	⌐	243	F3	1111 0011	≤
218	DA	1101 1010	⌐	244	F4	1111 0100	⌠
219	DB	1101 1011	■	245	F5	1111 0101	⌡
220	DC	1101 1100	■	246	F6	1111 0110	÷
221	DD	1101 1101	▮	247	F7	1111 0111	≈
222	DE	1101 1110	▮	248	F8	1111 1000	°
223	DF	1101 1111	▪	249	F9	1111 1001	•
224	E0	1110 0000	α	250	FA	1111 1010	·
225	E1	1110 0001	β	251	FB	1111 1011	√
226	E2	1110 0010	Γ	252	FC	1111 1100	ⁿ
227	E3	1110 0011	π	253	FD	1111 1101	²
228	E4	1110 0100	Σ	254	FE	1111 1110	■
229	E5	1110 0101	σ	255	FF	1111 1111	
230	E6	1110 0110	μ				
231	E7	1110 0111	γ				
232	E8	1110 1000	Φ				
233	E9	1110 1001	θ				

APPENDIX

F

Answers to Quizzes and Exercises

Day 1, "Introduction to SQL"

Quiz Answers

1. What makes SQL a nonprocedural language?

   SQL determines what should be done, not how it should be done. The database must implement the SQL request. This feature is a big plus in cross-platform, cross-language development.

2. How can you tell whether a database is truly relational?

   Apply Dr. Codd's 12 (we know there are 13) rules.

3. What can you do with SQL?

   SQL enables you to select, insert, modify, and delete the information in a database; perform system security functions and set user permissions on tables and databases; handle online transaction processing within an application; create stored procedures and triggers to reduce application coding; and transfer data between different databases.

4. Name the process that separates data into distinct, unique sets.

   Normalization reduces the amount of repetition and complexity of the structure of the previous level.

Exercise Answer

Determine whether the database you use at work or at home is truly relational.

(On your own.)

Day 2, "Introduction to the Query: The SELECT Statement"

Quiz Answers

1. Do the following statements return the same or different output:
   ```
   SELECT * FROM CHECKS;
   select * from checks;?
   ```

   The only difference between the two statements is that one statement is in lowercase and the other uppercase. Case sensitivity is not normally a factor in the syntax of SQL. However, be aware of capitalization when dealing with data.

2. None of the following queries work. Why not?

   a. `Select *`

      The FROM clause is missing. The two mandatory components of a SELECT statement are the SELECT and FROM.

b. `Select * from checks`

The semicolon, which identifies the end of a SQL statement, is missing.

c. `Select amount name payee FROM checks;`

You need a comma between each column name: `Select amount, name, payee FROM checks;`

3. Which of the following SQL statements will work?

a. `select *`

   `from checks;`

b. `select * from checks;`

c. `select * from checks`

   `/`

All the above work.

Exercise Answers

1. Using the CHECKS table from earlier today, write a query to return just the check numbers and the remarks.

   `SELECT CHECK#, REMARKS FROM CHECKS;`

2. Rewrite the query from exercise 1 so that the remarks will appear as the first column in your query results.

   `SELECT REMARKS, CHECK# FROM CHECKS;`

3. Using the CHECKS table, write a query to return all the unique remarks.

   `SELECT DISTINCT REMARKS FROM CHECKS;`

Day 3, "Expressions, Conditions, and Operators"

Quiz Answers

Use the FRIENDS table to answer the following questions.

```
LASTNAME          FIRSTNAME         AREACODE PHONE     ST ZIP
--------------    ----------------  -------- --------  -- -------
BUNDY             AL                     100 555-1111  IL 22333
MEZA              AL                     200 555-2222  UK
MERRICK           BUD                    300 555-6666  CO 80212
MAST              JD                     381 555-6767  LA 23456
BULHER            FERRIS                 345 555-3223  IL 23332
PERKINS           ALTON                  911 555-3116  CA 95633
BOSS              SIR                    204 555-2345  CT 95633
```

1. Write a query that returns everyone in the database whose last name begins with M.

```
SELECT * FROM FRIENDS WHERE LASTNAME LIKE 'M%';
```

2. Write a query that returns everyone who lives in Illinois with a first name of AL.

```
SELECT * FROM FRIENDS
WHERE STATE = 'IL'
AND FIRSTNAME = 'AL';
```

3. Given two tables (PART1 and PART2) containing columns named PARTNO, how would you find out which part numbers are in both tables? Write the query.

Use the INTERSECT. Remember that INTERSECT returns rows common to both queries.

```
SELECT PARTNO FROM PART1
INTERSECT
SELECT PARTNO FROM PART2;
```

4. What shorthand could you use instead of WHERE a >= 10 AND a <=30?

```
WHERE a BETWEEN 10 AND 30;
```

5. What will this query return?

```
SELECT FIRSTNAME
FROM FRIENDS
WHERE FIRSTNAME = 'AL'
  AND LASTNAME = 'BULHER';
```

Nothing will be returned, as both conditions are not true.

Exercise Answers

1. Using the FRIENDS table, write a query that returns the following:

```
NAME                ST
------------------- --
AL           FROM IL
```

INPUT

```
SQL> SELECT (FIRSTNAME || 'FROM') NAME, STATE
  2  FROM FRIENDS
  3  WHERE STATE = 'IL'
  4  AND
  5  LASTNAME = 'BUNDY';
```

2. Using the FRIENDS table, write a query that returns the following:

```
NAME                       PHONE
-------------------------- -----------
MERRICK, BUD               300-555-6666
MAST, JD                   381-555-6767
BULHER, FERRIS             345-555-3223
```

INPUT

```
SQL>SELECT LASTNAME || ',' || FIRSTNAME NAME,
  2        AREACODE || '-' || PHONE PHONE
  3 FROM FRIENDS
  4 WHERE AREACODE BETWEEN 300 AND 400;
```

Day 4, "Functions: Molding the Data You Retrieve"

Quiz Answers

1. Which function capitalizes the first letter of a character string and makes the rest lowercase?

   INITCAP

2. Which functions are also known by the name *group functions*?

   Group functions and aggregate functions are the same thing.

3. Will this query work?

   SQL> **SELECT COUNT(LASTNAME) FROM CHARACTERS;**

   Yes, it will return the total of rows.

4. How about this one?

   SQL> **SELECT SUM(LASTNAME) FROM CHARACTERS**

   No, the query won't work because LASTNAME is a character field.

5. Assuming that they are separate columns, which function(s) would splice together FIRSTNAME and LASTNAME?

   The CONCAT function and the || symbol.

6. What does the answer 6 mean from the following SELECT?

   INPUT   SQL> **SELECT COUNT(*) FROM TEAMSTATS;**

   OUTPUT   COUNT(*)

   6 is the number of records in the table.

F

7. Will the following statement work?

```
SQL> SELECT SUBSTR LASTNAME,1,5 FROM NAME_TBL;
```

No, missing () around lastname,1,5. Also, a better plan is to give the column an alias. The statement should look like this:

```
SQL> SELECT SUBSTR(LASTNAME,1,5) NAME FROM NAME_TBL;
```

Exercise Answers

1. Using today's TEAMSTATS table, write a query to determine who is batting under .25. (For the baseball-challenged reader, batting average is hits/ab.)

INPUT
```
SQL> SELECT NAME FROM TEAMSTATS
  2  WHERE (HITS/AB) < .25;
```

OUTPUT
```
NAME
- - - - - - - - - - - - - -
HAMHOCKER
CASEY
```

2. Using today's CHARACTERS table, write a query that will return the following:

OUTPUT
```
INITIALS_____CODE
K.A.P.                 32
```

```
1 row selected.
```

INPUT
```
SQL> select substr(firstname,1,1)||'.'||
            substr(middlename,1,1)||'.'||
            substr(lastname,1,1)||'.' INITIALS, code
     from characters
     where code = 32;
```

Day 5, "Clauses in SQL"

Quiz Answers

1. Which clause works just like LIKE(<exp>%)?

   STARTING WITH

2. What is the function of the GROUP BY clause, and what other clause does it act like?

   The GROUP BY clause groups data result sets that have been manipulated by various functions. The GROUP BY clause acts like the ORDER BY clause in that it orders the results of the query in the order the columns are listed in the GROUP BY.

3. Will this SELECT work?

```
SQL> SELECT NAME, AVG(SALARY), DEPARTMENT
     FROM PAY_TBL
     WHERE DEPARTMENT = 'ACCOUNTING'
     ORDER BY NAME
     GROUP BY DEPARTMENT, SALARY;
```

No, the syntax is incorrect. The GROUP BY must come before the ORDER BY. Also, all the selected columns must be listed in the GROUP BY.

4. When using the HAVING clause, do you always have to use a GROUP BY also?

   Yes.

5. Can you use ORDER BY on a column that is not one of the columns in the SELECT statement?

   Yes, it is not necessary to use the SELECT statement on a column that you put in the ORDER BY clause.

Exercise Answers

1. Using the ORGCHART table from the preceding examples, find out how many people on each team have 30 or more days of sick leave.

   Here is your baseline that shows how many folks are on each team.

INPUT
```
SELECT TEAM, COUNT(TEAM)
FROM ORGCHART
GROUP BY TEAM;
```

OUTPUT
```
TEAM                 COUNT
===============  ===========

COLLECTIONS          2
MARKETING            3
PR                   1
RESEARCH             2
```

Compare it to the query that solves the question:

INPUT
```
SELECT TEAM, COUNT(TEAM)
FROM ORGCHART
WHERE SICKLEAVE >=30
GROUP BY TEAM;
```

OUTPUT
```
TEAM                 COUNT
===============  ===========

COLLECTIONS          1
MARKETING            1
RESEARCH             1
```

The output shows the number of people on each team with a SICKLEAVE balance of 30 days or more.

F

2. Using the CHECKS table, write a SELECT that will return the following:

OUTPUT

```
CHECK#_____PAYEE_____AMOUNT__

   1     MA BELL          150
```

INPUT

```
SQL> SELECT CHECK#, PAYEE, AMOUNT
FROM CHECKS
WHERE CHECK# = 1;
```

You can get the same results in several ways. Can you think of some more?

Day 6, "Joining Tables"

Quiz Answers

1. How many rows would a two-table join produce if one table had 50,000 rows and the other had 100,000?

   5,000,000,000 rows.

2. What type of join appears in the following select statement?

   ```
   select e.name, e.employee_id, ep.salary
   from employee_tbl e,
        employee_pay_tbl ep
   where e.employee_id = ep.employee_id;
   ```

   The preceding join is an equi-join. You are matching all the employee_ids in the two tables.

3. Will the following SELECT statements work?

   ```
   select name, employee_id, salary
   from employee_tbl e,
        employee_pay_tbl ep
   where employee_id = employee_id
     and name like '%MITH';
   ```

   No. The columns and tables are not properly named. Remember column and table aliases.

   ```
   select e.name, e.employee_id, ep.salary
   from employee_tbl e,
        employee_pay_tbl ep
   where name like '%MITH';
   ```

   No. The join command is missing in the where clause.

   ```
   select e.name, e.employee_id, ep.salary
   from employee_tbl e,
        employee_pay_tbl ep
   where e.employee_id = ep.employee_id
     and e.name like '%MITH';
   ```

   Yes. The syntax is correct.

4. In the WHERE clause, when joining the tables, should you do the join first or the conditions?

   The joins should go before the conditions.

5. In joining tables are you limited to one-column joins, or can you join on more than one column?

   You can join on more than one column. You may be forced to join on multiple columns depending on what makes a row of data unique or the specific conditions you want to place on the data to be retrieved.

Exercise Answers

1. In the section on joining tables to themselves, the last example returned two combinations. Rewrite the query so only one entry comes up for each redundant part number.

INPUT/
OUTPUT

```
SELECT F.PARTNUM, F.DESCRIPTION,
S.PARTNUM,S.DESCRIPTION
FROM PART F, PART S
WHERE F.PARTNUM = S.PARTNUM
AND F.DESCRIPTION <> S.DESCRIPTION
AND F.DESCRIPTION > S.DESCRIPTION
```

```
    PARTNUM DESCRIPTION          PARTNUM DESCRIPTION
    ========== ================   ========== ====================

        76 ROAD BIKE                 76 CLIPPLESS SHOE
```

2. Rewrite the following query to make it more readable and shorter.

INPUT

```
select orders.orderedon, orders.name, part.partnum,
        part.price, part.description from orders, part
        where orders.partnum = part.partnum and orders.orderedon
     between '1-SEP-96' and '30-SEP-96'
     order by part.partnum;
```

   Answer:

```
SQL> select o.orderedon ORDER_DATE, o.name NAME, p.partnum PART#,
        p.price PRICE, p.description DESCRIPTION
     from orders o,
          part p
     where o.partnum = p.partnum
       and o.orderedon like '%SEP%'
     order by ORDER_DATE;
```

3. From the PART table and the ORDERS table, make up a query that will return the following:

OUTPUT

ORDEREDON	NAME	PARTNUM	QUANTITY
2-SEP-96	TRUE WHEEL	10	1

F

Answer:

```
select o.orderedon ORDEREDON, o.name NAME, p.partnum PARTNUM,
➡️o.quanity QUANITY
        from orders o,
             part p
        where o.partnum = p.partnum
          and o.orderedon like '%SEP%';
```

Many other queries will also work.

Day 7, "Subqueries: The Embedded SELECT Statement"

Quiz Answers

1. In the section on nested subqueries, the sample subquery returned several values:

```
LE SHOPPE
BIKE SPEC
LE SHOPPE
BIKE SPEC
JACKS BIKE
```

Some of these are duplicates. Why aren't these duplicates in the final result set?

The result set has no duplicates because the query that called the subquery

```
SELECT ALL C.NAME, C.ADDRESS, C.STATE,C.ZIP
FROM CUSTOMER C
WHERE C.NAME IN
```

returned only the rows where NAME was in the list examined by the statement IN. Don't confuse this simple IN statement with the more complex join.

2. Are the following statements true or false?

The aggregate functions SUM, COUNT, MIN, MAX, and AVG all return multiple values.

False. They all return a single value.

The maximum number of subqueries that can be nested is two.

False. The limit is a function of your implementation.

Correlated subqueries are completely self-contained.

False. Correlated subqueries enable you to use an outside reference.

3. Will the following subqueries work using the ORDERS table and the PART table?

```
SQL> SELECT *
     FROM PART;

     PARTNUM   DESCRIPTION   PRICE
         54    PEDALS        54.25
```

```
           42   SEATS              24.50
           46   TIRES              15.25
           23   MOUNTAIN BIKE     350.45
           76   ROAD BIKE         530.00
           10   TANDEM           1200.00
   6 rows selected.
```

```
SQL> SELECT *
     FROM ORDERS;

     ORDEREDON    NAME          PARTNUM   QUANITY   REMARKS
     15-MAY-96 TRUE WHEEL           23         6   PAID
     19-MAY-96 TRUE WHEEL           76         3   PAID
      2-SEP-96 TRUE WHEEL           10         1   PAID
     30-JUN-96 BIKE SPEC            54        10   PAID
     30-MAY-96 BIKE SPEC            10         2   PAID
     30-MAY-96 BIKE SPEC            23         8   PAID
     17-JAN-96 BIKE SPEC            76        11   PAID
     17-JAN-96 LE SHOPPE            76         5   PAID
      1-JUN-96 LE SHOPPE            10         3   PAID
      1-JUN-96 AAA BIKE             10         1   PAID
      1-JUN-96 AAA BIKE             76         4   PAID
      1-JUN-96 AAA BIKE             46        14   PAID
     11-JUL-96 JACKS BIKE           76        14   PAID
   13 rows selected.
```

a. ```
    SQL> SELECT * FROM ORDERS
         WHERE PARTNUM =
         SELECT PARTNUM FROM PART
         WHERE DESCRIPTION = 'TRUE WHEEL';
    ```

No. Missing the parenthesis around the subquery.

b.  ```
    SQL> SELECT PARTNUM
         FROM ORDERS
         WHERE PARTNUM =
         (SELECT * FROM PART
          WHERE DESCRIPTION = 'LE SHOPPE');
    ```

No. The SQL engine cannot correlate all the columns in the part table with the operator =.

c. ```
    SQL> SELECT NAME, PARTNUM
         FROM ORDERS
         WHERE EXISTS
         (SELECT * FROM ORDERS
          WHERE NAME = 'TRUE WHEEL');
    ```

Yes. This subquery is correct.

# Exercise Answer

Write a query using the table ORDERS to return all the NAMES and ORDEREDON dates for every store that comes after JACKS BIKE in the alphabet.

F
    ```

```
INPUT/     SELECT NAME, ORDEREDON
OUTPUT     FROM ORDERS
           WHERE NAME >
           (SELECT NAME
           FROM ORDERS
           WHERE NAME ='JACKS BIKE')

           NAME            ORDEREDON
           ==========  ===========

           TRUE WHEEL  15-MAY-1996
           TRUE WHEEL  19-MAY-1996
           TRUE WHEEL   2-SEP-1996
           TRUE WHEEL  30-JUN-1996
           LE SHOPPE   17-JAN-1996
           LE SHOPPE    1-JUN-1996
```

Day 8, "Manipulating Data"

Quiz Answers

1. What is wrong with the following statement?

   ```
   DELETE COLLECTION;
   ```

   If you want to delete all records from the COLLECTION table, you must use the following syntax:

   ```
   DELETE FROM COLLECTION;
   ```

   Keep in mind that this statement will delete all records. You can qualify which records you want to delete by using the following syntax:

   ```
   DELETE FROM COLLECTION
   WHERE VALUE = 125
   ```

   This statement would delete all records with a value of 125.

2. What is wrong with the following statement?

   ```
   INSERT INTO COLLECTION
   SELECT * FROM TABLE_2
   ```

   This statement was designed to insert all the records from TABLE_2 into the COLLECTION table. The main problem here is using the INTO keyword with the INSERT statement. When copying data from one table into another table, you must use the following syntax:

   ```
   INSERT COLLECTION
   SELECT * FROM TABLE_2;
   ```

   Also, remember that the data types of the fields selected from TABLE_2 must exactly match the data types and order of the fields within the COLLECTION table.

3. What is wrong with the following statement?

```
UPDATE COLLECTION ("HONUS WAGNER CARD",
25000, "FOUND IT");
```

This statement confuses the UPDATE function with the INSERT function. To UPDATE values into the COLLECTIONS table, use the following syntax:

```
UPDATE COLLECTIONS
SET NAME = "HONUS WAGNER CARD",
  VALUE = 25000,
  REMARKS = "FOUND IT";
```

4. What would happen if you issued the following statement?

```
SQL> DELETE * FROM COLLECTION;
```

Nothing would be deleted because of incorrect syntax. The * is not required here.

5. What would happen if you issued the following statement?

```
SQL> DELETE FROM COLLECTION;
```

All rows in the COLLECTION table will be deleted.

6. What would happen if you issued the following statement?

```
SQL> UPDATE COLLECTION
     SET WORTH = 555
     SET REMARKS = 'UP FROM 525';
```

All values in the COLLECTION table for the worth column are now 555, and all remarks in the COLLECTION table now say UP FROM 525. Probably not a good thing!

7. Will the following SQL statement work?

```
SQL> INSERT INTO COLLECTION
     SET VALUES = 900
     WHERE ITEM = 'STRING';
```

No. The syntax is not correct. The INSERT and the SET do not go together.

8. Will the following SQL statement work?

```
SQL> UPDATE COLLECTION
     SET VALUES = 900
     WHERE ITEM = 'STRING';
```

Yes. This syntax is correct.

Exercise Answers

1. Try inserting values with incorrect data types into a table. Note the errors and then insert values with correct data types into the same table.

Regardless of the implementation you are using, the errors that you receive should indicate that the data you are trying to insert is not compatible with the data type that has been assigned to the column(s) of the table.

2. Using your database system, try exporting a table (or an entire database) to some other format. Then import the data back into your database. Familiarize yourself with this capability. Also, export the tables to another database format if your DBMS supports this feature. Then use the other system to open these files and examine them.

See your database documentation for the exact syntax when exporting or importing data. You may want to delete all rows from your table if you are performing repeated imports. Always test your export/import utilities before using them on production data. If your tables have unique constraints on columns and you fail to truncate the data from those tables before import, then you will be showered by unique constraint errors.

Day 9, "Creating and Maintaining Tables"

Quiz Answers

1. True or False: The ALTER DATABASE statement is often used to modify an existing table's structure.

   False. Most systems do not have an ALTER DATABASE command. The ALTER TABLE command is used to modify an existing table's structure.

2. True or False: The DROP TABLE command is functionally equivalent to the DELETE FROM <table_name> command.

   False. The DROP TABLE command is not equivalent to the DELETE FROM <table_name> command. The DROP TABLE command completely deletes the table along with its structure from the database. The DELETE FROM... command removes only the records from a table. The table's structure remains in the database.

3. True or False: To add a new table to a database, use the CREATE TABLE command.

   True.

4. What is wrong with the following statement?

INPUT
```
CREATE TABLE new_table (
ID NUMBER,
FIELD1 char(40),
FIELD2 char(80),
ID char(40);
```

This statement has two problems. The first problem is that the name ID is repeated within the table. Even though the data types are different, reusing a field name within a table is illegal. The second problem is that the closing parentheses are missing from the end of the statement. It should look like this:

```
CREATE TABLE new_table (
ID NUMBER,
FIELD1 char(40),
FIELD2 char(80));
```

5. What is wrong with the following statement?

```
ALTER DATABASE BILLS (
COMPANY char(80));
```

The command to modify a field's data type or length is the ALTER TABLE command, not the ALTER DATABASE command.

6. When a table is created, who is the owner?

The owner of the new table would be whoever created the table. If you signed on as your ID, then your ID would be the owner. If you signed on as SYSTEM, then SYSTEM would be the owner.

7. If data in a character column has varying lengths, what is the best choice for the data type?

VARCHAR2 is the best choice. Here's what happens with the CHAR data type when the data length varies:

```
SQL> SELECT *
  2  FROM NAME_TABLE;

LAST_NAME       FIRST_NAME
JONES           NANCY
SMITH           JOHN
2 rows selected.


SQL> SELECT LAST_NAME
  2  FROM NAME_TABLE
  3  WHERE LAST_NAME LIKE '%MITH';

No rows selected.
```

F

You were looking for SMITH, but SMITH does exist in our table. The query finds SMITH because the column LAST_NAME is CHAR and there are spaces after SMITH. The SELECT statement did not ask for these spaces. Here's the correct statement to find SMITH:

```
SQL> SELECT LAST_NAME
  2  FROM NAME_TABLE
  3  WHERE LAST_NAME LIKE '%MITH%';

LAST_NAME
SMITH
1 row selected.
```

By adding the % after MITH, the SELECT statement found SMITH and the spaces after the name.

TIP

> When creating tables, plan your data types to avoid this type of situation. Be aware of how your data types act. If you allocate 30 bytes for a column and some values in the column contain fewer than 30 bytes, does the particular data type pad spaces to fill up 30 bytes? If so, consider how this may affect your select statements. Know your data and its structure.

8. Can you have duplicate table names?

   Yes. Just as long as the owner or schema is not the same.

Exercise Answers

1. Add two tables to the BILLS database named BANK and ACCOUNT_TYPE using any format you like. The BANK table should contain information about the BANK field used in the BANK_ACCOUNTS table in the examples. The ACCOUNT_TYPE table should contain information about the ACCOUNT_TYPE field in the BANK_ACCOUNTS table also. Try to reduce the data as much as possible.

   You should use the CREATE TABLE command to make the tables. Possible SQL statements would look like this:

   ```
   SQL> CREATE TABLE BANK
       2  ( ACCOUNT_ID      NUMBER(30)     NOT NULL,
            BANK_NAME       VARCHAR2(30)   NOT NULL,
            ST_ADDRESS      VARCHAR2(30)   NOT NULL,
            CITY            VARCHAR2(15)   NOT NULL,
            STATE           CHAR(2)        NOT NULL,
            ZIP             NUMBER(5)      NOT NULL;

   SQL> CREATE TABLE ACCOUNT_TYPE
          ( ACCOUNT_ID     NUMBER(30)     NOT NULL,
            SAVINGS        CHAR(30),
            CHECKING       CHAR(30);
   ```

2. With the five tables that you have created—BILLS, BANK_ACCOUNTS, COMPANY, BANK, and ACCOUNT_TYPE—change the table structure so that instead of using CHAR fields as keys, you use integer ID fields as keys.

   ```
   SQL> ALTER TABLE BILLS DROP PRIMARY KEY;
   SQL> ALTER TABLE BILLS ADD (PRIMARY KEY (ACCOUNT_ID));
   SQL> ALTER TABLE COMPANY ADD (PRIMARY KEY (ACCOUNT_ID));
   ```

3. Using your knowledge of SQL joins (see Day 6, "Joining Tables"), write several queries to join the tables in the BILLS database.

   Because we altered the tables in the previous exercise and made the key field the ACCOUNT_ID column, all the tables can be joined by this column. You can join the tables in any combination; you can even join all five tables. Don't forget to qualify your columns and tables.

Day 10, "Creating Views and Indexes"

Quiz Answers

1. What will happen if a unique index is created on a nonunique field?

   Depending on which database you are using, you will receive some type of error and no index at all will be created. The constituent fields of a unique index must form a unique value.

2. Are the following statements true or false?

   Both views and indexes take up space in the database and therefore must be factored in the planning of the database size.

   False. Only indexes take up physical space.

   If someone updates a table on which a view has been created, the view must have an identical update performed on it to see the same data.

   False. If someone updates a table, then the view will see the updated data.

   If you have the disk space and you really want to get your queries smoking, the more indexes the better.

   False. Sometimes too many indexes can actually slow down your queries.

3. Is the following CREATE statement correct?

   ```
   SQL> create view credit_debts as
        (select all from debts
        where account_id = 4);
   ```

   No. You do not need the parentheses; also the word all should been an *.

4. Is the following CREATE statement correct?

   ```
   SQL> create unique view debts as
        select * from debts_tbl;
   ```

   No. There is no such thing as a unique view.

5. Is the following CREATE statement correct?

   ```
   SQL> drop * from view debts;
   ```

   No. The correct syntax is

   ```
   drop view debts;
   ```

6. Is the following CREATE statement correct?

   ```
   SQL> create index id_index on bills
        (account_id);
   ```

   Yes. This syntax is correct.

F

Exercise Answers

1. Examine the database system you are using. Does it support views? What options are you allowed to use when creating a view? Write a simple SQL statement that will create a view using the appropriate syntax. Perform some traditional operations such as SELECT or DELETE and then DROP the view.

   Check your implementation's data dictionary for the proper tables to query for information on views.

2. Examine the database system you are using to determine how it supports indexes. You will undoubtedly have a wide range of options. Try out some of these options on a table that exists within your database. In particular, determine whether you are allowed to create UNIQUE or CLUSTERED indexes on a table within your database.

   Microsoft Access allows developers to use graphical tools to add indexes to a table. These indexes can combine multiple fields, and the sort order can also be set graphically. Other systems require you to type the CREATE INDEX statement at a command line.

3. If possible, locate a table that has several thousand records. Use a stopwatch or clock to time various operations against the database. Add some indexes and see whether you can notice a performance improvement. Try to follow the tips given to you today.

   Indexes improve performance when the operation returns a small subset of records. As queries return a larger portion of a table's records, the performance improvement gained by using indexes becomes negligible. Using indexes can even slow down queries in some situations.

Day 11, "Controlling Transactions"

Quiz Answers

1. When nesting transactions, does issuing a ROLLBACK TRANSACTION command cancel the current transaction and roll back the batch of statements into the upper-level transaction? Why or why not?

   No. When nesting transactions, any rollback of a transaction cancels all the transactions currently in progress. The effect of all the transactions will not truly be saved until the outer transaction has been committed.

2. Can savepoints be used to "save off" portions of a transaction? Why or why not?

   Yes. Savepoints allow the programmer to save off statements within a transaction. If desired, the transaction can then be rolled back to this savepoint instead of to the beginning of the transaction.

3. Can a COMMIT command be used by itself or must it be embedded?

A COMMIT command can be issued by itself or in the transaction.

4. If you issue the COMMIT command and then discover a mistake, can you still use the ROLLBACK command?

Yes and No. You can issue the command, but it will not roll back the changes.

5. Will using a savepoint in the middle of a transaction save all that happened before it automatically?

No. A savepoint comes into play only if a ROLLBACK command is issued—and then only the changes made after the savepoint will be rolled back.

Exercise Answers

1. Use Personal Oracle7 syntax and correct the syntax (if necessary) for the following:

```
SQL> START TRANSACTION
     INSERT INTO CUSTOMERS VALUES
     ('SMITH', 'JOHN')
SQL> COMMIT;
```

Answer:

```
SQL> SET TRANSACTION;
     INSERT INTO CUSTOMERS VALUES
     ('SMITH', 'JOHN');
SQL> COMMIT;
```

2. Use Personal Oracle7 syntax and correct the syntax (if necessary) for the following:

```
SQL> SET TRANSACTION;
     UPDATE BALANCES SET CURR_BAL = 25000;
SQL> COMMIT;
```

Answer:

```
SQL> SET TRANSACTION;
         UPDATE BALANCES SET CURR_BAL = 25000;
SQL> COMMIT;
```

This statement is correct and will work quite well; however, you have just updated everyone's current balance to $25,000!

3. Use Personal Oracle7 syntax and correct the syntax (if necessary) for the following:

```
SQL> SET TRANSACTION;
     INSERT INTO BALANCES VALUES
     ('567.34', '230.00', '8');
SQL> ROLLBACK;
```

This statement is correct. Nothing will be inserted.

F

Day 12, "Database Security"

Quiz Answers

1. What is wrong with the following statement?

   `SQL> GRANT CONNECTION TO DAVID;`

   There is no CONNECTION role. The proper syntax is

   `SQL> GRANT CONNECT TO DAVID;`

2. True or False (and why): Dropping a user will cause all objects owned by that user to be dropped as well.

   This statement is true only if the DROP USER *user name* CASCADE statement is executed. The CASCADE option tells the system to drop all objects owned by the user as well as that user.

3. What would happen if you created a table and granted select privileges on the table to public?

   Everyone could select from your table, even users you may not want to be able to view your data.

4. Is the following SQL statement correct?

   ```
   SQL> create user RON
        identified by RON;
   ```

   Yes. This syntax creates a user. However, the user will acquire the default settings, which may not be desirable. Check your implementation for these settings.

5. Is the following SQL statement correct?

   ```
   SQL> alter RON
        identified by RON;
   ```

   No. The user is missing. The correct syntax is

   ```
   SQL> alter user RON
        identified by RON;
   ```

6. Is the following SQL statement correct?

   `SQL> grant connect, resource to RON;`

   Yes. The syntax is correct.

7. If you own a table, who can select from that table?

   Only users with the select privilege on your table.

Exercise Answer

Experiment with your database system's security by creating a table and then by creating a user. Give this user various privileges and then take them away.

(On your own.)

Day 13, "Advanced SQL Topics"

Quiz Answers

1. True or False: Microsoft Visual C++ allows programmers to call the ODBC API directly.

   False. Microsoft Visual C++ encapsulates the ODBC library with a set of C++ classes. These classes provide a higher level interface to the ODBC functions, which results in an easier-to-use set of functions. However, the overall functionality is somewhat limited. If you purchase the ODBC Software Development Kit (SDK) (you can obtain the SDK by joining the Microsoft Developers Network), you can call the API directly from within a Visual C++ application.

2. True or False: The ODBC API can be called directly only from a C program.

   False. The ODBC API resides within DLLs that can be bound by a number of languages, including Visual Basic and Borland's Object Pascal.

3. True or False: Dynamic SQL requires the use of a precompiler.

   False. Static SQL requires a precompiler. Dynamic SQL is just that: dynamic. The SQL statements used with Dynamic SQL can be prepared and executed at runtime.

4. What does the # in front of a temporary table signify?

   SQL Server uses the # to flag a temporary table.

5. What must be done after closing a cursor to return memory?

   You must deallocate the cursor. The syntax is

   ```
   SQL> deallocate cursor cursor_name;
   ```

6. Are triggers used with the SELECT statement?

   No. They are executed by the use of UPDATE, DELETE, or INSERT.

7. If you have a trigger on a table and the table is dropped, does the trigger still exist?

   No. The trigger is automatically dropped when the table is dropped.

F

Exercise Answers

1. Create a sample database application. (We used a music collection to illustrate these points today.) Break this application into logical data groupings.

2. List of queries you think will be required to complete this application.

3. List the various rules you want to maintain in the database.

4. Create a database schema for the various groups of data you described in step 1.

5. Convert the queries in step 2 to stored procedures.

6. Convert the rules in step 3 to triggers.

7. Combine steps 4, 5, and 6 into a large script file that can be used to build the database and all its associated procedures.

8. Insert some sample data. (This step can also be a part of the script file in step 7.)

9. Execute the procedures you have created to test their functionality.

   (On your own.)

Day 14, "Dynamic Uses of SQL"

Quiz Answers

1. In which object does Microsoft Visual C++ place its SQL?

   In the CRecordSet object's GetDefaultSQL member. Remember, you can change the string held here to manipulate your table.

2. In which object does Delphi place its SQL?

   In the TQuery object.

3. What is ODBC?

   ODBC stands for open database connectivity. This technology enables Windows-based programs to access a database through a driver.

4. What does Delphi do?

   Delphi provides a scalable interface to various databases.

Exercise Answers

1. Change the sort order in the C++ example from ascending to descending on the State field.

   Change the return value of GetDefaultSQL as shown in the following code fragment:

```
CString CTyssqlSet::GetDefaultSQL()
{
return " SELECT * FROM CUSTOMER ORDER DESC BY STATE ";
}
```

2. Go out, find an application that needs SQL, and use it.

(On your own.)

Day 15, "Streamlining SQL Statements for Improved Performance"

Quiz Answers

1. What does *streamline an SQL statement* mean?

   Streamlining an SQL statement is taking the path with the least resistance by carefully planning your statement and arranging the elements within your clauses properly.

2. Should tables and their corresponding indexes reside on the same disk?

   Absolutely not. If possible, always store tables and indexes separately to avoid disk contention.

3. Why is the arrangement of conditions in an SQL statement important?

   For more efficient data access (the path with the least resistance).

4. What happens during a full-table scan?

   A table is read row by row instead of using an index that points to specific rows.

5. How can you avoid a full-table scan?

   A full-table scan can be avoided by creating an index or rearranging the conditions in an SQL statement that are indexed.

6. What are some common hindrances of general performance?

   Common performance pitfalls include

   - [ ] Insufficient shared memory
   - [ ] Limited number of available disk drives
   - [ ] Improper usage of available disk drives
   - [ ] Running large batch loads that are unscheduled
   - [ ] Failing to commit or rollback transactions
   - [ ] Improper sizing of tables and indexes

Exercise Answers

1. Make the following SQL statement more readable.

```
SELECT EMPLOYEE.LAST_NAME, EMPLOYEE.FIRST_NAME, EMPLOYEE.MIDDLE_NAME,
EMPLOYEE.ADDRESS, EMPLOYEE.PHONE_NUMBER, PAYROLL.SALARY, PAYROLL.POSITION,
EMPLOYEE.SSN, PAYROLL.START_DATE FROM EMPLOYEE, PAYROLL WHERE
EMPLOYEE.SSN = PAYROLL.SSN AND EMPLOYEE.LAST_NAME LIKE 'S%' AND
PAYROLL.SALARY > 20000;
```

F

You should reformat the SQL statement as follows, depending on the consistent format of your choice:

```
SELECT E.LAST_NAME, E.FIRST_NAME, E.MIDDLE_NAME,
       E.ADDRESS, E.PHONE_NUMBER, P.SALARY,
       P.POSITION, E.SSN, P.START_DATE
FROM EMPLOYEE E,
     PAYROLL P
WHERE E.SSN = P.SSN
  AND E.LAST_NAME LIKE 'S%'
  AND P.SALARY > 20000;
```

2. Rearrange the conditions in the following query to optimize data retrieval time. Use the following statistics (on the tables in their entirety) to determine the order of the conditions:

> 593 individuals have the last name SMITH.
>
> 712 individuals live in INDIANAPOLIS.
>
> 3,492 individuals are MALE.
>
> 1,233 individuals earn a salary >= 30,000.
>
> 5,009 individuals are single.
>
> Individual_id is the primary key for both tables.

```
SELECT M.INDIVIDUAL_NAME, M.ADDRESS, M.CITY, M.STATE, M.ZIP_CODE,
       S.SEX, S.MARITAL_STATUS, S.SALARY
FROM MAILING_TBL M,
     INDIVIDUAL_STAT_TBL S
WHERE M.NAME LIKE 'SMITH%'
  AND M.CITY = 'INDIANAPOLIS'
  AND S.SEX = 'MALE'
  AND S.SALARY >= 30000
  AND S.MARITAL_STATUS = 'S'
  AND M.INDIVIDUAL_ID = S.INDIVIDUAL_ID;
```

Answer:

According to the statistics, your new query should look similar to the following answer. Name like 'SMITH%' is the most restrictive condition because it will return the fewest rows:

```
SELECT M.INDIVIDUAL_NAME, M.ADDRESS, M.CITY, M.STATE, M.ZIP_CODE,
       S.SEX, S.MARITAL_STATUS, S.SALARY
FROM MAILING_TBL M,
     INDIVIDUAL_STAT_TBL S
WHERE M.INDIVIDUAL_ID = S.INDIVIDUAL_ID
  AND S.MARITAL_STATUS = 'S'
  AND S.SEX = 'MALE'
  AND S.SALARY >= 30000
  AND M.CITY = 'INDIANAPOLIS'
  AND M.NAME LIKE 'SMITH%';
```

Day 16, "Using Views to Retrieve Useful Information from the Data Dictionary"

Quiz Answers

1. In Oracle, how can you find out what tables and views you own?

   By selecting from USER_CATALOG or CAT. The name of the data dictionary object will vary by implementation, but all versions have basically the same information about objects such as tables and views.

2. What types of information are stored in the data dictionary?

   Database design, user statistics, processes, objects, growth of objects, performance statistics, stored SQL code, database security.

3. How can you use performance statistics?

   Performance statistics suggest ways to improve database performance by modifying database parameters and streamlining SQL, which may also include the use of indexes and an evaluation of their efficiency.

4. What are some database objects?

   Tables, indexes, synonyms, clusters, views.

Exercise Answers

Suppose you are managing a small to medium-size database. Your job responsibilities include developing and managing the database. Another individual is inserting large amounts of data into a table and receives an error indicating a lack of space. You must determine the cause of the problem. Does the user's tablespace quota need to be increased, or do you need to allocate more space to the tablespace? Prepare a step-by-step list that explains how you will gather the necessary information from the data dictionary. You do not need to list specific table or view names.

1. Look up the error in your database documentation.
2. Query the data dictionary for information on the table, its current size, tablespace quota on the user, and space allocated in the tablespace (the tablespace that holds the target table).
3. Determine how much space the user needs to finish inserting the data.
4. What is the real problem? Does the user's tablespace quota need to be increased, or do you need to allocate more space to the tablespace?
5. If the user does not have a sufficient quota, then increase the quota. If the current tablespace is filled, you may want to allocate more space or move the target table to a tablespace with more free space.

F

6. You may decide not to increase the user's quota or not to allocate more space to the tablespace. In either case you may have to consider purging old data or archiving the data off to tape.

These steps are not irrevocable. Your action plan may vary depending upon your company policy or your individual situation.

Day 17, "Using SQL to Generate SQL Statements"

Quiz Answers

1. From which two sources can you generate SQL scripts?

   You can generate SQL scripts from database tables and the data dictionary.

2. Will the following SQL statement work? Will the generated output work?

```
SQL> SET ECHO OFF
SQL> SET FEEDBACK OFF
SQL> SPOOL CNT.SQL
SQL> SELECT 'COUNT(*) FROM  ' || TABLE_NAME || ';'
  2  FROM CAT
  3  /
```

   Yes the SQL statement will generate an SQL script, but the generated script will not work. You need select 'select' in front of count(*):

```
SELECT 'SELECT COUNT(*) FROM ' || TABLE_NAME || ';'
```

   Otherwise, your output will look like this:

```
COUNT(*) FROM TABLE_NAME;
```

   which is not a valid SQL statement.

3. Will the following SQL statement work? Will the generated output work?

```
SQL> SET ECHO OFF
SQL> SET FEEDBACK OFF
SQL> SPOOL GRANT.SQL
SQL> SELECT 'GRANT CONNECT DBA TO ' || USERNAME || ';'
  2  FROM SYS.DBA_USERS
  3  WHERE USERNAME NOT IN ('SYS','SYSTEM','SCOTT')
  4  /
```

   Once again, yes and no. The statement will generate an SQL script, but the SQL that it generates will be incomplete. You need to add a comma between the privileges CONNECT and DBA:

```
SELECT 'GRANT CONNECT, DBA TO ' || USERNAME || ';'
```

4. Will the following SQL statement work? Will the generated output work?

```
SQL> SET ECHO OFF
SQL> SET FEEDBACK OFF
SQL> SELECT 'GRANT CONNECT, DBA TO ' || USERNAME || ';'
  2  FROM SYS.DBA_USERS
  3  WHERE USERNAME NOT IN ('SYS','SYSTEM','SCOTT')
  4  /
```

Yes. The syntax of the main statement is valid, and the SQL that will be generated will grant CONNECT and DBA to all users selected.

5. True or False: It is best to set feedback on when generating SQL.

False. You do not care how many rows are being selected, as that will not be part of the syntax of your generated statements.

6. True or False: When generating SQL from SQL, always spool to a list or log file for a record of what happened.

False. You should spool to an .sql file, or whatever your naming convention is for an SQL file. However, you may choose to spool within your generated file.

7. True or False: Before generating SQL to truncate tables, you should always make sure you have a good backup of the tables.

True. Just to be safe.

8. What is the ed command?

The ed command takes you into a full screen text editor. ed is very similar to vi on a UNIX system and appears like a Windows Notepad file.

9. What does the spool off command do?

The spool off command closes an open spool file.

Exercise Answers

1. Using the SYS.DBA_USERS view (Personal Oracle7), create an SQL statement that will generate a series of GRANT statements to five new users: John, Kevin, Ryan, Ron, and Chris. Use the column called USERNAME. Grant them Select access to history_tbl.

```
SQL> SET ECHO OFF
SQL> SET FEEDBACK OFF
SQL> SPOOL GRANTS.SQL
SQL> SELECT 'GRANT SELECT ON HISTORY_TBL TO ' || USERNAME || ';'
  2  FROM SYS.DBA_USERS
  3  WHERE USERNAME IN ('JOHN','KEVIN','RYAN','RON','CHRIS')
  4  /

GRANT SELECT ON HISTORY_TBL TO JOHN;
GRANT SELECT ON HISTORY_TBL TO KEVIN;
GRANT SELECT ON HISTORY_TBL TO RYAN;
GRANT SELECT ON HISTORY_TBL TO RON;
GRANT SELECT ON HISTORY_TBL TO CHRIS;
```

F

2. Using the examples in this chapter as guidelines, create some SQL statements that will generate SQL that you can use.

   There are no wrong answers as long as the syntax is correct in your generated statements.

WARNING

Until you completely understand the concepts presented in this chapter, take caution when generating SQL statements that will modify existing data or database structures.

Day 18, "PL/SQL: An Introduction"

Quiz Answers

1. How is a database trigger used?

   A database trigger takes a specified action when data in a specified table is manipulated. For instance, if you make a change to a table, a trigger could insert a row of data into a history table to audit the change.

2. Can related procedures be stored together?

   Related procedures may be stored together in a package.

3. True or False: Data Manipulation Language can be used in a PL/SQL statement.
   True.

4. True or False: Data Definition Language can be used in a PL/SQL statement.

   False. DDL cannot be used in a PL/SQL statement. It is not a good idea to automate the process of making structural changes to a database.

5. Is text output directly a part of the PL/SQL syntax?

   Text output is not directly a part of the language of PL/SQL; however, text output is supported by the standard package DBMS_OUTPUT.

6. List the three major parts of a PL/SQL statement.

   DECLARE section, PROCEDURE section, EXCEPTION section.

7. List the commands that are associated with cursor control.

   DECLARE, OPEN, FETCH, CLOSE.

Exercise Answers

1. Declare a variable called HourlyPay in which the maximum accepted value is 99.99/hour.

```
DECLARE
     HourlyPay number(4,2);
```

2. Define a cursor whose content is all the data in the CUSTOMER_TABLE where the CITY is INDIANAPOLIS.

```
DECLARE
     cursor c1 is
     select * from customer_table
     where city = 'INDIANAPOLIS';
```

3. Define an exception called UnknownCode.

```
DECLARE
     UnknownCode EXCEPTION;
```

4. Write a statement that will set the AMT in the AMOUNT_TABLE to 10 if CODE is A, set the AMT to 20 if CODE is B, and raise an exception called UnknownCode if CODE is neither A nor B. The table has one row.

```
IF ( CODE = 'A' ) THEN
     update AMOUNT_TABLE
     set AMT = 10;
   ELSIF ( CODE = 'B' ) THEN
     update AMOUNT_TABLE
     set AMT = 20;
   ELSE
     raise UnknownCode;
   END IF;
```

Day 19, "Transact-SQL: An Introduction"

Quiz Answers

1. True or False: The use of the word SQL in Oracle's PL/SQL and Microsoft/Sybase's Transact-SQL implies that these products are fully compliant with the ANSI standard.

   False. The word *SQL* is not protected by copyright. The products mentioned do comply with much of the ANSI standard, but they do not fully comply with everything in that standard.

2. True or False: Static SQL is less flexible than Dynamic SQL, although the performance of static SQL can be better.

   True. Static SQL requires the use of a precompiler, and its queries cannot be prepared at runtime. Therefore, static SQL is less flexible than dynamic SQL, but because the query is already processed, the performance can be better.

Exercise Answers

1. If you are not using Sybase/Microsoft SQL Server, compare your product's extensions to ANSI SQL to the extensions mentioned today.

   Because nearly all of Day 19 deals with Transact-SQL, we did not explore the many other extensions to ANSI SQL. Most documentation that accompanies database products makes some effort to point out any SQL extensions provided. Keep in mind that using these extensions will make porting your queries to other databases more difficult.

2. Write a brief set of statements that will check for the existence of some condition. If this condition is true, perform some operation. Otherwise, perform another operation.

   This operation requires an IF statement. There are no wrong answers as long as you follow the syntax for logical statements (IF statements) discussed today.

Day 20, "SQL*Plus"

Quiz Answers

1. Which commands can modify your preferences for an SQL session?

   SET commands change the settings available with your SQL session.

2. Can your SQL script prompt a user for a parameter and execute the SQL statement using the entered parameter?

   Yes. Your script can accept parameters from a user and pass them into variables.

3. If you are creating a summarized report on entries in a CUSTOMER table, how would you group your data for your report?

   You would probably break your groups by customer because you are selecting from the CUSTOMER table.

4. Are there limitations to what you can have in your LOGIN.SQL file?

   The only limitations are that the text in your LOGIN.SQL file must be valid SQL and SQL*Plus commands.

5. True or False: The DECODE function is the equivalent of a loop in a procedural programming language.

   False. DECODE is like an IF...THEN statement.

6. True or False: If you spool the output of your query to an existing file, your output will be appended to that file.

   False. The new output will overwrite the original file.

Exercise Answers

1. Using the PRODUCTS table at the beginning of Day 20, write a query that will select all data and compute a count of the records returned on the report without using the SET FEEDBACK ON command.

```
compute sum of count(*) on report
    break on report
    select product_id, product_name, unit_cost, count(*)
    from products
    group by product_id, product_name, unit_cost;
```

2. Suppose today is Monday, May 12, 1998. Write a query that will produce the following output:

```
Today is Monday, May 12 1998
```

Answer:

```
set heading off
select to_char(sysdate,' "Today is "Day, Month dd yyyy')
from dual;
```

3. Use the following SQL statement for this exercise:

```
1  select *
2  from orders
3  where customer_id = '001'
4* order by customer_id;
```

Without retyping the statement in the SQL buffer, change the table in the FROM clause to the CUSTOMER table:

```
12
c/orders/customer
```

Now append DESC to the ORDER BY clause:

```
14
append DESC
```

Day 21, "Common SQL Mistakes/Errors and Resolutions"

Quiz Answers

1. A user calls and says, "I can't sign on to the database. But everything was working fine yesterday. The error says invalid user/password. Can you help me?" What steps should you take?

   At first you would think to yourself, yeah sure, you just forgot your password. But this error can be returned if a front-end application cannot connect to the database. However, if you know the database is up and functional, just change the password by using the ALTER USER command and tell the user what the new password is.

2. Why should tables have storage clauses and a tablespace destination?

In order for tables not to take the default settings for storage, you must include the storage clause. Otherwise medium to large tables will fill up and take extents, causing slower performance. They also may run out of space, causing a halt to your work until the DBA can fix the space problem.

Exercise Answers

1. Suppose you are logged on to the database as SYSTEM, and you wish to drop a table called HISTORY in your schema. Your regular user ID is JSMITH. What is the correct syntax to drop this table?

Because you are signed on as SYSTEM, be sure to qualify the table by including the table owner. If you do not specify the table owner, you could accidentally drop a table called HISTORY in the SYSTEM schema, if it exists.

```
SQL> DROP TABLE JSMITH.HISTORY;
```

2. Correct the following error:

```
SQL> select sysdate DATE
  2  from dual;
```

```
select sysdate DATE
               *
ERROR at line 1:
ORA-00923: FROM keyword not found where expected
```

DATE is a reserved word in Oracle SQL. If you want to name a column heading DATE, then you must use double quotation marks: "DATE".

INDEX

W

MACMILLAN COMPUTER PUBLISHING USA
A VIACOM COMPANY

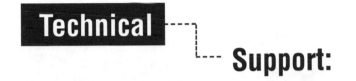

If you need assistance with the information in this book or with a CD/Disk accompanying the book, please access the Knowledge Base on our Web site at **http://www.superlibrary.com/general/support**. Our most Frequently Asked Questions are answered there. If you do not find the answer to your questions on our Web site, you may contact Macmillan Technical Support **(317) 581-3833** or e-mail us at **support@mcp.com**.

Microsoft BackOffice Unleashed, Second Edition

—Joe Greene et al.

This update of the highly successful first edition is an all-in-one, how-to guide that helps readers master the individual products within the BackOffice family and use those pieces to build a robust information resource for corporations. The book highlights the significant improvements in Exchange Server, including ActiveX programming support, and explores new commercial Internet servers, such as Proxy Server, Index Server, Merchant Server, and Conference Server. The CD-ROM includes source code, third-party products, and utilities to help readers take full advantage of Microsoft BackOffice.

Price: $75.00 USA/$105.95 CDN   *Accomplished–Expert*
ISBN: 0-672-31085-6   *1,500 pages*

Teach Yourself Transact-SQL in 21 Days

—Bennett Wm. McEwan & David Solomon

Based on the best-selling *Teach Yourself* series, this comprehensive book provides readers with the techniques they need to not only write flexible and effective applications that produce efficient results but also decrease the performance demands on the server. Readers quickly master methods that improve productivity and maximize performance. This book explores topics such as coding standards, the CASE function, and bitmaps. Q&A sections, exercises, and week-at-a glance previews make learning a breeze. The volume covers Transact-SQL for Microsoft SQL Server and Sybase SQL Server.

Price: $35.00 USA/$49.95 CDN   *New–Casual*
ISBN: 0-672-31045-7   *500 pages*

Windows NT Server 4 Unleashed, Professional Reference Edition

—Jason Garms et al.

Windows NT Server has been gaining tremendous market share over Novell and the new upgrade—which includes a Windows 95 interface—is sure to add momentum to its market drive. *Windows NT Server 4 Unleashed, Professional Reference Edition* addresses the growing market. It provides information on disk and file management, integrated networking, BackOffice integration, and TCP/IP protocols. The CD-ROM includes source code from the book as well as valuable utilities.

Price: $69.99 USA/$98.95 CDN   *Accomplished–Expert*
ISBN: 0-672-31002-3   *1,776 pages*

Windows NT 4 Administrator's Survival Guide

—Rick Sant'Angelo

This book is the one and only survival guide an NT network administrator needs. Written by best-selling author Rick Sant'Angelo, this concise, easy-to-use guide provides all the information users need to successfully implement and maintain a Windows NT 4 Server. The book has loads of tips and notes from the author on improving performance and saving money when implementing a Windows NT Server. It also includes a reference guide to third-party products, logon scripts programming, technical terms, and commonly used NT utilities. The CD-ROM contains demos of Windows NT applications, utilities, and source code from the book.

Price: $49.99 USA/$70.95 CDN   *Accomplished–Expert*
ISBN: 0-672-31008-2   *900 pages*

Add to Your Sams Library Today with the Best Books for Programming, Operating Systems, and New Technologies

The easiest way to order is to pick up the phone and call
1-800-428-5331
between 9:00 a.m. and 5:00 p.m. EST.
For faster service please have your credit card available.

ISBN	Quantity	Description of Item	Unit Cost	Total Cost
0-672-31085-6		Microsoft BackOffice Unleashed, Second Edition (Book/CD-ROM)	$75.00	
0-672-31045-7		Teach Yourself Transact-SQL in 21 Days	$35.00	
0-672-31002-3		Windows NT Server 4 Unleashed, Professional Reference Edition	$69.99	
0-672-31008-2		Windows NT 4 Administrator's Survival Guide	$49.99	
		Shipping and Handling: See information below.		
		TOTAL		

Shipping and Handling: $4.00 for the first book, and $1.75 for each additional book. If you need to have it now, we can ship product to you in 24 hours for an additional charge of approximately $18.00, and you will receive your item overnight or in two days. Overseas shipping and handling adds $2.00 per book. Prices subject to change. Call for availability and pricing information on latest editions.

201 W. 103rd Street, Indianapolis, Indiana 46290

1-800-428-5331 — Orders   1-800-835-3202 — Fax   1-800-858-7674 — Customer Service

Book ISBN 0-672-31110-0